Tales of the Future

I. F. Clarke

Third Edit...

TALE OF THE FUTURE

FROM THE BEGINNING TO THE PRESENT DAY

Third edition

An Annotated Bibliography

of

those satires, ideal states, imaginary wars and invasions, coming catastrophes and end-of-the-world stories, political warnings and forecasts, inter-planetary voyages and scientific romances – all located in an imaginary future period – that have been published in the United Kingdom between 1644 and 1976.

Collected and compiled

by

I F CLARKE

LONDON
THE LIBRARY ASSOCIATION
1978

The Library Association
7 Ridgmount Street
London WC1E 7AE

First published 1978

© I F Clarke 1978

British Library Cataloguing in Publication Data
Clarke, Ignatius Frederick
Tale of the future. – 3rd ed.
1. Science fiction, English – Bibliography
I. Title II. Library Association
016.823'0876   Z2014.S/

ISBN 0-85365-550-2

NB distributors in North America:
American Library Association
50 East Huron Street
Chicago, Illinois 60611

ISBN 0-8389-3225-8

Cover design by Philip Lloyd Smee

Set by Jubal Multiwrite, London

Printed and bound in Great Britain by
Biddles of Guildford

For Catherine

CONTENTS

ACKNOWLEDGEMENTS

I am pleased to have this opportunity of acknowledging my many debts to all those who have helped in the preparation of the third edition of this bibliography.

I am particularly indebted to the many librarians who have been of very great assistance to me, especially to Mr. W. A. G. Alison, FLA, Director of Libraries, Glasgow, and Mr. R. A. Gillespie, FLA, Librarian of the Mitchell Library, Glasgow, and Assistant Director of Libraries. I thank the Librarian of the Bodleian Library and the staff of the Radcliffe Camera for the bibliographical facilities they provided; I give the same grateful thanks to the staff of the National Library, Edinburgh,who were always most courteous and helpful; and I acknowledge with special gratitude the prompt and effective help of David Clements, BSc PhD, Head of Storage and Delivery Branch, British Library.

I make a special mention of those friends and correspondents who were most generous in their assistance and advice: Pat Adie and Petra Lewis who helped in compiling the author entries; Gerald Bishop who sent me his annual lists of science fiction publications; Professor Lyman Sargent who provided some new titles for the period before 1914; and G. A. Featherston and Colin Williamson, of Bromley Public Libraries, to whom I am much indebted for the annotations and suggestions they sent me.

The typing and final arranging of this book was a long and complicated task for Margaret Dalrymple and Margaret Philips. I am most grateful to them for the care and patience with which they laboured through many months and through several drafts. The checking of the bibliographical details was another exacting task to which my daughter, Catherine, was always equal; and it gives me great pleasure to dedicate this edition to her in acknowledgement of the help she gave.

Finally, I thank the publishers who sent information about their publications during the last six years; and I record my special debt to Janice Bryan of Futura Publications, Julia Stillwell of Granada Ltd, and John Bush of Victor Gollancz.

The University of Strathclyde
1978

THE ARRANGEMENT OF THIS BIBLIOGRAPHY

The publication of the third edition of *The tale of the future* is an appropriate occasion for recording the origin and explaining the principles of this bibliography. It goes back to the autumn of 1950, when I began a research project on 'The future in fiction' in the University of Liverpool; and by the time this was completed in 1953, it had become apparent that there was a number, probably a very large number, of futuristic stories still to be analysed and compared. There was, as they said in the 1950s, a new area of knowledge waiting to be delimited and explored; for in those days there was no more than a handful of studies on aspects of the tale of the future. One of these was *Pilgrims through time and space* (New York, 1947), a pioneer work by J. O. Bailey; another was Everett F. Bleiler's *Checklist of fantastic literature* (Chicago, 1948), which provided the first comprehensive listing of the various kinds of fantastic fiction published in the English language; and another excellent source was V. Dupont's *L'Utopie et le roman utopique dans la littérature anglaise* (Paris, 1944).

By 1953, however, it had become evident that the history of futuristic fiction was more complex and far older than had been supposed; and so I decided to follow my interest in the subject by establishing as full a listing as possible of all stories placed in some future period. For want of adequate bibliographies, I had to begin the hard way by examining all the titles entered in the annual editions of *The English catalogue*; and I confirmed and enlarged the preliminary check-lists by working through the many volumes of the first British Museum *Catalogue of printed books.* This task occupied me profitably and happily for some fourteen months; and most of the work was done with great economy in time by limiting the reading to the daily journeys by bus and train. I recall that my fellow passengers looked respectfully on the bulky volumes of the British Museum *Catalogue* as the visible sign of weighty and profound research.

By 1955 I had begun to sift through the original listings. About one-third of the titles (of the *Tomorrow comes* kind) had nothing to do with the future in any way; but the rest made up a formidable catalogue of imaginary wars, ideal states of the future, satires about future possibilities, exemplary tales and scientific romances. The investigation of these different areas of futuristic fiction has occupied me at intervals ever since. My intention was, and still is, to establish how the various forms of prophetic fiction originated and developed. Thus, the history of the imaginary wars of the future was given in *Voices prophesying war* (1966) and a survey of the evolution of futuristic literature – prophetic and predictive – will be found in *The pattern of expectation* (1978). If I last long enough, I may yet conclude with the biography of The Last Man in all his entrances and exits since the appearance of Cousin de Grainville's *Le Dernier Homme* in 1805.

I must now reveal that I was originally without any ambitions as a bibliographer; but friends and correspondents combined against me and I listened to flattering arguments that persuaded me half willingly to publish a bibliography of futuristic fiction. The first edition of *The tale of the future* came out in 1961, and ever since I have had frequent confirmation of a fact once hidden from me – that a bibliographer can hope for understanding only from the few who have attempted the difficult, never-ending work of compilation. Nothing is ever complete: certainly not the fiction entries in the annual volumes of the *British national bibliography*; and not even the more comprehensive entries in *Whitaker's cumulative book list* whose editors have had at times to complain about those publishers who do not send in notices of their books. Then, there is the hazard of the publisher who announces a title in the spring and allows it to vanish from his autumn list like a quiet ghost. There are publishers who fail to send copies to the copyright libraries; there are publishers who appear in one issue of *Whitaker's* only to be noted in the following year as "Gone from last known address"; and there are the publicity departments of some publishers which resist all enquiries about their publications. Completion is a moving target.

However, the work goes on; and in presenting this third edition it is prudent to begin by saying that it is not a bibliography of fantastic literature. Imaginary lands, parallel worlds, alternative histories, archaic romances, tales of terror or of witchcraft or of the occult – these do not appear unless the narrated events take place in some future period. The sole principle of selection is that a story should be located in a time – months, years, centuries, or millennia ahead – that follows after the date of publication. Fortunately most of the entries select themselves in that the dating of events and the accounts of changes in behaviour and social practices, or in technological developments and political systems, belong of set purpose to the shape of things to come. And then the borderline problems appear. With these the principle has been to include all those works (Graham Greene, *Our man in Havana*, for example) that the authors choose to place in the future, although the plots are not in any sense futuristic. The more difficult decisions relate to thrillers and spy stories – the Dr Palfrey yarns by John Creasey, for instance, or the *Fail-safe* stories of the 1960s, or the more recent style of the London flood described in *Deluge*. For these the test is a question of scale, and a title is entered whenever the events in the story are of such national or international importance that they could have changed the course of history or they would at least have become part of recorded history, had they taken place.

The entries in *Part 1* give the appropriate bibliographical information for first editions published in the United Kingdom. Variant editions are not recorded unless there has been a change of title or some major change in the text; and the annotations seek to give as briefly as possible the main theme of the narrative. These will undoubtedly be too brief for some and too banal for others; but I cannot find any good reason for providing longer accounts of the many third-rate stories that have appeared in the last thirty years, nor do I think it necessary to describe in detail such major works as Bellamy's *Looking backward*, Wells's *War of the worlds*, or Orwell's *Nineteen eighty-four*.

Finally, I am pleased to record that a number of major improvements have been made to this edition. The *Author index* now gives the full names of all writers, and the *Short-Title index* gives the surname of the author after each entry. The annotations now include the date of publication for American and British titles that were first published in the United States, and the original titles of foreign works published in English translation are entered together with the date of the first foreign edition.

THE TALE OF THE FUTURE: ORIGINS AND DEVELOPMENT

There can be no doubt that the idea of the future is one of the more obsessive preoccupations of modern times. Think-tanks, institutes of futurology, and government commissions forecast the state of the economy in the 1980s, of world population in the 1990s, and of urban life in the twenty-first century. Television programmes project their visions of the most varied and extraordinary possibilities in *Star Trek, Dr Who, The survivors*; and the cinema unites the viewers of the world in the shared excitements and exotic exploits of *Star Wars, 2001: A space odyssey, Planet of the Apes.*

There seems to be no end to the predicting and the inventing of possible futures for the inhabitants of Terra. Indeed, the phenomenal growth of futuristic fiction in the last thirty years is an unmistakeable sign that a planetary audience now exists, well versed in the mythologies of space fiction and skilled in elucidating the conventions of the nuclear disaster story, of oppressive police states, planetary wars, time travel adventures and the other familiar constants in contemporary tales of the future. At the same time there has been a parallel increase in studies of this literature. During the six years since the publication of the second edition of this bibliography some of the most informative accounts in the history of the genre have appeared: *Billion year spree*, an exhaustive and perceptive history of science fiction by Brian Aldiss; *New worlds for old* in which David Ketterer traces the course of American science fiction; *Fantastyka i futurologia*, a dogmatic and original investigation by the Polish writer, Stanislaw Lem; and there is an admirable encyclopedia by Pierre Versins, *Encyclopédie de l'utopie et de la science fiction*, in which the author writes with exceptional erudition on authors and topics as different as Edmond About and Roger Zelazny, 'Aerostation' and 'Zoologie'.

The tale of the future is the most social form of fiction. With rare exceptions the subject matter is drawn from the range of possible or probable developments that could affect – for good or ill – the future state of the nation, or of all mankind, or the entirety of some intergalactic civilization. The tale of the future is the popular literary product of a technological epoch. In all the varieties of the genre, from the entertainments of modern science fiction to Wellsian utopias and Orwellian dystopias, these anticipations of the future are the projective images of those social, political, scientific, or ecological changes that are only conceivable in a period of constant technological innovation. In consequence, the development of the genre during the last two hundred years has been a series of direct appeals to the nations, a history of an intimate association between writers and readers, an inventing of appropriate forms for specific themes, and the continuing influence of dominant ideas about the course of human history.

From the beginnings in the second half of the eighteenth century the authors have written – often in a very direct and candid way – for the nation and for the world, and from the earliest days they have had an international audience for their stories. This audience began with the educated minority in Europe that read Sebastien Mercier's *L'An 2440* with such enthusiasm in the 1770s, and it has grown into the science fiction associations, the fancons, worldcons, and fanzines of the present day. And here it is necessary to emphasize that, as the experience of the founding fathers shows, invention is the faithful partner of ideology; for the major innovators are those writers who have been most successful in adapting the manner of their anticipations to the hopes, fears, popular beliefs and principal convictions of their contemporaries. Thus, Sebastien Mercier's *L'An 2440* of 1771 ran to seventeen editions in French and went into foreign translations – English, Danish, Dutch, German – and inspired numerous European imitations, because the French author was able to describe an ideal state of the future that was the self-evident, prophetic conclusion of eighteenth century ideas about political liberty, technology, and the best order in human society. In like manner a long-forgotten author, Jean Baptiste François-Xavier Cousin de Grainville, had an extraordinary success in the first quarter of the nineteenth century with his account of the Last Man. In 1805 he found the central ideas for *Le Dernier Homme* in Christian tradition, in the then novel theories of Malthus about the growth of population and in Jenner's recent discovery of the smallpox vaccine. Grainville justified his projection by reference to contemporary science, telling his readers what they already knew about 'the profound improvements making in medical science by which the lives of thousands of the infantine world have been snatched from the empire of death, and who, in thus becoming the heads of numerous progenies, are laying the foundation of an immense population which the earth in after-ages will be inadequate to sustain.'

By the beginning of the nineteenth century the tale of the future had become an established form of fiction. For some writers, like the author of *Ini; ein Roman aus dem 21sten Jahrhundert* of 1810, the form was an opportunity to delight readers with the novelty of living in a more advanced society. So, Julius von Voss began with the declaration that 'a better future is coming, and we may at least be confident that we can expect our ever-developing civilization will be the salvation of all mortal souls.' And he proved his point with a pleasing vision of the twenty-first century when there is peace throughout the world and the sciences have improved life for all – submarines, underground cities lit by electricity, synthetic diamonds, flying machines, and balloon transports towed by eagles. In the same year of 1810 the Duc de Lévis attempted a more serious anticipation of the twentieth century in his *Les Voyages de Kang-hi*, where he described the ending of smallpox epidemics and the consequent growth of population, the building of a Suez canal and of railways across France, and major improvements in the health and well-being of all citizens.

In this way the aspirations of the early nineteenth century became the imagined realities of a later and more fortunate age. For some writers the probability of social and technological changes provided no more than a desirable background to their stories. This was the method of Mary Shelley in *The last man* of 1826 where she used a favourite theme of the day as a means of assuaging her grief for the death of Shelley. Most of the early prophets, however, found the sanction and substance of their stories in the idea of technological development. Jane Webb, for example, opens the elaborate adventures in *The mummy* of 1827 with an explanation of the galvanic techniques that bring the Pharaoh Cheops back to life; and in the subsequent adventures the mechanical marvels of her future world are a major entertainment for the reader. In like manner, long before Jules Verne, the author of *A hundred years hence* (1828) sends his hero on a journey round the world by means of kite-machines, steam barouchettes and fast transatlantic balloons.

By the 1830s, then, the tale of the future had become so well-known a literary device that a French historian brought out the first study of the genre; and in *Le Roman de l'avenir* of 1834 Félix Bodin claimed that the idea of progress was the primary cause of, and the necessary condition for, the new fiction. In the following year a striking demonstration of this vigorous faith in continued progress began in New York with the concoction of the first successful international hoax in newspaper history. On August 25 1835 the readers of the New York *Sun* were pleasantly surprised to read that the eminent astronomer Sir John Herschel had discovered an advanced civilization on the Moon by means of his new reflecting telescope. So powerful was the will-to-believe that the readers of the *Sun* accepted without question the daily reports of the temples, palaces, flying men and strange animals which Herschel and his assistant had observed on the Moon. The news was for most a welcome confirmation of what they expected. The sales of the *Sun* surpassed the optimistic calculations of the publisher. The story went into innumerable pamphlet editions; and later on, when the news reached Europe, there were similar demands for editions in English and for translations into Dutch, French, German, and Italian.

These expectations of constant progress were raised to the certainty of a scientific law after the publication of Darwin's *Origin of species* in 1859. As the new evolutionary theories spread the message of natural selection and the struggle for existence, they seemed to confirm the teaching of the new national histories – Macaulay, Buckle, Taine – that social and political progress would continue from age to age. At the same time a number of factors were working to start the tale of the future on the first major phase of its development as a means of propaganda and as a favoured medium for conjectures of every kind. First, the steady growth of population throughout the great technological nations and the parallel rise in the level of literacy had reached a point in the 1860s when publishers discovered that there was a vastly increased market for their products. One of the first to exploit the new opportunities was the astute and enterprising publisher, Pierre Jules Hetzel, who had plans for launching a new illustrated magazine for adolescents in 1862. Then Jules Verne, so the story goes, walked into his office with the first draft of *Five weeks in a balloon*, and a famous partnership began. Hetzel arranged that Verne was to write not less than one story a year for the *Magasin d'éducation et de récréation*, and each story was to be published as a book in the series of the *Voyages extraordinaires* which Hetzel started in 1867. The agreed scheme, Hetzel wrote, was for Verne 'to summarise all the knowledge of geography, geology, physics and astronomy which modern science has brought together, and in that attractive style of his to re-write the story of the universe.' Verne and Hetzel maintained that resolve for some forty years; and the heroic adventures and scientific wonders of *Twenty thousand leagues under the sea*, *From the Earth to the Moon*, *Around the world in eighty days*, *The Clipper of the clouds* – these gave adolescents of every age throughout the world an introduction to the powers of science and confirmation in the doctrine of progress.

The second factor at work in the evolution of futuristic fiction was the recent and rapid development of the war technologies – ironclads, breach-loading artillery, new rifles, the use of railways in the concentration and deployment of troops. The American Civil War, and more especially the Franco-German War of 1870, were a warning that the conduct of war was changing and, given the experimentation then going on, would continue to change. For an island people, dependent on foreign trade and unaccustomed to conscription, the defeat of the French was an omen that the British had to take seriously. So, a colonel of Engineers sent the editor of *Blackwood's Magazine* an admonitory tale about a future invasion of the United

Kingdom that ended in exemplary fashion with the destruction of British power. The uproar following on the publication of *The Battle of Dorking* in the May of 1871 showed that the tale of the future had once again discovered a prophetic model which was perfectly adapted to conveying serious messages about the state of the national defences. When Sir George Tomkyns Chesney's short story burst on the nation and the world, it was evident that the tale of the future had become a powerful and popular means of communication. For three months editions poured from the Blackwood presses in Edinburgh, and more than a dozen imitations and counterblasts appeared within weeks. There were voluminous reports in the European papers, and translations into Danish, Dutch, French, German, Italian, Portuguese; and special editions appeared in Australia, Canada, New Zealand, and the United States. Chesney had given the nineteenth century nation-states a potent device – *Der Zukunftskrieg, Les guerres imaginaires* – that proved to be a favoured means of propaganda in the decades before the First World War. Even more important, he had confirmed the tale of the future in its role as mediator between science and society, between the people and the possible.

Ever since the 1870s the course of futuristic fiction has been a process of constant development and increasing effectiveness – of new directions, the appearance of new styles of writing, and the regular introduction of new themes. After Verne and Chesney, the most important innovations were in utopian fiction. For many Victorians the ideal state of the future was both the pattern and the promise of the coming reign of social justice. And here it was once more a matter of a consensus of enthusiasms inspired by two widely-read books which for a time had a decisive influence on contemporary thinking. The first was a most famous, poorly written projection of the ideal socialist state, *Looking backward* by the American Edward Bellamy, which first appeared in 1888; and the second was an even more influential book (at least in Europe) which came out in Vienna in 1890 – *Freiland: ein soziales Zukunftsbild* – in which the Austrian economist and editor Theodor Hertzka set out a capitalist scheme for a more perfect future. The postscript to Bellamy's book explained that he meant *Looking backward* to be read 'in all seriousness, as a forecast, in accordance with the principles of evolution, of the next stage in the social and industrial development of humanity'. And that was how the world saw *Looking backward* which aroused immense enthusiasm on both sides of the Atlantic, inspired the founding of many Bellamy Clubs in the United States, and was translated into most of the major world languages, including Russian and Chinese.

By 1890 everything was ready for the appearance of H. G. Wells, the most original and inventive writer in the history of futuristic fiction. From the start in *The time machine* Wells developed his own remarkable variations on the established forms. In the style of earlier dystopias the Wellsian time-traveller discovers humanity in decline and goes on to observe the end of life upon Earth; and in *The war of the worlds* Wells showed that he had learnt from Chesney how to adapt the imaginary war story to the spectacular conditions of an interplanetary conflict. Wells was fortunate in his education, his imagination and his times. The biology he had learnt from T. H. Huxley was the core of his best fiction, and his exceptional capacity for ordered, logical fantasy gave his stories a vigour and coherence beyond the reach of all contemporary writers of science fiction. As Arnold Bennett noted in his journal for January 19 1904: 'No future novelist will be able to 'fudge' science now that Wells has shown how it can be done without fudging'.

Since the appearance of H. G. Wells, the tale of the future has continued to respond to the conditions of society and to the potentialities of the sciences. The fearful experiences of the First World War carried over into a series of new, admonitory projections. In a celebrated play of 1921, *RUR*, the Czech writer Karel Capek introduced the modern myth of the dangerous robots who represent the misuse of science. Then the Russian writer Zamyatin produced in *We* a famous premonitory story of the all-powerful and self-sufficient state; and this gave the German film director Fritz Lang material for *Metropolis* of 1926, one of the masterpieces of the early cinema. The mood of futuristic fiction between the two world wars was not optimistic. The old-style utopian visions of the steel-and-concrete worlds of brotherly love had vanished. The new fiction presented a sequence of devastating wars in *Ragnarok, Death rattle, The poison war*; prophecies of the destruction of the entire human race in *Unthinkable, Man alone, The last man*; and alarming forecasts of the political perils to come in *Revolution, The Battle of London, Traitor's way*. At their best the new writers spoke out for all mankind against the dangers that menaced the world in their time. One of the most eloquent was Aldous Huxley who devised *Brave new world* as the counter-image of the Wellsian world state; and in the 1930s that became the symbol of a renewed questioning of the once happy union between science and society.

This questioning has continued since 1945. The visions of the future have been more deadly wars, atomic disasters, fearful epidemics, and the last days of the human race. The grand old constructive and progressive ideal state has vanished; its place has been taken by *Nineteen eighty-four, Ape and essence, Player piano, Limbo '90* and the rest of the ominous prophecies of the 1950s and 1960s. The tale of the future has certainly kept its pact with mankind in so far as the shape of things to come is so often the salutary consummation of our worst fears. At the same time there has been a sustained outpouring of science fiction stories in the last thirty years. And here again the seriousness of many able writers – Brian Aldiss, Philip K. Dick, Ursula Le Guin, Stanislaw Lem, Kurt Vonnegut – appears in their stories of the future. These are allegories, dreams, visions, parables and prophetic warnings for a world united more than ever before by the communication sciences and divided by the ancient antagonisms of *Homo sapiens*. The tale of the future continues in its prophetic, admonitory role, observing all observers, seeking to anticipate all possibilities.

PART I CHRONOLOGICAL LIST WITH ANNOTATIONS

This list gives the first date of publication, the author wherever known, title, publisher and a brief note for all tales of the future (so far discovered) that have been published in the United Kingdom between 1644, the date of the earliest specimen as far as is known, and 1976.

Full titles have only been given where they seemed to be required. This means, in effect, that most of the political tracts, the satires and ideal states carry their full titles; in adventure stories and romances, all sub-titles have been omitted. Further, entries are strictly limited to prose fiction; all plays and poems set in a future period have been excluded. Similarly, juvenile fiction has been excluded; but there will, without doubt, be some stories especially in the field of the scientific romance that might be considered to be juvenile.

The list includes all known translations from foreign languages. Works by American authors and works by British authors that were first published in the United States are indicated by [U.S. and year of publication] at the end of the annotation. The names of the translators of foreign publications are given wherever they are known.

1644   **Anonymous (Cheynell, F.)** *Aulicus his dream of the Kings sudden comming to London*, London, 6p.
An anti-royalist forecast of the perils to be expected if Charles I returned to London.

1733   **Madden, S.** *The memoirs of the twentieth century: being the original letters of state under George the Sixth . . .revealed in the year 1728.* Vol. 1. Printed for Messieurs Osborn and Longman, x, 527p.
Pedestrian forecast of Europe about 1997: Mohammedanism is almost extinct; the Jesuits control Italy; Britain dominates Russia. (Only Vol. 1. published.)

1763   **Anonymous** *The reign of George VI, 1900–1925.* Printed for W. Nicoll, xxi, 192p.
Tory description of the ideal monarch, George VI, who defeats all European powers and becomes king of France. Frigates, ships-of-the-line and coaches are still part of life in the twentieth century. (See Oman, C., 1899.)

1769   **Anonymous** *Private Letters from an American in England to his Friends in America.* Printed for J. Almon, 163p.
Britain in decline: its harbours are empty, religion degenerate, great buildings in ruins. This has been caused by Scottish immigrants, idle bishops, fanatical Methodists.

1772   **Anonymous (Mercier L. S.)** *Memoirs of the year two thousand five hundred.* Translated from the French by W. H. (W. Hooper, M.D.) 2v. Printed for G. Robinson, 472p.

The first English translation of Sebastian Mercier's forecast of *L'An deux mille quatre cent quarante,* 1771, the first utopia of the future in which the idea of progress is dominant. The world is united in the brotherhood of man; France has a constitutional monarchy; Deism is the true religion; canals and other technological advances have improved life for all. A most influential utopia – there were many imitations, some seventeen editions in France, translations into English, Dutch and German. See *Note 1.*

1778   **Anonymous (Tickell, R.)** *Anticipation: Containing the Substance of His M------Y'S Most Gracious Speech to both H----S of P--------T.* Printed for T. Becket, 74p.

Arguments about the state of the nation and the conduct of the war with the American colonists placed in the mouths of the more eminent politicians of the day on the occasion of the opening of Parliament, 26 November 1778. Fox speaks on the 'impracticability of an offensive war in America'. Lord North proclaims 'that America is still the offspring of Great Britain.' See *Note 2.*

1780   **Anonymous (Croft Sir H.)** *The Abbey of Kilkhampton; or, monumental records for the year 1980.* G. Kearsly, 75p.

The text is a collection of eulogistic and satirical epitaphs on the author's contemporaries – from Burke to Boswell.

1781   **Anonymous** *Anticipation; or, the voyage of an American to England in the year 1899, in a series of letters, humorously describing the supposed situation of this kingdom at that period.* W. Lane, 163p.

A re-issue of *Private Letters,* 1769.

1788   **Anonymous (Croft, Sir H.)** *The wreck of Westminster Abbey: being a selection from the monumental records of the most conspcuous personages, who flourished towards the latter end of the eighteenth century.* Printed for C. Stalker, 60p.

In the same vein as the publication of 1780.

1797   **Anonymous (Mercier, L. S.)** *Astraea's return; or the halcyon days of France in the year 2440: a dream.* Translated from the French by Harriot Augusta Freeman. Printed for the translator; and sold by her at . . . Lambeth, 308p.

Another translation of *L'An 2440.*

1806   **Anonymous** *The last man; or, Omegarus and Syderia. A romance in futurity.* 2v. Printed for R. Dutton, 424p.

An unacknowledged translation from the French of Jean-Baptiste François-Xavier Cousin de Grainville, *Le Dernier Homme,* 1805: after centuries of progress, the world comes to an end.

1807   **Cassandra Non-Reveur** (*pseud.*) *The Red Book; or, the government of Francis the First, Emperor of the English . . . a dream.* J. J. Stockdale, 76p.

An attack on Sir Francis Burdett; the French Revolution repeats itself in Britain.

1819   **Anonymous** *One thousand eight hundred and twenty nine; or, "Shall it be so?"* J. J. Stockdale, 36p.
An attack on the claims of Catholic Emancipation; in 1829 the Stuarts are restored by Papal bull.

1824   **Anonymous (Banim, J.)** *Revelations of the dead-alive.* W. Simpkin & R. Marshall, 376p.
A satire, placed in the year A.D. 2023 and aimed at writers of the Romantic period.

1825   **A Late Fellow of St. John's, Cambridge (Hunt. L.?)** *The rebellion of the beasts.* G. & H. L. Hunt, xii, 166p. Illus.
The beasts of England rise against their masters.

1826   **Anonymous (Shelley, M.)** *The last man. By the author of Frankenstein.* 3v. H. Colburn, xi, 1038p.
Begins with the abdication of the last British monarch and ends with a plague that wipes out most of Europe.

1827   **Anonymous (Webb. J.)** *The mummy! A tale of the twenty-second century.* 3v. H. Colburn, viii, 951p.
A Gothic romance set in the highly advanced world of A.D. 2130. The story is one of the earliest examples of science fiction.

1828   **Moresby, Lord C.** (*pseud*?) *A hundred years hence; or the memoirs of Charles, Lord Moresby, written by himself.* Longman, Rees, Orme, 210p.
A tale of travel and romance in the advanced world of the twentieth century.

1831   **Anonymous** *Great Britain in 1841; or, the results of the Reform Bill.* Roake & Varty, 21p.
An account of the horrors expected to follow on the Reform Bill.

1831   **Anonymous** *A leaf from the future history of England on the subject of reform in Parliament.* Roake & Varty, 12p.
The evils of "Radical Reform" demonstrated.

1836   **Anonymous,** *Mrs. Maberly; or, the world as it will be.* John Macrone, 3v, (287 + 288 + 291p.)
Domestic tale of world-wide travels and romantic encounters set in the year 2036.

1837   **Anonymous (Williams, R. F)** *Eureka: a prophecy of the future.* 3v. Longman, Rees, Orme, 960p.
A German empire stretches from the Vistula to the Adriatic; Africa is a series of republics; and Britain is a forgotten land.

1838   **R. P. (Walker. R.)** *Oxford in 1888: a fragmentary dream by a Sub-Utopian. Published from the original MS. by the editor, R. P.* H. Slatter, 70p. Map.
A description of the reformed Oxford of the future.

1845   **Anonymous** *1945: a vision.* F. & J. Rivington. 39p.
The nation learns to repent of its "faithless days" after a disastrous war.

1847   **Anonymous (Henningsen, C. F.)** *Sixty years hence.* 3v.
T. Cautley Newby, 1070p.
A satire on the divisions in society.

1848   **Lamartine De Prat, M.L.A.** *France and England: a vision of the future.*
Translated from the French. H. G. Clarke, viii, 155p.
Political and utopian prophecy of a progressive, united Europe in which the
United Kingdom has no part.

1850   **Anonymous** *The Times, 333,379, 6th January, 1950.* 4p.
One of the several burlesque editions of *The Times* that appeared during the
second half of the last century. This issue, like the issue of 1862, made mild fun
of matters of general interest at the time.

1850   **Hovenden, R.** *A tract of future times or, the reflections of posterity on*
[1851]   *the excitement, hypocrisy, and idolatry of the nineteenth century.*
C. Gilpin, 190p.
A religious and moral lecture on the evils of the times.

1851   **Anonymous** *The last peer.* 3v. T. Cautley Newby, 1140p.
The development of machinery has reduced the demand for labour; decline of the
aristocracy and the monarchy follows.

1851   **Anonymous** *History of the sudden and terrible invasion of England by*
the French in . . . May, 1852. T. Bosworth, 23p.
A demonstration of the dangers of military unpreparedness; the French, under
"that little Corsican, Louis Napoleon Bonaparte", capture London.

1857   **Anonymous** *Imaginary history of the next thirty years.* Sampson Low,
72p.
A series of forecasts: Australia declares her independence; Chinese missionary
society established in London, etc.

1859   **Lang, H.** *The air battle: a vision of the future.* W. Penny, 112p.
Britain, now a backward country, is protected by the Black Saharans, the most
powerful nation on Earth.

1859   **Penny, Mrs S. J.** *A dream of the day that must come.* W. Penny, 58p.
A moral fantasy about Christian duty and the universal judgement.

1862   **Anonymous** *The Times No. 55,567, 1962.* 4p.
A forecast of the days when the House of Ladies and the House of Peeresses
rule Britain. The Thames at last a pure river; the International Exhibition covers
fourteen and a half miles of ground.

1867   **Mohoa (Fairburn, E.)** *The ships of Tarshish: being a sequel to Sue's*
"Wandering Jew". Hall & Co., 104p.
A romance built round the construction of a new type of battleship.

1867   **Wykehamicus Friedrich (Gale, F.)** *Anno Domini 3867. The history of the English Revolution. By Lord Macaulay's New Zealander. Edited by Wykehamicus Friedrich, Esq.* London 3867.P. S. King, 31p.
A blast against the Reform Bill of 1867.

1868   **O'Neil, H.** *Two thousand years hence.* Chapman and Hall, 351p. Illus.
[1867]   The consequences of the Reform Bill of 1867; "the reins of government were transferred . . . into the hands of poverty and ignorance".

1871   **Anonymous (Chesney, Sir G. T.)** *The Battle of Dorking: reminiscences of a Volunteer.* Blackwoods, 64p.
The Battle of Dorking episode is the most interesting example of pamphleteering in the last century. The original story, written when Chesney was president of the Royal Indian Civil Engineering College at Staines, was published anonymously in the May issue of *Blackwood's Magazine, 1871.*
The story described a successful invasion of Britain by Prussia. The British forces are easily defeated, thanks to antiquated equipment and obsolete tactics. This demonstration of the need for Army reform caught the public attention at a moment of great nervousness; it caused such dismay that Gladstone felt it necessary to make a speech against its 'alarmism'.
The number of pamphlets provoked by Chesney's story and the large number of foreign translations indicate the effectiveness of his ominous predictions. See *Note* 3.

1871   **Anonymous** *After the Battle of Dorking; or what became of the invaders?* G. Maddick, 23p.
The enemy are decisively repulsed.

1871   **Anonymous** *The Battle of Dorking: a myth.* Style, 31p.
A facetious account of how the battle was never really fought.

1871   **Anonymous** *The Battle of the ironclads; or, England and her foes in 1879.* G. J. Palmer, 32p.
How the Royal Navy saved Britain.

1871   **Anonymous** *Britannia in council.* Grant, 36p.
A facetious discussion of the Battle of Dorking.

1871   **Anonymous** *The cruise of the Anti-Torpedo.* Tinsley Bros., 48p.
A British submarine comes to the rescue after the Battle of Dorking.

1871   **Anonymous** *The hens who tried to crow.* Robert Hardwicke, 48p.
A Battle of Dorking fable set in a chicken run.

1871   **Anonymous** *Our hero: or, who wrote "The Battle of Dorking".* Bradbury, Evans, 48p.
A humorous repudiation of Chesney's story.

1871   **Anonymous** *The official despatches and correspondence relative to the Battle of Dorking, as moved for in the House of Commons, 21st July, 1920,* W. H. Elliott, 8p.
A fake gazette: shows that Britain was not defeated at the Battle of Dorking.

1871   **Anonymous** *The suggested invasion of England by the Germans.*
Houlston, 16p.

Translation of a German fantasy: Trutz-Baumwoll, J. M. (*pseud.*) *Sendschreiben des deutsch-englischen Zukunfts-politiker . . . S. M. den Deutschen Kaiser (Allgemeine Zeitung,* 3 June, 154, 1871)
A German variation on the Battle of Dorking.

1871   **Anonymous (Stone, C.)** *What happened after the Battle of Dorking; or, the Victory of Tunbridge Wells.* Routledge, 60p.

Continues where Chesney left off: the British forces recover and make a successful counter-attack.

1871   **Anonymous (Hayward, A.)** *The second Armada: a chapter of future history.* Harrison & Sons, 16p.

The Royal Navy defeats an invasion in 1874.

1871   **Dioscorides, Dr. (Harting, Pieter)** *Anno Domini 2071.* Translated from the Dutch by Dr. A. V. Bikkers. W. Tegg, 132p.

Roger Bacon conducts the author round the perfect world of the future.

1871   **Hemyng, B.** *The Commune in London: or, thirty years hence, a chapter of anticipated history.* C. H. Clarke, 45p.

After a British defeat, the mob rises and proclaims a republic; Gladstone is held responsible for all the disasters.

1871   **M., J. W.** *The coming Cromwell.* British and Colonial Publishing Co., 48p.

A new Cromwell establishes a republic and defeats a German invasion.

1871   **M., J. W.** *The Siege of London.* Robert Hardwicke, 64p.

Another version of 'the old woman's story that lately appeared in print . . . an account of the invasion of England.'

1871   **McCauley, M. R.** (*pseud.*) *Chapters from future history: the Battle of Berlin.* Tinsley Brothers, 54p

A German republican movement ruins enemy plans to conquer Britain.

1871   **Maguire, J. F.** *The next generation.* 3v Hurst & Blackett, 997p.

A better world in 1891: Ireland has self-government, women have the vote, and Britain has obtained "nearly half of the once great Empire of China".

1871   **Moltruhn, M.** (*pseud.*) *The other side at the Battle of Dorking.* Whittaker, 84p.

Although the enemy have taken London, the Royal Navy cuts them off from their bases.

1871   **Sketchley, A. (Rose, G.)** *Mrs. Brown on the Battle of Dorking.* G. Routledge, 58p.

A humorous account of the battle.

1872   **Octogenarian** (*pseud.*) *The British Federal Empire: how it was founded. A speech . . . in a certain city of the Empire.* C. H. Clarke, 32p.
After defeating Russia and Germany, the British people create a federal empire.

1873   **Maitland, E.** *By and by: an historical romance of the future.* 3v. R. Bentley, iv, 1034p.
An ideal state of the future: socialism, world government, careers for women, a smoke-free London, etc.

1873   **N., J.** *Cuttings from 'The Times' of 1900.* John Hodges, 28p.
Series of forecasts about contemporary evils: immoral journalism, financial manipulations, German military ambitions, sectarian education, etc.

1873   **Verne, J.** *From the Earth to the Moon direct in 97 hours 20 minutes.*Translated from the French by L. Mercier and E. E. King. Sampson Low, Marston, 323p. Illus.
The Gun Club of Baltimore fires the first passenger-carrying projectile at the Moon. First published 1865 as *De la Terre à la Lune.*

1874   **Anonymous (Blair, A.)** *Annals of the twenty-ninth century: or, the autobiography of the tenth president of the World Republic.* 3v. S. Tinsley, 758p.
A perfect world of Christian concord, scientific advances, space travel, and universal peace.

[1874]   **Macaulay, C. (Adams, W. M.)** *The carving of Turkey. A chapter of European history, from sources hitherto unpublished.* Mead & Co., 80p.
Italy, France, Scandinavia join with the United Kingdom in a war against Germany and Russia.

1875   **Anonymous** *The Battle of Pluck.* A. S. Humphfrey, 31p.
A repudiation of the Battle of Dorking proposition: the Germans are decisively repulsed.

1875   **Anonymous** *In the future: a sketch in ten chapters.* "Express" Office, Hampstead, 66p.
A European commonwealth under one supreme king has emerged from the destruction of Rome.

1876   **Anonymous** *The Invasion of 1883.* J. Maclehose (Glasgow), 62p.
Another anti-Chesney story: once again the German invaders are totally repulsed, thanks to a reformed Army system.

1876   **Anonymous** *A parallel case; or, the Straits of Dover question A.D. 2345.* Bell, Darlington, 11p.
A political lesson: Britain is conquered in the twenty-fourth century by the mighty Ashantee nation.

1876   **Anonymous** *1975: a tradition. By my great grandson.* E. West, Simpkin, Marshall, 163p.
A romance set in the future.

1876   **Cassandra** (*pseud.*) *The Channel Tunnel; or, England's ruin.* W. Clowes, 37p.
A successful German invasion by means of the Channel Tunnel.

1877   **Anonymous** *Fifty years hence: an old soldier's tale of England's downfall.* G. W. Bacon, 32p.
Because Britain had become involved in the Turkish question, the Russians and Germans attacked and conquered the United Kingdom.

1877   **Anonymous (Dyas, R. H.)** *The Upas: a vision of the past, present and future.* Charles Watts, 438p.
Spirit of the future takes narrator on tour of all history, closing with future triumph of free thought.

1877   **Merlin Nostradamus (Cobbe, F. P.)** *The age of science: a newspaper of the 20th century.* Ward, Lock & Tyler, 50p.
Ironic forecasts of future developments.

1878   **Anonymous** *Democracy by telephone; or, Parliament a year hence.* G. Taylor, 16p.
A farce based on the introduction of telephones to the Commons.

1878   **Anonymous** *Gortschakoff and Bismarck; or, Europe in 1940.* J. Parker, 14p.
German and Russian victories in Europe.

1878   **Verne, J.** *Hector Servadac.* Translated from the French by E. E. Frewer. Sampson Low, Marston, 370p. Illus.
A comet grazes the earth and carries off part of North Africa into space. Originally published 1877 as *Hector Servadac.*

1879   **Anonymous (Chesney, Sir G.T.)** *The new ordeal.* W. Blackwood, 140p.
The nations revert to ordeal by combat, since weapons have become too destructive.

1879   **Anonymous (Watson, H. C. M.)** *Erchomenon; or, the republic of materialism.* Sampson Low, 226p.
The future consequences of irreligion and Darwinism.

1879   **Dekhnewallah, A.** (*pseud.*) *The great Russian invasion of India: a sequel to the Afghanistan campaign of 1878-9* Harrison, 69p.
A warning of the possibilities to be expected from "the subjection of India to a Secretary of State in England".

1880   **Anonymous** *Back again; or five years of Liberal rule.* Sampson Low, 32p.
Collapse of the British Empire follows granting of Home Rule to Ireland.

1880   **Hay, W. D.** *The doom of the great city: being the narrative of a survivor, written A.D. 1942.* Newman, 52p.
A London fog suffocates the wicked inhabitants of the city.

1880   **Verne, J.** *The Begum's fortune.* Translated by W. H. G. Kingston.
[1879]   Sampson, Low, Marston, 239p. Illus.
         The virtuous Frenchman, Dr. Sarrasin, and the wicked Professor Schultz of Jena construct their ideal cities in North America. First published 1879 as *Les cinq millions de la Bégum.*

1881   **Budge** *(pseud.) The eastern question solved.* W. H. Allen, 82p.
         The European powers occupy Constantinople which becomes "an international capital, governed by a permanent congress . . . of all the European nations".

1881   **Hay, W. D.** *Three hundred years hence; or, a voice from posterity.*
         Newman, xv, 356p.
         A remarkable forecast of the highly organized and scientific world of the future.

1881   **Lang-Tung** *(pseud.) The decline and fall of the British Empire . . .*
         Written for the use of junior classes in schools by Lang-Tung, Professor
         of History at the Imperial University of Pekin. F. V. White, 32p.
         How the Chinese conquered Britain.

1881   **M. Pee** *(pseud.) Hibernia's House; a forecast of the Irish Commons*
         assembled at Dublin. E. W. Allen, 30p.
         Comic debates in an Irish parliament.

1881   **Prophet** *(pseud.) The Wearing o' the Green in 1890.* E. Stanford, 10p.
         Political independence does not benefit the Irish.

1882   **Anonymous** *The dawn of the twentieth century.* 3v. Remington, 781p.
         In the better world of the future the Pope has repudiated infallibility, Europe is a federation of states, and population everywhere has become "polished, reasonable and tractable".

1882   **Anonymous (Butler, Sir W. F.)** *The invasion of England, told twenty*
         years after by an old soldier. Sampson Low, Marston, Searle, 190p.
         The Germans conquer because Britain had failed to develop "the stout stock of English yeomen and peasant life".

1882   **Anonymous (Besant, Sir W.)** *The revolt of man.* W. Blackwood, 258p.
         A satire directed against the emancipation of women.

1882   **The Demure One** *(pseud.) The Battle of Boulogne; or how Calais*
         became English again. C. F. Roworth, 51p.
         The Volunteers defeat a French attempt to invade the United Kingdom through the Channel Tunnel.

1882   **Grip** *(pseud.) How John Bull lost London; or, the capture of the*
         Channel Tunnel. Sampson Low, 127p.
         French troops, disguised as tourists, pour through the Channel Tunnel and take London.

1882   **Grip** (*pseud.*) *The monster municipality, or, Gog and Magog reformed. A dream.* Sampson Low, 128p.
An attack on methods of municipal reform.

1882   **Nunsowe Greene** (*pseud.*) A thousand years hence. Sampson Low, xii, 397p.
Air travel, planetary journeys, etc. in the scientific world of the future.

1882   **Trollope, A.** *The fixed period.* 2v. W. Blackwood, 403p.
Steam-bowlers and mechanical catchers for cricket in 1980; a poor attempt by Trollope.

1882   **Vindex** (*pseud.*) *England crushed; the secret of the Channel Tunnel revealed.* P. S. King, 16p.
An account of an imaginary scheme for a German invasion by way of the Tunnel.

1883   **Anonymous** *The Battle of the Moy; or, how Ireland gained her independence in 1892–1894.* W. S. Sonnenschein, 123p. Illus.
After a British defeat in war, an Irish ideal state emerges: "No more landlords, no more agents, with their blighting and withering trains of tithes, distrains and evictions". [U.S. 1883]

1883   **Anonymous** *The Battle of Port Said.* Reprinted from "Engineering", 72p.
Author writes: "The object of the story is to expose certain weaknesses in the construction of our warships".

1883   **Anonymous** *King Bertie, A.D. 1900.* Crown Pub. Co.
From the *English Catalogue*; no copy available.

1883   **Forth, C.** *The surprise of the Channel Tunnel.* H. Wightman, 22p.
The French treacherously attempt to invade by way of the Channel Tunnel.

1883   **Ulidia** (*pseud.*). *The Battle of Newry.* Hodges, Figgis, 42p.
Liberal legislation confiscates all large estates and replaces the House of Lords by an elected Upper House. Other repressive measures cause Ulster to rise in rebellion.

1884   **Anonymous** *England in 1910.* Willing & Co., 16p.
A brief account of the ideal future: practical education for all, Atlantic balloon services, the Thames a clean river.

1884   **Anonymous** *How Glasgow ceased to flourish: a tale of 1890.* Wilson & McCormick, Glasgow, 28p.
An invasion story – Russian warships on the Clyde – designed to argue for a better defence policy.

1884   **Anonymous (Brookfield A. M.)** *Simiocracy: a fragment from future history.* W. Blackwood, viii, 186p.
A satire on the Liberals; they give the vote to all aged fifteen and over with disastrous consequences.

1884   **Anonymous (Fairfield, ?.?.)** *The socialist revolution of 1888, by an Eye-witness.* Harrison, 35p.
The consequences of "the extravagant doctrines of Mr. Henry George".

1884   **Anonymous (Ouseley, Rev. G. J.)** *Palingenesia; or the earth's new birth.* H. Nisbet, xi, 359p.
The new world of justice and brotherly love is ruled over by one king who resides in Jerusalem.

1884   **Anonymous (Wise, C.)** *Darkness and dawn: the peaceful birth of a new age.* Kegan Paul, 141p.
An aristocrat leads the nation to a juster form of society; rest of the country follows his example; property divided equally.

1884   **Posteritas** *(pseud.) The siege of London.* Wyman, 68p.
Gladstone held responsible for the French invasion of Britain.

1884   **Robinson, E. A. & Wall, G. A.** *The Disk, a Prophetic reflection.* Griffith, Farran, Okeden, 182p.
The invention of the photo-electrophone gives the world television.

1885   **Anonymous** *The battle of tomorrow.* Chappell, 54p.
A demonstration of "the horrors of war into which the nations are drifting".

1885   **Anonymous (Lang, A. and Kendall, M.)** *That very Mab.* Longmans, Green, 215p.
Queen Mab comes from the Southern Ocean to England, where she discovers the oddities of civilized life.

1885   **Coverdale, Sir H. S.** *(pseud.) The fall of the Great Republic.* Sampson, Low, Marston etc., 226p.
Socialism and Irish immigrants cause the downfall of government in the United States and bring on the triumvirate of O'Hallaran, Wagner and Van Liest. European Coalition declares war and occupies the United States. [U.S. 1885].

1885   **Greer, T.** *A modern Daedalus.* Griffith, Farran, xvi, 261p.
The hero discovers the secret of winged flight and forms a flying brigade to fight for Ould Ireland's liberty.

1885   **Jefferies, R.** *After London.* Cassell, vii, 442p.
A fantasy of the barbaric and feudal world that emerges after the destruction of the great cities.

1885   **S. L. S. (St. Loe Strachey, J.)** *The great bread riots; or, what came of fair trade.* Simpkin, Marshall, 60p.
The Corn Laws are re-introduced and prices soar disastrously.

1885   **Tuckwell, Rev. W.** *The new utopia; or, England in 1985.* Birmingham Sunday Lecture Society, 16p.
The new world of science and democracy.

1886   **Anonymous** *The great Irish rebellion of 1886.* Harrison, 48p.
The Orangemen rally to the cause of Queen and nation.

1886   **Anonymous** *Newry Bridge; or, Ireland in 1887.* W. Blackwood, 72p.
A civil war in Ireland forces the British government to treat Ireland justly.

[1886]   **Anonymous** *Openings and proceedings of the Irish Parliament; two visions.* Reeves & Turner, 24p.
One vision shows an Irish parliament in 1887. The other, set in 1894, shows the Irish members back at Westminster.

1886   **Anonymous** *A radical nightmare; or, England forty years hence.* Field & Tuer, 62p.
As a result of radical government "almost every Conservative . . . had been compelled to leave the country."

1886   **Innominatus** *(pseud.) In the light of the twentieth century.* John Hodges, 153p.
Moral and religious projection in protest against the belief that "whatever the spirit of the age appears most conspicuously to be is the last word of social progress . . ."

1886   **Lester, E.** *The siege of Bodike: a prophecy of Ireland's future.* J. Heywood, 140p.
Although given self-government, the Irish rise in rebellion and have to be put down.

1886   **Minto, W.** *The crack of doom.* 3v. W. Blackwood, 885p.
A romance set at a time when a comet is expected to hit the earth.

1886   **Parnell, J.** *Cromwell the Third.* Published by the author, 11p.
Tertius Cromwell inaugurates a Socialist millennium, peace on earth and universal prosperity.

1886   **Watlock, W. A.** *The next 'Ninety-three; or, crown, commune and colony. Told in a citizen's diary.* Field & Tuer, 36p.
The horrors of a socialist Britain.

1887   **Anonymous (Fox, S. Middleton)** *Our own Pompeii.* 2v. W. Blackwood, 498p.
A satire on contemporary attitudes in art and literature.

1887   **Anonymous (Hudson, W. H.)** *A crystal age.* T. F. Unwin, iv, 287p.
In his preface to the second edition (1906) Hudson writes: "Romances of the future, however fantastic they may be, have for most of us a perennial if mild interest, since they are born of a very common feeling – a sense of dissatisfaction with the existing order of things combined with a vague faith in or hope of a better one to come". An arcadian utopia set in the remote future.

1887   **Captain of the Royal Navy.** *The battle off Worthing; why the invaders never got to Dorking.* London Literary Society, 96p.
The Royal Navy repulses all enemy attempts at invasion.

[1887]   **Clowes, W. L. and Burgoyne, A. H.** *The great naval war of 1887.*
Hatchards, 60p. Map.
A French conquest of Britain is "the natural result of years of indifference,
mismanagement, and parsimony".

1887   **Gay, J. Drew.** *The mystery of the shroud: a tale of socialism.* J. W.
Arrowsmith, 134p.
Mining and smelting activities in south east England create permanent fog that
provides cover for revolutionists.

1887   **Gopcevic, S.** *The conquest of Britain in 1888, and the sea fights and
battles that led to it.* Translated from the German by Commander F. H.
E. Crowe, R. N. Griffin, 54p. Illus.
A tactical description of naval warfare.

[1887]   **Hope, Lt. Col. W.** *An omitted incident in the "Great Naval War of
1887".* George Redway, 24p.
An answer to the story by Clowes & Burgoyne: successful operations by an
improvised merchant cruiser.

1887   **North, D.** *The last man in London.* Hodder & Stoughton, 118p.
A mediocre fantasy.

[1887]   **Peddie, J.** *The capture of London.* General Publishing Co. 15p.
In 1905 the French Army invades Britain by way of the Channel Tunnel.

1887   **Verne, J.** *Clipper of the clouds.* Translated from the French. Sampson
Low, Marston, Searle, 234p. Illus.
How the first aeronef flew round the world. Originally published 1886 as *Robur le
Conquérant.*

1887   **W., E.** *The Island of Anarchy.* Lovejoy's Library, Reading, 105p.
An early twentieth century reforming Parliament deals in a radical and religious
manner with criminals and anarchists.

1887   **Watten, B.** *Stratharran; or, the Crofters' Revolt.* Oliphant, Anderson &
Ferrier, 190p.
Scottish crofters combine to force justice on the Laird.

1888   **Anonymous** *The dawn of the twentieth century, 1st January, 1901.*
Field & Tuer, 156p.
The author presents a very rosy picture of the future of the British Empire.

1888   **Anonymous** *"Down with England!"* Translated from the French.
Chapman & Hall, 152p.
A translation of the popular anti-British prophecy, *Plus d'Angleterre.* The French
destroy the Royal Navy; the British Empire is dissolved.

1888   **Anonymous** *The Great Irish "Wake".* Clement-Smith, (London and New
York), 23p.
The granting of independence proves no blessing to the Irish.

1888   **Anonymous** *Plus encore d'Angleterre; or, repulse of the French.* J. W. Arrowsmith, 16p.
The introduction states: "This little brochure is a reply to the French pamphlet *Plus d'Angleterre,* which describes an imaginary invasion and conquest of England."

1888   **Anonymous** *The "Russia's Hope"; or Britannia no longer rules the waves.* Translated from the Russian by C. J. Cooke, with a preface by William Beatty-Kingston. Chapman & Hall, iv, 175p.
Exploits of a Russian cruiser in a successful war against the United Kingdom.

[1888]   **Besant, W.** *The inner house.* Arrowsmith, 198p.
Rediscovery of the romantic past provokes rebellion against a communist dictatorship.

1888   **Clapperton, J. H.** *Margaret Dunmore, or a Socialist Home.* Swan, Sonnenschein, 204p.
Idealists collaborate in establishing a socialist community.

1888   **Lester, H. F.** *The taking of Dover.* J. W. Arrowsmith, 44p.
The French conquer Britain.

1888   **Lyon, Captain, E. D.** *Ireland's dream: a romance of the future.* 2v, Swan, Sonnenschein, 520p.
Gladstone gives Ireland her liberty; and general misery is the result.

1888   **Mackay, D.** *The dynamite ship.* Illus. Page, Pratt & Turner, 209p.
A self-righteous tale ("Saints protect us") of the bombardment of London by the Irish League, followed by the Lord Mayor's surrender and an Irish rising.
[U.S. 1888]

[1889]   **Anonymous** *The bombardment of Scarbro' by the Russian fleet in 1891.* Crown Printing Co., 36p.
A facetious account of a bombardment and landing at Scarborough.

1889   **Anonymous** *England's danger; or, rifts within the lute. A Russian plot.* Griffin (Portsmouth), 98p.
Russian agents plan to blow up Woolwich Arsenal, Upnor Castle, and the Medway magazines in support of a Russian invasion scheme.

1889   **Bellamy, E.** *Looking backward, 2000–1887.* W. Reeves, 249p.
Bellamy's description of an organized and socialistic future world was the most influential ideal state to appear in the United States in the last century; it was probably the most important specimen of its kind in Europe. It was translated into most European languages; it started off a flood of more than fifty utopias in the United States; and it provoked William Morris so much that he wrote his own idea of a better future, *News from nowhere.* [U.S. 1888]

[1889]   **Corbett, E. B.** *New Amazonia: a foretaste of the future.* Lambert, 146p.
In A.D. 2472 Ireland is the New Amazonia, colonised by surplus women from Britain. A land of peace, vegetarianism, and no men.

1889   **Cromie, R.** *For England's sake.* F. Warne, 154p.
An heroic maharajah defeats a Russian invasion force in "the year of grace 189–".

1889   **Dalton, H. R. S.** *Lesbia Newman.* George Redway, 327p.
A tale of the reunion of the Christian churches, of world peace, and the emancipation of women.

1889   **Grove, W.** *The wreck of a world.* Digby & Long, xi, 151p.
A Darwinian tale of the time when the machines rebel and threaten to destroy mankind.

1889   **Hayes, W. D.** *Mr. Boyton: merchant, millionaire and king.* Simpkin, Marshall, Hamilton, 266p.
American millionaire becomes King of Poland and leads his people to victory against the Germans.

1889   **Laurie, A. (Grousset, P.)** *The conquest of the Moon.* Translated from the French. Sampson, Low, 354p. Illus.
Space travel and lunar exploration. Originally published 1887 as *Les Éxilés de la terre.*

1889   **Stockton, F. R.** *The great war syndicate.* Longmans, 160p.
A syndicate directs operations for America in an Anglo-American war; their motor-bomb causes Britain to surrender. [U.S. 1889].

1889   **"V"** *The swoop of the eagles. Ward & Downey, 88p.*
The United Kingdom faces an invasion by the continental powers.

1889   **Vogel, Sir J.** *Anno Domini 2000; or, woman's destiny.* Hutchinson, viii 331p.
Equality of the sexes in the Federated Empire of the future.

1890   **Anonymous** *The angel and the idiot: a story of the next century.*
No copy available.

1890   **Anonymous (Watson, H. C. M.)** *Decline and fall of the British Empire; or, the witches cavern.* Trischler, 291p.
Irreligion and socialism have ruined Britain.

1890   **Anonymous** *Pope Booth: the Salvation Army, A.D. 1950.* W Lucas., 16p.
A tale of consequences: "Let the 'General' stick to his first idea –teaching men sobriety and the need of purity; but when he enters into the arena of Socialism . . . it is time for all men to pause and think".

1890
[1889]   **Bleunard, A.** *Babylon electrified. The history of an expedition undertaken to restore Ancient Babylon by the power of electricity and how it resulted.* Translated from the French by Frank Linstow White. Illus. 284p.
An extraordinary fantasy of the attempt to make Mesopotamia a centre of civilization. Originally published 1888 as *La Babylone électrique.*

1890   **Dixie, Lady F.** *Gloriana; or, the revolution of 1900.* Henry, x, 350p.
A melodramatic romance written round a campaign for women's rights.

1890   **Laurie, A. (Grousset. P.)** *New York to Brest in seven hours.*
Translated from the French. Sampson Low, Marston, 302p. Illus.
An engineering genius builds an oil pipe-line from America to Europe. Originally
published 1888 as *De New-York à Brest en sept heures.*

1890   **Thiusen, I. (MacNie, J.)** *Looking forward; or, the Diothas.*
G. P. Putnam, viii, 258p.
In the 96th century war is an anachronism; and poverty has been abolished.
Originally published U.S. 1883 as *The Diothas.*

1890   **Walsh, R.** *The fate of the Triple Alliance.* Simpkin, Marshall, 64p.
Formation of an "Anti-War Union" brings a European war to a rapid end.

1891   **Anonymous** *The Christ that is to be.* Chapman, 350p.
By A.D. 2100 Europe is a socialist community, China a great power, and Britain
has lost her colonies. In a successful, materialistic world the Second Coming
takes place.

1891   **Anonymous** *The Ingathering: a fiction of social economy.* Waterlow and
Sons, 56p.
Brief account of a communal and family system of social organization.

1891   **Anonymous (Morris, A.)** *Looking ahead: a tale of adventure (not by
the author of "Looking Backward").* Henry, 264p.
An anti-Bellamy forecast in which the author demonstrates "that the plans
adopted to bring about the industrial millenium had instead only brought about
the shoddy feudalism which I saw around me."

1891   **Arnold-Forster, H. O.** *In a conning tower.* Cassell, 54p. Illus.
The author intends to give 'a faithful idea of the possible course of action
between two modern ironclads.' A famous story in its day. Reprinted from
Murray's Magazine, 1888.

[1891] **Bland, C. A.** *Independence: a retrospect.* Harrison & Sons, 56p.
Political consequences of Australian demands for independence.

1891   **Boisgilbert, E. (Donnelly, I.)** *Caesar's column.* Ward & Lock, xii, 242p.
See next entry: Donnelly's story was first published U.S. April 1890 under a
pseudonym in order to stimulate sales. The author's identity was revealed in
November 1890.

1891   **Donnelly, I.** *Caesar's column.* Sampson, Low, 367p.
A socialist revolution overthrows an oppressive government. [U.S. 1890]

[1891] **Folingsby, K.** *Meda: a tale of the future.* Printed for private circulation.
Aird & Coghill, 325p.
By A.D. 5575 cities have been abandoned and physiological development has
reached the stage when mankind can live on air.

1891   **Herbert, W.** *The world grown young: being a brief record of*
[1892]   *reforms . . . by the late Mr. Philip Adams.* W. H. Allen, 304p.
         A philanthropist creates a better Britain.

1891   **Hertzka, Dr. T.** *Freeland: a social anticipation.* Translated from the
         German by A. Ransom. Chatto & Windus, xxiv, 443p.
         A description by the Viennese economist, Theodor Hertzka, of the establishment
         of an ideal state on a sound economic basis in Kenya; the work had considerable
         influence in Europe. Originally published 1889 as *Freiland: ein soziales
         Zukunftsbild.*

1891   **Hume, F. W.** *The year of miracle: a tale of the year one thousand nine
         hundred.* Routledge, 148p.
         A fanatical socialist spreads the germs of a plague in London. Eventually an ideal
         state emerges.

[1891]   **Jerome, J. K.** *The new utopia* in *Diary of a pilgrimage.*
         J. W. Arrowsmith, 80p. Illus.
         An ironical account of life under a socialist government in the twenty-ninth
         century.

[1891]   **Michaelis, R.** *A sequel to Looking backward; or, "Looking further
         forward".* Translated from the German. W. Reeves, vi, 110p.
         A demonstration that Bellamy's ideal state "stripped of its fine colouring is
         nothing but communism". Originally published 1890 as *Ein Blick in die Zukunft.*

1891   **Miller, G. N.** *The strike of sex.* W. H. Reynolds, 63p.
         The women go on strike so that "no woman from this time forth and forever shall
         be subjected to the woes of maternity without her free and specific
         endorsement."

1891   **Morris, W.** *News from nowhere: an epoch of rest, being some chapters
         from a utopian romance.* Reeves & Turner, 238p.
         Morris produced his own characteristic account of an arcadian future world as a
         reply to Bellamy's *Looking backward.* "I wouldn't care to live in such a Cockney
         paradise as he imagines." First issued serially in the *Commonweal* in 1890.

1891   **Oakhurst, W.** *The universal strike of 1899.* William Reeves, 90p.
         A general strike leads to better understanding between classes and greater
         justice for all.

1891   **Strachey, J. St. L.** *How England became a republic: a romance of the
         constitution.* Arrowsmith, 71p.
         Strachey writes that he has "endeavoured to work out a scheme by which we
         might maintain our existing institutions intact, even should we no longer be
         able . . . to employ the services of a personal monarch."

1891   **Thomas, C.** *The crystal button.* Routledge, 160p.
         Life in the advanced, scientific world of the forty-seventh century. [U.S. 1891]

1891   **Verne, J.** *The purchase of the North Pole.* Sampson, Low, Marston etc.
[1890]   182p. Illus.
 The Baltimore Gun Club plans to shift the Earth's axis. First published 1889 as *Sans dessus dessous.*

1891   **X.Y.Z.** *The Vril staff.* David Stott, 298p.
 An idealist uses a secret weapon to support the European League of Peace.

1892   **Anonymous** *The doom of the County Council of London.* W. H. Allen, 38p.
 How the London County Council became too powerful.

1892   **Clowes, W. L.** *The captain of the "Mary Rose": a tale of tomorrow.* Tower Publishing Co., xvi, 308p. Illus.
 The author declares his intention of giving an answer to the question: "What will the sea-fighting of tomorrow be like?"

1892   **Donnelly, I.** *The golden bottle.* Sampson, Low & Co., 246p.
 The hero, given power to turn iron into gold, overthrows capitalism, defeats the European powers, and finally establishes a world state. [U.S. 1892].

1892   **Farningham, M. (Hearne, M. A.)** *Nineteen hundred?* J. Clarke, viii, 318p.
 The Christian Party secures control of Parliament and a perfect state begins.

1892   **J.A.C.K.** *Golf in the Year 2000.* Fisher Unwin, 159p.
 A comic tale of golf in the future – mechanical caddies, more powerful clubs, better balls.

1892   **L'Estrange, M.** *(pseud.) What we are coming to?* David Douglas, 124p.
 A voluminous forecast ranging from decimal currency to phonetic spelling.

[1892]   **Morgan, A. and Brown, C.** *The disintegrator.* Digby & Long, 220p.
 A scientist runs into unexpected troubles when he seeks to control nature.

[1892]   **Seaforth, A. N. (Clarke, G. S.)** *The last great naval war.* Cassell, 120p. Maps.
 The story of a Franco-British war which opens in 189–.

1892   **Strongi'th'arm, C. (Armstrong, C. W.)** *The yorl of the Northmen; or, the fate of the English race, being the romance of a monarchical Utopia.* Reeves & Turner, 127p.
 An ideal state in the style of William Morris.

1893   **Anonymous** *1895: under Home Rule.* Simpkin, Marshall, 18p.
 The miseries of Home Rule for Ireland fully demonstrated.

1893   **Bennett, A.** *The dream of an Englishman.* Simpkin, Marshall, 190p.
 Vision of future greatness ending with forecast of space travel.

1893   **Bramston, M.** *The Island of Progress* in *The Wild Lass of Estmere and other stories.* Seeley & Co. pp.201–227.
Brief ironic vision of a progressive, technological future in which everything is subordinated to the demands of science.

1893   **Colomb, Rear-Admiral P. and others.** *The great war of 189–: a*
[1892] *forecast.* W. Heinemann, x, 308p. Illus.
The author begins: "In the following narrative an attempt is made to forecast the course of events preliminary and incidental to the Great War which, in the opinion of military and political experts, will probably occur in the near future".

[1893] **Mr. Dick** *(pseud.) James Ingleton: the history of a social state A.D. 2000.* J. Blackwood, 450p.
A monarchical restoration ends the miseries of life under a socialist government.

1893   **Donovan, Rev. A.** *The Irish Rebellion of 1898.* Hodges, Figgis, 12p.
The story of "a cruel and treacherous rebellion", the result of "the sinister influence of Mr. Gladstone".

[1893] **Ex-revolutionist** *(pseud.) "England's downfall"; or, the last great revolution.* Digby, Long, 175p.
A Revolutionary League seizes power with disastrous results.

1893   **Fawcett, E. D.** *Hartmann the anarchist; or, the doom of the great city.* E. Arnold, 214p. Illus.
How the anarchists attacked the capitalist countries.

1893   **Griffith, G.** *The angel of the revolution.* Tower Publishing Co., viii, 393p. Illus.
An international conspiracy of nihilists overthrows the Czar.

1893   **Hayes, F. W.** *The great revolution of 1905; or, the story of the Phalanx.* R. Forder, lxviii, 316p.
The dedicated idealists of the Phalanx secure power in Parliament and begin a programme of nationalisation.

1893   **Hayes, F. W.** *The Phalanx League. State Industrialism: the story of the Phalanx. With an account of civilization in Great Britain at the close of the nineteenth century.* William Reeves. Bellamy Library No. 34, 316p.
Another edition of the above.

1893   **L'Estrange, H.** *Platonia.* J. W. Arrowsmith, 190p.
A space-craft powered by electricity visits the planet Platonia where the inhabitants live in an utopian state.

1893   **Mael, P. (Causse, C. & Vincent, C.)** *Under the sea to the North Pole.* Translated from the French. Sampson, Low, Marston, 244p. Illus.
Adventure story of a journey to the Pole by a submarine.

1893   **Moffat, W. G. & White, J.** *What's the world coming to?* E. Stock, 172p.
A world war ushers in an International Federation, universal peace, and an age of scientific marvels.

1893   **O'Flannagan, Right Hon. P.** *(pseud.) Ireland a nation!* Olley, 37p.
A humorous account of Ireland under Home Rule, written from the Ulster point of view.

1893   **Richter, E.** *Pictures of the socialistic future.* Translated from the German by H. Wright, with an introduction by T. Mackay. Sonnenschein, 134p.
A satirical description of life under socialism in a future Germany: another broadside in the anti-Bellamy battle. Originally published 1891 as *Sozialdemokratische Zukunftsbilder.*

1894   **Anonymous** *Story of my dictatorship.* Bliss & Co., 22p.
A fantasy of socialism and land reform. [U.S. 1894].

1894   **Bingham, F.** *The cap becomes a coronet.* Simpkin, Marshall, 50p. Illus.
A farcical tale of domestic service.

[1894]   **Clowes, W. L.** *The double emperor.* E. Arnold, 238p.
A Ruritanian romance of the future.

1894   **Eardley-Wilmot, Capt. S.** *The next naval war.* E. Stanford, 74p. Illus.
The French defeat Britain in a war over the evacuation of Egypt.

1894   **Griffith, G.** *Olga Romanoff.* Tower Publishing Co., viii, 377p.
A romantic sequel to the novel of 1893.

1894   **Griffith, G.** *The syren of the skies.* C. Arthur Pearson, 118p.
Paperback edition of the above.

[1894]   **Hayes, F. W.** *State industrialism: the story of the Phalanx.* W. Reeves, lxviii, 316p.
Another edition of the publication of 1893.

[1894]   **Hertzka, T.** *A visit to Freeland; or, the new paradise regained.* Translated from the German. W. Reeves, vi, 155p.
A sequel to *Freeland,* 1891. First published 1893 as *Eine Reise nach Freiland.*

1894   **Lazarus, H.** *The English revolution of the twentieth century: a prospective history.* T. Fisher Unwin, xi, 463p.
A demonstration of the effects to be expected from social reforms.

1894   **Le Queux, W.** *The great war in England in 1897.* Tower Publishing Co., 330p. Illus.
French and Russian troops invade Britain, but are decisively repulsed.

1894   **McIver, G.** *Neuroomia*. Swan Sonnenschein, 307p.
Explorers discover a highly advanced civilisation at the South Pole.

1894   **Mitchell, J. A.** *The last American*. Gay & Bird, 78p.
A Persian expedition in the third millenium unearths what was once the
flourishing civilisation of the United States. [U.S. 1889]

1895   **Allen, G.** *The British barbarians*. J. Lane, xxiii, 202p.
A tourist from the twenty-fifth century comes to Britain to study customs and
conventions.

1895   **Cromie, R.** *The crack of doom*. Digby & Long, 214p.
A demon scientist plans to blow up the world.

1895   **Danyers, G.** *Blood is thicker than water: a political dream*. Tower
Publishing Co., 160p.
The Franco-German war of 1901 ends in an Anglo-American Commonwealth.

1895   **Eastwick, J.** *The new Centurion: a tale of automatic war*. Longmans,
93p. Illus.
A detailed account of "what fighting with automatic weapons would be like"

1895   **Ellis, T. M.** *Zalma*. Tower Publishing Co., 438p.
An anarchist plot to contaminate European cities with anthrax germs.

1895   **Geissler, L. A.** *Looking beyond*. Reeves, 194p.
Continues the story of Bellamy's *Looking backward*, and is an answer to *Looking
further forward* by Richard Michaelis. [U.S. 1891].

1895   **Griffith, G.** *The outlaws of the air*. Tower Publishing Co., 376p. Illus.
The Aerial Navigation Syndicate saves Britain from a Franco-Russian attack.

1895   **Jane, F. T.** *Blake of the "Rattlesnake"; or, the man who saved
England: a story of torpedo warfare in 189-*. Tower Publishing Co.,
269p. Illus.
The author states his intention has been "to work into story form some of the
romance that clings thick around the torpedo service".

1895   **Mackay, K.** *The yellow wave; a romance of the Asiatic invasion of
Australia*. R. Bentley, xii, 435p.
The story of the defence of Australia in 1954.

1895   **Mears, A. G.** *Mercia, the astronomer royal*. Simpkin, Marshall, 349p.
A romance of A.D. 2002 when women have gained complete equality with men.

1895   **Nisbet, H.** *The great secret*. F. V White, xi, 288p.
The survivors from an ocean liner, blown up by anarchists, discover an ideal
state.

1895   **Wells, H. G.** *The time machine: an invention*. W. Heinemann, 152p.
The first of Wells's many tales of the future.

1895   **X (Fawkes, F. A.)** *Marmaduke, Emperor of Europe, political and social reformer.* E. Durrant, vii, 271p.
A British idealist becomes Emperor of Europe and inaugurates an age of universal peace.

1896   **Andreae, P.** *The vanished emperor.* Ward, Lock and Bowden, 310p.
Sir John Templeton solves the case of the missing German emperor.

1896   **Anonymous** *The Jacobite Doctors: a story of the Second Restoration.* By a member of the Legitimist Club. Box & Gilham, 16p.
The Stuart line is restored in the person of the young queen, Maria IV.

1896   **Anson, Capt.** *(ed?) The great Anglo-American war of 1900.* E. Stanford, v, 88p.
Britain defeated by the United States.

1896   **Burton, F. G.** *The Naval Engineer and the Command of the Sea.* Technical Publishing Co., 231p.
The author writes: "The growing importance to the Navy of highly trained engineer officers and skilled mechanics has not yet been sufficiently recognised by the Authorities." The story demonstrated his point.

1896   **Cromie, R.** *The next crusade.* Hutchinson, 240p.
Britain and Russia are victorious in a war against Turkey and Austria.

1896   **Glyn, C.** *A woman of tomorrow.* The Women's Printing Society, 172p.
Woman buried 1896 awakes in 1996 to discover that women rule the world.

1896   **Grier, S. C. (Gregg, H. C.)** *An uncrowned king.* W. Blackwood, 487p.
Political adventures in the Balkans.

[1896]   **Miller, G. N.** *After the strike of a sex.* Bellamy Library, No. 26. 63p.
Another edition of *The strike of a sex*, 1891.

1896   **Tracy, L.** *The final war: a story of the great betrayal.* Pearson, x, 372p. Illus.
Lord Roberts defeats a Russo-French attack.

[1896]   **Traill, H. D.** *The barbarous Britishers.* John Lane, 95p.
Parody of Grant Allen's *The British barbarians*, 1895.

1897   **Anonymous** *Posterity: its verdicts and its methods; or democracy A.D. 2100.* William & Norgate, 171p.
A concoction of the most diverse reformist ideas, set out as a discussion.

1897   **Bellamy, E.** *Equality.* W. Heinemann, viii, 365p.
A sequel to *Looking backward*. [U.S. 1897].

1897   **Gleig, C.** *When all men starve.* J. Lane, 192p.
The half-trained crews and defective ships of the Royal Navy prove to be no match for the French and Russian fleets.

[1897]   **Gorst, H. E.** *Without bloodshed: a probability of the twentieth century.*
Roxburghe Press, 109p.
An American millionaire buys up "four-fifths of the real property in the United
Kingdom".

1897   **Griffith, G.** *Briton or Boer?* F. V. White, ix, 296p. Illus.
Boers defeated and the British conquer South Africa.

[1897]   **Hendow, Z. S.** *The future power; or, the great revolution of 190-.*
Roxburghe Press, 79p.
A socialist utopia in which "the state finds everyone something to do, and feeds,
clothes, and lodges everyone as well".

1897   **Jane, F. T.** *To Venus in five seconds.* A. D. Innes, 130p. Illus.
A facetious and highly improbable account of space travel.

1897   **Munro, J.** *A trip to Venus.* Jarrold, 254p.
Space journey in an "ariel car".

[1897]   **Palmer, J. H.** *The invasion of New York; or, how Hawaii was annexed.*
F. T. Neely, iv, 248p.
The defeat of a Japanese attempt to invade the United States. [Published
simultaneously in U.K. and U.S.A.].

1897   **Spence, J. C.** *The dawn of civilisation.* Watts & Co., 176p.
An attack on abuses of the 19th century projected into the better world of 2243
when Herbert Spencer's ideas have led to a more perfect existence.

1897   **Thorburn, S. S.** *His Majesty's greatest subject.* Constable, 324p.
India plays her part in a war fought by the United Kingdom against France and
Germany.

1897   **Tracy, L.** *An American emperor.* Pearson, x, 336p. Illus.
The romance of an American who organises the flooding of the Sahara and is
offered the crown of France.

1897   **Verne, J.** *For the flag.* Translated from the French by Mrs. C. Hoey.
Sampson Low, 312p.
Scientist invents a super-bomb and joins with a pirate against the world. First
published 1896 as *Face au drapeau.*

1898   **Augustinus** *(pseud.) Two brothers.* Chapple and Kemp, 88p.
Britain returns to Catholicism; the end of the world follows.

1898   **Benham, C.** *The fourth Napoleon.* W. Heinemann, 600p.
[1897]   How Walter Sadler, barrister, became Napoleon IV.

1898   **Buchanan, R.** *The Rev. Annabel Lee.* Pearson, vi, 255p.
In the world of the twenty-first century the heroine sets out to restore the
forgotten precepts of Christianity.

1898   **Gerrare, W. (Greener, W. W.)** *The warstock.* W. W. Greener, 234p.
An ideal state organized by inventors.

1898   **Gorst, H.** *Sketches of the future.* J. MacQueen, 218p.
Includes four 'Sketches of the future' – whimsical and ironic.

1898   **Graves, C. L. and Lucas, E. V.** *The war of the Wenuses. Translated from the Artesian of H. G. Pozzuoli.* Arrowsmith, 140p.
An amusing burlesque of Wells's *War of the worlds;* the Wenuses (all females) arrive in crinoline-shaped projectiles and cause havoc with "the Mash Glance".

1898   **Grier, S. C. (Gregg, H. C.)** *A crowned queen.* W. Blackwood, 590p.
The Balkans under Russia.

1898   **Hannan, C.** *The bethrothal of James.* Bliss, Sands. 243p.
Doctor develops rejuvenation serum.

1898   **Morris, J.** *What will Japan do?* Lawrence & Bullen, xii, 190p.
A perceptive forecast of the Russo-Japanese War. Includes an account of a fleet engagement off Tsushima.

1898   **Oppenheim, E. P.** *Mysterious Mr. Sabin.* Ward, Lock, 397p. Illus.
Secret agents plan the invasion of the United Kingdom.

1898   **Perry, W. C.** *The revolt of the horses.* Grant Richards, 229p. Illus.
How the horses created the Houyhnhnm State of Great Britain.

1898   **Reeves, B.** *The divines of Mugtown.* Stockwell, 30p.
An ironic account of attempts at inter-church communion and the confusion that follows.

1898   **Shiel, M. P.** *The yellow danger.* Grant Richards, vi, 345p.
A romance of the Chinese attempt to conquer the world. [U.S. 1895].

1898   **Stead, W. T.** *Blastus, the King's Chamberlain.* Grant Richards, xvi, 302p.
A study of the way African questions and French interests in Africa affect British politics.

1898   **Stockton, F. R.** *The great stone of Sardis.* Harper, 341p. Illus.
In 1947 a scientist leads a submarine expedition to the North Pole. [U.S. 1898].

1898   **Tracy, L.** *The lost provinces.* Pearson, 388p.
A sequel to *An American emperor,* 1897.

1898   **Wells, H. G.** *The war of the worlds.* W. Heinemann, viii, 303p.
The Martian invasion of the world; still the best of its kind.

1898   **Wilson, H. W. and White, A.** *When war breaks out.* Harper, 94p.
Forecast of a naval war: the United Kingdom versus the Allied Powers of France and Russia.

1899   **Augustinus** *(pseud.) Paul Rees: a story of the coming Reformation.*
Simpkin, Marshall, 126p.
Britain is converted to Catholicism.

1899   **Griffith, G.** *Gambles with destiny.* F. V. White, 232p.
[1898]   Short stories: a President of the United States confines all criminals to one town;
a comet comes close to earth; a mad scientist tries to corner the world's
electricity supplies.

1899   **Griffith, G.** *The great pirate syndicate.* F. V. White, 310p.
British industrialists and financiers gain control of the world by means of new
scientific weapons.

1899   **Jane, F. T.** *The violet flame: a story of Armageddon and after.* Ward,
Lock, vi, 245p. Illus.
A demon scientist threatens Britain with his disintegrating machine.

1899   **Mendes, H. P.** *Looking ahead: twentieth century happenings.* Gay &
Bird, 382p.
The nations of the world united in peace and brotherhood. [U.S. 1898]

1899   **Oman, C.** *(ed.) The reign of George VI, 1900–1925 . . . Reprinted with
preface and notes.* Rivingtons, xxxii, 106p. See *Note 4.*

1899   **Stevenson, P. L.** *How the Jubilee Fleet escaped destruction, and the
Battle of Ushant.* Simpkin, Marshall, 68p. Illus.
Entirely taken up with naval tactics.

1899   **Wells, H. G.** *Tales of space and time.* Harper, 360p.
Contains one very interesting story of a future technological paradise.

1899   **Wells, H. G.** *When the sleeper wakes.* Harper, 330p. Illus.
Wells has stated that this novel "was our contemporary world in a state of highly
inflamed distension". A small group of very wealthy men controls the masses.

1899   **Wright, H.** *Depopulation: a romance of the unlikely.* George Allen,
166p.
Purposive prediction to show how "industrial centralisation was only paving the
way to individualist ruin".

1900   **Anonymous (Maude, Col. F. N.)** *The new Battle of Dorking.* Grant
Richards, 255p. Illus.
Grant Richards writes that the book had been commissioned "in the hope that it
might have had the same kind of success that its predecessor had had three or
four decades earlier". The story demonstrates the ease with which the French
· could invade Britain.

[1900]   **Allen, F. M. (Downey, E.)** *London's peril.* Downey & Co., 96p.
The French are engaged in building a Channel Tunnel for the purpose of
attacking the United Kingdom. See Pemberton, M. 1901.

1900   **Cole, R. W.** *The struggle for empire: a story of the year 2236.* Elliot Stock, 213p.
The Anglo-Saxons dominate the world; and as they begin to colonize the planets, a war in space begins.

1900   **Ellis, H.** *The Nineteenth Century.* Grant Richards, 166p.
Criticisms of Nineteenth Century society, science, religion, social practices etc. set in an undated future period.

1900   **Fryers, A. (Clery, W. A.)** *The Devil and the inventor.* C. Arthur Pearson, 272p.
An inventor makes a bargain with the Devil – for a price.

1900   **Gorst, H. E.** *Farthest south.* Greening, 181p.
A facetious variation on the "cycling novel" of the period: the tale of a cycling expedition to the South Pole.

1900   **Grier, S. C. (Gregg, H. C.)** *The kings of the east.* W. Blackwood, 363p.
A romance of the time when European Jews colonise Palestine.

1900   **Lafargue, P. (Philpot, J. H.)** *The forsaken way.* Hurst & Blackett, 287p.
A romantic tale about a young celibate who leaves a Eugenist lay community to explore the world.

1900   **March, R.** *A second coming.* Grant Richards, 296p.
Christ appears in London to the consternation of many.

1900   **Netterville, L. (O'Grady, S. J.)** *Queen of the world; or, under tyranny.* Lawrence & Bullen, vi, 293p.
In A.D. 2174 the Chinese rule the world by means of air power.

1900   **Newcomb, S.** *His wisdom, the defender.* Harper Bros. (New York and London), 328p. Illus.
A scientist invents new weapons with which he defeats the European nations; he abolishes war and establishes justice throughout the world.

1900   **Offin, T. W.** *How the Germans took London.* Simpkin, Marshall, 64p.
The Germans invade Britain.

1900   **Peck, B.** *The world a department store.* Gay & Bird, viii, 311p. Illus.
A better world of the future, much influenced by Bellamy's ideas. [U.S. 1900]

1900   **Serviss, G. P.** *The moon metal.* Harper Bros. (New York and London), 163p.
A wicked scientist gains almost dictatorial powers because he alone controls the metal that has replaced gold.

1900   **West, J. (Müller, E.)** *My afterdream: a sequel to the late Mr. Edward Bellamy's "Looking Backward".* T. F. Unwin, 247p.
An anti-Bellamy demonstration of the need for "a higher ideal among the toiling masses". First published 1891 as *Aus den Errinerungen des Herrn Julian West.*

1900   **White, F. M.** *The white battalions.* Pearson, 341p.
The Gulf Stream diverted; arctic conditions in Europe enable Britain to defeat her enemies.

1900   **Zola, E.** *Fruitfulness.* Translated and edited with a preface by E. A. Vizetelly. Chatto and Windus, ix, 412p.
First of the unfinished sequence of *Les Quatres Évangiles* in which the action advances towards 1980. Although the stories primarily deal with the lives of the children of Pierre Froment, there are occasional references to future political and technological developments both in Europe and in the French colonies in Africa. First published 1899 as *Fécondité.*

1901   **Anonymous** *The sack of London in the great French war of 1901.* F. V. White, 126p.
The French and Russians invade Britain.

1901   **Caine, H.** *The eternal city.* W. Heinemann, 606p. Illus.
Love and politics in a future papal Rome.

1901   **Cairnes, Capt.** *The coming Waterloo.* Constable, 364p.
Britain and Germany in alliance against France and Russia.

1901   **Conrad, J. and Hueffer, F. M.** *The Inheritors.* W. Heinemann, 324p.
A visitor from the Fourth Dimension, a parallel universe, takes a hand in European schemes for the colonization of Greenland – in order to prepare the way for the Dimensionists.

1901   **Ford, W. W.** *Psyche, 1902.* Spiers & Pond, 75p.
Caesar's invasion, as if it had taken place in 1902.

1901   **Fletcher, J. S.** *The three days' terror.* J. Long, 307p.
A secret society holds the nation to ransom.

1901   **Green, A. L.** *The end of an epoch.* W. Blackwood, 391p.
The experiences of the solitary able-bodied survivor after a bacillus has wiped out all but the aged and weak.

1901   **Griffith, G.** *A honeymoon in space.* Illus. by Stanley Wood & Harold Piffard. C. Arthur Pearson, 302p.
Lord Redgrave takes his bride on a tour of the Solar System.

1901   **Pemberton, M.** *Pro patria.* Ward, Lock, 316. Illus.
The French, with the help of a British renegade, attempt to drive a tunnel under the Channel in order to invade Britain.

1901   **Shiel, M. P.** *The lord of the sea.* Grant Richards, 496p.
A Jewish idealist attempts to dominate the world.

1901   **Shiel, M. P.** *The purple cloud.* Chatto & Windus, 463p.
The adventures of the new Adam after the human race has been wiped out.

1901   **Tracy, L.** *The invaders.* Pearson, 428p. Illus.
Disguised French and German soldiers emerge from hiding and seize British towns.

1901   **Zola, E.** *Work.* Translated and edited with preface by E. A. Vizetelly. Chatto & Windus, vii, 500p.
Continues the Froment story; includes mention of a great European war. First published 1901 as *Travail.*

1902   **Cromie, R.** *A new Messiah.* Digby, Long, 320p.
A secret society attempts to control the world.

1902   **Curtis, A. C.** *A new Trafalgar.* Smith & Elder, 301p.
Another German invasion story.

1902   **Devinne, P.** *The day of prosperity: a vision of the century to come.* T. F. Unwin, 271p.
An American perfect world of the future: no idle persons, votes for all, size of towns limited. (U. S. 1902)

1902   **Kuppord, S. (Adams, J.)** *A fortune from the sky.* Nelson, 230p.
An electrical apparatus makes war absolete.

1902   **Oppenheim, E. P.** *The traitors.* Ward, Lock. 304p. Illus.
An imaginary war against the Turks in the Balkans.

1902   **Pinkerton, T. A.** *No rates and taxes: a romance of five worlds.* Arrowsmith, 125p.
The Jews defeat the Turks and begin a period of universal peace; the decline of man follows rapidly.

1902   **Stowe, H. B.** *He's coming tomorrow.* Oliphant, 22p.
A brief tale of the Second Coming by the author of *Uncle Tom's Cabin.* [U.S. 1901]

1903   **Anonymous (James, L.)** *The boy galloper: by the Intelligence Officer.* W. Blackwood, 319p. Illus.
A German invasion story.

1903   **Griffith, G.** *The lake of gold.* F. V. White, 320p.
The discovery of vast gold deposits enables an idealist to create a perfect world.

1903   **Griffith, G.** *A woman against the world.* F. V. White, 320p.
Lady Sybil Morrant puts to sea and holds up ships on the oceans.,

1903   **Griffith, G.** *The world masters.* J. Long, 303p.
The members of the International Electric Power and Storage Trust establish Anglo-American control of the world.

1903   **Platts, W. Carter** *Up-to-To-morrow.* With seventy illustrations by The
Author, F. Holmes, R. Brownley, and other artists. John Long, 222p.
Comic tales about the extraordinary activities of an eccentric inventor.

1903   **Ubique (Guggisberg, Capt. F. G.)** *Modern warfare; or, how our
soldiers fight.* Nelson, 487p. Illus.
Part II describes a German attack on Belgium and the part British troops play in
the defeat of Germany.

1903   **Hill, H. (Grainger, F. E.)** *Seaward for the foe.* Ward, Lock, 378p. Illus.
In the days when "Great Britain stood face to face with allied France and Russia
for the death-grip".

1903   **Stanley, W. F.** *The case of The. Fox.* Truslove & Hanson, 200p. Illus.
The United States of Europe established in 1934; armies have been disbanded,
and crime is almost unknown.

1903   **Thorne, G. (Gull, C. A. R.)** *When it was dark.* Greening, 427p.
A national crisis follows on evidence that apparently indicates there was no
Resurrection.

1903   **Wells, H. G.** *Twelve stories and a dream.* Macmillan, 377p.
Short stories.

1903   **Zola, E.** *Truth.* Translated and edited with a preface by E. A. Vizetelly.
Chatto & Windus, x, 587p.
Advances theme of *Les Quatre Évangiles* to separation of State and Church, and
the reconciliation of all Frenchmen. First published 1903 as *Vérite.*

1904   **[1903] Bullock, S. F.** *The red leaguers.* Methuen, 322p.
The struggle for Irish liberty fails because of disunity.

1904   **Calderon, G.** *Dwala.* Smith, Elder, 244p.
The Missing Link becomes prime minister of Great Britain.

1904   **Chesterton. G. K.** *The Napoleon of Notting Hill.* Lane, 302p. Illus.
By a characteristic Chestertonian paradox, an ideal state of the Wellsian type
sparks off an explosion of liberty, individualism, and local patriotism.

1904   **Clarke, A.** *Starved into surrender.* C. W. Daniel, 276p.
A Franco-Russian attack on Britain fails because of a revolution in Russia. Britain
becomes "a cooperative commonwealth".

1904   **Dickberry, F. (De Bury, F. B.)** *The storm of London.* J. Long, 313p.
A dream in which a storm destroys most of London.

1904   **Griffith, G.** *A criminal Croesus.* J. Long, 320p.
A fantastic story of gold produced by gnome-like creatures living in a submarine
world; used to create the United States of South America.

1904   **Guttenberg, V.** *A modern exodus.* Greening, 328p.
A Jewish state established in Palestine as the result of a Jewish Expulsion Bill.

1904   **Hall, G. R.** *Black fortnight; or, the invasion of 1915.* Sonnenchein, 128p.
The European war has "been caused by the great international financiers".

1904   **Hamilton, C.** *The passing of Arthur.* Nash, 220p.
An ironical account of the events in the life of a Liberal government.

1904   **Hastings, G. G.** *The first American king.* Smart Set Publishing Co., 260p. (New York and London).
Socialist revolution destroys an oppressive government.

1904   **Niemann, A.** *The coming conquest of England.* Translated from German by J. H. Freese. G. Routledge, vii, 384p.
The author writes: "My dreams, the dreams of a German, show me the war that is to be, and the victory of the three great allied nations –Germany, France and Russia." Britain, of course, is totally defeated. Originally published 1904 as *Der Weltkrieg – Deutsche Träume.*

1904   **Ralli, C.** *Vanessa.* Cassell, 344p.
Rebellion in the days when three millionaires own New York.

1904   **Rolfe, Fr. (Rolfe, F. W.)** *Hadrian the Seventh.* Chatto & Windus, 413p.
An Englishman is elected Pope; renounces temporal sovereignty, sells the Vatican treasures, denounces socialism.

1904   **Upward, A.** *The fourth conquest of England.* Tyndale Press, 72p.
All the horrors of a Catholic renaissance in Britain, complete with Inquisition.

1904   **Wells, H. G.** *The food of the gods and how it came to earth.* Macmillan, vii, 317p.
A growth accelerator produces a race of giants. After much confusion, a better world begins to develop.

1904   **X (Fawkes, F. A.)** *The setting sun.* Skeffington, 167p.
British expedition to East Midasland is an opportunity for ridiculing nationalism, militarism, and imaginary war stories.

1905   **Anonymous (Mills, E. E.)** *The decline and fall of the British Empire. A brief account . . . Appointed for use in the National Schools of Japan, Tokio, 2005.* Simpkin, Marshall, iv, 50p.
The evils that have brought about the end of the British Empire examined and listed.

1905   **Barnes, J.** *Unpardonable war.* Macmillan, (London & New York) 356p.
A war between Britain and America ends in a union of the two countries.

1905   **Byatt, H.** *Purple and white.* R. A. Everett, 316p.
After the Great War of the future, the White Kaiser brings peace to the world.

1905   **Farrow, G. E.** *The food of the dogs.* Brinsley Johnson. 95p. Illus.
A pardoy of the H.G. Wells' story of 1904.

1905   **Kernahan, C.** *A world without a child.* Hodder and Stoughton, 91p.
A future Britain peopled by "the Pleasurists and the Pessimists".

1905   **Middleton, J. B.** *The god of this world.* Kegan Paul, 205p.
The preaching of the New Testament in the corrupt Britain of 1986 eventually
leads to universal brotherhood.

1905   **Mill, G. (Miller, M.)** *In the hands of the Czar.* W. Blackwood, 362p.
A romance of the Russia of 1907.

1905   **Tarde, G.** *Underground man.* Translated from the French by C.
Brereton; foreword by H. G. Wells. Duckworth, 198p.
A new ice age begins in A.D. 2490; the remnants of humanity go underground.
Originally published 1904 as *Fragment d'histoire future.*

1905   **Turner, R.** *Peace on earth.* Alston Rivers, 336p.
A philanthropist organizes a Congress of Peace.

1905   **Wintle, H.** *The cleansing of the Lords.* Lane, 296p.
The effect on British politics of a bill "to cleanse the House of Lords."

1905   **Young, F. E. M.** *The war of the sexes.* J. Long, 208p.
A dream of a world from which men have vanished.

1906   **Anonymous** *Star of the morning: a chronicle of Karyl the Great and the
revolt of 1920-22.* T. Burleigh, 242p.
Women enter Parliament and obtain equality with men.

1906   **Anonymous (Ford, D. M.)** *A time of terror.* Greening, 340p.
A mysterious league brings about a great upheaval.

1906   **Anonymous (Lang, A.?)** *When it was light: a reply to "When it was
dark."* J. Long, 208p.
A counterblast to the tale by G. Thorne published in 1903.

1906   **Blyth, J.** *The aerial burglars.* Ward, Lock, 255p. Illus.
A winged flying machine is the means of setting the world right.

1906   **Caine, W. and Fairbairn, J.** *The confectioners.* Arrowsmith, 315p.,
Illus.
An amusing and ironic tale about scientific advances: artificial foods, the
Universal Substance, tobacco substitutes, and other examples of human folly.

1906   **General Staff (*pseud.*)** *The writing on the wall.* W. Heinemann, viii,
228p. Maps.
The author declares: "The object of this work is to call the attention of the public
to the absolute unpreparedness of our land forces for the tasks which they may
be called upon to perform." Britain is defeated in the usual manner.

1906   **Griffith, G.** *The great weather syndicate.* F. V. White, vi, 312p.
A young British scientist foils the plots of wicked American financiers.

1906   **Harris, J. H.** *A romance in radium.* Greening, 235p.
An immortal from another planet comes to visit earth.

1906   **Hernaman-Johnson, F.** *The Polyphemes.* Ward, Lock, 318p.
A race of rational ants, far more intelligent than human beings, almost conquers the world.

1906   **Holt-White, W.** *The earthquake.* Grant Richards, 334p.
An international conspiracy plans to ruin Britain.

1906   **Kernahan, C.** *The dumpling: a detective love story of a great Labour rising.* Cassell, 339p. Illus.
Revolution in London when the Labour legions take to the barricades.

1906   **Le Queux, W.** *The invasion of 1910.* E. Nash, xiv, 550p. Illus.
Field-Marshall Earl Roberts introduces the book: "The catastrophe that may happen if we still remain in our present state of unpreparedness is vividly and forcibly illustrated in Mr. Le Queux's new book which I recommend to the perusal of everyone who has the welfare of the British Empire at heart." The story, first serialised in the *Daily Mail,* March 1906, was the most notorious of all the tales of a German invasion. It was translated into 26 languages and sold over a million copies as a book.

[1906]   **Long, G.** *Valhalla.* H. J. Drane, 280p.
A fantastic romance of a world mostly submerged by floods. The spirits of the dead work for the survivors.

1906   **Mastin, J.** *The stolen planet.* P. Wellby, 282p.
A romance of space travel.

1906   **Oldmeadow, E.** *The North Sea bubble.* Grant Richards, ix, 353p. Illus.
The Royal Navy defeats a German invasion.

1906   **Seymour, C.** *Comet chaos.* Chatto & Windus, 335p.
A professor hopes to escape extinction of all life on Earth by taking to a submarine.

1906   **Shiel, M. P.** *The last miracle.* T. W. Laurie, 320p.
The future of Catholicism – reformed and purified.

1906   **Sutphen, V. T.** *The doomsman.* Harper Bros. (New York and London).
An adventure story of life in the days after a great catastrophe.

1906   **Tems Dyvirta (***pseud.***)** *London's transformation: a suggestive sketch of days to come.* King, Sell & Olding, 72p.
An American millionaire moves the Thames; Britain and the United States form a union.

1906   **Thorne, G. (Gull, C. A. R.)** *Made in his image.* Hutchinson, viii, 360p.
A slave world of the future is redeemed by the teachings of Christianity.

1906   **Vaux, P.** *The shock of battle.* Putnam, 379p.
How the Royal Navy defeated Germany.

1906   **Wells, H. G.** *In the days of the comet.* Macmillan, viii, 305p.
One of Wells's poorer stories: the mysterious gases of a comet cause the moral
regeneration of the world.

1906   **Wood, W.** *The enemy in our midst.* J. Long, 320p.
The operations of the German fifth column: "every registered alien
German . . . was an authority on the topography and resources of the district in
which he dwelt".

1907   **Anonymous** *A second Franco-German war and its consequences for
England.* Simpkin, Marshall, 146p.
Consists of two parts. Part I (*The invasion of Belgium* by a Belgian Officer)
describes an imaginary German invasion. Part II (*Belgian neutrality and British
naval supremacy* by Civis Britannicus) is not fiction but an examination of the
need for adequate military preparation.

1907   **Anonymous (Bramah, E.)** *What might have been: the story of a social
war.* J. Murray, viii, 380p.
How Britain learnt the perils of socialism.

1907   **Adderley, J.** *Behold the days come.* Methuen, x, 243p.
The Church of England leads the movement for socialism and social justice.

1907   **Bennett, A.** *The City of Pleasure.* Chatto & Windus, vi, 309p.
Millionaire builds a "City of Pleasure" on the Thames.

1907   **Benson, R. H.** *Lord of the world.* Pitman, 384p.
Catholicism is the only surviving form of religion in an atheistic world state.

1907   **Blyth, J.** *The tyranny.* W. Heinemann, 275p.
A tyrant rules Britain; a war with Germany leads to a mass rising against the
tyranny.

1907   **Byatt, H.** *The flight of Icarus.* Sisley's, 247p.
A fantastic story of a king of the Jews who converts Britain to Judaism.

1907   **Cole, R. W.** *The death trap.* Greening, 312p.
Another German invasion: our Japanese allies land at Liverpool and save the
situation.

1907   **Dawson, A. J.** *The message.* Grant Richards, viii, 386p. Illus.
And another German invasion; military defeat leads to "a mighty revival of
Puritanism, backed by the awakened twentieth century spirit of Imperial
patriotism".

1907   **Grier, S. C.** *The power of the keys.* W. Blackwood, 360p.
The "Scythians" invade India.

1907   **Griffith, G.** *The world peril of 1910.* F. V. White, 320p.
A German invasion story.

1907   **Macpherson, J. F.** *A Yankee Napoleon.* J. Long, 318p.
The Royal Navy prevents an American from becoming ruler of the world.

1907   **Newte, H. W. C.** *The master beast.* Rebman, 249p.
The horrors of socialism in A.D. 2020.

1907   **Oppenheim, E. P.** *The secret.* Ward, Locke, 317p. Illus.
A German plot for the invasion of the United Kingdom.

1907   **Scot, H.** *The way of war.* J. Long, 318p.
And another German invasion, this time in Scotland.

1907   **Seestern (Grautoff, F. H.)** *Armageddon 190–.* Translated from the
German by G. Herring. Kegan, Paul, xxiii, 402p.
The history of Britain's defeat closes with Mr. Balfour lamenting that: "the Navy of
the Kaiser has accomplished far more than we ever expected". Originally
published 1906 as *1906 – Der Zusammenbruch der alten Welt.*

1907   **Straus, R.** *The dust which is God.* Samurali Press, 62p.
The vision of a cosmic evolutionary process which "is striving towards
perfectness".

1907   **Vaux, P. and Yexley, L.** *When the eagle flies seaward.* Hurst &
Blackett, 343p.
Once again the Royal Navy saves the day.

1908   **Agricola** *(pseud.)* *How England was saved: history of the years 1910–
1925.* Sonnenschein, 172p.
A demonstration of the fact that "England was doomed to economic disaster if
she continued to depend almost entirely on her exports of manufactured goods".

1908   **Anonymous** *The future Prime Minister.* Grant Richards, 258p.
A sentimental story, beginning in 1895 and closing in the near future, about an
idealistic young man who risks everything for the free trade movement.

1908   **Belloc, H.** *Mr. Clutterbuck's election.* E. Nash, 329p.
An amusing satire on the corruptions, as Belloc saw them, of parliamentary
government.

1908   **Burgoyne, A. H.** *The war inevitable.* F. Griffiths, 313p.
The author concludes: "The war, forced on us by a jealous power, wrought
nothing but good at its termination, for . . . the income tax dropped to a
bearable maximum of sixpence".

1908   **Cleeve, L. (Kingscote, A. G.)** *A woman's aye and nay.* J. Long, 318p.
A romance of the "Woman's Enfranchisement Bill".

1908   **Coutts, T.** *The prodigal city.* Greening, vi, 298p.
An idealist learns the follies of socialism.

[1908]   **Crabapple, J.** *The war of 1908 for the supremacy of the Pacific.*
W. H. Smith, 23p.
The United States defeat a Japanese attempt to seize Manila.

1908   **Dawson, W. J.** *A soldier of the future.* Hodder & Stoughton, viii, 312p.
The reunion of the churches.

1908   **Flecker, J. E.** *The last generation.* New Age Press, 56p.
After children have been forbidden on pain of death, the human race dies out.

1908   **Grace, S.** *Dennis Martin, traitor.* Western Morning News, 277p.
Irish rebellion and German invasion.

1908   **Harding, E.** *The woman who vowed.* T. F. Unwin, 315p.
The Demetrian cult aims to purify the race and to improve the institution of
marriage. Published U.S. 1907 as *The Demetrian.*

1908   **Harris-Burland, J. B.** *Workers in darkness.* Greening & Co. 323p.
A Society of Criminals threatens the safety of London.

1908   **Hodgson, W. H.** *The house on the borderland.* Chapman & Hall, xii,
300p.
Time-travel through the remote future to the end of the Solar System.

1908   **Junius, J.** *(pseud.) Pope Pacificus.* S.P.C.K., 64p.
A very early specimen of the ecumenical movement: a liberal-minded Pope works
for the reunion of Christendom.

1908   **Kernahan, C.** *The red peril.* Hurst & Blackett, 328p.
A variation on the German invasion theme.

1908   **Kipling, A. W.** *The new dominion.* F. Griffiths, 292p.
An American-Japanese war in the Pacific.

[1908]   **London, J.** *The iron heel.* Everett, 374p.
An attempted rising against an oppressive totalitarian regime. [U.S. 1907]

1908   **Mayne, J. D.** *The triumph of socialism.* Sonnenschein, 139p.
A German invasion is the signal for a mass rising against the socialist
government of Great Britain.

1908   **Navarchus (Vaux, P. and Yexley, L.)** *The world's awakening.* Hodder
& Stoughton, 463p.
How "the electorate of Great Britain and Ireland began to reap the fruits of so-
called economy in both Services".

[1908]   **Omen, E.** *Nutopia; or, Nineteen-twenty-one.* Henry Drane, 181p.
A humorous tale of imaginary lands and future wars. Action takes place about an
imaginary island in the Pacific.

1908   **Oriel, A.** *The miracle.* Archibald Constable, 271p.
War in the Balkans and the collapse of Turkey.

1908   **Serjeant, C.** *When the saints are gone.* J. Long, 221p.
The reign of Antichrist in Britain and the Second Coming.

1908   **Wallace, E.** *The Council of Justice.* Ward, Lock, 319p. Illus.
A dedicated group work against the criminals of the world.

1908   **Wells, H. G.** *The war in the air.* G. Bell, vii, 389p. Illus.
German air fleets destroy New York and a world war follows.

1908   **Wilson, J.** *When the women reign, 1930.* A. Stockwell, 159p.
[1909]   A lesson for suffragettes: women gain political power but learn that men still matter.

1909   **Andrew, S. (Layton, F. G.)** *The Serpent and the Cross.* Greening, 320p.
A plot to overthrow Christianity in Britain.

1909   **Anonymous** *An amazing revolution and after.* G. Allen, 165p.
The Progressive Party leads the nation to a socialistic ideal state.

1909   **Anonymous** *Red England: a tale of the socialist terror.* J. Milne, 223p.
All the horrors of socialism fully demonstrated.

1909   **Belloc, H.** *A change in the Cabinet.* Methuen, 308p.
An amusing satire on political and party machinations: a Cabinet minister tells the truth with disastrous consequences.

1909   **Blyth, J.** *The swoop of the vulture.* Digby, Long, 315p.
A German fleet flying the White Ensign raids Lowestoft and Yarmouth: war follows.

[1909]   **Bramah, E. (Smith, E. B.)** *The secret of the League: the story of a social war.* Nelson, 287p. Front.
Another edition of *What might have been,* published anonymously in 1907.

1909   **Brant, J. I.** *The new regime, A.D. 2202.* T. W. Laurie, 122p.
A world state on scientific lines: international research programmes, industrial corporations independent of government, political control of continents by a world parliament. [U.S. 1909]

1909   **Caine, H.** *The White Prophet.* Heinemann, 2 vols, 381 & 371p. Illus.
Espionage, mutiny and romance in Egypt.

1909   **Collins, C.** *The human mole.* Greening, 338p.
Adventures with an earth-boring machine.

1909   **Curties, Capt. H.** *When England slept.* Everett, 312p.
German fifth column assists an invasion attempt.

1909   **Everett, F.** *John Bull, socialist.* Sonnenschein, 188p.
The miseries of socialism revealed.

1909   **Fox-Davies, A. C.** *The sex triumphant.* G. Routledge, 166p.
The struggle for women's rights succeeds.

1909   **France, A. (Thibault, J. A.)** *Penguin island.* Translated by
E. W. Evans. J. Lane, 236p.
A satiric allegory which concludes with a chapter on 'Future Times'. First
published 1908 as *L'Ile des Pingouins.*

1909   **France, A. (Thibault, F. A.)** *The White Stone.* Translated from the
French by C. E. Roche. J. Lane, 240p.
Concludes with a long utopian vision of the Year CCXX of the Federation of the
Peoples. First published 1905 as *Sur la pierre blanche.*

1909   **Haig, J. C.** *In the grip of the trusts.* Methuen, 111p.
The disasters expected from Protection.

[1909]   **Hawke, N.** *The invasion that did not come off.* Drane, 128p.
Once again the Royal Navy defeats the enemy.

1909   **Holt-White, W.** *The man who stole the earth.* T. F. Unwin, 382p. Illus.
A new type of airship is used to dominate the world and eventually to establish
universal peace.

1909   **Hookham, A. E.** *Amid the strife.* Andrew Prickett, 323p. Illus.
A moral tale about a war between Britain and Bryghtland.

1909   **Kipling, R.** *With the Night Mail.* 37p. (in Actions and Reactions,
Macmillan, 302p.)
A short story forecasting the air traffic of the future, its direction and control.

1909   **Kirmess, C. H.** *The Australian cisis.* W. Scott, 335p.
Japanese invasion of Australia.

[1909]   **Mastin, J.** *Through the sun in an airship.* C. Griffin, vii, 317p.
Space travel in the future.

1909   **Parabellum (Grautoff, F. H.)** *Banzai!* Translated from the German.
Stanley Paul, 320p.
Japanese invasion of America. Originally published 1908 as *Bansai!*

1909   **Sedgwick, S. N.** *The last persecution.* Grant Richards, 314p.
By 1940 the Chinese have conquered all Eurasia. In Britain they persecute
Christians.

1909   **Sladen, D.** *The tragedy of the Pyramids.* Hurst & Blackett, 428p.
The author presents his book as a counterblast to Hall Caine's *White Prophet;* it
is intended 'to give a different picture of the Egyptian mutiny which both he, and
I, believe to be inevitable.'

1909   **Verne, J.** *The chase of the golden meteor.* Translated from the French by Frederick Lawton. Grant Richards, 291p. Illus.
Solid gold meteor causes world-wide excitement as it draws near Earth. First published posthumously 1908 as *La Chasse au météore.*

1909   **Williams, L.** *The great raid.* Black & White Publishing Co., 151p. Illus.
Another German invasion story.

1909   **Wodehouse, P. G.** *The swoop! or, how Clarence saved England: a tale of the great invasion.* Alston Rivers, 122p. Illus.
A story to end all invasion stories: the epic of Clarence MacAndrew Chugwater "one of General Baden-Powell's Boy Scouts", who defeats the forces of Germany, Russia, the Mad Mullah, the Swiss Navy, China, Monaco, the Young Turks, and Moroccan brigands.

[1910]   **Anonymous** *The German invasion of England.* By a French Staff Officer. D. Nutt, 86p.
A "staff appreciation" in fiction.

1910   **Anonymous** *The next crusade.* Hutchinson, vi, 176p.
The National Association for the Exposure and Removal of Legal Anomalies campaigns for a reform of the legal system.

1910   **Anonymous (Ford, D. M.)** *The raid of Dover: a romance of the reign of woman, A.D. 1940.* King, Sell & Olding, 188p.
Life in the days when women rule.

1910   **Applin, A.** *The Priest of Piccadilly.* F. V. White, 312p.
A social and religious reformer seeks to change the world for the better.

1910   **Belloc, H.** *Pongo and the bull.* Constable, 305p.
A satire on the party system.

1910   **Beresford, L.** *The second rising.* Hurst & Blackett, 328p.
A rising against British rule in India.

[1910]   **Carter, J. L. J.** *Peggy the aeronaut.* Everett, 254p.
Adventure in the days when Britain's airfleet is inferior to the German air force.

1910   **Collins, C.** *The Blinding Light.* Greening, 319p.
The Black Fog and the Blinding Light enable criminals to raid the Bank of England.

[1910]   **Cutcliffe-Hyne, C. J.** *Empire of the world.* Everett, 314p. Illus.
The inventor of a mysterious "ray" compels the nations to disarm.

1910   **Glendon, G.** *The emperor of the air.* Methuen, 311p. Illus.
International anarchists wage a war of revenge on the world.

1910   **Godfrey, H.** *The man who ended war.* Ward, Lock, 301p. Illus.
A scientist discovers "a new type of radio-active energy which effects the ultimate decomposition of matter". He uses his invention to force the nations to disarm. [U.S. 1908].

1910 **Hale, Col. L. A.** *The horrors of war in Great Britain.* Love & Malcolmson, 16p.
A description of the horrors of war in order to demonstrate the need for 'the immediate adoption of universal liability for service.'

1910 **Herbert, E. G.** *Newaera: a socialist romance.* P. S. King, 212p.
An idealist establishes a socialist community and learns the bitter lesson of the clash between principle and practice.

1910 **Horner, D. W.** *By aeroplane to the sun.* Century Press, 268p. Illus.
The aether-ships of A.D. 2000 are powered by radium and journey to the planets.

1910 **Kipling, A. W.** *The shadow of glory, 1910–1911.* Alston Rivers, xvi, 440p.
The author writes: "This book is intended to show both the glories and the horrors of modern warfare."

1910 **Le Queux, W.** *The unknown tomorrow.* F. V. White, vii, 305p.
All the horrors of socialism in 1935.

1910 **Michelson, M.** *The awakening of Zojas.* Hodder & Stoughton (New York printed), 268p.
Suspended animation: the hero revives and leads a revolt against an oppressive government. [U.S. 1910]

1910 **Pocock, R.** *The chariot of the sun.* Chapman & Hall, 305p.
An incoherent tale of the days when Queen Margaret reigns.

1910 **Prince, E.** *Wake up England! being the amazing story of John Bull–socialist.* St. Stephen's Press, 188p.
More miseries of life under socialism.

1910
[1909] **Reynolds, S.** *The Holy Mountain.* John Lane (London and New York), 309p.
A man makes a wish and causes a mountain to move from Wiltshire to London.

1910
[1911] **Watson, S.** *In the twinkling of an eye.* W. Nicholson, vii, 266p.
The beginning of the end of the world: all the true Christians vanish, as God gives the world the 'opportunity of being prepared for the return of the Lord.'

1910 **Wells, H. G.** *The sleeper awakes.* Nelson, 288p.
In the preface Wells writes: 'I have taken the opportunity afforded by this reprinting to make a number of excisions and alterations.' Revised and shortened version of *When the sleeper wakes*, 1899.

[1911] **Benson, R. H.** *The dawn of all.* Hutchinson, vi, 339p.
A Catholic ideal state of the future.

1911 **Collins, C.** *Four millions a year.* Greening & Co., 314p.
An altruist discovers a new source of power. The millionaires of the world follow his example and give their money away.

1911   **Emanuel, W.** *100 years hence.* Nash, 74p.
A comic version of a future newspaper.

1911   **Griffith, G.** *The lord of labour.* F. V. White, vii, 310p.
A German invasion is defeated by "submarine destroyers" and "aerial destroyers".

1911   **Minnett, C.***The day after tomorrow.* F. V. White, 310p.
A romance set in the socialist world of 1975.

1911   **Morice, C.** *He is risen again.* Translated from the French. Nash, 230p.
Christ appears in Paris. First published 1911 as *Il est ressuscité!*

1911   **Pirret, C.** *Queen Flora's recollections.* E. Stock, 240p.
The restoration of the Stuarts in 1998.

1911   **Pollock, Lieut. Colonel A.** *Lord Roastem's Campaign in North-Eastern France.* Hugh Rees, 63p. Map. Illus.
Strategical account of a war fought by Germany against France and Great Britain.

1911   **Serviss, G. P.** *A Columbus of space.* Appleton (New York and London), 297p. Illus.
Space travel and romantic adventures on Venus.

1911   **Silberrad, U. L.** *The affairs of John Bolsover.* T. Nelson, 288p. Illus.
A journalist investigates the mysterious career of a British prime minister.

1911   **Trevena, J. (Henham, E. G.)** *The reign of the saints.* Alston Rivers, vi, 376p.
An object lesson of the attempt "to make all things equal, to seize lands, railways and every kind of property".

1911   **Ward, W. J.** *Shanghaied socialists.* Maritime Review, Cardiff, 374p.
Forty selected socialists are transported to the South Seas for the good of the nation.

1911   **Watson, S.** *The mark of the Beast.* W. Nicholson, 276p.
The reign of Antichrist, Lucien Apleon, who acts out the prophecies of the Beast in *Revelations.*

1911   **Wicks, M.** *To Mars via the moon.* Seeley & Co., 327p. Illus.
Space travel.

1912   **Anonymous (Begbie, E. H.)** *The day that changed the world.* Hodder & Stoughton, vii, 289p.
A mysterious moral impulse improves the world out of all recognition.

1912   **Blyth, J.** *The peril of Pines Place.* F. V. White, 311p.
Enemy agents attempt to foment rebellion in Britain.

1912   **Brex (Twells, J.)** *The civil war of 1915.* Pearson, 159p.
More consequences of socialism.

1912   **Campbell, S.** *Under the Red Ensign.* Andrew Melrose, 128p.
A war between Britain and Germany is decided by one great fleet engagement.

1912   **Chambers, R. W.** *The green mouse.* Amalgamated Press, 128p.
Satirical account of a scientific apparatus for promoting happy marriages. [U.S. 1910]

1912   **Fawkes, F. A.** *Found – a man.* Kegan Paul, 254p.
The rulers of Europe and the President of the United States are persuaded to sign an international treaty of peace and friendship in King's College Chapel.

1912   **Fendall, P.** *Lady Ermintrude and the plumber.* S. Swift, 276p.
A romance of the days of socialism.

1912   **Hodgson, W. H.** *The night land.* E. Nash, 583p.
An extraordinary fantasy of the time when the sun is dead and mankind maintains itself in two vast metal pyramids.

[1912] **Holt-White, W.** *The world stood still.* Everett, 312p.
How the world came close to war when the richest men in Europe and the United States decided to withdraw from business.

1912   **Horner, D. W.** *Their winged destiny.* Simpkin, Marshall, 316p.
Adventures in space.

1912   **Janson, G.** *Pride of war.* Translated from the Swedish. Sidgwick & Jackson, 350p.
Short stories on themes of future warfare. First published 1912 as *Lognerna; berattelser om Kriget.*

[1912] **Kennedy, R. A.** *The triuneverse.* C. Knight, 221p.
In 1950 the planet Mars splits in two.

[1912] **Lamport, R. F.** *Veeni the master.* Stanley Paul, 305p.
The end of all human life on Earth save for the few who are reincarnated in the world of Zan.

1912   **Lurgan, L. (Knowles, M. W.)** *A message from Mars.* Greening, 288p.
A virtuous Martian visits Earth to teach lessons of peace, brotherly love and unselfishness. Based on the play of the same name by Richard Ganthony.

1912   **Mark Time (Irwin, H. C.)** *A derelict empire.* W. Blackwood, 303p.
A British officer saves India from chaos after a socialist government has ordered the withdrawal of all troops.

1912   **Naval Officer, A.** *Great was the fall.* J. Long, 320p. Map.
The United States saves Britain from conquest by Germany.

1912   **Palmer, W.** *Under Home Rule.* Simpkin, Marshall, 170p.
A horror story to demonstrate the folly of granting Home Rule to Ireland.

1912   **Potter, M. H.** *Life the jade.* Everett, 319p.
The secret of immortality is discovered, but mortality is found to have some remarkable advantages.

1912   **Searchlight (Eardley-Wilmot, Rear Admiral)** *The battle of the North Sea in 1914.* H. Rees, 80p.
A British naval victory in which "the big ship had justified her existence".

1912   **Serviss, G. P.** *The second deluge.* Grant Richards, 399p. Illus.
A new flood covers the Earth. [U.S. 1912]

1912   **Wallace, E.** *Private Selby.* Ward, Lock. 319p.
A comic tale which includes an invasion episode.

1912   **Wintle, H.** *Until that day.* John Ousely, 349p.
The ideal means of ending political strife is to restore the absolute power of the King.

1913   **Austin, F. B.** *In action: studies in war.* Nelson, 293p. Frontis.
Short stories about events in imaginary wars.

1913   **Beresford, J. D.** *Goslings.* W. Heinemann, 325p.
A plague wipes out most of the male population of the world. The new society is adjusted in favour of women and against old-fashioned conventions.

1913   **Burkitt, W. T.** *The coming day.* Drane's, 96p.
Brief, enthusiastic account of the establishment of a socialist state in the United Kingdom: "crime was gradually dying out for the simple reason that people could afford to be honest".

1913   **Doyle, A. C.** *The poison belt.* Hodder & Stoughton, viii, 199p. Illus.
The world enters a zone of mysterious gas, and all life apparently comes to an end.

1913   **Fleming, B.** *Masks.* Everett, 320p.
A new aeroplane may lead to world-domination.

1913   **Gastine, L.** *War in space: a grand romance of aircraft warfare between France and Germany.* Translated from the French by G. H. Marchat. Walter Scott Publishing Co., 339p.
Adventure and romance in the days of the biplane and the monoplane. First published 1912 as *Les Torpilleurs de l'air.*

1913   **Lamszus, W.** *The human slaughterhouse: scenes from the war that is sure to come.* Translated from German by O. Williams. Hutchinson, 127p.
A description of the horrors of war. First published 1912 as *Das Menschenschlachthaus.*

1913   **Mattingley, S.** *The terror by night.* Pearson, 158p.
Britain and France successfully resist German attack.

1913   **Pollock, Lt. Col. A. W.** *In the cockpit of Europe.* Smith, Elder, 340p.
Map.
Britain sends an expeditionary force to help France when Germany attacks.

1913   **Raphael, J. N.** *Up above.* Hutchinson, 271p.
Inhabitants of the upper atmosphere come down to earth in a 'subaerine'.

1913   **Saki (Munro, H. H.)** *When William came.* J. Lane, 322p.
The best of all the "German invasion" stories: a merciless and very effective
analysis of moral, social, and military weaknesses.

1913   **Shiel, M. P.** *The Dragon.* Grant Richards, 356p.
The Prince of Wales saves Europe from the yellow hordes.

1913   **Snaith, J. C.** *An affair of state.* Methuen, 351p.
A Prime Minister saves the nation from industrial unrest and civil war.

1913   **Tinseau, L. de** *Duc Rollon.* Translated from the French by F. B.
Gilmour.Harpers, 302p.
In the year 2000, on the fiftieth anniversary of "the Columbian Empire", an
expedition goes from America to collect old iron in Normandy. First published
1913 as *Le Duc Rollon.*

1913   **Wallace, E.** *The Fourth Plague.* Ward, Lock, 303p.
The Red Hand threatens the safety of the world.

[1914]   **Anonymous (Carrel, F.)** *2010.* T. W. Laurie, 249p.
A super-scientist leads the world towards peace and happiness: "human nature
was divested of its weakness, its baseness, its cruelty and crime".

1914   **Chesterton G. K.** *The flying inn.* Methuen, vii, 310p.
A well-known satire on the power of politicians and the wickedness of all who do
not like beer, cheese and English inns.

1914   **Fletcher, J. S.** *The ransom for London.* J. Long, 295p.
International criminals threaten to destroy London.

1914   **Focus** *(pseud.) Larry; or England's coming danger.* E. Constans, 96p.
The threat of civil war brings in a reign of peace, justice, and brotherly love.

1914   **Gubbins, H.** *The elixir of life. H. J. Drane, 254p.*
The scientific world of A.D. 2905

1914   **Holt-White, W.** *The woman who saved the Earth.* Everett, 222p.
The struggle against anarchists in London.

1914   **Newton, W. D.** *The North afire: a picture of what may be.* Methuen,
200p.
Ulster rises against Home Rule for Ireland.

1914   **Newton, W. D.** *War*. With a preface by Fr. R. H. Benson. Methuen, xvi, 236p.
A war story to demonstrate the need for peace.

1914   **Pain, B.** *Futurist fifteen*. T. W. Laurie, 115p.
"An Old Moore or Less Accurate Forecast of certain events in the year 1915".
Alas! they were unusually inaccurate.

1914   **Palmer, F.** *The last shot*. Chapman & Hall, 517p.
A war between imaginary countries.

1914   **Taber, A. E.** *Work for all*. Arthur Wigley (Leeds), 96p.
A cooperative commonwealth based on Ruskin's ideas.

1914   **Vanewords, J. P.** *The great miracle*. S. Paul, 316p.
Hero applies his preternatural powers in the cause of international understanding.

1914   **von Suttner, Baroness B.** *When thoughts will soar*. Translated from the German by N. H. Dale. Constable, v, 448p.
A description of the consequences of modern warfare. First published 1911 as *Der Menschheit Hochgedanken*.

1914   **Wells, H. G.** *The world set free*. Macmillan, 286p.
As a result of atomic warfare, the world learns that "the old tendencies of human nature . . . were incompatible with the monstrous destructive power of the new appliances the inhuman logic of science had produced."

1915   **Cowen, L.** *"Wake up!": a dream of tomorrow*. Everett, 256p.
A demonstration that "only in universal military service can Britain find safety".

[1915]   **Cutcliffe-Hyne, C. J.** *Emperor of the world*. Newnes, 254p.
A new edition of *Empire of the world*, first published in 1910.

1915   **Floyd, A.** *The woman's harvest*. T. W. Laurie, 224p.
Ex-servicemen lead a revolt and oblige the government to introduce legislation that makes Britain a self-supporting country.

1915   **Grahame-White, C. and Harper, H.** *The invisible war-plane*. Blackie, 272p. Illus.
A professor invents "a thick and glutinous paint which neither reflects, deflects, nor absorbs light"; he uses it to make an airship invisible.

1915   **Haines, D. H.** *Clearing the seas; or, the last of the warships*. Harper (London & New York) 281p. Illus.
The forces of "the Blues" attack the United States.

1915   **Higginbottom, W. H.** *King of Kulturia*. Walter Scott Publishing Co. 160p.
A weak satire on Germany.

1915   **Kellerman, B.** *The tunnel.* Translated from the German. Hodder & Stoughton, 319p.
Europe and the United States collaborate in the building of a transatlantic tunnel railway. Originally published 1913 as *Der Tunnel.*

[1915]   **London, J.** *The scarlet plague.* Mills & Boon, 153p.
In the twenty-first century a plague wipes out most of mankind. [U.S. 1915]

1915   **Sommerfeld, A.** *"How Germany crushed France" (The story of 1915, the greatest conspiracy in history).* A translation from the German with preface by L. G. Redmond-Howard. Everett, 159p.
An imaginary invasion and conquest of France. First published 1912 as *Frankreichs Ende im Jahre 19 . .*

1915   **Thorne, G. (Gull, C. A. R.)** *The secret sea-plane.* Hodder & Stoughton, 243p.
The invention of a powerful sea-plane prevents the German zeppelins from dominating the North Sea.

1915   **Walker, J. B.** *America fallen! The sequel to the European War.* Putnam, x, 158p. Illus.
How the Germans invaded the United States and the lessons to be drawn from this. [U.S. 1915]

1915   **Wallace, E.** *"1925": the story of a fatal peace.* Newnes, 128p.
The failure to secure "the complete subjugation of Germany" results in a German invasion.

1916   **Abdullah, Achmed** *The red stain.* Simpkin, Marshall, 309p.
Hussain Khan leads a secret organization against all the forces of the West. [U.S. 1915]

1916   **Anonymous (Münch, P. G)** *Hindenburg's march into London: being a translation from the German original.* Edited with a preface by L. G. Redmond-Howard. J. Long, 254p.
The Germans land on the south coast and rapidly overrun Britain. First published 1915 as *Hindenburgs Einmarsch in London.*

1916   **Dixon, T.** *The fall of a nation.* D. Appleton (New York and London) 361p.
A German conquest of the United States.

1916   **Gentle Joseph** *A peaceful revolution.* E. J. Adams (Bath), 104p.
The happy world of A.D. 2016: emancipation of women, better education, a just economic system.

1916   **Gouvrieux, M.** *With wings outspread.* Translated from the French by Bernard Miall. Heinemann, 243p.
Aerial warfare in 1920.

1916   **Moffett, C.** *The conquest of America: a romance of disaster and victory; U.S.A., A.D. 1921.* Hodder & Stoughton, 310p. Illus.
"The purpose of this story is to give an idea of what might happen to America, being defenceless as at present, if she should be attacked, say at the close of the great European war, by a mighty and victorious power like Germany." [U.S. 1916]

[1917]   **Allen, R.** *Captain Gardiner of the International Police.* Hodder and Stoughton, 320p.
The International Federation of civilized nations repels a Chinese attack.

1917   **Gerard, M. (Teague, J. J.)** *The new order.* Hodder & Stoughton, viii, 269p.
A former army chaplain begins a campaign for the moral regeneration of the nation.

1917   **Kipling, R.** *As easy as A.B.C.* 42p.
(In *A Diversity of creatures.* Macmillan 442p.)
This short story, first published in the *London Magazine* in 1912, presents a Wellsian future world controlled by the Aerial Board of Communications.

1917   **Rousseau, V. (Emanuel, V. R.)** *The messiah of the cylinder.* C. Brown, 319p.
A Christian underground of the twenty-first century, when materialism has apparently conquered. [U.S. 1917]

1917   **von Kartoffel, Baron** *(pseud.) The Germans in Cork: being the letters of his Excellency, the . . . Military Governor of Cork in the year 1918.* T. F. Unwin, 112p.
A moral lesson for Ireland: the Germans will not be liberators.

1917   **Stead, F. H.** *No more war!* Simpkin, Marshall, 424p.
The Kaiser is killed by conspirators.

1918   **Brussoff, V.** *The Republic of the Southern Cross.* Translated from the Russian. Constable, 32p.
The title story (the first of nine) relates how the *mania contradicens* destroys an Antarctic dictatorship.

1918   **Corelli, M. (Mackay, M.)** *The young Diana.* Hutchinson, 320p
Romantic tale of a woman who takes part in an experiment to extend human life.

1918   **Doyle, Sir A. C.** *Danger!*
(In *Danger! and other stories.* John Murray, 246p.)
A famous forecast of unrestricted submarine warfare, first published in *The Strand Magazine*, July 1914. The story predicted with considerable accuracy the effects of submarine attacks on British shipping.

1918   **Gregory, O.** *Meccania: the super-state.* Methuen, xviii, 298p.
A remarkable forecast of the origin and development of totalitarian government in Meccania (i.e. Germany).

[1918] **Onions, O. (Oliver, G.)** *New moon.* Hodder & Stoughton, 312p.
An ideal state emerges in Britain on the lines of More's *Utopia.*

1918 **Pan (Beresford, L.)** *The kingdom of content.* Mills & Boon, 278p.
A small community settles down to a new life after civilization has been wiped out.

[1918] **Rousseau, V. (Emanuel, V. R.)** *The apostle of the cylinder.* Hodder & Stoughton, 312p.
A new title for the edition of 1917.

[1918] **Sladen, D.** *Fair Inez.* Hutchinson, 283p.
A romance of the third millenium when Australia is only five days' travel by airship from Britain. .

1918 **Swayne, M. (Nicoll, M.)** *The blue germ.* Hodder & Stoughton, 279p.
An "immortality bacillus" has disastrous consequences.

1918 **Watchman (Draper, W.)** *The Tower.* Headley Bros., 143p.
A vision of the better & happier Britain of the future: village settlements, manual industries, new towns, justice for all.

1919 **Bleackley, H.** *Anymoon.* J. Lane, 327p.
The miseries of life under communism.

[1919] **Colwyn, J.** *A city without a church.* Stockwell, 117p.
The revolution of 1938 leads to a realization of the need for religion.

1919 **Draper, W.** *The new Britain.* Headley Brothers, 143p.
First published as *The Tower,* 1918.

1919 **Garratt, E. R.** *The cry.* C. J. Thynne, 467p.
A story of the Second Coming.

1919 **Gull, C. A. R.** *The air pirate.* Hurst & Blackett, 287p.
An airship raids Atlantic shipping.

1919 **Lucian** *(pseud.) Dips into the near future.* Headley, 98p.
Comic projections.

1919 **Macaulay, R.** *What not.* Constable, xiii, 236p.
An ironic account of the time when the Ministry of Brains controls Britain.

1919 **Motta, L.** *The Princess of the Roses.* Translated from the Italian by William Collinge. Stanley Paul, 288p. Illus.
Written in 1910: a war between East and West in which scientific discoveries give victory to the West. First published 1912 as *La Principessa delle rose.*

[1919] **Munn, B.** *The skeleton man.* Angold's, 118p.
A cheap thriller: death rays threaten the world.

1919   **Newte, H. W. C.** *The red fury: Britain under Bolshevism.* Holden & Hardingham, 249p.
First published as *The Master Beast* in 1907.

1919   **Sharp, E.** *Somewhere in Christendom.* Allen & Unwin, 256p.
Christian principles put an end to the horrors of war.

1919   **Winsor, G. M.** *Station X.* H. Jenkins, 317p.
Wireless communication with Mars & Venus; the Martians try to gain a footing on Earth. [U.S. 1919]

1920   **Beck, C. (Bridges, T. C.)** *The brigand of the air.* Pearson, 224p. Illus.
An airship adventure story.

1920   **Beresford, J. D.** *A world of women.* Collins, 128p.
New edition of *Goslings*, 1913, which was published U.S. 1913 as *A world of women*.

[1920]   **Blake, S.** *Beyond the blue.* Books Ltd., 221p.
Space travel adventure.

1920   **Cournos, J.** *London under the Bolsheviks.* Reprinted from the *Nineteenth Century.* Russian Liberation Committee, 12p.
A dream of the horrors of living under a revolutionary regime.

1920   **Hambrook, E. C.** *The red tomorrow.* The Proletarian Press, viii, 325p.
The war of 1942 ends in a Red terror.

1920   **Le Queux, W.** *The terror of the air.* Lloyds, 278p.
German air pirates threaten the safety of the world.

1920   **Richmond, W. B.** *Democracy – false or true?* Cecil Palmer, 172p.
Vision of the ideal Britain of the future.

1920   **Shanks, E.** *The people of the ruins.* Collins, 252p.
The barbaric life of A.D. 2074 is a punishment for the folly of war.

1921   **Bannerman, Sir A.** *Leaders of the blind.* The National Review, 352p.
The League of Universal Brotherhood works for revolution in the United Kingdom.

1921   **Beresford, J. D.** *Revolution.* Collins, 252p.
A general strike leads to bloodshed and revolution.

[1921]   **Bernard, J.** *The new race of the devils.* Anglo-Eastern Publishing Co., 191p.
What came of a German attempt to breed a race of supermen by means of artificial insemination.

1921   **Blayre, C. (Allen, E. H.)** *The Purple Sapphire, and other posthumous papers selected from the unofficial records of the University of Cosmopoli by Christopher Blayre,, sometime Registrar of the University.* Philip Allan, 210p.
The 'Antescript' is dated from Cosmopoli, January 1952; a series of short stories, mostly on science fiction themes and communications with the planets.

1921   **Gull, C. A. R.** *The city in the clouds.* Hurst & Blackett, 288p.
A wealthy scientist builds a pleasure city two thousand feet above ground level.

[1921]   **Nedram** *(pseud.) John Sagur.* Heath Cranton, 272p.
How the world was organized in a scientific manner and universal peace began.

[1921]   **Pallen, C. B.** *Crucible Island.* Harding & Moore, 215p.
Utopian romance of a socialist state that is not destined to succeed. [U.S. 1921]

1921   **Pan (Beresford, L.)** *The great image.* Odham's, 288p.
The tyranny of the great combines provokes a revolution.

1921   **Ross, Major-General C.** *The Fly-by-nights.* J. Murray, 250p.
Prohibition and Bolshevism in post-war Britain.

1922   **A. E. (Russell, G. W.)** *The Interpreters.* Macmillan, 180p.
A symposium, placed in a future century, on "what relations the politics of Time may have to the politics of Eternity."

1922   **Barbor, H. R.** *Against the red sky: silhouettes of revolution.* C. W. Daniel, 272p.
A revolution in Britain overthrows the government.

1922   **Beresford, L.** *The last woman.* Odham's.
No copy available.

1922   **Hamilton, C.** *Theodore Savage.* L. Parsons, 320p.
The new Stone Age of the future.

1922   **Scrymsour, E.** *The perfect world.* Nash & Grayson, 320p.
An inner-world discovered; the end of our world follows. [U.S. 1922]

1922   **Hext H. (Phillpotts, E.)** *Number 87.* Thornton Butterworth, 287p.
An apparition, known as 'The Bat ', terrifies the world.

[1922]   **Van Pedroe-Savidge, E.** *The flying submarine.* A. Stockwell, 255p.
Spies and secret weapons in the battle against the Red Army.

1923   **Anonymous** *When woman rules: a tale of the first women's government by a well-known Member of Parliament.* J. Long, 352p.
A comedy of the days when women control the nation.

[1923]   **Addison, H. (Owen, H. C.)** *The battle of London.* H. Jenkins, 312p.
The author explains: the book "was written with the frank intention of shocking what the friends of Red Russià call the bourgeoisie into a realization of the only means of meeting the revolution".

1923   **Broomhead, R.** *A voice from Mars.* A. Stockwell, 176p.
A space-journey to Mars, where the inhabitants speak English.

1923   **Campbell, D.** *The last millionaire.* H. Cranton, 244p.
A beneficent millionaire leads the nations to a new life of equality and happiness.

1923   **Connington, J. J. (Stewart, A. W.)** *Nordenholt's million.* Constable, 303p.
A classic of its kind: the story of how the *Bacillus diazotans* threatens all life on Earth.

1923   **Graham, P. A.** *The collapse of homo sapiens.* Putnam, 276p.
Civilization has collapsed as the result of "a succession of bloody, ruthless, annihilating wars".

1923   **Joscelyne, C.** *When Gubbins ruled.* Fortune & Merriman, 95p.
A crude satire on the Labour Party.

1923   **Knox, R. A.** *Memories of the future.* Methuen, 244p.
An amusing satire on the latest fads in education, literature, philosophy, religion.

1923   **Lynch, Col. A.** *Seraph wings.* J. Long, 318p.
How Austin Grainge became dictator of Great Britain and began a rule of social justice.

1923   **Maurice, M. (Skinner, C. A.)** *Not in our stars.* Fisher Unwin, 288p.
Only one man knows that a gigantic meteorite has disturbed the course of time.

1923   **Nichols, R.** *Fantastica.* Chatto & Windus, 515p.
Contains a long novella (340p.), *Golgotha & Co.,* about the exploitation of religious beliefs and sentiments.

1923   **Odle, E. V.** *The clockwork man.* W. Heinemann, 213p.
A human automaton arrives in the present from the year 8000.

[1923]   **Turner, C. C.** *The secret of the desert.* Hurst & Blackett, 285p.
A small band of survivors from a world catastrophe adopts the simple, agricultural life.

1923   **Tyson, J. A.** *The scarlet tanager.* Mills & Boon, 308p.
[1922]   Secret Service adventures.

1923   **Wharton, A. (McAllister, A.)** *The man on the hill.* T. F. Unwin, 316p.
The government troops defeat the People's Army.

1923   **Wignall, T. C. and Knox, G. D.** *Atoms.* Mills & Boon, 288p.
Exploitation of atomic energy attracts the criminal interest.

1924   **Choate, P.** *The king who went on strike.* Eveleigh Nash & Grayson, 287p.
A sentimental tale of the young king, Alfred II, who goes on strike when the British workers are on strike. [U.S. 1924]

1924   **Davey, N.** *Yesterday. A Tory fairytale.* Chapman & Hall, 240p.
Isle of Wight declares itself independent, and the nation prepares for war.

[1924]   **Egbert, H. M. (Emanuel, V. R.)** *Draught of eternity.* J. Long, 254p.
Love and adventure in the days when New York is in ruins.

1924   **Egbert, H. M. (Emanuel, V. R.)** *The sea demons.* J. Long, 254p.
Sea creatures menace the safety of the world.

1924   **Fraser, R.** *The flying draper.* T. Fisher Unwin, 316p.
Albert Codling astounds the nation when he wills himself to fly.

1924   **Hussingtree, M. (Baldwin, O. B.)** *Konyetz.* Hodder & Stoughton, 320p.
A Bolshevist attack on Europe, followed by the Black Plague and end of the world.

1924   **Kingsmill, H. (Lunn, H. K.)** *The dawn's delay.* Elkin Mathews, 203p.
Three novellas: two look into the future – *The end of the world* and *W. J.*

1924   **Kitchell, J. G.** *The Earl of Hell.* Century Co. (New York and London) 325p.
Adventures of a man who can control gravity.

1924   **Leblanc, M. E. M.** *The tremendous event.* Translated from the French by A. T. de Mattos. Hurst & Blackett, 283p.
Adventure story set in the days after a great upheaval of the Channel bed has created a causeway between England and France. Originally published 1920 as *Le Formidable événement.*

[1924]   **MacClure, V.** *Ultimatum.* Harrap, 327p.
The League of the Covenant uses secret weapons and airships to force peace on the world. Published U.S. 1924 as *The Ark of the Covenant.*

1924   **Sieveking, L. de G.** *Stampede.* Illus. by G. K. Chesterton. The Cayme Press, 305p.
A comedy of politicians, ray guns and international diplomacy.

1924   **Tayler, J. L.** *The last of my race.* J. W. Ruddock, 131p.
A future world of intelligent creatures far above men.

1924   **Thorne, G. (Gull, C. A. R.)** *When the world reeled.* Ward, Lock, 313p.
A mysterious enemy creates snow, fog and cyclones in order to damage Britain.

1924   **Wells, H. G.** *The dream.* J. Cape, 320p.
A man living two thousand years in the future dreams of 'the wars and diseases, the shortened, crippled lives, the ugly towns' of the past.

1925   **Belloc, H.** *Mr. Petre.* With twenty-two drawings by G. K. Chesterton. Arrowsmith, 310p.
An ironic tale of high finance, politics, and the problems caused by amnesia.

1925   **Bywater, H. C.** *The great Pacific war*. Constable, ix, 317p.
A remarkably accurate forecast of the pattern of a naval war between Japan and the United States.

1925   **Capek, K.** *Krakatit*. Translated from the Czech. Geoffrey Bles, 416p.
A young engineer discovers a new and immensely powerful explosive; and struggles to hide his secret from the world. Originally published 1924 as *Krakatit*.

1925   **Coron, H.** *Ten years hence?* J. M. Ouseley, 255p.
A new aeroplane saves Britain from air attack.

1925   **Cox, E.** *Out of the silence*. John Hamilton, 319p.
A woman from the past is prepared to use any means to cure the world of evil and disease.

1925   **Craig, H.** *A hazard at Hansard: the speech from the Throne, Ottawa, Fourth August, 2014*. Arthur Stockwell, 31p.
A forecast of the social, political and moral improvements to come.

1925   **Hadfield, R. L. and Farncombe, F. E.** *Ruled by radio*. H. Jenkins, 256p.
An adventure story of the "Z ray".

[1925]   **Long, P. and Wye, A.** *The remnants of 1927*. Long's Publications, 191p.
Political demonstration of the consequences of socialism and communism.

1925   **Lynch, B.** *Menace from the Moon*. Jarrolds, 305p.
Lunar inhabitants use heat rays to endanger the Earth.

1925   **Madariaga, S. de.** *The sacred giraffe*. M. Hopkinson, 269p.
[1926]   By the year 6922 there has been a reaction to feminism; "hominism" is considered immoral.

1925   **Murray, V. T.** *The rule of the beasts*. S. Paul, 191p.
A plague removes most of mankind, and a new race of rational animals emerges.

1925   **Oppenheim, E. P.** *Gabriel Samara*. Hodder and Stoughton, 319p.
A romance of the restored monarchies.

1925   **Oppenheim, E. P.** *The wrath to come*. Hodder and Stoughton, 318p.
German and Japanese plans for the conquest of the world. [U.S. 1924]

1925   **Samuel, H. B.** *The Quisto-Box*. A. M. Philpot, 284p.
A thought-reading machine fails to help mankind.

1925   **Shaw, S.** *The locust horde*. Hodder and Stoughton, 319p.
The Soviet begins to transport the "entire female population of Russia" across the Bering Strait.

1925   **Sieveking, L. de.** *The ultimate island.* Routledge, 340p.
An airman discovers that Atlantic shipping is being drawn to a group of unknown islands by a vast whirlpool.

1925   **Tregarron, Y.** *Murderer's Island.* Methuen, 250p.
A romantic tale of the next century when murderers are sentenced to transportation for life.

1925   **Vivian, E. C.** *Star dust.* Hutchinson, 287p.
A scientist applies his knowledge of the electron to transmute matter into gold – with catastrophic results.

[1925]   **Wright, S. F.** *The amphibians.* Merton Press, 279p.
A time traveller discovers new types of rational animals in the distant future.

1926   **Austin, F. B.** *The war-god walks again.* Williams & Norgate, vii, 247p.
A warning against complacency in military thinking: eight short stories.

1926   **Baxter, G. (Ressich, J. S. M. and De Banzie, E.)** *Blue lightning.* Cassell, 329p.
Invention of an annihilation device causes world-wide upheavals and leads to race warfare.

1926   **Boswell, D.** *Posterity.* J. Cape, 254p.
In the days when the unions have set a limit on the number of children to be born.

1926   **Dent, G.** *The emperor of the if.* W. Heinemann, 333p.
Pterodactyls over London; Sigillaria engulf the Albert Hall.

1926   **Desmond, S.** *Ragnarok.* Duckworth, 351p.
After a disastrous world war what is left of mankind takes to caves, sewers and underground dwellings.

1926   **Glossop, R.** *The orphan of space.* G. MacDonald, 310p.
A fantastic tale of a future period when a wicked dictator is favoured by Satan.

[1926]   **Grant, I. F.** *A candle in the hills.* Hodder & Stoughton, 319p.
The Highlanders lead the revolt against the Soviet Government of Great Britain.

1926   **Haldane, C.** *Man's world.* Chatto & Windus, 299p.
War abolished; birth and parenthood no longer haphazard; mothers chosen by the state.

1926   **Halsbury, Earl of.** *1944* T. Butterworth, 302p.
After a world war in which all the great cities are destroyed, a remnant of mankind survives.

[1926]   **J. J. J.** *The Blue Shirts.* Simpkin, Marshall, 280p.
The rise and fall of the Socialist Republic of Great Britain.

1926   **Jacomb, C. E.** *And a new Earth*. Routledge, 239p.
An ideal scientific world of the distant future has developed out of the work of an engineer on Easter Island.

1926   **Jaeger, M.** *The question mark*. Hogarth Press, 252p.
In the ideal world of the twenty-second century all needs are satisfied.

1926   **O'Duffy, E.** *King Goshawk and the birds*. Macmillan, ix, 319p.
A satire on plutocracy, the press, etc.

1926   **Oldrey, J.** *The Devil's henchmen*. Methuen, 250p.
An airship comes down into an advanced community in the Himalayas.

1926   **Powell, G.** *All things new*. Hodder & Stoughton, 320p.
A scientist struggles for the peace of the world.

1926   **Radcliffe, G. (Travers, S.)** *The return of the Ceteosaurus*. Drane's Ltd., 310p.
Short stories.

1926   **Roger, N. (Pittard, H.)** *The new Adam*. S. Paul, 256p.
A moral tale: gland-grafting, hyperuranium, and the powers of science. First published as *Le Nouvel Adam*, 1924.

1926   **Spanner, E. F.** *The broken trident*. Williams & Norgate, 309p.
A detailed forecast of the effect of air power on naval warfare.

1926   **Spanner, E. F.** *The naviators*. Williams & Norgate, vi, 302p.
Only the Air Force is able to prevent a Japanese invasion of Australia.

[1926]   **Wallace, E.** *The Day of Uniting*. Hodder & Stoughton, 314p.
A new comet seems bound to collide with Earth.

1927   **Blakemore, F. J.** *The coming hour (?)*. Sands, vii, 226p.
In 1946, after experimenting with socialism, the nation votes "for the abolition of state control".

1927   **Capek, K.** *The absolute at large*. Translated from the Czech. Macmillan, viii, 294p.
An engineer's invention leads to a religious revival, a prodigious growth of industry, and a world war. Originally published 1922 as *Tovãrna na Absolutno*.

1927·   **Chesterton, G. K.** *The return of Don Quixote*. Chatto & Windus, viii, 312p.
Britain returns to a medieval pattern of society. [U.S. 1926].

[1927]   **Dellbridge, J.** *The Moles of Death*. Diamond Press, 303p.
The Moles of Death plot to conquer the Indian Empire.

[1927]   **Hadfield, R. L. and Farncombe, F. E.** *Red Radio*. H. Jenkins, 256p.
A death ray foils a Russian attempt to secure world power.

1927   **Legge, J. G.** *The millennium.* Blackwell, 164p.
A Ministry of Hygiene tries to force health upon the nation.

1927   **Margrie, W.** *The story of a great experiment: how England produced the first superman.* Watts & Co., 119p.
How Donald Fraser ended poverty and made Britain the first eugenic country in the world.

1927   **Maurois, A.** *The next chapter: the War against the Moon.* Kegan Paul *(Today and Tomorrow Series)* 74p.
An ironic tale of the preparations to attack the Moon.

1927   **Montague, C. E.** *Right off the map.* Chatto & Windus, 312p.
War in the imaginary republic of Ria.

1927   **Murray, W.** *The Messiah.* Arthur H. Stockwell, 112p.
A religious reformer changes the world.

1927   **Ollivant, A.** *To-morrow.* A. Rivers, 320p.
An ideal socialist Arcadia of the future.

1927   **One of the Unemployed.** *The brain box.* Hurst & Blackett, 287p.
An inventor uses a device to detect the most secret thoughts of politicians.

1927   **Oxenham, J. (Dunkerley, W. A.)** *The man who would save the world.* Longmans, 210p.
A devout Christian brings about world disarmament and a reign of brotherly love.

1927   **Spanner, E. F.** *The harbour of death.* Williams & Norgate, v, 310p.
Air and naval battles in the near future.

1927   **Von Harbou, T.** *Metropolis.* Translated from German. Hutchinson, 250p.
Revolt against the oppressive, inhuman, mechanical world of the future. The story, which draws on Capek's *RUR* (1921), was the source for the famous film, *Metropolis* (UFA 1926), by the Austrian director Fritz Lang.

1927   **Wright, S. F.** *Deluge.* F.Wright, 320p.
A great flood submerges most of the world.

1928   **Belloc, H.** *But soft – we are observed.* Arrowsmith, 312p. Illus. by G. K. Chesterton.
A satire on parliamentary government: the communists and anarchists of 1979 prove to be no different from the old parties.

[1928]   **Bentley, N. K.** *Drake's mantle.* Jarrold's, 286p.
A gallant admiral thwarts a Russian plot to invade Britain.

1928   **Brent, L. (Worts, G. F.)** *The return of George Washington.* Hodder & Stoughton, 320p.
George Washington brought back to life by a scientific process.

1928   **Creswick, P.** *The turning wheel*. Heath Cranton, 285p.
A dream of the floods that submerge the world.

1928   **Davey, N.** *Judgement Day*. Constable, 305p.
The Book of Judgement is opened for the inhabitants of the English village of Quaire.

1928   **Dudley, E.** *The challenge*. Longmans, ix, 133p.
A socialist revolution ends in the conversion of Europe to Catholicism.

1928   **Elmore, E.** *The Steel Grubs*. Selwyn & Blount, 287p.
A professor saves the country from a plague of steel-destroying grubs and the perils of the People's Government.

1928   **Forster, E. M.** *The machine stops,* 61p. In *The eternal moment and other stories*. Sidgwick & Jackson, 187p.
Written as "a reaction to one of the earlier heavens of H. G. Wells", this story examines the miseries of technological perfection. First published 1909 in the *Oxford and Cambridge Review*.

1928   **Grierson, F. D.** *Heart of the Moon*. Alston Rivers, 287p.
Interplanetary adventure.

1928   **Hamilton, C.** *Lest ye die*. J. Cape, 285p.
First published in 1922 as *Theodore Savage*.

1928   **Lazlo, G.** *Spires, bells and dreams!* Cassell, 306p.
The Jews of the world accept Christ as the Messiah and join with Christians to oppose materialism.

1928   **Lindsay, Capt. C. McD.** *Betrayed!! or what might come to pass.* H. J. Drane, 299p.
A socialist government reduces the armed forces in 1934 and in consequence the Empire is lost.

1928   **Sadler, A.** *Red ending*. Ward, Lock, 314p.
A communist invasion threatens the safety of India.

1928   **Snell, E.** *Kontrol*. Ernest Benn, 288p.
A wicked scientist on a secret island plans to create a race of supermen.

1928   **Wentworth-James, G. de S.** *The television girl*. Hurst & Blackett, 288p.
Romantic tale set in the near future.

1929   **Burdekin, K.** *The rebel passion*. Thornton Butterworth, 316p.
Giraldus the Monk looks into the future even unto the end of the machine age.

1929   **Edwards, G. (Pendray, G. E.)** *The earth tube*. Appleton, (New York & London), 308p.
The highly advanced Eastern world attacks the Americas by means of a subterranean tunnel.

1929   **Graham, H. E. (Hamilton, E. G.)** *The defence of Bowler Bridge.*
William Clowes, vi, Maps, 56p.
A tactical study of operations in modern warfare.

1929   **Guest, E.** *At the end of the world.* Matthews & Marrot, 112p.
Mankind finally becomes perfect; the end of the world follows.

1929   **Hodgson, J.** *The time-journey of Dr. Barton.* Author, 89p. Illus.
An engineer's vision of the future: heat machines, rocket planes, the
Mediterranean largely drained.

1929   **Kingsmill, H. (Lunn, A. K.)** *The return of William Shakespeare.*
Duckworth, 254p.
A comic and not very serious tale.

1929   **Lepper, G. H.** *Lion's hold.* Stockwell, 192p.
Australia and New Zealand prevent the handing over of Tanganyika to the
Germans.

1929   **Lincoln, M.** *The man from up there.* John Hamilton, 255p.
National commotion follows on arrival of a man from the Moon.

1929   **Macaulay, L.** *The decadence: an excerpt from "A history of the
triumph and the decay of England", dateable 1949.* Watts & Co., 108p.
A Free Trade attack on government policy in the 1920s.

1929   **McKay, H.** *A camouflage revolution.* Gardner, Darton, 262p.
A communist-directed rising in Britain.

1929   **Oppenheim, E. P.** *Matorni's vineyard.* Hodder & Stoughton, 307p.
Secret service adventures in 1940. [U.S. 1928]

1929   **Penmare, W. (Nisot, M. E.)** *The man who could stop war.* Hodder &
Stoughton, 308p.
A new gas which can immobilize all living things is used to stop a Russian
invasion.

1929   **Pertwee, R.** *MW – XX3* W. Heinemann, 335p.
A gallant naval officer thwarts a communist dominated general strike.

1929   **Rohmer, S. (Wade, A. S.)** *The Emperor of America.* Cassell, 294p.
Criminal conspiracy to control the United States.

1929   **Shiel, M. P.** *The Yellow Peril.* V. Gollancz, 367p.
First published 1913 as *The Dragon.*

1929   **Sinclair, U.** *The millennium: a comedy of the year 2000.* T. W. Laurie,
246p.
A farce aimed at the author's principal dislikes.

1929   **Slack, S. (Muir, J. R. B.)** *Robinson the Great. A political fantasia on the problems of today and the solutions of to-morrow.* Christopher's, 149p.
Author states that he has written "for the purpose of setting forth, in a concrete way, certain criticisms and ideas which he holds about the working of our system of government."

[1929]   **Wright, S. F.** *The world below.* Collins, 314p.
First published in 1925 as *The Amphibians.*

1930   **Belloc, H.** *The man who made gold.* Arrowsmith, 296p. Illus. by G. K. Chesterton.
An amusing satire on politicians, big business, science.

1930   **Blair, H.** *1957.* W. Blackwood, 354p.
A rising in India on the centenary of the Mutiny.

1930   **Delmont, J.** *The submarine city.* Translated from the German. Hutchinson, 288p.
German survivors from the First World War develop secret weapons in submarine caves off the Ligurian coast. First published 1925 as *Die Stadt unter dem Meer.*

[1930]   **Elmore, E.** *This siren song.* Collins, 285p.
Discovery of a new source of motive power.

1930   **Gibbons, F. P.** *The red Napoleon.* Brentano, 352p.
A military genius directs the communist and Asian hordes in the conquest of the world. [U.S. 1929].

1930   **Miles (Southwold, S.)** *The seventh bowl.* E. Partridge, 254p.
A history of the future from the Great Gas War of 1940 to the discovery of the power behind the universe and the end of life on Earth.

1930   **Morton, J. B.** *Drink up, Gentlemen!* Chapman & Hall, 282p.
Hilarious tale of the revolt against the efficiency movement that had curtailed drinking hours and turned pubs into cafeterias.

1930   **Rohmer, S. (Wade, A. S.)** *The day the world ended.* Cassell, 319p.
A mad scientist threatens to destroy the world.

1930   **Sims, A.** *Anna Perenna.* Chatto & Windus, 316p.
An ironic tale of life in the days when all grievances of the workers have been satisfied.

1930   **Stapledon, O.** *Last and first men.* Methuen, xi, 355p.
One of the most remarkable imaginative works in the field of futuristic fiction: an account of human development during the next hundreds of millions of years.

1930   **Sutherland, M. (Morris, G. S.)** *Second storm.* T. Butterworth, 319p.
A Russian Reconstruction League overthrows the communist government and liberates Russia.

1930   **Tillyard, A.** *Concrete*. Hutchinson, 288p.
What happened in the materialistic world of A.D. 2100 when the son of the
President of England rediscovered Christianity.

[1930]   **Von Harbou, T.** *The girl in the Moon*. Translated from the German by
Baronness von Hutten. Hutchinson, 250p.
Of interest as the source for Fritz Lang's film, *Die Frau im Mond* (UFA 1928). Lang
was married to Von Harbou; this story of a rocketship journey to the Moon first
appeared as *Die Frau im Mond*, 1928

1930   **Wells, H. G.** *The autocracy of Mr. Parham*. W. Heinemann, 370p. Illus.
by David Low.
How a history don became Lord Paramount of Great Britain.

1930   **Wright, S. F.** *Dawn*. Harrap, 363p.
A sequel to *Deluge*, first published in 1927. [U.S. 1929].

1931   **Berkeley, R.** *Cassandra*. V. Gollancz, 288p.
Admonitory tale of war and destruction in order to demonstrate necessity of a
national government.

1931   **Blair, H.** *Governor Hardy*. W. Blackwood, 303p.
Sir John Hardy saves India in 1957.

1931   **Blair, H.** *The great gesture*. W. Blackwood, 295p.
War in the days of the United States of Europe.

1931   **Collier, J.** *No traveller returns*. White Owl Press, 62p.
Dystopian account of a scientific society in which the rebels seek a more natural
life.

1931   **Crump, C. G.** *The red king dreams*. Faber & Faber, 383p.
A cumbersome satire on university life.

1931   **Eidlitz, W.** *Zodiak*. H. Hamilton, 319p.
The Russians attempt to stir up a world revolution by dropping propaganda
pamphlets from a giant plane.

[1931]   **Gibbs, A.** *The new crusade.* Hutchinson, 287p.
A millionaire plans to convert Britain to nudism.

1931   **Graham, H. E. (Hamilton, E. G.)** *The Battle of Dora*. William Clowes,
xii, 75p. Maps.
Tactical study of infantry and tank tactics in warfare.

1931   **Johnhett (Hettinger, J.)** *Our glorious future*. C. W. Daniel, 308p.
A wonder child reconciles all classes, ends war and reunites science and religion.

1931   **King-Hall, S.** *Post-war pirate*. Methuen, 252p.
Philanthropic idealist takes to piracy on the high seas.

1931   **Lambourne, J.** *The kingdom that was.* J. Murray, 302p.
In a future world the animals are civilized and man is a hunted creature.

1931   **Le Pretre, W.** *The Bolshevik.* H. Walker, 291p.
A rising against the Bolshevists who control all France and most of Britain.

1931   **McKenna, S.** *Beyond Hell.* Chapman & Hall, 353p.
The League of Nations agrees to send convicted murderers to a penal island.

1931   **Miles (Southwold, S.)** *The gas war of 1940.* Scholartis Press, 302p.
Universal destruction shows that "man has created a peril which he must now at all costs avoid . . . the perfection of instruments of destruction".

1931   **Miller, A.** *The king of men.* Nash & Grayson, 320p.
A mysterious disease conveniently kills off all debauchees.

1931   **Moxley, F. W.** *Red snow.* Jarrolds, 287p.
Red snow in 1935; and no more babies after 1936, [U.S. 1930]

[1931]   **Newman, B.** *Armoured doves.* Jarrolds, 288p.
An international league of scientists uses secret weapons to put an end to war.

1931   **Walsh, J. M.** *Vandals of the void.* J. Hamilton, 288p.
The Mercurian space-fleet threatens the planets.

1932   **Anthony, K.** *The passionate Calvary.* Hurst & Blackett, 286p.
England conquered by the Forces of the Unknown, and then restored to be another Eden.

1932   **Bailey, A. J.** *The Martian Emperor-President.* Printed for private distribution by William James Ray, 262p. Portrait.
Martians visit Earth in an immense spaceship.

1932   **Belloc, H.** *The Postmaster-General.* Arrowsmith, 286p. Illus. by G. K. Chesterton.
A very amusing satire on corruption in the party system.

1932   **Blayre, C. (Allen, E. H.)** *The strange papers of Dr. Blayre.* Philip Allan, 271p.
Reprint of *The Purple Sapphire* (1921) with additional papers from various professors of the University of Cosmopoli.

1932   **Buchan, J.** *The gap in the curtain.* Hodder & Stoughton, 255p.
An experiment in time projection: five men see a copy of *The Times* for a year ahead.

[1932]   **Delmont, J.** *Mistress of the skies.* Translated from the German. Hutchinson, 288p.
A romance of science and love. First published 1928 as *Der Ritt auf dem Funken*.

[1932] **Dyson, S. S.** *The melting pot.* Dover Printing and Publishing Co., 200p.
A National Party solves the problems of unemployment and creates a better Britain.

1932   **Edmonds, H.** *The riddle of the Straits.* Ward, Lock, 319p.
[1931] The Channel Tunnel saves Britain.

1932   **Freese, S.** *The ten year plan: a dream of 1940.* C. Palmer, 235p.
Town-planning for a smokeless and all-electric London of the future.

1932   **Furnill, J.** *Culmination.* Elkin Matthews & Marrot, viii, 534p.
A fantastic tale of the invention of an Ether-bridge, "designed to serve as a means of direct oral communication" between the living and the dead.

1932   **Gloag, J.** *To-morrow's yesterday.* Allen & Unwin, 184p.
Rational animals, descended from the cat tribe, return from the distant future to view with disgust our world today.

1932   **Gobsch, H.** *Death rattle.* Translated from the German by I. F. D. Morrow. Faber & Faber, 322p.
Death and destruction in 1934. First published 1931 as *Wahn-Europa 1934.*

[1932] **Godwin, G.** *Empty victory.* J. Long, 288p.
The story attempts to answer the question: "What would happen, as the world is today, if a first-class Power, completely disarmed . . . became the victim of a military aggressor?".

1932   **Helders, Major (Knauss, R.)** *The war in the air, 1936.* Translated from the German by C. W. Sykes. J. Hamilton, 254p. Illus.
An account of the air battles in which Britain defeats France. First published 1932 as *Luftkrieg 1936: Die Zertrümmerung von Paris.*

1932   **Howard, C.** *Paris Prelude.* J. Bale, 229p.
In 1961 a doctor looks back over his life.

1932   **Huxley, A.** *Brave new world.* Chatto & Windus, 306p.
The most famous satire of the 'thirties; Huxley suggests that man cannot live by technology alone.

1932   **James, R.** *While England slept.* J. Bale, vii, 246p.
A successful Anglo-Catholic plot to turn Britain into a Catholic state.

1932   **Lawrence, J. C.** *The year of regeneration.* Harper (New York and London), 220p.
Author writes that the book "represents an effort to create two characters, an historian, writing in 1983, and a suppositious Master of the Sons of Liberty, working in 1932–33." An ideal reorganization of life and politics in the United States.

1932   **Morison, F. (Ross, A. H.)** *Sunset.* Faber & Faber, 286p.
An English scientist communicates with another planet and is then put to death. [U.S. 1932]

1932   **Nicolson, H.** *Public faces*. Constable, 350p.
International political upheavals follow when it is discovered that Britain has the secret of atomic bomb manufacture.

1932   **Phillips, M. K.** *Trustees of the Empire*. Houghton Publishing Co., 190p.
Romantic and religious tale of the search for universal peace and unity.

1932   **Ray, J.** *The scene is changed*. J. Heritage, 294p.
A plague leaves three hundred men to face two million women.

1932   **Sibson, F. H.** *The survivors*. W. Heinemann, 292p.
Adventure follows when ships are stranded on a volcanic island that has appeared in the Atlantic.

1932   **Stapledon, O.** *Last men in London*. Methuen, viii, 312p.
The author writes: "a member of a much more developed human species, living on Neptune two thousand million years hence, enters into our minds to observe the Terrestrial field through our eyes but with his own intelligence".

[1932]   **Tillyard, A.** *The approaching storm*. Hutchinson, 286p.
A Red revolution has turned Britain into a communist state.

[1932]   **Vines, S.** *Return Belphegor!* Wishart, 310p.
A fundamentalist revival in Britain.

1932   **Wright, S. F.** *Beyond the rim*. Jarrolds, 319p.
Descendants of a Puritan community discovered in the Antarctic.

1932   **Wright, S. F.** *The new gods lead*. Jarrolds, 288p.
Short stories about an "eugenic" society.

1933   **Alexander, R.** *The pendulum of fate*. Daniel, 192p.
Fantasies of time and space.

1933   **Anonymous (Snow, C. P.)** *New lives for old*. V. Gollancz, 399p.
Discovery of a rejuvenation drug is not a blessing for mankind.

1933   **Arlen, M. (Kuyumjian, D.)** *Man's mortality*. W. Heinemann, xx, 379p.
Revolt against the world authority in the days when International Aircraft and Airways is the only government.

[1933]   **Balmer, E. and Wylie, P.** *When worlds collide*. S. Paul, 287p.
Only the occupants of a space-ship escape when a planet collides with the Earth. [U.S. 1933].

1933   **Bell, N. (Southwold, S.)** *The Lord of life*. Collins, 320p.
An atmospheric catastrophe destroys most of the human race. [U.S. 1933]

1933   **Black, L.** *The poison war*. S. Paul, 288p.
World war, bombing and poison gas attacks.

1933   **Clouston, J. S.** *Button brains.* H. Jenkins, 312p.
Humorous narrative centred on an ingenious robot.

1933   **Collier, J.** *Tom's a-cold.* Macmillan, iii, 320p.
The barbaric Britain of A.D. 2000. Published U.S. 1933 as *Full Circle.*

1933   **Dearmer, G.** *Saint on holiday.* W. Heinemann, 337p.
Life in the days when the "Ministry of Grace" controls the country.

1933   **Dilnot, F.** *I warmed both hands.* Lovat Dickson, 316p.
International turmoil follows on the discovery of a growth accelerator.

1933   **Edmonds, H.** *Red invader.* Ward, Lock, 318p.
Plot and counter-plot as Russia and Germany prepare a sudden air raid on Britain.

1933   **Ellis, A. W.** *To tell the truth.* J. Cape, 229p.
A young Russian discovers the truth.

1933   **Faraday, W. B.** *The milk in the cocoanut.* Denis Archer, 260p.
Whimsical tale about survival after death.

[1933]   **Frazer, S.** *A corned hog.* Chapman & Hall, 295p.
Charles Stewart, an American film star, is elected King of England.

1933   **Gloag, J.** *The new pleasure.* Allen & Unwin, 304p.
What happens when everyone develops an acute sense of smell.

1933   **Hannay, J. F. W.** *Rebel's triumph.* Methuen, 280p.
Collapse of American capitalism: guerilla warfare, starvation and disease.

1933   **Kaul, F.** *Contagion to this world.* Translated from the German by Winifred Ray. Geoffrey Bles, 317p.
A disaster story: civilized life is wiped out. First published 1930 as *Die Welt ohne Gedächtnis.*

1933   **Keeler, H. S.** *The box from Japan.* Ward, Lock, 384p.
The Zell process causes an international upheaval. [U.S. 1932]

1933   **Kendall, J. (Brash, M. M.)** *Unborn tomorrow.* Collins, 319p.
How the revolt began against the socialist and regimented world of 1995.

1933   **Knowles, W. P.** *Jim McWhirter.* C. W. Daniel, 282p.
An idealist reforms the government and establishes an utopian scheme of social improvements.

[1933]   **Lewis, H.** *The way out: the social revolution in retrospect, viewed from A.D. 2050.* Elliot Stock, 60p.
Plans for improving society.

1933 **O'Duffy, E.** *Asses in clover.* Putman (London & New York), 331p.
A satire on everything from big business and fashionable religions to films and modern poetry.

1933 **Sibson, F. H.** *Unthinkable.* Methuen, 272p.
Members of an Antarctic expedition return to find that war has wiped out civilization.

1933 **Simpson, H.** *The woman on the Beast.* W. Heinemann, 492p.
Three linked stories, the last set in 1999: Mrs. Sopwith, or Antichrist, a thinly disguised Aimée Macpherson, becomes world ruler and the end of the world follows.

1933 **Sterne, J.** *The secret of the Zodiac.* Boswell, 256p.
Bolshevists and Freemasons destroy the British Empire.

1933 **Stuart, F.** *Glory.* V. Gollancz, 287p.
Love and adventure in the days when Trans-Continental Aero-routes control the skies of the world.

1933 **Tweed, T. F.** *Rinehard* A. Barker, 311p.
An American president dissolves Congress, establishes a National Reconstruction Corps and introduces an authoritarian regime. First published U.S. 1933 as *Gabriel over the White House.*

1933 **Viereck, G. S. and Eldridge, P.** *Prince Pax.* Duckworth, 319p.
Capital cities bombed to encourage peace.

1933 **Wells, H. G.** *Scientific Romances.* V. Gollancz, 1222p.
Contains: *The Time Machine, Island of Dr. Moreau, Invisible Man, War of the Worlds, First men in the Moon, Food of the Gods, In the days of the Comet.*

1933 **Wells, H. G.** *The shape of things to come: the ultimate revolution.* Hutchinson, 431p.
The last of the great Wellsian plans for a better world.

1933 **Williams, C.** *Shadows of ecstasy.* V. Gollancz, 287p.
The emergence of the Allied Supremacies of Africa and the attack on London.

1933 **Wright, S. F.** *Power.* Jarrolds, 381p.
In the days when Stanley Maitland rules Britain by Orders in Council.

1934 **Balmer, E. and Wylie, P.** *After worlds collide.* S. Paul, 287p.
The few surviving groups from the destruction of Earth establish themselves on another planet. [U.S. 1934].

1934 **Beeding, F. (Palmer, J. L. and Saunders, H. St. G.)** *The one sane man.* Hodder & Stoughton, 318p.
One man tries to use weather control in order to force a reform on the nations.

1934 **Bell, N. (Southwold, S.)** *Valiant clay.* Collins, 250p.
Originally published in 1931 under the title of *The gas war of 1940.*

1934   **Beverley, B.** *The air devil.* Philip Allan, 252p.
Sabotage hits the world airlines.

1934   **Blayre, C. (Allen, E. H.)** *Some women of the University.* Nubiana, Tip.
Sorelle, Nessuno, 171p.
Continues the themes of *The Purple Sapphire*, 1921.

1934   **Brown, R. B.** *A broth of a boy.* Fortune Press, 373p.
An odd tale about the Empire of Ratagonia in 1980.

1934   **Buchanan, A.** *He died again.* Arthur Barker, 283p.
A moral tale of arms manufactures, international belligerence, and the need for peace.

1934   **Christie, D.** *The striking force.* Rich & Cowan, 310p.
War between Russia and the United Kingdom from Persia to Afghanistan.

1934   **Constantine, M.** *(pseud.) Proud man.* Boriswood, 318p.
Ironic impressions of the human race presented as a dream about the future.

1934   **Cozzens, J. G.** *Castaway.* Longman, 182p.
Experiences of the only survivor from the destruction of New York. [U.S. 1934].

1934   **Curtis, M.** *Landslide.* V. Gollancz, 286p.
Politics and love in the days when Leo Steele is dictator of the Confederation of the West.

[1934]   **Dalton, M.** *The Black Death.* Sampson Low, 316p.
Air raids destroy all life in Britain.

1934   **Forester, C. S.** *The peacemaker.* W. Heinemann, 341p.
A scientist invents a means of stopping wars and tries to persuade the British Government to disarm.

1934   **Gloag, J.** *Winter's youth.* Allen & Unwin, 312p.
By 1960 the power of modern weapons has forced peace on the world.

1934   **Harvey, W.** *Strange conquest.* Lincoln Williams, 255p.
Fear compels mankind to unite.

1934   **Hedges, S. G.** *Plague panic.* H. Jenkins, 311p.
Scientists of the world unite to fight a deadly disease.

1934   **Hubbard, T. O'Brien** *To-morrow is a new day.* With eight wood engravings by Blair Hughes-Stanton. Lincoln Williams, 125p.
A prophet preaches salvation to a world that does not heed him.

1934   **Levett, A.** *A Martian examines Christianity.* Watts, 118p.
Pedestrian examination of "time-honoured absurd beliefs" presented through a visitor from Mars.

1934   **Llewellyn, A.** *The strange invaders*. Bell, vii, 309p.
Life in the new ice age somewhere in Russia, where a residual Communism is the religion of a primitive people.

1934   **MacIlraith, F. and Connolly, R.** *Invasion from the air*. Grayson & Grayson, 320p.
The introduction states: "We endeavour to show that the first result of an air offensive in a city like London will be the demoralisation of the population, especially when it finds that there is practically no protection from the deadly gases . . . carried by bombing aircraft".

1934   **Mitchell, J. L.** *Gay Hunter*. W. Heinemann, 286p.
Civilisation has collapsed; man now leads a peaceful life as a hunter, but has to fight the menace of re-industrialisation.

1934   **Mitchison, G. R.** *The first worker's government; or, new times for Henry Dubb*. Foreword by Stafford Cripps. V. Gollancz, 528p. Index.
The history of the General Election of 1936 and the establishment of a socialist economic system.

1934   **Moseley, M.** *War upon women*. Hutchinson, 286p.
The effects of modern warfare are examined in the lives of a colonel, his wife and his daughter.

1934   **Reid, L.** *Cauldron bubble*. V. Gollancz, 448p.
An admonitory tale about a war between two imaginary contries.

[1934]   **Sibson, F. H.** *The stolen continent*. A. Melrose, 288p.
A sequel to *The survivors*.

1934   **Sinclair, U.** *I, Governor of California, and how I ended poverty; a true story of the future*. T. W. Laurie, 64p.
A characteristic piece from Upton Sinclair. [U.S. 1933]|

1934   **Spencer, D. A. and Randerson, W.** *North Sea Monster*. Houghton & Scott-Nell, 245p.
A secret society forces disarmament on the world.

1934   **Troubetzkoy, Princess P. and Nevinson, C. R. W.** *Exodus, A. D. A warning to civilians*. Hutchinson, 288p.
Air attacks on London cause the breakdown of civilization.

1934   **Weston, G.** *Comet "Z"*. Methuen, 280p.
A comet causes the sterilization of all but two males. Published U.S. 1934 as *His first million women*.

[1934]   **Wheatley, D.** *Black August*. Hutchinson, 349p
The Prince Regent defeats communism in Britain.

1935   **Balsdon, D.** *Have a new master*. Eyre & Spottiswoode, 278p.
A hilarious tale of school life set in the future.

1935   **Beynon, J. (Harris, J. B.)** *The secret people.* Newnes, 256p.
Adventures with the pigmy people discovered under the Sahara in 1964.

1935   **Brockway, F.** *Purple plague: a tale of love and revolution.* Sampson Low, Marston, 310p.
An outbreak of the "Purple Plague" compels a liner to stay at sea; a revolutionary ship's council takes control.

1935   **Browne, D. G.** *The stolen boat-train.* Methuen, 281p.
A general strike and an attempt to kidnap the king.

1935   **Channing, M.** *The poisoned mountain.* Hutchinson, 304p.
Oriental villains plot to subjugate India.

1935   **Charles, J.** *The man without a mouth.* A. H. Stockwell, 224p.
A professor's invention opens the way to world peace.

1935   **Connell, J. (Robertson, J. H.)** *David go back.* Cassell. 301p
A Scottish rebellion in the mid-twentieth century.

1935   **Conquest, J.** *With the lid off.* T. Werner Laurie, 463p.
Vision of a better Britain of the future: Christian principles, concern for the poor, justice for all.

1935   **Corbett, J.** *Devil-Man from Mars.* H. Jenkins, 312p.
A Martian visits London, bringing the Death Ray with him.

[1935]   **Cornwallis-West, G.** *The woman who stopped war.* Hutchinson, 286p.
The women of Europe form "The Women's Save the Race League" and force the world to live in peace.

1935   **Cross, V. (Cory, V.)** *Martha Brown M.P.* T. W. Laurie, 256p.
A woman's world of the thirtieth century, when women are the stronger sex.

1935   **Divine, A. D.** *They blocked the Suez Canal.* Methuen, 218p.
A conspiracy to block the Canal in order to cut off Italian supplies to Abyssinia.

1935   **Edmonds, H.** *The professor's last experiment.* Rich & Cowan, 311p.
An inventor is able to stop a war.

[1935]   **Ertz, S.** *Woman alive.* Hodder & Stoughton, 206p. Illus.
The only surviving woman refuses to take a mate – at first.

1935   **Frazer, S.** *A shroud as well as a shirt.* Chapman & Hall, 343p.
A satire on Fascism.

1935   **Greenwood, E.** *Miracle in the drawing room.* Skeffington, 320p.
Miraculous events meet with a mixed reception in a believing and unbelieving nation.

1935   **Gresswell, E. K.** *When Yvonne was dictator.* J. Heritage, 306p.
How women gained equality with men.

1935   **Hubbard,W. D.** *The thousandth frog.* Blackie, 233p.
A plague of gigantic insects and frogs in the United States.

1935   **Hyder, A.** *Vampires overhead.* Philip Allan, 248p.
Vampires destroy most of life on earth.

1935   **Lancing, G. (Hunter, B. M.)** *Fraudulent conversion: a romance of the gold standard.* S. Paul, 335p.
A professor reforms Britain's economics and politics.

1935   **Lewis, S.** *It can't happen here.* J. Cape, 413p.
What happened when "Buzz" Windrip became dictator of the United States. [U.S. 1935]

1935   **Mitchell, M.** *Traveller in time.* Sheed & Ward, 324p.
The invention of Tempervision by an Irishman permits viewers to have an Irish vision of the past.

1935   **Nathan, R.** *Road of ages.* Constable, 245p.
A new Exodus: the Jews trek to the land set aside for them in "the deserts of Asia where these unhappy people . . . had been offered a haven by the Mongols".

1935   **Noel, L. (Barker, N. L.)** *The golden star.* S. Paul, 288p.
War breaks out when an asteroid, believed to be solid gold, approaches earth.

1935   **Pollard, L.** *Menace.* T. W. Laurie, 256p.
A Russian air attack on Britain leads to a rising in Russia.

1935   **Russell, A. J.** *Christ comes to town.* Cassell, 374p.
The New Testament story retold in a modern setting.

1935   **Stuart, F.** *The Angel of Pity.* Grayson & Grayson, 284p.
A tale of future warfare.

1935   **Stokes, S. (Fawcett, F. D.)** *Air-Gods' parade.* Arthur Barron, 180p. Frontis.
Russians attack London in 1945 with 'flying torpedos' and 'flying bombs'.

1935   **Sykes, W. S.** *The ray of doom.* Hodder & Stoughton, 312p.
The Liberator threatens all organic life with his Death Ray.

1935   **Trevarthen, H. P. (Heydon, J. K.)** *World D.* Sheed & Ward, 320p.
A scientist discovers the laws of Psycho-Physics and establishes a new world beneath the bed of the Pacific Ocean.

1935   **Ward, R. H.** *The sun shall rise.* Nicholson & Watson, 363p.
The Fascists secure control of Britain.

1935   **Wedlake, G. E. C.** *The wrecking ray.* H. Jenkins, 312p.
Pirate ship holds up Atlantic shipping.

1935   **White, T. H.** *Gone to ground.* Collins, 266p.
Tales told in a bomb-proof shelter by a party following the Flat Hat Hounds.

1935   **Wood, S. A.** *I'll blackmail the world.* Hodder & Stoughton, 312p.
From a secret island a fanatic sends out his aeroplanes to dominate Europe.

[1935]   **Wright, S. F.** *Prelude in Prague: a story of the war of 1938.* G. Newnes, 317p.
A German attack on Czechoslovakia is followed by a German ultimatum to Britain. Published U.S. 1936 as *The War of 1938.*

1936   **Ambler, E.** *The dark frontier.* Hodder & Stoughton, 320p.
Political intrigue and revolution in an imaginary European country.

1936   **Baker, F.** *The birds.* Peter Davies, 346p.
The birds unite against mankind and civilization almost comes to an end.

1936   **Balsdon, D.** *Sell England?* Eyre & Spottiswoode, 278p.
The author writes: ". . . this thirtieth-century world offers little more than, at the best a satire, at the worst a burlesque, of our twentieth-century life".

1936   **Beverley, B.** *The space raiders.* P. Allen, 245p.
The League of Nations organizes the defence of the world against attacks from outer space.

[1936]   **Beynon, J. (Harris, J. B.)** *Planet plane.* Newnes, 248p.
By rocket-ship to Mars in 1981.

1936   **Bradford, J. S.** *Even a worm.* Arthur Barker, 302p.
The animals of the world rebel against mankind.

1936   **Burke, N.** *The scarlet vampire.* S. Paul, 288p.
Future warfare in the imaginary land of Swartzalia.

1936   **Collins, D.** *Race the sun.* Constable, 311p.
Adventures with the first stratospheric aeroplane.

[1936]   **Cunningham, B.** *Wide, white page.* Hutchinson, 288p.
Prince Alexis founds an utopian community in the Antarctic.

1936   **Detre, Professor L.** *War of two worlds.* Translated from the German. Jarrolds, 253p.
Intelligent ants menace the regimented and scientific world of A.D. 2000. Originally published 1935 as *Kampf zweier Welten.*

1936   **Edwards, C. (Edwards, F. A.)** *Fear haunts the roses.* Ward Lock, 314p.
Political implications of the discovery of a death-ray.

1936   **Gérard, F.** *The Black Emperor.* Rich & Cowan, 278p.
An attempt by negroes to conquer the world.

1936   **Gérard, F.** *The Dictatorship of the Dove.* Rich & Cowan, 280p.
Members of the Apostleship of Peace try to prevent war.

1936   **Hamilton, E.** *The horror on the asteroid.* P. Allen, 256p.
Six short stories.

1936   **Herbert, B.** *Crisis 1992!* Richards, 286p.
A new planet comes dangerously close to the earth.

1936   **Hill, W. B.** *A new Earth and a new Heaven.* Watts, 312p.
Account of the foundation of ideal communities based on "ideas which, if put into practice, would result in big and beneficial consequences to the human race."

1936   **Howell Smith, A.D.** *Gods divide.* Watts & Co., 314p.
Account of one man's search for faith told in the year 1946.

1936   **Jaeger, M.** *Retreat from Armageddon.* Duckworth, 224p.
A house-party takes refuge in the Welsh borders during the three-days war.

1936   **Jameson, S.** *In the second year.* Cassell, 300p.
A Fascist Britain of the future.

1936   **Macleod, J. G.** *Overture to Cambridge.* Allen & Unwin, 244p.
A future world rent by the everlasting wars of the Blues and the Yellows; peace is found only by those who abandon the cities.

1936   **MacPherson, I.** *Wild harbour.* Methuen, 250p.
A couple seek refuge from war in 1944.

1936   **Masefield, L.** *Cross double cross.* Putnam, 331p.
The struggle between Socialists and Conservatives in 1950.

1936   **Meredith, E.** *Our stranger: a kinemato-romance.* Grayson & Grayson, 407p.
Life in New London in 1971.

1936   **O'Neil, J.** *Day of wrath.* V. Gollancz, 288p.
Wars which end with "Europe going up in flames. South and East the Yellow men were pouring death on the remnants of our White civilisation."

1936   **Painter, T. and Laing, A. K.** *The glass centipede.* Butterworth, 285p.
A criminal plot to dominate the world by causing an epidemic.

[1936]   **Phillpotts, E.** *The owl of Athene.* Hutchinson, 198p.
Mankind unites to fight an invasion of enormous crabs.

1936   **Smith, W.** *The machine stops.* R. Hale, 284p.
What happened when all the metal in the world disintegrated.

1936 **Speaight, R. W.** *The angel in the mist.* Cassell, 324p.
A tale of theatrical life.

1936 **Spitz, J.** *Sever the Earth.* Translated from the French by M. Mitchiner.
J. Lane, viii, 167p. Illus.
A comedy of world upheavals. World split into two separate hemispheres.
Originally published 1936 as *L'Agonie du globe.*

1936 **Stevenson, D. E.** *The empty world.* H. Jenkins, 312p.
A handful of people, survivors from a world disaster, begin a new life.

1936 **Tolstoi, A.** *The deathbox.* Translated from the Russian. Methuen,
375p. Illus.
The engineer Garin uses his deathbox to become Dictator of the World.

1936 **Tunstall, B.** *Eagles restrained.* Allen & Unwin, 320p.
How the International Air Police put an end to a war between Germany and
Poland.

1936 **Wootton, B.** *London's burning: a novel for the decline and fall of the
Liberal age.* Allen & Unwin, 284p.
The political world in 1940.

1936 **Wright, S. F.** *Four days' war.* R. Hale, 288p.
Russia and Germany unite against Britain in 1938.

1937 **Adam, R.** *War on Saturday Week.* Chapman & Hall, 311p.
Reactions of ordinary people to the outbreak of an imaginary war.

1937 **Allott, K. and Tait, S.** *The rhubarb tree.* Cresset Press, 293p.
An ironic story of Fascism in the United Kingdom.

1937 **Campion, S. (Coulton, M. R.)** *Thirty million gas masks.* Peter Davies,
313p.
The horrors of modern warfare described in the context of an imaginary war.

1937 **Capek, K.** *War with the newts.* Translated from the Czech by M. and R.
Weatherall. Allen & Unwin, 348p.
What happened when the newts became rational . . . Capek writes: 'The Newts
are simply the Multitude; their epoch-making achievement is in the number there
are of them.' Originally published 1936 as *Válka s mloky.*

1937 **Clark, C.** *Sky-raft.* Newnes, 247p.
Adventures in a craft which cruises in the stratosphere.

1937 **Constantine, M.** *(pseud.) Swastika night.* V. Gollancz, 288p.
A story of the days when the Holy German Empire rules over Europe, Africa and
part of Asia.

1937 **Eton, R. (Meynell, L. W.)** *Not in our stars.* Nicholson & Watson, 318p.
To escape the expected destruction of London, a group of people flee to an
Atlantic island.

1937   **Ford, F. M. (Hueffer, F. M.)** *Vive le roy*. Allen & Unwin, 321p.
The struggle for power in a future monarchical France.

1937   **Hawker, C.** *The great peril*. Blackie, 255p. Illus.
How the United Kingdom was saved from the Krandan air invasion.

1937   **Ingham, L. H.** *The unknown dictator*. A. H. Stockwell, 199p.
A mysterious dictator in the Himalayas plots the downfall of Britain.

1937   **Jones, G.** *The blue bed*. J. Cape, 245p.
A Bolshevist rising in Wales.

1937   **Kingsmill, H., (Lunn, H. K.) and Muggeridge, M.** *1938: a pre-view of next year's news*. Eyre & Spottiswoode, 160p. Illus.
A comic version of the news.

1937   **Lamb, W.** *The world ends*. Dent, 204p. Illus.
The tranquil life of the last of the human race.

1937   **Lindsay, D. T.** *The Green Ray*.
Borderline entry. See *Note 5*

1937   **Low, A. M.** *Adrift in the stratosphere*. Blackie, 224p. Illus.
Space travel and adventure.

1937   **Low, A. M.** *Mars breaks through*. H. Joseph, 251p.
A Martian gains control of earth.

1937   **Oppenheim, E. P.** *The dumb gods speak*. Hodder & Stoughton, 319p.
Intrigue, future warfare and the 'ultimate' weapon.

1937   **Shiel, M. P.** *The young men are coming!* Allen & Unwin, 375p.
Civil war in Britain. The Young Men win.

1937   **Stapledon, O.** *Star maker*. Methuen, xii, 339p.
An evolutionary history of the future universe to the end of the galaxies.

[1937]   **Sutter, A. O.** *The Super-woman*. A. H. Stockwell, 235p.
The perfect woman proclaims the 'spiritual dynamic of all true moral being' and so ends disease, poverty and discord throughout the world.

1937   **Taunton, E. C.** *If twelve today*. Chapman & Hall, 261p.
A dedicated Christian reforms the nation.

1937   **Wright, S. F.** *Megiddo's Ridge*. R. Hale, 284p.
The final battle in "The Great War of 1938".

1938   **Anson, A.** *When woman reigns*. Pen-in-hand, 206p.
By A.D. 2525 men have become totally subservient to women.

1938 **Beaujon, P. (Ward, B. L.)** *Peace under earth: dialogues from the year 1946.* Megaw, 47p. Frontis.
An ironic dialogue on the Christmas theme, set in 1946 when everyone is living in underground cities.

[1938] **Clouston, J. S.** *Not since Genesis.* Jarrolds, 287p.
The state of Europe examined, as a gigantic meteorite speeds towards earth.

1938 **Cosier, C. H. T.** *The mighty millstone.* Arthur Stockwell, 228p.
A world disaster follows after a planetoid hits earth.

[1938] **Desmond, S.** *Chaos.* Hutchinson, 484p.
A German air raid on London starts a world war.

1938 **Desmond, S.** *World-birth.* Methuen, 404p.
Forecasts of future warfare and of the coming of the ideal world.

1938 **Gérard, F.** *Wotan's wedge.* Rich & Cowan, 278p.
British Intelligence foils German plans against the United Kingdom.

1938 **Hamilton, B.** *Traitor's way.* Cresset Press, 252p.
The struggle to combat the Fascist movement in Britain.

1938 **Linklater, E.** *The impregnable women.* J. Cape, 348p.
The women of Europe organize a "love-strike", and so end a war.

1938 **Marvell, A.** *Minimum man; or, time to be gone.* V. Gollancz, 350p.
How the New Freedom Party brought totalitarianism to Britain and how it was overcome.

1938 **Maurois, A.** *The thought-reading machine.* Translated from the French by James Whittall. J. Cape, 191p.
An ironic tale: "Thus, the invention which I at one time imagined would transform human relationships had accomplished nothing of the sort." First published 1937 as *La Machine à lire les pensées.*

1938 **Pavlenko, P.** *Red planes fly east.* Translated from the Russian by S. Garry. Routledge, 523p.
The colonization of Siberia ends in a war with Japan. First published 1937 as *Na Vostokye.*

1938 **Phillpots, E.** *Saurus.* John Murray, 281p.
A rational iguana from space gives the world good advice.

1938 **Pollard, Capt. A. O.** *Air reprisal.* Hutchinson, 272p.
The Vandalian air attack on Britain and what came of it.

1938 **Priestley, J. B.** *The doomsday men.* W. Heinemann, 312p.
Religious fanatics plan to destroy the world by an atomic explosion, but are prevented at the last minute.

1938   **Radcliffe, G.** *The sky wolves.* Thornton Butterworth, 252p.
The Royal Air Force saves London from destruction.

1938   **Rand, A.** *Anthem.* Cassell, 147p.
The search for individuality in a rigidly conformist world.

1938   **Seton, G. (Hutchison, G. S.)** *According to plan.* Rich & Cowan, 302p.
Colonel Grant saves Britain from foreign domination.

1938   **Street, A. G.** *Already walks tomorrow.* Faber & Faber, 432p.
Britain faces starvation as the result of a wrong agricultural policy.

1938   **Wright, S. F.** *The adventure of Wyndham Smith,* H. Jenkins, 284p.
The futility of living in a world where all work is done by machines drives mankind to suicide.

1938   **Young, R. (Payne, P. S. R.)** *The war in the marshes.* Faber & Faber, 353p.
Revolution in North Wales.

1939   **Bennett, A. G.** *The demigods.* Jarrolds, 384p.
A species of giant ants, highly organized and highly intelligent, threatens mankind.

1939   **Buckle, R.** *John Innocent at Oxford.* Chatto & Windus, 150p. Illus. by the author.
Fantasy of love and personal relations in the ideal Oxford of the future.

1939   **Chadwick, P. G.** *The death guard.* Hutchinson, 431p.
Synthetic creatures are used in a future war.

1939   **Corbett, J.** *The ghost plane.* Herbert Jenkins, 284p.
A mysterious phantom-plane attacks London; nation held to ransom.

[1939]   **Craig, T.** *Plague over London.* Hutchinson, 256p.
A Russian agent spreads typhoid germs through Britain.

1939   **Dane, C. (Ashton, W.)** *The arrogant history of White Ben.* Heinemann, 420p.
A scarecrow comes to life in a time of war and gives the nation the leadership it needs.

1939   **Edwards, C. (Edwards, F. A.)** *Drama of Mr. Dilly.* Robert Hale, 288p.
An ironic tale of the dictator who takes over the People's Republic in the Britain of 1976.

1939   **George, V. (Vernon, G. S.)** *The crown of Asia.* S. Paul, 286p.
The Secret Service and a volcanic eruption foil attempts to invade India.

1939   **Howorth, M.** *This is Armageddon.* Arthur H. Stockwell, 288p.
A Secret Voice speaks to the world and a professor establishes a Model State in the Valley of the Mountains.

1939   **Marsh, C.** *And wars shall cease.* Broadway Publishing, 351p.
Members of the Cosmic Brotherhood help to establish peace throughout the world.

1939   **Marvell, A.** *Three men make a world.* V. Gollancz, 286p.
Britain becomes an agricultural nation when petrol-destroying bacteria end the career of the internal combustion engine.

1939   **Oppenheim, E. P.** *Exit a dictator.* Hodder & Stoughton, 288p.
The Russian people rebel against their government.

1939   **Parkinson, H. F.** *They shall not die.* Constable, 277p.
The hero discovers a death-preventing serum and lives on into the twenty-first century.

1939   **Peskett, S. J.** *Back to Baal.* Illustrated by the author. Francis Aldor, 177p.
An ironic account about the revival of the cult of Baal in darkest London.

1939   **Ramseyer, E.** *Airmen over the suburb.* Translated from the French by
[1938]   Norah Bickley. V. Gollancz, 287p.
The horrors of air raids in a war between France and Germany.

1939   **St. John, A.** *Why not now?* With introductory note by Dugald Semple. C. W. Daniel, 333p. Illus.
A dream of the creation of a just, Christian society in the United Kingdom.

1939   **Sherriff, R. C.** *The Hopkins manuscript.* V. Gollancz, 352p.
The Moon collides with the Earth: Europe goes down under a flood of Asiatic barbarians.

[1939] **Shute, N. (Norway, N. S.)** *What happened to the Corbetts.*
W. Heinemann, 267p.
The author states: "I wrote this story to tell people what the bombing attacks would really be like . . . I was right in my guess that gas would not be used and in the disruption of civil life that would be caused by high explosive. I overlooked the importance of fire".

1939   **Watts, N.** *The man who did not sin.* H. E. Walter, 216p.
The application of Christian principles leads to universal peace, justice and prosperity.

1939   **Wells, H. G.** *The holy terror.* M. Joseph, 447p.
The poorest of Wells' utopian stories: how Rudolf Whitlow became the founder of the World State.

[1939] **Wheatley, D.** *Sixty days to live.* Hutchinson, 391p.
How a tiny group escaped the universal destruction when a comet strikes the earth.

1940 **Best, H.** *The twenty-fifth hour.* J. Cape, 285p.
Adventures in the desolate world after the Second World War.

[1940] **Bridges, T. C.** *The death star.* Collins, 288p. Illus.
A small group survives on Earth after a new star has approached too closely.

1940 **Brown, D. and Serpell, C.** *Loss of Eden.* Faber & Faber, 251p.
Britain makes peace with Nazi Germany and pays the full price for this folly.

1940 **Gloag, J.** *Manna.* Cassell, 280p.
A new fungus threatens to upset the economic system.

1940 **Horsnell, H.** *Man alone.* H. Hamilton, 159p.
The life of "the sole survivor of a catastrophe as universal as it was inexplicable"

1940 **Noyes, A.** *The last man.* J. Murray, 272p.
The experiences of the few survivors of a press-button war; a moral lesson on man's failure to base his life on "the eternal grounds of the moral law". Also published U.S. 1940 as *No other man.*

1940 **Wells, H. G.** *All aboard for Ararat.* Secker & Warburg, 106p.
An allegory for the times: ends with another flood and a new Noah.

[1941] **Beresford, J. D.** *A common enemy.* Hutchinson, 208p.
Out of a natural catastrophe comes a general change of heart and a federated Europe is founded.

[1941] **Beresford, J. D.** *What dreams may come.* Hutchinson, 256p.
An ideal state in a future age when mankind has passed through several biological changes.

1941 **Bishop, M.** *The star called Wormwood.* V. Gollancz, 288p.
Fascism in the year 2839.

1941 **Brown, D. and Serpell, C.** *If Hitler comes* . . . Faber & Faber, 251p.
A reissue of *Loss of Eden*, 1940.

1941 **Hamlyn, W. A.** *Strange weather!* Knole Park Press, 272p.
A weather-machine, which can produce hurricanes and blizzards, saves Britain from invasion.

1941 **Lynn, G.** *The return of Karl Marx.* Foreword by Herbert Read. Chancery Books, 48p.
Karl Marx returns to London and, after experiences with left-wing parties, is expelled for political deviation.

1941 **Nathan, R.** *They went on together.* W. Heinemann, 191p.
An invasion of the United States.

1941   **Newman, B.** *Secret weapon.* V. Gollancz, 189p.
A new explosive brings the war to an end.

1941   **Van Loon, H. W.** *Invasion.* Harrap, 171p.
Nazi invasion of the United States. [U.S. 1940].

1942   **Boshell, G.** *John Brown's Body.* Secker & Warburg, 175p.
A heroic Englishman leads the peoples of Europe against Nazi domination.

1942   **Divine, A. D.** *Tunnel from Calais.* Collins, 192p.
The Germans attempt to invade Britain by means of a secret tunnel under the Channel.

1942   **Jameson, S.** *Then we shall hear singing.* Cassell, 232p.
In a nameless country, "five years after the end of the war", German medical methods fail to crush the sense of individuality in the conquered.

1942   **Morton, H. V.** *I, James Blunt.* Methuen, 56p.
A warning to the complacent – a diary written in 1944 describes life in Nazi-occupied Britain.

1942   **Sackville-West, V.** *Grand Canyon.* M. Joseph, 206p.
The author's intention is to demonstrate "the terrible consequences of an incomplete conclusion or indeed of any peace signed by the Allies with an undefeated Germany".

1942   **Stapledon, O.** *Darkness and light.* Methuen, viii, 181p.
An imaginative picture of possible developments and struggles in the future.

1943   **Allan, M.** *Change of heart.* G. Harrap, 288p.
A sentimental account of the moral and political re-education of the German people.

1943   **Armstrong, A. (Willis, G. A.) and Graeme, B. (Jeffries, G. M.)** *When the bells rang.* Harrap, 240p.
Fantastic tale of a German invasion of Great Britain.

[1943] **Atholl, J.** *The man who tilted the Earth.* Mitre Press, 63p.
A plot to destroy the world with Explosive Z.

1943   **Cassius (Foot, M.)** *The trial of Mussolini: being a verbatim report of the first great trial for war criminals held in London sometime in 1944 or 1945.* V. Gollancz, 82p.
An attack on men and policies the author did not like.

[1943] **Cummings, R.** *Into the Fourth Dimension.* Gerald Swann, 128p.
Space travel adventures. [U.S. 1941].

1943   **Fearn, J. R.** *The intelligence gigantic.* World's Work, 100p.
In A.D. 2064 a superhuman intelligence seeks to dominate mankind.

[1943]   **Finigan, G. L.** *Anno Domini 1963*. Direct Publicity Co., 39p.
A brief account of a better future world.

1943   **Hawkin, M.** *When Adolf came*. Jarrolds, 176p.
The German conquest of Britain and the British underground movement.

1943   **Kearney, C.** *Erone*. Biddles Ltd, (Guildford), 253p.
An ideal state organised by scientists, engineers and economists.

1943   **Kent, C. H.** *Armistice or total victory?* Arthur Stockwell, 36p.
Written "to show to my fellow countrymen and women why this war must end by
the absolute and final destruction of the German spirit of everlasting strife and
bloodshed."

1943   **Maugham, R.** *The 1946 Ms*. War Facts Press, 44p.
A political warning – a general defeats Germany and establishes a dictatorship in
the United Kingdom.

1943   **Oppenheim, E. P.** *Mr. Mirakel*. Hodder & Stoughton, 224p.
Nature rebels against man and the war comes to an end.

1943   **Russell, E. F.** *Sinister barrier*. World's Work, iv, 135p.
How mankind fought an alien race.

1944   **Askham, F.** *The heart consumed*. J. Lane, 234p.
Ideas on education in the twenty-first century.

1944   **Beresford, J. D. and Wynne-Tyson, E.** *The riddle of the tower*.
Hutchinson, 152p.
A time-traveller moves through the future history of humanity.

1944   **Borodin, G. (Milkomane, A. M.)** *Peace in nobody's time*. Hutchinson,
151p.
How James B. Brotherby "challenged the existing order without an army, with a
united proletariat, without a revolution from the left or a counter revolution from
the right or a compromise from the centre."

1944   **Collins, E.** *Mariners of space*. Lutterworth Press, 240p.
The Earth space-fleet is victorious in an interplanetary war.

[1944]   **Desmond, S.** *Black dawn*. Hutchinson, 224p.
How the Anglo-Saxon Confederation united with the other great world powers.

1944   **Fearn, J. R.** *The Golden Amazon*. World's Work, 117p.
Marvellous adventures of the Superwoman.

1944   **Ingram, K.** *The Premier tells the truth*. Quality Press, 164p.
What happens when a Conservative prime minister reveals what he really thinks.

1944   **King-Hall, L.** *Fly envious time*. P. Davies, 176p.
A history of the progressive improvement of society in the future.

1944   **Lea, R.** *The outward urge.* Rich & Cowan, 216p.
The British Freedom Party rises against the Workers' Government – "a minor, if unpleasant, incident in the country's advance towards full Federal freedom in the Community of Nations."

1944   **Stapledon, O.** *Old man in new world.* Allen & Unwin, 36p.
Brief vision of a better Britain in the future – diversity, originality, self-expression promoted by the New Educational Policy.

1945   **Cross, J. K.** *The angry planet.* P. Lunn, 200p.
Experiences of the first expedition to Mars.

1945   **Fowler, S. (Wright, S. F.)** *The adventure of the Blue Room.* Rich & Cowan, 192p.
War in 1990 between two of the three remaining world power groups, under rules that prevent direct injury to human life.

[1945]   **Alexander, R. W.** *Back to nature.* Stanley Paul, 192p.
Two hundred young people abandon the comfortable city life of 2044 A.D. to face the realities of nature.

1945   **Ardrey, R.** *World's beginning.* H. Hamilton, 204p.
A chemical company, organized on a just social basis, eventually gives the United States a new form of society. [U.S. 1944]

1945   **Harrison, M.** *Higher things.* MacDonald, 187p.
Man discovers he can defy gravity.

1945   **Lewis, C. S.** *That hideous strength.* J. Lane, 476p.
The last of the trilogy that began with *Out of the silent planet.* Ransom fights for the safety of humanity against the plots of an immoral group of scientists who have the help of "the dark Eldils". See *Note 6.*

1946   **Arnold, F. E.** *Wings across time.* Pendulum Series, 120p.
Four stories.

1946   **Baker, G.** *None so blind.* N. Wolsey, 207p.
An idealist directs the re-education of the German people and defeats a Nazi underground movement.

[1946]   **Chetwynd, B.** *Future imperfect.* Hutchinson, 174p.
A romance of the days when "it would kill men to keep up the pace women have set politically and professionally"

1946   **Cummings, R.** *The shadow girl.* Gerald Swann, 186p.
Time travel and warfare in the third Millennium.

1946   **Hanley, J.** *What Farrar saw.* Nicholson & Watson, 202p.
Traffic jams have become so serious that bombing is the only solution to the problem of untangling them.

1946   **Kuehnelt-Leddihn, E. and C.** *Moscow 1979.* Translated from the
German. Sheed & Ward, v, 314p.
A comet helps to bring freedom to the Russian people. [U.S. 1940]

1946   **Martin, P.** *Summer in three thousand.* Quality Press, 184p.
Earth divided into the still bad old world of America and the progressive ideal
state of the World Island.

1946   **Mottram, R. H.** *The visit of the princess.* Hutchinson, 174p.
The effect of a visit from a Ruritanian princess on the regimented Britain of the
nineteen-sixties.

1946   **Ramuz, C. F.** *The triumph of death.* With an introduction by Denis de
Rougemont. Frontis. by Edward Burra. Translated from the French by
Allan Ross Macdougall and Alex Comfort. Routledge, xvi, 155p.
Vision of the end of all life on Earth. First published 1925 as *Présence de la mort.*

1946   **Rose, F. H.** *The maniac's dream.* Duckworth, 237p.
A vision of the world destroyed by atomic bombs.

1947   **Cowie, D.** *The rape of man.* Tantivy Press, 222p.
Animals and vegetables of the world rebel against mankind.

1947   **De Chair, S.** *The Teetotalitarian State.* Falcon Press, 175p.
An ironic tale of Mr. Bang who leads the Teetotalitarian Front to victory against
the Neighbour Party.

1947   **Faulconbridge, P.** *(pseud.) Commissars over Britain.* Beaufort Press,
[1948]   84p. Illus.
The British Resistance Movement save the nation from Soviet domination.

1947   **Fearn, J. R.** *Liners of time.* World's Work, 156p.
Scientific wonders in A.D. 2000.

1947   **Frank, P. (Hart, H.)** *Mr. Adam.* V. Gollancz, 191p.
The consequences of an explosion in an American nuclear fission plant. [U.S.
1946]

1947   **Green, F. L.** *A fragment of glass.* M. Joseph, 263p.
A strip cartoon character is the means of reforming the nation.

1947   **Jones, A. M. K.** *When Smuts goes.* V. Gollancz, 232p.
The end of white power in South Africa.

1947   **Maxwell, C. F.** *Plan 79.* John Gifford, 214p.
Wicked Germans devise Plan 79, a scheme for germ warfare, with catastrophic
results for humanity.

1947   **Neville, D.** *Bright morrow.* John Crowther, 157p.
An idealist shows the world how to avoid wars.

1947   **Remenham, J. (Vlasto, J. A.)** *The peacemaker.* MacDonald, 256p.
The world's wealthiest industrialist finds a way to make the nations unite.

1947 **Stacpoole, H. de V.** *The story of my village.* Hutchinson, 124p.
A virus infection destroys the vision of all men and kills large numbers of people. As a result the cities are emptied and "the whole world has become a village".

1947 **Staniland, M.** *Back to the future.* N. Vane, 264p.
A depressing future world of identity cards, queues for food, etc.

1947 **Venning, H. (Van Zeller, C. H.)** *The end: a projection, not a prophecy.* D. Organ, 298p.
The appearance of Antichrist is followed by the arrival of the Pope in England and the end of the world.

1948 **Borodin, G. (Milkomane, G. A. M.)** *Spurious sun.* T. Werner Laurie, 281p.
Cosmic effects, after the explosion of a Scottish Atomic Station.

1948 **Colvin, I.** *Domesday village.* Falcon Press, 126p.
The socialist Britain of 1986 discovers the happiness of "the bad old days of laissez faire".

1948 **Farjeon, J. J.** *Death of a world.* Collins, 192p.
The Earth is destroyed.

1948 **Fearn, J. R.** *The Golden Amazon returns.* World's Work, 133p.
The Super-woman fights interplanetary gangsters.

1948 **Gandon, Y.** *The last white man.* Translated from the French. Cassell, 254p.
Save for one man, the entire white race dies out. First published 1945 as *Le Dernier Blanc*.

1948 **Gibbs, H.** *Pawns in ice.* Jarrolds, 222p.
A world war of the future.

1948 **Green, H. (Yorke, H. V.)** *Concluding.* Hogarth Press, 254p.
A day in the life of a septuagenarian scientist, fifty years hence.

1948 **Groom, P.** *The purple twilight.* T. W. Laurie, 282p.
The first men to reach Mars discover a dying civilisation; atomic warfare has made all its females sterile.

1948 **Heard, G.** *Doppelgangers.* Cassell, 256p.
By 1997 psychological knowledge has made considerable advances; the nation is separated into psychological types and the masses are controlled by subtle means. [U.S. 1947].

1948 **Kearney, C. B.** *The great calamity.* Author, 23p.
A universal disaster wipes out all the great cities and most of Britain as well.

1948 **Laski, M.** *Tory heaven; or, thunder on the right.* Cresset Press, 172p.
An amusing dream of a future Tory Britain.

1948   **Newman, B.** *The flying saucer.* V. Gollancz, 250p.
A league of scientists stages fake Martian attacks on Earth in order to compel the nations to unite.

1948   **Parkman, S.** *Life begins tomorrow.* Hodder & Stoughton, 319p.
Devastation in Britain; a man and woman struggle against great odds.

1949   **Chappell, C.** *The arrival of Master Jinks*, The Falcon Press, 220p.
The serum RA 65 makes possible the One Month Baby.

1949   **Dahl, R.** *Sometime never.* Collins, 255p.
A somewhat grim comedy of the period after the third world war when Gremlins take possession of any empty world. [U.S. 1948]

1949   **Del Martia, A. (Fearn, J. R.)** *The trembling world.* Gaywood Press, 128p.
Radiations from Mars menace life on Earth. See *Note 7.*

1949   **Desmond, H.** *Terrible awakening.* Wright & Brown, 220p.
An interplanetary flight to escape a collision between Earth and another planet.

1949   **Eldershaw, M. B. (Eldershaw, F. S. and Barnard, M. F.)** *Tomorrow and Tomorrow.* Phoenix Press, 468p.
A writer in Australia four hundred years hence describes life in the bad old days of 1920–50.

1949   **Graves, R.** *Seven days in New Crete.* Cassell, 281p.
Love, magic and metaphysics in an archaic future world. Also published U.S. 1949 as *Watch the North Wind rise.*

1949   **Hesse, H.** *Magister Ludi.* The Nobel Prize Novel *Das Glasperlenspiel*, translated by Mervyn Savil. Aldus Publications, 502p.
This philosophical romance, first published in 1943, attempts to give a design for an ideal way of life. In a very different world of the future, the aristocratic hierarchy of intellectuals who belong to the Castalian Order aims at the co-ordination of all arts and sciences; music and mathematics are the basis of their synthesis.

1949   **Huxley, A.** *Ape and essence.* Chatto & Windus, 153p.
This story is the first major statement, within the tale of the future, of post-war anxiety at humanity's failure to control itself and its tremendous powers of destruction. [U.S. 1948]

1949   **Jameson, S.** *The moment of truth.* Macmillan, 176p.
Another war in which Europe is defeated and largely destroyed.

1949   **Moore, W.** *Greener than you think.* V. Gollancz, 320p.
A growth-accelerator covers the world with grass. England and the British monarchy are the last to go. [U.S. 1947]

1949   **Newman, B.** *Shoot.* V. Gollancz, 241p.
How the Western powers defeated a sudden Russian attack.

1949   **Orwell, G. (Blair, E.)** *Nineteen eighty-four*. Secker & Warburg, 312p.
Undoubtedly the most famous futuristic fiction that has appeared since 1945. Winston Smith, O'Brien and the whole apparatus of the police state have become part of our political folk-lore.

1949   **Phillpotts, E.** *Address unknown*. Hutchinson, 219p.
Discovery of an inhabited planet.

1949   **Temple, W. F.** *Four-sided triangle*. J. Long, 239p.
Complications follow the invention of a matter-duplicator.

1950   **Capon, P.** *The other side of the sun*. W. Heinemann, 321p.
On Antigeos, a newly-discovered planet near the Sun, there is an ideal state.

1950   **Creasey, J.** *The man who shook the world*. Evan Bros., 286p.
Dr. Palfrey prevents the plot to shake the world.

1950   **Fearn, J. R.** *Operation Venus!* Scion Press, 128p.
Interplanetary adventures.

1950   **Fitzgibbon, C.** *Iron hoop*. Cassell, 220p.
Life in an occupied city during the "Third World War". [U.S. 1949]

1950   **Guthrie, J. (Brodie, J.)** *Is this what I wanted*. T. W. Laurie, 153p.
Illus.
A tale of love and personal relationships in the near future, when war is coming.

1950   **Hickling, H.** *The furious evangelist*. A. Redman, 384p.
The struggle for freedom against a totalitarian regime.

[1950]   **Rayer, F. G.** *Worlds at war*. Tempest Publishing Co., 128p.
Science fiction stories.

1950   **Ryves, T. E.** *Bandersnatch*. The Gray Walls Press, 299p.
A visit to a most unattractive world of the future.

1950   **Sea-Lion (Bennett, G. M.)** *This creeping evil*. Hutchinson, 176p.
The forces of evil seek to destroy Britain.

1950   **Statten, V. (Fearn, J. R.).**
The late John Russell Fearn was responsible for a large number of science fiction stories. Many of them appeared under his pseudonyms – Statten, Gridban, and Magroon; and all of these were published as cheap paper-backs by the Scion Press. The fantastic stories narrated by Fearn are worth no more than a brief mention. See *Note* 7. The following were published in 1950:

Annihilation. End of the earth.
The cosmic flame. Flying saucers.
Inferno. Future intrigue.
The micro men. Earth saved from tyranny.
Nebula X. Plot and counter-plot in 1970.
Sun makers. Creation of artificial suns.
2,000 years on. Future adventures.
Wanderer of space. Space travel.

[1950] **Stewart, G. R.** *Earth abides.* V. Gollancz, 334p.
The adventures of the new Abraham after the population of America has been wiped out by a plague. [U.S. 1949]

1951 **Bleiler, E. F. and Dikty, T. E.** *(eds.) The best science fiction stories.* Grayson & Grayson, 256p.
Eight stories selected from the original thirteen of the U.S. 1950 edition.

1951 **Brackett, L. (Hamilton, E. L.)** *Shadow over Mars.* World Distributors, Manchester, 128p.
Amorous and adventurous exploits on Mars [U.S. 1944]

1951 **Bradbury, R.** *The silver locusts.* R. Hart-Davis, 232p.
The first men on Mars and the end of life on Earth. Published U.S. 1951 as *The Martian Chronicles.*

1951 **Brede, A.** *Sister Earth.* Scion Press, 112p.
Space travel adventures.

1951 **Brown, F.** *What mad universe.* T. V. Boardman, 223p.
Earth is involved in a war with Arcturus: satirical treatment of science fiction themes. [U.S. 1949]

1951 **Clarke, A. C.** *The sands of Mars.* Sidgwick & Jackson, 219p.
The life of the first men on Mars.

1951 **Coblentz, S. A. (Stanley, A. C.)** *The sunken world.* Fantasy Books, 190p.
Adventure in Atlantis. [U.S. 1950]

1951 **Cummings, R.** *The princess of the atom.* T. V. Boardman, 191p.
A fantastic tale of microscopic human beings and a race of giants who attack the United States. [U.S. 1950]

1951 **Dunsany, Lord** *The last revolution.* Jarrolds, 192p.
The revolt of the machines and what came of it.

1951 **Edmonds, H.** *The rockets (Operation Manhattan).* MacDonald, 286p.
A tale of love and adventure which closes with a rocket attack on New York.

1951 **Ehrlich, M.** *The big eye.* T. V. Boardman, 256p.
An earth-destroying comet is used as a means of compelling the world to live in peace. [U.S. 1949],

1951 **Friend, O. J.** *The kid from Mars.* Fantasy Books, 190p.
Effects of a visitor from Mars. [U.S. 1949]

1951 **Gibbs, L.** *Late final.* Dent, 216p.
Life in the devastated Britain of 1960.

1951 **Greenberg, M.** *(ed.) Men against the stars.* Grayson & Grayson, xvi, 253p.
Editorial preface, introduction by W. Ley; eight stories from original twelve of U.S. 1950 edition.

1951   **Guerard, A. J.** *Night journey.* Longmans, 357p.
An indictment of ideological wars presented in terms of an imaginary war in a
nameless country. [U.S. 1950]

1951   **Hamilton, E.** *The star kings.* Museum Press, 220p.
Adventure with the Interstellar Patrol in the Mid-Galactic Empire. [U.S. 1949]

1951   **Herbert, A. P.** *Number Nine; or the mind-sweepers.* Methuen, 244p.
Comic tale of naval operations and manoeuvres in the Civil Service.

1951   **Koestler, A.** *The age of longing.* Collins, 448p.
Koestler writes: "it is not a visionary tale of the distant future; it merely carries the
present one step further in time".

1951   **Long, F. B.** *John Carstairs: space detective.* Fantasy Books, 192p.
Detectives at work in the space age.

1951   **Matthews, R.** *Red sky at night.* Hollis & Carter, 219p.
A mass pilgrimage to Russia ends with the Russians proclaiming themselves to
be Christians; world parliament established.

1951   **Pilkington, R.** *Stringer's folly.* Dennis Yates, 256p.
A foreign power plans the invasion of the United Kingdom.

1951   **Rayer, F. G.** *Tomorrow sometimes comes.* Home & Van Thal, 256p.
A moral tale on the consequences of the atomic bomb and the need for a sense
of individual responsibility.

1951   **Slater, H. J.** *Ship of destiny.* Jarrolds, 200p.
Adventures on a luxury liner when floods have submerged most of Europe.

1951   **Smith, G. O.** *Pattern for conquest.* Clerke & Cockeran, 203p.
Interstellar battles begin when man moves through the planets. [U.S. 1949]

1951   **Sowden, L.** *Tomorrow's comet.* R. Hale, 302p.
A comet approaches the earth and all life is doomed.

1951   **Statten, V. (Fearn, J. R.)** See remarks on Statten under 1950. See
Note 7. Following are all from the Scion Press:
The avenging Martian. Destruction of all Venusians.
Born of Luna. Adventure with the Selenites.
Cataclysm. The Black Terror threatens earth.
The catalyst. Destruction of Mercury.
Deadline to Pluto. Planetary Peril.
The devouring fire. The fight for earth.
The new satellite. Earth in danger.
Petrified planet. Space adventure.
The red insects. Giant termites and time machines.
The renegade star. Earth out of orbit.

1951   **Van Vogt, A. E.** *The voyage of the "Space Beagle"*. Grayson & Grayson, 256p.
Extraordinary adventures during the exploration of outer space. [U.S. 1950]

1951   **West, A.** *Another kind*. Eyre & Spottiswoode, 351p.
Trade unionism, strikes, and a civil war in the near future.

[1951]   **Wollheim, D. A.** *(ed.) Flight into space*. Cherry Tree Books, 190p.
Short stories. [U.S. 1950]

1951   **Wright, S. F.** *The throne of Saturn*. W. Heinemann, 208p.
Twelve stories; foreword by author.

1951   **Wylie, P.** *The disappearance*. V. Gollancz, 351p.
In an instant all the men in the world become invisible to the women and the women to the men. [U.S. 1951]

1951   **Wyndham, J. (Harris, J. B.)** *The day of the Triffids*. M. Joseph, 302p.
The Triffids – mobile and dangerous hybrid plants – imperil the safety of all that is left of mankind after radio-active weapons have done their worst.

1952   **Ashton, F. and Ashton, S.** *Wrong side of the Moon*. T. V. Boardman, 191p.
Adventure story of the attempt to send the first spaceship to the Moon.

1952   **Asimov, I.** *I, robot*. Grayson & Grayson, 224p.
Life in the age of the robots. [U.S. 1950]

1952   **Berry, B.** *And the stars remain*. Panther, 112p.
Space exploration reveals the powers behind the universe.

1952   **Berry, B.** *Born in captivity*. Panther, 192p.
The underground movement in the days when policemen are Environmental Psychologists.

1952   **Berry, B.** *Dread visitor*. Panther, 128p.
Lemurs threaten the safety of Earth.

1952   **Berry, B.** *Return to Earth*. Panther, 111p.
Visit to a desolate Earth.

1952   **Bleiler, E. F. and Dikty, T. E.** *(eds.) The best science fiction stories. Second series*. Grayson & Grayson, 240p.
Fourteen stories from original eighteen of the U.S. 1951 edition.

1952   **Bradbury, R.** *The illustrated man*. R. Hart-Davis, 192p.
Prologue, epilogue, sixteen stories. [U.S. 1951]

[1952] **Branley, F. M.** *Lodestar; rocket ship to Mars.* W. Heinemann, 213p.
Space adventure story. [U.S. 1951]

1952 **Bulmer, H. K.** *Encounter in space.* Panther, 128p.
Spaceships of the Solar Commonwealth defeat the enemy.

1952 **Bulmer, H. K.** *Space treason.* Panther, 114p.
Battles for the control of space.

1952 **Campbell, H. J.** *Beyond the visible.* Panther, 189p.
Earth will not heed warnings and is destroyed.

1952 **Campbell, J. W.** *(ed.) From unknown worlds.* Atlas Publishing Co.,
128p.
Short stories.

1952 **Campbell, J. W.** *The thing and other stories.* Cherry Tree Books,
192p.
Introduction – 'Basically, science fiction is an effort to predict the future on the
basis of the known facts, culled largely from present-day science laboratories' –
seven stories. First published U.S. 1948 as *Who goes there?*

1952 **Capon, P.** *The other half of the planet.* W. Heinemann, 255p.
A sequel to *The other side of the Sun* of 1950.

1952 **Carnell, J.** *(ed.) No place like Earth.* T. V. Boardman, 256p.
Ten stories.

1952 **Clarke, A. C.** *Islands in the sky.* Sidgwick & Jackson, 190p.
First experiences in an Earth satellite.

1952 **Clarke, A. V. and Bulmer, H. K.** *Cybernetic Controller.* Panther, 112p.
Mankind revolts against regimentation.

1952 **Conklin, G.** *(ed.) Possible worlds of science fiction.* Grayson &
Grayson, xii, 256p.
Editorial introduction: thirteen stories on themes of space travel and planetary
existence. [U.S. 1951].

1952 **Conroy, R.** *Mission from Mars.* Panther, 112p.
Martians intervene in an Earth war.

1952 **Deegan, J. J.** *(pseud.) Amateurs in alchemy.* Panther, 128p.
Revolt on the planet Hamman II.

1952 **Deegan, J. J.** *(pseud.) Underworld of Zello.* Panther, 128p.
Adventures on the planet Zello.

1952 **Du Bois, T.** *Solution T-25.* Kemsley, 190p.
A secret weapon ends the Russian domination of the world. [U.S. 1951]

1952   **Duncan, R.** *The last Adam*. D. Dobson, 93p.
One man survives the hydrogen bomb.

1952   **Flackes, B.** *Duel in nightmare worlds*. Panther, 112p.
Space adventure.

1952   **Fysh** *(pseud.) Planetary war*. Archer Press, 96p.
Space adventure.

1952   **Gernsback, H.** *Ralph 124C41 +*. Fantasy Books, 190p.
This account of the technological marvels of the future represents an important stage in the development of American science fiction. First serialised 1911 in Gernsback's magazine, *Modern Electrics*, and first published U.S. 1925.

1952   **Gridban, V. (Tubb, E. C.)** See remarks on Statten, 1950; and see *Note* 7 for the use of the Gridban pseudonym by Fearn and Tubb. The following were published by the Scion Press in 1952; E. C. Tubb writing as Volsted Gridban:
Alien universe. Adventures in hyper-space.
Debracy's drug. The fight for a free world.
Reverse universe. Space adventures.

1952   **Hamilton, E.** *City at world's end*. Museum Press, 192p.
The inhabitants of a small town in the Middle West are suddenly projected into the future. [U.S. 1951]

1952   **Hay, G.** *Flight of "The Hesper"*. Panther, 112p.
Difficulties and dangers in the long journey through space.

1952   **Hay, G.** *This planet for sale*. Panther, 111p.
Interplanetary adventures.

1952   **Hazlitt, H.** *Time will run back*. E. Benn, 256p.
The world dictator's son restores freedom and justice. First published U.S. 1951 as *The great idea*.

1952   **Healy, R. J.** *(ed.) New tales of space and time*. Weidenfeld & Nicolson, xiii, 279p.
Introduction (G. Heard, 'Why science fiction?') and ten stories on human futures. [U.S. 1951]

1952   **Healy, R. J. and MacComas, J. F.** *(eds.) Adventures in time and space*. Grayson & Grayson, vii, 327p.
Eleven stories from original thirty-three of U.S. 1946 publication.

1952   **Lederman, F.** *Tremor*. Gaywood Press, 112p.
Space adventure.

1952   **Leinster, M. (Jenkins, W. F.)** *The last space ship*. Fantasy Books, 190p.
The struggle against the tyrants of the Galactic Planets. [U.S. 1949]

1952   **Niall, I.** *The boy who saw tomorrow.* W. Heinemann, 259p.
The effect on a community when a boy has visions of the future.

1952   **Noel, S.** *I killed Stalin.* R. Hale, 224p.
Cloak-and-dagger work in the near future. [U.S. 1951]

1952   **Reynolds, P.** *It happened like this.* Translated from the French by
[1953]   J. F. McCrindle. Eyre & Spottiswoode, 191p.
Atomic warfare followed by the collapse of Russia. First published 1950 as *Ce pourrait se passer comme ça* and published U.S. 1952 as *When and if.*

1952   **Sarban (Wall, J. W.)** *The sound of his horn.* P. Davies, 154p.
An unusually able story of "the hundred and second year of the First German Millennium as fixed by our First Fuehrer and Immortal Spirit of Germanism, Adolf Hitler"

1952   **Scott, W. (Dudley-Smith, T.)** *The Domesday story.* P. Davies, 256p.
Romance and adventure as men strive to prevent the explosion of a new hydrogen bomb.

1952   **Sheldon, R.** *The menacing sleep.* Panther, 128p.
Martian investigator saves Earth.

1952   **Slater, H. J.** *The smashed world.* Jarrolds, 221p.
A fantasy of life after thirty centuries of peace and world government.

1952   **Statten, V. (Fearn, J. R.)** See remarks on Statten under 1950. See *Note 7.* Following are all from the Scion Press:
Across the ages. A time journey.
Eclipse express. Selenite civilization.
The G-bomb. The Martians attack Earth.
Inner Cosmos. Space adventure.
Laughter in space. Adventure in A.D. 2006.
The last Martian. Space adventures.
The man from tomorrow. Time travel.
The space warp. Science fiction adventures.
The time bridge. Time travel.
The time trap. Science fiction adventures.
Worlds to conquer. Space adventures.

1952   **Tubb, E. C.** *Atom wars on Mars.* Panther, 112p.
War between Earth and Mars.

1952   **Tweed, T. F.** *Gabriel over the White House.* Cherry Tree Books, 190p.
First published U.K. 1933 as *Rinehard.*

1952   **Van Vogt, A. E.** *The weapon shops of Isher.* Weidenfeld & Nicholson, 231p.
For generations the gunmaker's guild has been mankind's only protection against enslavement. [U.S. 1949]

1952   **Walsh, J. M.** *Vanguard to Neptune*. Fantasy Books, 190p.
Crusoe adventures on Neptune in A.D. 2235.

1952   **Ward, J.** *We died in Bond Street*. Hodder & Stoughton, 191p.
The mob rule of the New England Party terrifies the nation.

1952   **Williams, I.** *Dangerous waters*. Gryphon Books, 224p.
The underwater forces of Neptunia attempt to conquer Britain.

1952   **Williams, I.** *Newbury in Orm*. Gryphon Books, 191p.
Adventures on the planet Orm.

1953   **Asimov, I.** *Foundation*. Weidenfeld & Nicolson, 246p.
First in the *Foundation* series: history of the grand design to save the Galactic
Empire from self destruction. [U.S. 1951]

1953   **Berry, B.** *From what far star*. Panther, 143p.
An alien race endangers earth.

1953   **Berry, B.** *The venom-seekers*. Panther, 160p.
A man goes back in time to find a weapon that could mean life or death for
mankind.

1953   **Bester, A.** *The demolished man*. Sidgwick & Jackson, 224p.
A tale of love and adventure in a world of telepaths. [U.S. 1953]

1953   **Blair, A.** *Cosmic conquest*. C. Warren. No information available. See
Note 8.

1953   **Bleiler, E. F. and Dikty, T. E.** *(eds,) The best science fiction stories.
Third series*. Grayson & Grayson, 264p.
Sixteen stories from original eighteen of the U.S. 1952 edition.

1953   **Bleiler, E. F. and Dikty, T. E.** *(eds.) Imagination unlimited*. J. Lane,
185p.
First six stories from original U.S. 1952 edition.

1953   **Bleiler, E. F. and Dikty, T. E.** *(eds) Men of space and time*. J. Lane,
224p.
Last seven stories from *Imagination unlimited* U. S. 1952.

1953   **Bleiler, E. F. and Dikty, T. E.** *(eds) The year's best science fiction
novels*. Grayson & Grayson, 264p.
Introduction; four stories. [U.S. 1952]

1953   **Bounds, S. J.** *Dimension of horror*. Panther, 160p.
The struggle to prevent the outbreak of war between Earth and Venus.

1953   **Bradbury, R.** *The golden apples of the sun*. R. Hart-Davis, 192p.
Twenty stories from the twenty-two of the U.S. 1953 edition.

1953   **Brown, F.** *Space on my hands*. Transworld, 239p.
Nine stories. [U.S. 1951]

1953   **Bulmer, H. K.** *Empire in chaos*. Panther, 160p.
Illegal trafficking in space and the danger to the Galaxy.

1953   **Bulmer, H. K.** *Galactic intrigue*. Panther, 160p.
An interplanetary struggle for a matter transmitter.

1953   **Bulmer, H. K.** *Space salvage*. Panther, 144p.
Space wrecks start an interstellar war.

1953   **Bulmer, H. K.** *The stars are ours*. Panther, 160p.
In the days of the robots an unseen danger menaces mankind.

1953   **Campbell, H. J.** *Another space: another time*. Panther, 160p.
A scientist opposes Science Security.

1953   **Campbell, H. J.** *Brain ultimate*. Panther, 160p.
A scientist attempts to smash a dictatorship and to contact other intelligences in the universe.

1953   **Campbell, H. J.** *The red planet*. Panther, 160p.
Two men, space-wrecked on a planet, find that the only food is a red grass.

1953   **Campbell, H. J.** *(ed.) Sprague de Camp's new anthology*. Panther, 159p.
Six stories based on the theme of Brazil as the largest world power of the future.

1953   **Campbell, H. J.** *Tomorrow's universe*. Panther, 224p.
Eight stories.

1953   **Capon, P.** *The world at bay*. W. Heinemann, 199p.
Invaders from another planet.

1953   **Charles, N.** *(pseud?)* In 1953 the firm of Curtis Warren, reported by *Whitaker's* as 'Gone from last known address', brought out a number of paperbacks by Charles Neil. These are not obtainable in any of the copyright libraries, and there is no information on: *Beyond Zoaster, The land of Esa, Planet Tha, Pre-Gargantua, Research Opta, Twenty-four hours, World of gold*.

1953   **Clarke, A. C.** *Prelude to space*. Sidgwick & Jackson, 176p.
Preparations to send the first rocket-ship into space.

1953   **Conklin, G.** *(ed.) Invaders of earth*. Weidenfeld & Nicolson, 256p.
Fourteen stories from original twenty-two of the U.S. 1952 edition.

1953   **Crossen, K. F.** *(ed.) Adventures in tomorrow*. J. Lane, 240p.
Editorial introduction: thirteen stories on atomic, galactic, and interstellar themes. [U.S. 1951]

1953   **Deegan, J. J.** *(pseud.) Antro: the life-giver.* Panther, 160p.
Space travellers discover the secret of evolution on the planets.

1953   **Deegan, J. J.** *(pseud.) Corridors of time.* Panther, 160p.
Opens trilogy on themes of travel and adventure.

1953   **Deegan, J. J.** *(pseud.) The great ones.* Panther, 160p.
Invaders from space seek to conquer earth.

1953   **Desmond, H.** *Fear rides the air.* Wright & Brown, 160p.
Flying saucers pursued into space.

1953   **Divine, D. (Divine, A. D.)** *Atom at Spithead.* Robert Hale, 176p.
An atomic bomb thriller.

1953   **Elliot, L.** *Overlord New York.* C. Warren, 160p.
An invasion story.

1953   **Elliot, L.** *The third mutant.* C. Warren, 160p.
Spying in an inter-galactic war.

1953   **Fearn, J. R.** *The Amazon's diamond quest.* World's Work, 175p.
Detective work in space.

1953   **Fearn, J. R.** *The Golden Amazon's triumph.* World's Work, 192p.
The super-woman triumphs in space.

1953   **Frankau, G.** *Unborn tomorrow.* MacDonald, 302p.
In the world of "A.D. forty-nine fifty-two" Catholicism is the universal religion and
monarchies rule in Europe.

1953   **Garner, R. (Berry, B.)** *The immortals.* Panther, 160p.
Continues trilogy begun in *Resurgent dust*: the discovery of science on Venus.

1953   **Garner, R. (Berry, B.)** *Resurgent dust.* Panther, 160p.
Opens a trilogy: mankind on Venus after destruction of life on earth.

1953   **Gold, H. L.** *(ed.) Galaxy reader of science fiction.* Grayson & Grayson,
240p.
Thirteen stories. [U.S. 1952].

1953   **Goodchild, G.** *Doctor Zil's experiment.* Ward, Lock, 206p.
Millions of years ahead in time, when mankind no longer exists, a race of highly
intelligent and mobile Yuccas are the crown of life.

1953   **Greenberg, M.** *(ed.) The crucible of power.* J. Lane, 240p.
Three stories from the original five of the U.S. 1952 edition, *Five science fiction
novels.*

1953   **Grey, C. (Tubb, E. C.)** In 1953–54 the Milestone press brought out
eight titles under the pseudonym of Charles Grey. Some, perhaps all,

can be attributed to E. C. Tubb. No information is available on the following: *Dynasty of doom, Sometime never, Space hunger, Tormented city, The wall.*

1953   **Gridban, V. (Fearn, J. R.)** See remarks on Statten (1950). Following are all from the Scion Press:
The dyno-depressant. Earth in danger.
Exit life. Inhabitants of Earth vanish.
The genial dinosaur. Venusians attempt to invade Earth.
Magnetic brain. Brain operations on Mars.
The master must die. Life and death adventure in 1990.
Moons for sale. Space travel.
The purple wizard. Time travel.
Scourge of the atom. Review of human history.

1953   **Gridban, V. (Tubb, E. C.)** See remarks on Gridban, 1952. see also *Note 7.* The Milestone Press published the following by E. C. Tubb writing as Volsted Gridban:
Fugitive of time. Time travel adventures.
Planetoid Disposals Ltd. Space adventures.

1953   **Harrison, M.** *The brain.* Cassell, 287p.
An atomic-bomb cloud assumes the shape of a human brain and, therefore becomes intelligent.

1953   **Heinlein, R.** *The man who sold the Moon.* Sidgwick & Jackson, 256p.
Opens the 'Future History' series: six stories on space themes [U.S. 1950]

1953   **Heinlein, R.** *The puppet masters.* Museum Press, 191p.
Creatures from outer space take possession of human bodies and threaten mankind. [U.S. 1951]

1953   **Leinster, M (Jenkins, W. F.)** *(ed.) Great stories of science fiction.* Cassell, 318p.
Introduction by Clifton Fadiman, Editorial Preface, twelve stories [U.S. 1951]

1953   **Lorraine, P. (Fearn, J. R.)** *Dark boundaries.* C. Warren, 160p.
Civil war between intellectuals and helots. See *Note 8.*

1953   **Lorraine, P.** *(Pseud.) Two worlds.* C. Warren, 128p.
Science fiction adventures. See *Note 9.*

1953   **Magroon, V. (Fearn, J. R.)** *Burning void.* Scion Press, 128p.
Inter-stellar struggles.

1953   **Maine, C. E. (McIlwain, D.)** *Spaceways.* Hodder & Stoughton, 191p.
Adventures in the space age.

1953   **Merril, J.** *(ed.) Beyond human ken.* Grayson & Grayson, 240p.
Fifteen stories. [U.S. 1952]

1953   **Merril, J.** *Shadow on the hearth.* Sidgwick & Jackson, 287p.
Family life, its anxieties and terrors, in the time when atomic rockets hit New York. [U.S. 1950]

[1953]   **Richmond, M.** *The grim tomorrow.* Wright & Brown, 224p.
Atomic bombs cause a world disaster.

1953   **Russell, E. F.** *Dreadful sanctuary.* Museum Press, 254p.
Detective work in A.D. 1972. [U.S. 1951].

1953   **Shaw, B. (Fearn, J. R.)** *Z formations.* Curtis Warren, 159p.
Four men flung through space to land on unknown planet. See *Note* 9.

1953   **Shaw, B.** *(pseud.)* Curtis Warren published the following under the name of Bryan Shaw – no information is available:
Lost world, Ships of Vero, Z formations. See *Note* 8.

1953   **Sheldon, R.** *Atoms in action.* Panther, 160p.
Adventures in a far-distant stellar system.

1953   **Sheldon, R.** *House of entropy.* Panther, 160p.
Life on a planet where a giant brain controls the inhabitants.

1953   **Shute, N. (Norway, N. S.)** *In the wet.* W. Heinemann, 364p.
Life under an anti-royalist Labour government when over·ten million Britons have emigrated.

1953   **Stanford, J. K.** *Full moon at Sweetenham.* Faber & Faber, 238p. Illus.
A whimsical tale set in the days of the Bookmakers' Government; the Prime Minister is "one of the most popular and highly trusted figures on the Turf".

1953   **Statten, V. (Fearn, J. R.)** See remarks on Statten (1950). Following are all from the Scion Press:
Black avengers. Outlaws in space.
Black-wing of Mars. Dangers on Mars.
Black bargain. The world in peril.
The dust destroyer. How Earth was saved.
The interloper. Space adventure.
Man in duplicate. New race experiments.
Man of two worlds. Space adventure.
Odyssey of nine. Space adventure.
Pioneer 1990. Space travel.
Science Metropolis. Planetary struggles.
To the ultimate. Space travel.
Zero hour. Experiments in time.

1953   **Tucker, W.** *The long loud silence.* J. Lane, 192p.
Atomic and bacteriological warfare wipes out all the major cities east of the Mississippi. [U.S. 1952]

1953   **Van Vogt, A. E.** *Destination: universe.* Eyre & Spottiswoode, 247p.
Introduction, ten stories [U.S. 1952]

1953   **Van Vogt, A. E.** *The house that stood still.* Weidenfeld & Nicolson, 247p.
The immortals come to the rescue of earth and prevent an atomic war. [U.S. 1950]

1953   **Van Vogt, A. E.** *Slan.* Weidenfeld & Nicolson, 247p.
The struggle between mankind and the Slans, a mutation of the human species. [U.S. 1946]

1953   **Vonnegut, K.** *Player piano.* Macmillan, vii, 352p.
The anxieties and problems of living in an epoch when machines do most of the work: the American equivalent of *Nineteen eighty-four.* [U.S. 1952]

1953   **Waugh, E.** *Love among the ruins.* Chapman & Hall, 64p. Illus.
A satire on the welfare state; criminals are considered to be "victims of inadequate social services".

1953   **Wellard, J.** *Night in Babylon.* Macmillan, vi, 298p.
The struggle between Christian and totalitarian ideas in a "liberated" Europe.

1953   **Williamson, J.** *The humanoids.* Museum Press, 191p.
Invincible creatures take over earth for the eventual good of mankind. [U.S. 1949]

1953   **Wolfe, B.** *Limbo '90.* Secker & Warburg, 438p.
A nightmare world of cybernetics and human beings physically reshaped. The story, Wolfe writes, is "about the overtone and undertow of *now* – in the guise of 1990". [U.S. 1952]

1953   **Wollheim, D. (ed.)** *Prize stories of space and time.* Weidenfeld & Nicolson, 256p.
Short stories. [U.S. 1953]

1953   **Wyndham, J. (Harris, J. B.)** *The Kraken wakes.* M. Joseph, 288p.
The world fights the menace from space and from the depths of the oceans. Published U.S. 1953 as *Out of the deeps.*

1953   **Yorke, P.** *Space-time Force.* H. Kelly, 192p.
Adventures with the Galactic Patrol.

1954   **Asimov, I.** *The caves of steel.* T. V. Boardman, 224p.
Detective work in the subterranean New York of the future. [U.S. 1954]

1954   **Bennett, M.** *The long way back.* J. Lane, 206p.
An expedition from civilized Africa discovers the legendary island of Britain, destroyed long ago by atomic explosions.

1954   **Bernard, R.** *The wheel in the sky.* Ward, Lock, 191p.
How they built the first space satellite.

1954   **Black, D.** *Candles in the dark.* Cassell, 188p.
Romantic adventures after the bombing of New York.

1954   **Brackett, L. (Hamilton, L. B.)** *The starmen.* Museum Press, 168p.
Space travel and intergalactic co-operation. [U.S. 1952]

1954   **Bradbury, R.** *Fahrenheit 451.* Hart-Davis, 158p.
An Orwellian future world in which a few independent thinkers keep the old values alive by reading forbidden books. [U.S. 1953]

1954   **Brown, F.** *Project Jupiter.* T. V. Boardman, 222p.
Congress proves reluctant to vote the money required to send an expedition to Jupiter. First published U.S. 1953 as *The lights in the sky are stars.*

1954   **Brown, F.** *What mad universe.* T. V. Boardman, 192p.
Life in a parallel world. [U.S. 1949].

1954   **Browne, G. S.** *The yellow planet.* E. Self, 100p.
Space adventures.

1954   **Bulmer, K.** *Challenge.* C. Warren, 160p.
A spaceship journeys to Saturn.

1954   **Bulmer, K.** *World aflame.* Panther, 144p.
World-wide earthquakes reveal the existence of another race of rational beings.

1954   **Burke, J.** *The echoing worlds.* Panther, 160p.
A parallel universe and the danger of an invasion of Earth.

1954   **Burke, J.** *Hotel Cosmos.* Panther, 144p.
A detective tracks down a criminal from Urania.

1954   **Burke, J.** *Pattern of shadows.* Museum Press, 128p.
Adventure in the days when the Interplanetary Federation controls space travel.

1954   **Burke, J.** *Twilight of reason.* Panther, 160p.
Evolutionary retrogression and the loss of intelligence.

1954   **Campbell, H. J.** *Once upon a space.* Panther, 142p.
A struggle against dictatorship.

1954   **Campbell, J. W.** *(ed.) The firsy "Astounding science fiction" anthology.* Grayson & Grayson, 239p.
Seven stories from original U.S. 1952 edition.

1954   **Campbell, J. W.** *(ed.) The second "Astounding science fiction" anthology.* Grayson & Grayson, 224p.
Twelve stories from original U.S. 1952 edition.

1954   **Capon, P.** *Down to Earth.* W. Heinemann, 196p.
A continuation of *The other side of the Sun,* 1950.

1954   **Carnell, J.** *(ed.) Gateway to tomorrow.* Museum Press, 192p.
Ten stories.

1954   **Carr, C. (Mason, S. C.)** *Colonists of space.* Ward, Lock, 192p.
Space travel adventures.

1954   **Castle, J. L.** *Satellite E One.* Eyre & Spottiswoode, 190p.
The building of the first space-satellite in A.D. 2017.

1954   **Chilton, C.** *Journey into space.* H. Jenkins, 220p.
Adventures with Jet Morgan in space. First of the Jet Morgan trilogy and book of
the BBC serial.

1954   **Christopher, J. (Youd, C. S.)** *The twenty-second century.* Grayson &
Grayson, 239p.
Three novellas

1954   **Clarke, A. C.** *Childhood's end.* Sidgwick & Jackson, 253p.
Overlords from a distant planet take control of Earth and give it peace and
prosperity; humanity advances in the evolutionary scale. [U.S. 1953]

1954   **Clarke, A. C.** *Expedition to Earth.* Sidgwick & Jackson, 167p.
Eleven stories. [U.S. 1953]

1954   **Conklin, E. G.** *(ed.) Strange adventures in science fiction.* Grayson &
Grayson, 248p.
Nine stories from original U.S. 1952 edition, *The omnibus of science fiction.*

1954   **Conklin, E. G.** *(ed.) Strange travels in science fiction.* Grayson &
Grayson, 256p.
Thirteen stories from 1952 U.S. edition.

[1954]   **Cross, J. K.** *SOS from Mars.* Hutchinson, 216p.
The story of the second and third expeditions to Mars.

1954   **Crossen, K. F.** *(ed.) Future tense.* J. Lane, 216p.
Seven stories from original fourteen of U.S. 1952 edition.

1954   **Crowcroft, P.** *The fallen sky.* P. Nevill, 222p.
Life in a devastated Britain.

1954   **De Camp, L. S.** *Rogue queen.* W. H. Allen, 160p.
Adventures with the Terran Space Authority. [U.S. 1951]

1954   **Deegan, J. J.** *(pseud.) Beyond the fourth door.* Panther, 160p.
Continues the theme of the earlier stories: a young couple travel from a city of
the future to explore other worlds.

1954   **Deegan, J. J.** *(pseud.) Exiles in time.* Panther, 160p.
Continues the above story.

1954   **Derleth, A.** *(ed.) Beachheads in space.* Weidenfeld & Nicolson, 224p.
Seven stories – space travel and space warfare from original fourteen
of the U.S. 1952 edition.

1954   **Derleth, A.** *(ed.) Worlds of tomorrow.* Weidenfeld & Nicolson, 224p.
Fifteen stories from original nineteen of the U.S. 1953 edition.

1954   **Dexter, W. (Pritchard, W. T.)** *World in eclipse.* P. Owen, 195p.
The last members of the human race fight to prevent the Vulcanid occupation of earth.

1954   **Dorman, G.** *Swooping vengeance.* Hutchinson, 176p.
Sabotage and espionage adventures.

1954   **Fearn, J. R.** *The Amazon strikes again.* World's Work, 175p
The wonder-woman struggles against the powers of outer space.

1954   **Fearn, J. R.** *Twin of the Amazon.* World's Work, 159p.
The struggle to save world civilization.

1954   **Garner, R. (Berry, B.)** *The indestructible.* Panther, 160p.
Concludes the Venus trilogy, begun with *Resurgent dust*, 1953: the remnants of Earth's population freed from tyranny.

1954   **Golding, W.** *Lord of the flies.* Faber & Faber, 248p.
Set in an undated period of the near future when war has brought a group of children to a deserted tropical island; a remarkable study of children's rapid advance to savagery.

1954   **Greenberg, M.** *(ed.) The robot and the man.* J. Lane, 224p.
Ten stories. [U.S. 1953]

1954   **Grey, C. (Tubb, E., C.)** *Enterprise 2115.* Merit Books, 160p.
Astronaut comes back to a changed Earth and is involved in a struggle for the future of mankind.

1954   **Gridban, V. (Fearn, J. R.)** *Frozen limit.* Scion Press, 158p.
Deep-freeze operations.

1954   **Gridban, V. (Fearn, J. R.)** *The lonely astronomer.* Scion Press, 160p.
Murder in 1991.

1954   **Heinlein, R.** *The green hills of Earth.* Sidgwick & Jackson, 224p.
Second in the 'Future History' series: ten stories. [U.S. 1951]

1954   **Karp, D.** *One.* V. Gollancz, 256p.
Another Orwellian world in which the supreme heresy is man's "pride, his vanity, his unwarranted belief that he is a creature apart". [U.S. 1953]

1954   **Kuttner, H.** *Ahead of time.* Weidenfeld & Nicolson, 192p.
Ten stories. [U.S. 1953]

1954   **Kuttner, H.** *Fury.* D. Dobson, 186p.
Foreword by Groff Conklin: In the twenty-seventh century the Immortals, a new human species, return from Venus to colonize the Earth. [U.S. 1950]

1954   **Kuttner, H.** *Mutant.* Weidenfeld & Nicolson, 224p.
After the "Great Blow-up", a race of telepathic mutants presents mankind with a problem. [U.S.]

1954   **MacDonald, J. D.** *Planet of the dreamers.* R. Hale, 175p.
[1955]   The inhabitants of a dying planet try to prevent the first space-ship from leaving the earth. First published U.S. 1951 as *Wine of the dreamers.*

1954   **MacGregor, G.** *From a Christian ghetto.* Longmans, 140p.
In the materialistic world of A.D. 2453 only a few persecuted Christians survive.

1954   **Mackenzie, N.** *Invasion from space.* Wright & Brown, 158p.
Martians invade Earth in flying saucers.

1954   **Malaquais, J.** *The joker.* Translated from the French by H. Briffault.
V. Gollancz, 320p.
Life in the conformist state. First published 1953 as *Le Gaffeur.*

1954   **Merak, A. J.** *Dark Andromeda.* Panther, 160p.
Space-fleets from Andromeda set out to attack the Earth.

1954   **Miller, P. S.** *The titan and other stories.* Weidenfeld & Nicolson, 224p.
Seven stories. [U.S. 1952]

1954   **Mines, S.** *(ed.) Startling stories.* Cassell, 301p.
Introduction by Robert A. Heinlein: eleven short stories.

1954   **Newman, B.** *The wishful think.* R. Hale, 192p.
An English civil servant discovers that he can control the mind of the Russian dictator, Granitov.

1954   **Pangborn, E.** *West of the sun.* R. Hale, 191p.
Colonists in a strange new world. [U.S. 1953].

1954   **Pohl, F.** *(ed.) Star science fiction stories.* T. V. Boardman, 207p.
Fifteen stories. [U.S. 1953].

1954   **Pratt, F.** *Double in space.* T. V. Boardman, 224p.
Contains two stories: the hypnotic conditioning of space pilots and life on a space station. [U.S. 1951].

1954   **Rochester, G. E.** *The black octopus.* Frederick Warne, 257p.
Submarine operations against international criminals.

1954   **Russell, E. F.** *Sentinels from space.* Museum Press, 208p.
An interplanetary struggle between Mars and Venus. First published U. S. 1951 as *The star watchers.*

1954   **Sheldon, R.** *The metal eater.* Panther, 160p.
Scientists fight against strange forces on a distant planet.

1954   **Shiras, W. H.** *Children of the atom.* T. V. Boardman, 216p.
The unforeseen consequences of the explosion of an atomic plant. [U.S. 1953].

1954   **Simak, C. D.** *City.* Weidenfeld & Nicolson, 248p.
A race of dogs preserves the memory of the human race, long since passed away. [U.S. 1952].

1954   **Smith, E. E.** *Triplanetary.* T. V. Boardman, 287p.
Prodigious space adventures throughout the galaxy. First in the *Lensman* series. [U.S. 1948]

1954   **Statten, V. (Fearn, J. R.)** See remarks on Statten 1950. The following are from the Scion Press:
A time appointed. Space adventures.
Wealth of the void. Discovery of a golden planetoid.

1954   **Stewart, W. (Williamson, J.)** *Seetee shock.* World's Work, 159p.
The mastering of anti-matter leads to the prodigious exploits of the space engineers. See this title under Williamson, J. 1969. [U.S. 1950]

1954   **Sturgeon, T.** *More than human* V. Gollancz, 232p.
Evolution of a new kind of human being and invention of an anti-gravity generator. [U.S. 1953]

1954   **Tubb, E.C.** *City of no return.* Scion Press, 144p.
Adventures on Mars.

1954   **Tubb, E. C.** *The hell planet.* Scion Press, 144p.
Adventures on Mercury.

1954   **Tubb, E. C.** *The resurrected man.* Dragon Books, 120p.
Spaceman restored to life with extraordinary results.

1954   **Tubb, E. C.** *The Stellar Legion.* Scion Press, 144p.
Adventure in the epoch of the Federation of man.

1954   **Tubb, E. C.** *World at bay.* Panther, 159p.
A fight for survival.

1954   **Tucker, W.** *City in the sea.* Nova Publications, 154p.
Long after World War III an expedition into the interior of North America discovers that women have become the dominant sex. [U.S. 1951]

1954   **Vandel, J. G.** *Enemy beyond Pluto.* Translated from the French. H. Kelly, 192p.
An attempt to invade Earth from outer space. First published 1953 as *Attentat cosmique.*

1954   **Van Vogt, A. E.** *The weapon makers.* Weidenfeld & Nicolson, 224p.
The clash between the Isher Empire and the weapon makers. [U.S. 1947]

1954   **Vercors (Bruller, J.)** *Borderline.* Translated from the French by Rita Barisse. Macmillan, 231p.
Discovery of *Paranthropus*, the almost-human link between animals and men, raises grave questions about the nature of man. First published 1952 as *Les Animaux dénaturés.*

1954   **Wilding, P.** *Spaceflight Venus.* H. Locke, 190p.
The adventures of the first men to reach Venus.

1954   **Williamson, J.** *Dragon's island.* Museum Press, 224p.
A race of un-men is discovered in New Guinea. [U.S. 1951]

1954   **Wyndham, J. (Harris, J. B.)** *Jizzle.* D. Dobson, 251p.
Fifteen stories.

1955   **Adams, W. S.** *The Fourth Programme.* Lawrence & Wishart, 63p. Illus.
A broadcast by God and the reactions of Church and Government.

1955   **Anderson, P.** *Brain wave.* W. Heinemann, 212p.
What happens when the neuronic response to all animal and human life on earth is suddenly speeded up. [U.S. 1954]

1955   **Ash, A.** *Conditioned for space.* Ward, Lock, 192p.
The world faces an attack from space, and a one-time jet pilot is called back to life.

1955   **Asimov, I.** *The currents of space.* T. V. Boardman, 217p.
The struggle to save the planet Florina. [U.S. 1952]

1955   **Atkins, J.** *Tomorrow revealed.* Neville Spearman, 254p.
One of the few literates in 3750 A.D. reconstructs the history of the past out of science fiction stories. Elaborate and amusing.

1955   **Barr, D. N.** *The man with only one head.* Rich & Cowan, 192p.
An atomic fog covers entire world and leaves all males – save one – infertile.

1955   **Bleiler, E. F. and Dikty, T. E.** *(eds.) The best science fiction stories. Fourth series.* Grayson & Grayson, 239p.
Thirteen stories from original fifteen of the U.S. 1953 edition.

1955   **Bleiler, E. F. and Dikty, T. E.** *(eds.) Category Phoenix.* J. Lane, 192p.
Three stories from the original five in U. S. 1953 edition of *Year's best science fiction novels 1953.*

1955   **Bleiler, E. F. and Dikty, T. E.** *(eds.) The year's best science fiction novels. Second Series.* Grayson & Grayson, 240p.
Four stories from the original five in U.S. 1954 edition of *Year's best science fiction novels 1954.*

1955   **Blish, J.** *Jack of eagles.* Nova Publications, 159p.
A struggle between two groups both endowed with paranormal powers. [U.S. 1952]

1955   **Boland J.** *White August.* M. Joseph, 239p.
An unknown enemy uses wireless waves to bury Britain under snow.

1955   **Bounds, S. J.** *The Moon raiders.* Foulsham, 160p.
Flying saucers and raiders from outer space.

1955   **Brown, A.** *(pseud?) Angelo's moon.* J. Lane, 224p.
The "natural" way of life triumphs over the subterranean civilisation of Hypolitania.

1955   **Brown, F.** *Angels and spaceships.* V. Gollancz, 224p.
Seventeen stories. [U.S. 1954]

1955   **Burke, J.** *Alien landscapes.* Museum Press, 160p.
Six stories.

1955   **Burke, J.** *Deep freeze.* Panther, 144p.
After the destruction of Earth the women of planet Demeter are left to carry on the human race.

1955   **Burke, J.** *Revolt of the humans.* Panther, 144p.
Mankind fights for freedom.

1955   **Capon, P.** *The wonderbolt.* Ward, Lock, 206p.
Cloak-and-dagger work to secure a dangerous meteorite.

1955   **Carnell, J.** *(ed.) The best from New worlds science fiction.* T. V. Boardman, 190p.
Introduction by John Wyndham, editorial foreword, eight stories.

1955   **Carnell, J.** *(ed.) Gateway to the stars.* Museum Press, 192p.
Nine stories.

1955   **Carr, C. (Mason, S. C.)** *Salamander war.* Ward, Lock, 192p.
Colonists from Earth fight for survival on a distant planet.

1955   **Christopher, J. (Youd, C. S.)** *The year of the comet.* M. Joseph, 272p.
Plot and counter-plot in the managerial world of the future.

1955   **Churchill, R. C.** *A short history of the future.* Werner Laurie, 192p.
History of the future up to the sixty-seventh century composed from postwar forecasts and prophecies.

1955   **Clarke, A. C.** *Earthlight.* F. Muller, 222p.
A conflict of loyalties in the planetary society of the future.

1955   **Clement, H. (Stubbs, H. C.)** *Mission of gravity.* R. Hale, 192p.
Adventures on the planet Mesklin where the gravitational pressures are immense and the rational animals very different from human beings [U.S. 1954]

1955   **Conklin, G.** *(ed.) Adventures in dimension.* Grayson & Grayson, vi, 240p.
Thirteen stories – past, present, future – from original twenty-three of the U.S. 1953 edition, *Science fiction adventures in dimension.*

1955   **Conquest, R.** *A world of difference.* Ward, Lock, 192p.
Love and adventure in A.D. 2007.

1955   **Crane, R. (Robertson, F. C.)** *Hero's walk.* Cresset Press, 223p.
Mysterious warnings from space forbid mankind to enter outer space. [U.S. 1954]

1955   **Crispin, E. (Montgomery, R. B.)** *(ed.) Best SF.* Faber & Faber, 368p.
Introduction; fourteen stories.

1955   **Derleth, A.** *(ed.) New worlds for old.* Weidenfeld and Nicolson, 224p.
Fifteen stories from *Worlds of tomorrow*, first published U.S. 1953.

1955   **De Rouen, R. R.** *Split image.* Allan Wingate, 283p.
The first spaceship from Earth makes contact with the robots of Dextar.

1955   **Dexter, W. (Pritchard, W. T.)** *Children of the void.* P. Owen, 195p.
Life on the planets after life on Earth has ended.

1955   **Dick, P. K.** *A handful of darkness.* Rich & Cowan, 224p.
Fifteen stories on the theme of the ordinary man's struggle to exist. Not previously published U.S.

1955   **Dorman, G.** *Shattering silence.* Hutchinson, 176p.
1954]   A Russian plot to steal plans for a sonic ray.

1955   **Duncan, D.** *Dark dominion.* W. Heinemann, 234p.
The United States builds the first space satellite. [U.S. 1954]

1955   **Elton, J.** *The green plantations.* Ward, Lock, 192p.
Earth revolts against Ollodian tyranny.

1955   **Falkner, J.** *Overlords of Andromeda.* Panther, 144p.
Struggles in the galaxies.

1955   **Falkner, J.** *Untrodden streets of time.* Panther, 144p.
Science fiction adventure.

1955   **Finney, J.** *The body snatchers.* Eyre & Spottiswoode, 192p.
An alien life-form attempts to take possession of minds and bodies in California. [U.S. 1955]

1955   **Frazee, S.** *The sky block.* Bodley Head, 191p.
Adventure story of electronic weather control and enemy agents. [U.S. 1953]

1955   **Gold, H. L.** *(ed.) Science fiction omnibus.* Grayson & Grayson, 350p.
Twenty stories from original U.S. 1954 edition of *Second galaxy reader of science fiction.*

1955   **Gordon, R. (Hough, S. B.)** *Utopia 239.* W. Heinemann, 208p.
An anarchic ideal state emerges after the destruction of Britain in an atomic war.

1955   **Haynes, J. R. (Wilding, P.)** *The scream from outer space.* Rich & Cowan, 176p.
Adventure on the planet Diana, newly arrived in the solar system.

1955   **Healy, R. J.** *(ed.) Nine tales of space and time.* Weidenfeld & Nicolson, 274p.
Original stories from nine authors. [U.S. 1954]

1955   **Heinlein, R.** *Assignment in eternity.* Museum Press, 224p.
Four novellas. [U.S. 1953]

1955   **Jones, R. F.** *This island Earth.* T. V. Boardman, 220p.
An alien v. Earth men story. [U.S. 1952]

1955   **Kee, R.** *A sign of the times.* Eyre & Spottiswoode, 256p.
Another regimented world of the future, halfway to 1984.

1955   **Kornbluth, C. M.** *The mindworm and other stories.* M. Joseph, 256p.
Twelve stories first published in this edition.

1955   **Lesser, M.** *(ed.) Looking forward.* Cassell, 400p.
Twenty stories – yesterday, tomorrow, and "imagination unlimited." [U.S. 1953]

1955   **Lin Yutang.** *The unexpected island.* W. Heinemann, 351p.
Survivors from the fourth world war establish an ideal state based on the wisdom of Greece and China.

1955   **McIntosh, J. T. (Macgregor, J. M.)** *Born leader.* Museum Press, 190p.
Democrats and tyrants in the planets. [U.S. 1954]

1955   **McIntosh, J. T. (Macgregor, J. M.)** *World out of mind.* Museum Press, 189p.
Another race plans the conquest of Earth. [U.S. 1953]

1955   **Mackenzie, N.** *The terror in the sky.* Wright & Brown, 158p.
The first space flight.

1955   **Mackenzie, N.** *World without end.* Wright & Brown, 159p.
The end of the world draws near, as a part of the sun hurtles through space.

1955   **Maine, C. (McIlwain, D.)** *Crisis 2000.* Hodder & Stoughton, 192p.
The Saturnians arrive for the world festival.

[1955]   **Maine, C. E. (McIlwain, D.)** *Timeliner.* Hodder & Stoughton, 192p.
Love and adventure in the space age. Based on a BBC sound play 'The Einstein Highway' 1954

1955   **Mars, A. (Gillespie, A. C.)** *Artic submarine.* Elek Books, 240p.
The Admiralty orders an experimental journey through the Arctic Circle.

1955   **Mead, H.** *The bright phoenix.* M. Joseph, 302p.
Another brutal and regimented future world.

1955   **Mead, S.** *The big ball of wax.* T. V. Boardman, 222p.
Advertising dominates the United States of 1992. [U.S. 1954]

1955   **Melling, L.** *The great beyond A.D. 2500.* Foreword by Sir John
Anderson. Torch Publishing Company, 102p.
Author writes that "this small book attempts to show . . . a conception of God
and the way that leads to a balanced, rational way of living."

1955   **Merril, J.** *(ed.) Beyond the barriers of space and time.* Sidgwick &
Jackson, xiii, 292p.
Introduction by T. Sturgeon, nineteen stories about the mind. [U.S. 1954]

1955   **Mingston, R. G. (Stamp, R. G.)** *Ten days to the Moon.* Maclellan,
Glasgow, 217p. *diagrs.*
"It is the story of the problems which beset a man who planned to build a space
ship . . ."

1955   **The Observer.** *"A.D. 2500"; The Observer Prize stories.* Heinemann,
241p.
The prize-winning entries in a national competition for stories of the future.

1955   **Oliver, C.** *Shadows in the Sun.* Reinhardt, 184p.
An invasion from space. [U.S. 1954]

1955   **Pangborn, E.** *A mirror for observers.* F. Muller, 191p.
Good and bad aliens struggle for the destiny of Earth. [U.S. 1954]

1955   **Pawle, H.** *Before dawn.* Hutchinson, 248p.
A soldier-priest leads the nations to peace and happiness.

1955   **Pohl, F. and Kornbluth, C. M.** *The space merchants.* W. Heinemann,
186p.
The battle of the advertising agencies in time to come. [U.S. 1953]

1955   **Rein, H.** *Few were left.* Methuen, 219p.
Experiences of a group of survivors trapped in the New York Underground after a
gigantic catastrophe. [U.S. 1955]

1955   **Savage, R.** *When the moon died.* Ward, Lock, 192p.
The revolt against the world tyranny.

1955   **Shafer, R.** *The conquered place.* Putnam, 320p.
Adventure in the conquered United States.

1955   **Sheckley, R.** *Untouched by human hands.* M. Joseph, 254p.
Thirteen stories. [U.S. 1954]

1955   **Sieveking, L.** *A private volcano.* Ward, Lock, 254p.
An idealist leads the world to peace.

1955   **Smith, E. E.** *First Lensman.* T. V. Boardman, 306p.
Second in *Lensman Series:* Virgil Samms brings another sector of the galaxy into
the Solarian system. [U.S. 1950]

1955   **Smith, G. O.** *Hellflower.* Bodley Head, 250p.
Interstellar drug smuggling [U.S. 1953]

1955   **Spencer, G. F.** *Heavens for all.* Mitre Press, 191p.
Romance in the space age.

1955   **Statten, V.** *1000-year voyage.* Dragon Publications, 128p.
Earth dictator condemned to voyage to Alpha Centauri.

1955   **Sturgeon, T. (Waldo, E. H.)** *Way home.* Mayflower, xi, 335p.
Eleven stories; selection and introduction by Groff Conklin. [U.S. 1955]

1955   **Taine, J. (Bell, E. T.)** *G.O.G. 666.* Rich & Cowan, 224p.
American scientists investigate the Russian fifty-year plan in genetics. [U.S.
1954]

1955   **Taine, J. (Bell, E. T.)** *Seeds of life.* Rich & Cowan, 192p.
A scientist produces a superman. [U.S. 1951]

1955   **Tubb, E. C.** *Alien dust.* T. V. Boardman, 224p.
The first thirty-five years of colonization on Mars.

1955   **Verron R.** *The point of no return.* Wright and Brown. 190p.
An unknown submarine race menaces our world.

1955   **Vidal, G.** *Messiah.* W. Heinemann, 286p.
The preaching of the new ethic that death is desirable. [U.S. 1954]

1955   **Water, S.** *The man with absolute motion.* Rich & Cowan, 208p.
Love and warfare in the galaxies.

1955   **Wibberley, L.** *The wrath of grapes.* Hale 191p.
Grand Fenwick (population 6000) defeats the United States and brings sanity to
the world.

1955   **Wyndham, J. (Harris, J. B.)** *The Chrysalids.* M. Joseph, 239p.
Mutants and telepaths in the days after the atom bomb has wiped out twentieth-
century civilisation. Published U.S. 1955 as *Re-birth.*

[1956]   **Bester, A.** *Tiger! Tiger!* Sidgwick & Jackson, 232p.
Elaborate, exciting tale of a search for vengeance through the planets and of
secrets in the war between the planets. Published U.S. 1956 as *The stars my
destination.*

1956   **Bleiler, E. F. and Dikty, T. E.** *(eds.) The best science fiction stories. Fifth series.* Grayson & Grayson, 207p.
Ten stories from original thirteen of the U.S. 1954 edition *The best science fiction stories 1954.*

1956   **Blish, J.** *Earthman, come home.* Faber & Faber, 256p.
Third of the *Cities in flight* series: polarity generators speed whole cities through space. [U.S. 1955]

1956   **Blish, J.** *They shall have stars.* Faber & Faber, 181p.
First of the *Cities in flight* series: *Homo americanus* as the conqueror of space. [U.S. 1954]

1956   **Boland, J.** *No refuge.* Michael Joseph, 254p.
Bank robbers find their way to the strange country of Yademos.

1956   **Bounds, S. J.** *The world wrecker.* Foulsham, 159p.
An alien race threatens to destroy earth.

1956   **Brackett, L. (Hamilton, E. L.)** *Sword of Rhiannon,* T. V. Boardman, 208p.
The theft of a Martian relic. [U.S. 1953]

1956   **Bradbury, R.** *The October country.* With drawings by J. Mugniani. Hart Davis, 306p.
Short stories. [U.S. 1955]

1956   **Burke, J.** *Pursuit through time.* Ward, Lock, 214p.
Opens in A.D. 1996 and then goes back to 1946.

1956   **Capon, P.** *Into the tenth millennium.* W. Heinemann, 280p.
An ideal state in which everyone is happy and there are neither roads nor railways.

1956   **Chilton, C.** *The red planet.* H. Jenkins, 208p.
Jet Morgan makes the first journey to Mars. Second in the Jet Morgan trilogy.

1956   **Christopher, J. (Youd, C. S.)** *The death of grass.* M. Joseph, 231p.
The adventures of the few who survived the great catastrophe.

1956   **Clarke, A. C.** *The city and the stars.* F. Muller, 256p.
In a decadent future world a man discovers the history of earth's vigorous and heroic past. Revised and enlarged version of *Against the fall of night* first published U.S. 1953.

1956   **Creasey, J.** *The flood.* Hodder & Stoughton, 191p.
The super-detective, Dr. Palfrey, foils a mad scientist's attempt to wipe out the human race by flooding the world.

1956   **Crispin, E. (Montgomery, R. B.)** *(ed.) Best SF two.* Faber & Faber, 296p.
Introduction, fourteen stories.

1956   **Derleth, A.** *(ed.) The other side of the Moon.* Grayson & Grayson, 232p.
Eleven stories. [U.S. 1949]

1956   **Derleth, A.** *(ed.) Portals of tomorrow.* Cassell, 214p.
Introduction, sixteen stories. [U.S. 1954]

1956   **Dick, P. K.** *The world of chance.* Rich & Cowan, 160p.
A variation on Orwellian themes. First published U.S. 1955 as *Solar Lottery.*

1956   **Duncan, D.** *Another tree in Eden.* W. Heinemann, 192p.
The flooding of the Mohave Desert leads to the discovery of *Spectralium probioticum,* the source of life itself. [U.S. 1955]

1956   **Fagan, H. A.** *Ninya.* J. Cape, 224p. Illus.
The first explorers of the Moon discover our own problems are there also.

1956   **Gordon, R. (Hough, S. B.)** *No Man Friday.* W. Heinemann, 201p.
Crusoe experiences on Mars.

1956   **Gowland, J. S.** *Beyond Mars.* Gryphon Books, 191p.
Space travel.

1956   **Hingley, R.** *Up Jenkins!* Longmans, 226p.
A hilarious comedy of the police state in Great Britain.

1956   **Hough, S. B.** *Extinction bomber.* Bodley Head, 191p.
A moral lesson on the danger of atomic warfare and the need for individual responsibility.

1956   **Kornbluth, C. M.** *Christmas Eve.* M. Joseph, 206p.
How the first military satellite stopped the Russo-Chinese conquest of the United States. First published U.S. 1955 as *Not this August.*

1956   **Lott, S. M.** *Escape to Venus.* Rich & Cowan, 221p.
The colonization of Venus after the disastrous war of 1980.

1956   **Low, A.M.** *Satellite in space.* H. Jenkins, 190p.
Adventures of the first men in space.

1956   **McIntosh, J. T. (MacGregor, J. M.)** *One in three hundred.* Museum Press, 192p.
The selection of the few who are to escape the destruction of the earth. [U.S. 1954]

1956   **Mackenzie, N.** *Day of judgement.* Wright & Brown, 191p.
A millionaire tries to dominate the world.

1956   **Maine, C. E. (McIlwain, D.)** *Escapement.* Hodder & Stoughton, 224p.
An invention in recording and the trouble it causes.

1956   **Mantley, J.** *The twenty-seventh day.* M. Joseph, 272p.
Creatures from outer space reveal means of bringing peace to the world.

1956 **Matheson, R.** *Born of man and woman.* M. Reinhardt, 164p.
Thirteen stories. [U.S. 1954]

1956 **Matheson, R.** *I am Legend.* Transworld, 192p.
A vampire horror tale. [U.S. 1954]

1956 **Russell, E. F.** *Deep space.* Eyre & Spottiswoode, 249p.
Nine stories. [U.S. 1954]

1956 **Russell, E. F.** *Men, Martians and machines.* D. Dobson, 191p.
The exploration of the outer galaxies. [U.S. 1956]

1956 **Sellings, A. (Ley, A.)** *Time transfer.* M. Joseph, 240p.
Sixteen stories.

1956 **Simak, C.** *Time and again.* W. Heinemann, 239p.
The struggle between mankind and a new race of androids. [U.S. 1951]

1956 **Sloane, W.** *(ed.) Stories for tomorrow.* Eyre & Spottiswoode, xii, 476p.
Short stories. [U.S. 1954]

1956 **Smith, H. A.** *The Age of the Tail.* Arthur Barker. 159p. Illus.
An ironic story of what happens when all children are born into the world
complete with tails.

1956 **Stark, R.** *Crossroads to nowhere.* Ward Lock, 208p.
An anarchist society gives place to a dictatorship.

1956 **Stuart, W. J.** *Forbidden planet.* Transworld, 192p.
The story is based of the M.G.M. film *Forbidden Planet* (1956), which recounts the
exploration of the planet Altair 4. [U.S. 1956]

1956 **Tenn, W.** *Of all possible worlds.* M. Joseph, 255p.
Eight stories. [U.S. 1955]

1956 **Waller, R.** *Shadow of authority.* J. Cape, 223p.
In the days when the National Publishing Authority controls all literature.

1956 **Walter, W. G.** *Further outlook.* G. Duckworth, 224p.
A time-journey into the better and happier world of the twenty-first century.

1956 **Wilding, P.** *Shadow over the Earth.* H. Locke, 160p.
A minor planet approaches the Earth and the Sun is blotted out.

1956 **Wyndham, J. (Harris, J. B.)** *The seeds of time.* M. Joseph, 253p.
Foreword, ten stories.

1957 **Aldiss, B.** *Space, time and Nathaniel.* Faber & Faber, 208p.
Fourteen stories – space, time, people.

1957 **Barlow, J.** *One half of the world.* Cassell, 224p.
Life under the Occupiers at a time when Britain has lost an atomic war. [U.S. 1957]

1957 **Blish, J.** *Fallen star.* Faber & Faber, 224p.
An anticipatory tale of the International Geophysical Year. Published U.S. 1957 as *The Frozen Year.*

1957 **Bloch-Michel, J.** *The flight into Egypt.* Translated from the French. Longmans, 234p.
The experiences of a family in flight after a bombing attack. First published 1952 as *La fuite en Egypte.*

1957 **Bowers, R. L.** *This second Earth.* Cobra Books, 160p.
Space travel and ideal worlds.

1957 **Clarke, A. C.** *The deep range.* F. Muller, 224p.
Adventures with the Bureau of Whales.

1957 **Dye, C.** *Prisoner in the skull.* Transworld, 224p.
A thriller of man and superman in A.D. 2000. [U.S. 1952]

1957 **Frank, P. (Hart, H.)** *Seven days to never.* Constable, 252p.
The Russians attempt to invade U.S.A. First published U.S. 1956 as *Forbidden area.*

1957 **Hoyle, F.** *The black cloud.* W. Heinemann, x, 250p.
All life on Earth is in danger.

1957 **Hubbard, L. R.** *Return to tomorrow.* Panther, 144p.
Space travel adventures. [U.S. 1954]

1957 **Larsen, E. (Lehrburger, E.)** *You'll see.* Rider, 172p. Illus.
An optimistic account of life in 1982.

1957 **Leinster, M. (Jenkins, W. F.)** *Operation outerspace.* Grayson & Grayson, 190p.
The "Dabney Field" makes travel to the stars possible. [U.S. 1954]

1957 **Mackenzie, N.** *The wrath to come.* Wright & Brown, 188p.
The invasion of earth and how it was defeated.

1957 **MacLaren, B.** *Day of misjudgement.* V. Gollancz, 272p.
An unpleasant farce.

[1957] **Maine, C. E. (McIlwain, D.)** *High vacuum.* Hodder & Stoughton, 192p.
Adventures of the first men on the Moon.

1957 **Mars, A. (Gillespie, A. C.)** *Atomic submarine.* Elek books, 192p.
Love and adventure in the very near future when a solitary submarine saves Britain from a Russo-Chinese attack.

1957   **Maxwell, E.** *(pseud.) Quest for Pajaro.* W. Heinemann, 115p.
A test pilot lands in an ideal Spanish community.

1957   **Mead, H.** *Mary's country.* M. Joseph, 288p.
The adventures of a group of children of the "Guardian Class" after an epidemic has wiped out most of the population.

1957   **Powys, J. C.** *Up and out.* Macdonald, 224p.
Two novellas: the first takes place after a hydrogen bomb has wiped out all but four of the human race.

1957   **Ray, R.** *The strange world of Planet X.* H. Jenkins, 190p.
Scientists discover the Fourth Dimensional world of Planet X.

1957   **Richards, G.** *Brother Bear.* M. Joseph, 206p.
The Russian invasion of New York and what followed. First published U.S. 1956 as *Two Roubles to Times Square.*

1957   **Russell, E. F.** *Three to conquer.* D. Dobson, 224p.
What happens when the Venusians take possession of the bodies of three space pilots. [U.S. 1957]

1957   **Shute, N. (Norway, N. S.)** *On the beach.* W. Heinemann, 320p.
The survivors of the first and last atomic war await the end of humanity.

1957   **Sisson, M.** *The cave.* Hemingford Grey (Hunts.), Vine Press, 25p. With engravings on wood by Frank Martin.
A new Adam and Eve visit a devastated earth.

1957   **Steinbeck, J.** *The short reign of Pippin IV.* W. Heinemann, 164p.
The French deputies elect a monarch to govern but results are not what they expected. [U.S. 1957]

1957   **Sturgeon, T. (Waldo, E. H.)** *Thunder and roses.* M. Joseph, 255p.
Eight stories selected and edited by Groff Conklin.

1957   **Swain, D. V.** *The transposed man.* Panther, 143p.
Revolt against the all-powerful Society of Mechanists.

1957   **Wyndham, J. (Harris, J. B.)** *The Midwich cuckoos.* M. Joseph, 239p.
Xenogenesis in an English village.

1958   **Aldiss, B.** *Non-stop.* Faber & Faber, 252p.
An able, imaginative story of lost tribes and a fallen civilization. Published U.S. 1959 as *Starship.*

1958   **Asimov, I.** *The naked Sun.* M. Joseph, 237p.
Sequel to *Caves of Steel,* 1954. [U.S. 1957]

1958   **Asimov, I.** *Pebble in the sky.* Transworld, 220p.
Adventures in Galactic Era 827. [U.S. 1950]

1958   **Asimov, I.** *Second Foundation*. Brown, Watson, 160p.
Completes the history of the Galactic Empire begun in *Foundation* [U.S. 1953]

1958   **Asimov, I.** *stars like dust*. Panther, 192p.
Interplanetary intrigue and murder. [U.S. 1951]

1958   **Blackburn, J.** *A scent of new-mown hay*. Secker & Warburg, 224p.
Scientists fight a world peril.

1958   **Bounds, S. J.** *The robot brains*. Brown, Watson, 158p.
Automata invade Earth.

1958   **Bowen, J.** *After the rain*. Faber & Faber, 203p.
A second deluge: floods cover the Earth; and a new Ark and a new Noah.

1958   **Brebner, W.** *Doubting Thomas*. R. Hart-Davis, 184p.
Life in an electronically controlled totalitarian state. [U.S. 1956]

1958   **Bryan, P. H. H.** *The Barford cat affair*. Abelard-Schuman, London and New York, 152p.
The cats of Barford go on strike: dreadful consequences for the population.

1958   **Bryant, P. (George, P. B.)** *Two hours to doom*. T. V. Boardman, 192p.
An atomic bomb story. Published U.S. 1958 as *Red Alert*. This was the source for the film *Dr. Strangelove*.

1958   **Cole, B.** *Subi: the volcano*. W. H. Allen, 240p.
A beleaguered U.S. base in the Far East during the third world war. [U.S 1957]

[1958]   **Conyers, B.** *Never forever*. Regency Press, 200p.
Life in A.D. 2050 after an elixir has been discovered.

1958   **Cooper, E.** *The uncertain midnight*. Hutchinson, 224p.
Man rises against the Androids. Also published U.S. 1958 as *Deadly image*.

1958   **Creasey, J.** *The plague of silence*. Hodder & Stoughton, 188p.
Dr. Palfrey saves the world from a lethal plague.

1958   **Crispin, E. (Montgomery, R. B.)** *(ed.) Best SF three*. Faber & Faber, 224p.
Introduction by editor; eleven stories.

1958   **Dexter, J. B.** *The time kings*. Badger Books, 160p.
Time travel adventures.

1958   **Duncan, D.** *Occam's razor*. V. Gollancz, 200p.
A scientist breaks through the barriers of space and time with almost disastrous consequences.

1958   **Fear, W. H.** *Lunar flight*. Badger Books, 160p.
Life in Space Station One.

1958   **Fear, W. H.** *Operation satellite*. Badger Books, 160p.
Man against the stars.

1958   **Fear, W. H.** *Return to space*. Badger Books, 160p.
The first colony on the Moon.

1958   **Fear, W. H.** *The ultimate*. Badger Books, 160p.
The Martians invade earth.

1958   **Finney, J.** *The clock of time*. Eyre & Spottiswoode, 189p.
Twelve stories of time travel. First published U.S. 1956 as *The third level*.

1958   **Greene, G.** *Our man in Havana*. W. Heinemann, 273p.
Although this comedy of the reluctant spy does not follow the usual style of tales of the future, it is entered here because the author states that it is "set at some indeterminate date in the future."

1958   **Haggard, W. (Clayton, R. H. M.)** *Slow burner*. Cassell, 192p.
Trouble begins when Britain draws ahead in the development of atomic power.

1958   **Heinlein, R. A.** *Double star*. M. Joseph, 208p.
Politics and adventure in the galactic epoch. [U.S. 1956]

1958   **Jackson, S.** *The sundial*. M. Joseph, 254p.
A group of people await the end of the world. [U.S. 1958]

1958   **Jones, E.** *Head in the sand*. Barker, 223p.
Britain under Russian rule.

1958   **Jones, M.** *On the last day*. J. Cape, 266p.
During the third world war the Allies strive to build the first inter-continental missile.

1958   **Leinster, M. (Jenkins, W. F.)** *War with the Gizmos*. Frederick Muller, 159p.
The Gizmos, gaseous dynamic systems, threaten all life in North America. [U.S. 1958].

1958   **Lundberg, K.** *The Olympic hope*. Translated from the Danish by E. Hansen and W. Luscombe. S. Paul, 172p.
An account of the 800-metre event at the Olympic Games of 1966. First published 1956 as *Det Olympiske Håb*.

1958   **Mackenzie, N.** *The Moon is ours*. Wright & Brown, 192p.
Space travel adventures.

1958   **Mackenzie, N.** *A storm is rising*. Wright & Brown, 189p.
Revolt and rebellion on the planet Sivos.

1958   **Maine, C. E. (McIlwain, D.)** *The tide went out*. Hodder & Stoughton, 190p.
H-bomb tests cause the oceans to run dry.

1958   **Manning, P. L.** *The destroyers*. Badger Books, 160p.
Life continues on Mars after earth has been destroyed.

1958   **Matheson, R.** *The shores of space*. Transworld, 184p.
Thirteen stories. [U.S. 1957]

1958   **Merak, A.J.** *Hydrosphere*. Badger Books, 160p.
Intergalactic conflict and colonization.

1958   **Phelps, G.** *The centenarians*. W. Heinemann, 224p.
The world's greatest artists and scientists are flown for safety to a mountain retreat. All is perfect until destructive elements break into the new Eden.

[1958] **Pohl, F. and Kornbluth, C. M.** *Gladiator-at-law*. Digit Books, 160p.
Public combats fought with all the latest weapons. [U.S. 1955]

1958   **Russell, E. F.** *Wasp*. D. Dobson, 202p.
Espionage in a space war. [U.S. 1957]

1958   **Sherriff, R.C.** *The cataclysm*. Pan Books, 253p.
A revised edition of *The Hopkins manuscript*, 1939.

1958   **Simak, C. D.** *Strangers in the universe*. Faber & Faber, 264p.
Seven stories. [U.S. 1956]

1958   **Wallace, D.** *Forty years on*. Collins, 256p.
Out of terror and destruction a new community emerges in the Isle of Ely.

1958   **Young, A. M.** *The Aster disaster*. A. H. Stockwell, 250p.
Adventures in space.

1958   **Young, M.** *The rise of the meritocracy*. Thames & Hudson, 160p.
The coming of the new mandarins and the bureaucrats of the future. A famous story: has given the language a word and an idea.

1959   **Aldiss, B.** *The canopy of time*. Faber & Faber, 221p.
Eleven stories linked by notes: the human race in the next few million years.

1959   **Asimov, I.** *The end of eternity*. Panther, 192p.
Adventures with the time-travellers. [U.S. 1955]

1959   **Barr, T. C.** *Split worlds*. Digit Books, 156p.
Crew of a space station return to a desolate world.

1959   **Bester, A.** *The stars my destination*. Panther, 192p.
First published U.K. 1956 as *Tiger! Tiger!*

1959   **Blish, J.** *A case of conscience*. Faber & Faber, 208p.
Moral problems in a planetary paradise. [U.S. 1958]

1959   **Blish, J.** *A clash of cymbals*. Faber & Faber, 197p.
Scientists of a wandering planet discover an anti-matter universe which threatens the existence of their world. Concludes *Cities in flight* series. Published U.S. 1958 as *The triumph of time*.

1959   **Blish, J.** *Vor*. Transworld, 160p.
A machine-like creature from outer space comes to Earth. [U.S. 1958]

1959   **Bradbury, R.** *The day it rained for ever*. R. Hart-Davis, 252p.
Twenty-three stories. First published U.S. 1958 as *A medicine for melancholy*.

1959   **Brunner, J.** *The brink*. V. Gollancz, 192p.
How the world came close to World War III.

1959   **Chapkin, P.** *Light of Mars*. Badger Books, 160p.
The Earth is threatened with destruction by another world.

1959   **Coon, H.** *43,000 years later*. Panther, 160p.
Explorers from a later age discover a destroyed earth. [U.S. 1958]

1959   **Cooper, E.** *Deadly image*. Panther, 192p.
A new edition of *The uncertain midnight*, 1958.

1959   **Cooper, E.** *Seed of light*. Hutchinson, 224p.
The last human beings journey through space for centuries and return to Earth through the time dimension.

1959   **Cooper, E.** *Tomorrow's gift*. Digit Books, 160p.
A ghost story set in the future.

[1959]   **Crisp, F.** *The ape of London*. Hodder & Stoughton, 192p.
A deadly power from outer space masters the minds of men and gives them inhuman strength.

1959   **Desmond, H.** *Suicide Fleet*. Wright & Brown, 190p.
A party of idealists try to prevent the explosion of an atomic device on a Pacific island.

1959   **Fanthorpe, R. L.** *Alien from the stars*. Badger Books, 160p.
Flying saucers land on Earth. See *Note 10*.

1959   **Fanthorpe, R. L.** *Fiends*, Badger Books, 160p.
Giant ants invade the world.

1959   **Fanthorpe, R. L.** *Hyperspace*. Badger Books, 160p.
An electronic gateway leads to the fourth dimension.

1959   **Fanthorpe, R. L.** *Space-borne*. Badger Books, 160p.
Volunteers set out on a mission of no-return.

1959   **Frank, P. (Hart, H.)** *Alas, Babylon!* Constable, 256p.
The U.S.A. is wiped out save for a few survivors here and there. [U.S.1959]

1959   **Fullerton, C.** *The man who spoke dog*. With drawings by Anton. Harvill Press, 159p.
An understanding of dog-language brings fame and fortune to one lucky man.

1959   **Hamilton, E.** *The Star of Life*. Muller, 160p.
First man to orbit the Moon meets the Vramen. [U.S. 1959]

[1959]   **Heinlein, R.** *Revolt in 2100*. Digit Books, 160p.
Three stories, intrigue in tomorrow's U.S.A. [U.S. 1953]

1959   **Hodder-Williams, C.** *Chain reaction*. Hodder & Stoughton, 224p.
Disaster in an atomic energy centre.

1959   **Hoyle, F.** *Ossian's ride*. W. Heinemann, 252p.
Investigation of a secret industrial community.

1959   **Kenton, L. P.** *Destination Moon*. Badger Books, 160p.
The first manned space rocket to the Moon.

1959   **Lymington, J. (Chance, J. N.)** *Night of the big heat*. Hodder & Stoughton, 160p.
Spider-like creatures from outer space invade Earth.

1959   **Mackenzie, Sir C.** *The lunatic republic*. Chatto & Windus, 224p.
In 1997 the Celestial Chinese Republic sends a rocket to the Moon.

[1959]   **Maine, C. E. (McIlwain, D.)** *Count-down*. Hodder & Stoughton, 191p.
Murder reaches out of the future.

1959   **Merak, A. J.** *No dawn and no horizon*. Badger Books, 160p.
Man turns towards the alien world of Alpha Centauri.

1959   **Mittelholzer, E.** *A tinkling in the twilight*. Secker & Warburg, 270p.
The hero, an ascetic, repeatedly slips into the future at various times in the twenty-first century.

[1959]   **Roberts, L.** *Time echo*. John Spencer, 157p.
Fugitive from twenty-fourth century changes places with a nineteenth century diplomat.

1959   **Roshwald, M.** *Level 7*. W. Heinemann, 191p.
How World War III happened. [U.S. 1959]

1959   **Russell, E. F.** *Next of kin*. D. Dobson, 187p.
The psychological counter-attack in a space war.

1959   **Sheckley, R.** *Pilgrimage to Earth*. Corgi, 190p.
Fifteen stories. [U.S. 1957]

1959   **Smith, E. E.** *The Skylark of space*. Brown, Watson, 159p.
Scientist builds super-spaceship—space adventures follow. First in the *Skylark* series. [U.S. 1946].

1959   **Updike, J** *The poorhouse fair*. V. Gollancz, 192p.
An allegorical tale of life in an American institution: that is, the United States. The author "meant the future it portrays to be no less a predictive blue-print than a caricature of contemporary decadence." [U.S. 1958]

1959   **Wallop, D.** *What has four wheels and flies*. P. Davies, 192p.
Life in U.S.A. when dogs are taught to drive. [U.S. 1959]

1959   **Wyndham, J. (Harris, J. B.) and Parkes, L.** *The outward urge*.
M. Joseph, 192p.
Man's advance through space, told in the experiences of the Troon family. *Note* Lucas Parks was another pseudonym of John Beynon Harris.

1960   **Asimov, I.** *Earth is room enough*. Panther, 176p.
Fifteen stories about the dangerous world of the future. [U.S. 1957]

1960   **Barzman, B.** *Out of this world*. Collins, 320p.
Interplanetary communication and envoys from another world. Published U.S. 1960 as *Twinkle, twinkle, little star*.

1960   **Blish, J.** *Galactic cluster*. Faber & Faber, 233p.
Six stories. [U.S. 1959]

1960   **Chilton, C.** *The world in peril*. H. Jenkins, 222p.
Jet Morgan saves the world from a Martian invasion. Concludes the Jet Morgan trilogy.

1960   **Colquhoun, K.** *Point of stress*. H. Hamilton, 188p.
An ironic examination of attitudes to a new American missile site.

1960   **Condon, R.** *The Manchurian candidate*. M. Joseph, 285p.
An American hero, brain-washed in Korea, returns to play his planned part in an American presidential election. [U.S. 1959]

1960   **Cooper, E.** *Voices in the dark*. Brown, Watson, 157p.
Flying saucers over London.

1960   **Drury, A.** *Advise and consent*. Collins, 628p.
Unflattering views of the U.S. Senate and government set in the near future. [U.S. 1959]

1960   **Fitzgibbon, C.** *When the kissing had to stop*. Cassell, 256p.
Political apathy and anti-nuclear campaigners provide the means for establishing the British People's Republic. [U.S. 1960]

1960   **Foley, J.** *Man in the Moon*. Four Square, 160p.
Anticipation of a lunar landing.

1960   **Foster, R. (Crossen, K. F.)** *The rest must die*. F. Muller, 162p.
Survival story–after the atomic bombing of New York. [U.S. 1959]

1960   **Haile, T.** *Galaxies ahead*. Digit Books, 160p.
A lost-in-space adventure story.

1960   **Hartley, L. P.** *Facial justice*. H. Hamilton, 256p.
A powerful story of life in the New State after World War III where all are apparently free and equal; inspectors enforce orders designed to remove all opportunity for envy, pride and greed. And then an individual foments rebellion.

1960   **Heinlein, R. A.** *Lost legacy*. Digit Books, 156p.
Contains title story and *Jerry was a man*, first published in *Assignment in eternity*, U.K. 1955.

1960   **Herbert, F.** *The dragon in the sea*. V. Gollancz, 208p.
Psychosis, espionage and homing torpedoes all combine against the lone venture of a nuclear submarine in the days of World War III. [U.S. 1956]

1960   **Iggulden, J.** *Breakthrough*. Chapman & Hall, 240p.
Spy adventures in the World Police State of A.D. 2009.

1960   **King-Hall, S.** *Men of destiny*. King-Hall, 204p.
East German communists start a world crisis.

1960   **Lawrence, H. L.** *The children of light*. MacDonald, 192p.
A tale of the consequences of atomic radiation.

[1960]   **Leiber, F.** *The green millennium*. Abelard-Schuman, 256p.
An odd tale about an extra-terrestial cat and its telepathic influence. [U.S. 1953]

1960   **Lymington, J. (Chance, J. N.)** *The giant stumbles*. Hodder & Stoughton, 160p.
What happens when a scientist discovers that the entire human race is in danger.

1960   **Lymington, J. (Chance, J. N.)** *The grey ones*. Hodder & Stoughton, 159p.
Strange forces in nature begin to fight against mankind.

1960   **Maine, C. E. (McIlwain, D.)** *Calculated risk*. Hodder & Stoughton, 191p.
Visitors from the twenty-fourth century.

1960   **Margulies, L.** *(ed.) Get out of my sky*. Crest Books, 176p.
Three novellas: Blish, J. *Get out of my sky*; Anderson, P. *Sister Planet*; Scortia, T. N. *Alien night*.

1960   **Margulies, L.** *(ed.) Three from out there*. Panther, 192p.
Contains: Azimov, I. *Mother Earth*; Knight, D. *Double meaning*; Hamilton, E. *Son of two worlds*. [U.S. 1959]

1960   **Merwin, S.** *Killer to come*. Abelard-Schuman, 252p.
Thrills and space-travel. [U.S. 1953],

1960   **Miller, W.** *A canticle for Leibowitz*. Weidenfeld & Nicolson, 320p.
A remarkable story of the new Dark Ages, when the Church is the only effective international organisation and the only guardian of science and technology. Man rediscovers the lost sciences and once again splits the atom. [U.S. 1960]

1960   **Moore, C. L.** *Doomsday morning.* World Distributors, 191p.
Revolution in the United States. [U.S. 1957]

1960   **Morel, D.** *Moonlight red.* Secker & Warburg, 287p.
A pestilence drives the world mad.

1960   **Pohl, F.** *Slave ship.* D. Dobson, 148p.
The new-style warfare of the future: combat animals, extra-sensory perception,
electronic devices. [U.S. 1957]

1960   **Pohl, F. and Kornbluth, C. M.** *Wolfbane.* V. Gollancz, 200p.
In a regimented society of the far future, a group of rebels defy all rules and
conventions in their struggle for liberty. [U.S. 1957]

1960   **Queffelec, H.** *Frontier of the unknown.* Translated from the French by
Jonathan Griffin. Secker & Warburg, 319p.
Frightening experiences of work in a nuclear power plant. First published as
Combat contre l'invisible.

1960   **Roberts, L.** *The in-world.* Badger Books, 142p.
Earth is invaded by aliens from the caves at the core.

1960   **Simak, C.** *Ring around the Sun.* World Distributors, 190p.
Discovery of parallel worlds in the near future. [U.S. 1953]

1960   **Sinclair, A.** *The Project.* Faber & Faber, 192p.
A moral tale about preparations for launching a rocket.

1960   **Smith, S.** *The village that wandered.* T. V. Boardman, 223p.
A Devon village floats away and arrives in New York Harbour.

1960   **Sturgeon, I. (Waldo, E. H.)** *E pluribus unicorn.* Abelard-Schuman,
276p.
Essay on Sturgeon by Groff Conklin, thirteen stories. [U.S. 1959]

1960   **Sully, K.** *Skrine.* P. Davies, 156p.
A fantasy of life in a destroyed world.

1960   **Tsiolkovsky, K.** *Beyond the planet Earth.* Pergamon Press. Translated
from the Russian by K. Syers, 190p.
A story of the first men in space: originally published in Russia in 1920 as *Vne
Zemli.*

1960   **Valentine, V. (Eaton, B. V.)** *Cure for death.* Sidgwick & Jackson,
238p.
What happens when the scientists discover how to make the body-cells immortal.

1960   **Van Mierlo, H. A.** *By then mankind ceased to exist.* Stockwell
(Ilfracombe), 112p.
The author writes: "This small work gives the average reader an idea of atomic
warfare, and it urges the importance of the banning of atom power for war
purposes."

1960   **Van Vogt, A. E.** *The mind cage.* Panther, 191p.
Interplanetary intrigue and detection. [U.S. 1957]

1960   **Van Vogt, A. E.** *Mission to the stars.* Brown, Watson, 160p.
A space-ship from Earth searches for inhabited planets in distant star systems.
First published U.S. 1952 as *The mixed men.*

1960   **Ward, H.** *Hell's above us.* Translated from the French by A. Neame.
Sidgwick & Jackson, 319p.
The International Scientific Monitoring Office compels the world to make peace
and to plan the sharing of world resources. First published 1958 as *L'Enfer est
dans le ciel.*

1960   **Wyndham, J. (Harris, J. B.)** *Trouble with lichen.* M. Joseph, 190p.
A new type of lichen appears; it has the extraordinary effect of being able to
treble the normal life-span.

1961   **Aldiss, B.** *Equator.* Brown, Watson, 160p.
Plot and counterplot as the alien Rosk seek living space on Earth. First published
U.S. 1959 as *Vanguard from Alpha.*

1961   **Aldiss, B.** *The Interpreter.* Brown, Watson, 155p.
Interstellar politics when Earth is victim of intergalactic exploitation. First
published U.S. 1960 as *Bow down to Nul.*

1961   **Aldiss, B.** *(ed.) Penguin Science Fiction.* Penguin Books, 236p.
Introduction in which Aldiss writes that "Science-fiction – 'SF' to its adherents –
concerns anything that has not happened; it may be something that is very likely
to happen, or something that is very unlikely to happen." Twelve stories.

1961   **Allighan, G.** *Verwoerd – the end.* T. V. Boardman, xxvii, 228p. Illus.
Review of South African history up to 1987 – a change of heart leads to a just
and equal society.

1961   **Amis, K. and Conquest, R. (eds.)** *Spectrum.* V. Gollancz, 317p.
Introduction, ten stories.

1961   **Anderson, P.** *Guardians of time.* V. Gollancz, 176p.
Four stories of the Time Patrol. [U.S. 1960]

1961   **Asterley, H. C.** *Escape to Berkshire.* Pall Mall Press, 247p.
A moral tale of life after the nuclear bombs have destroyed London.

1961   **Ball, F. N.** *Metatopia.* Thames Bank, Ipswich, 244p.
An ideal state of the future – advanced technology, high efficiency, freedom for
all. Notes on the text p.229–44.

1961   **Balsdon, J. P. V. D.** *The day they burned Miss Termag.* Eyre &
Spottiswoode, 251p.
A witty tale of life in an oppressive Oxford of the future.

1961 **Berriault, G.** *The descent.* Arthur Barker, 167p.
Bomb frenzy and shelter mania in the United States of the near future. [U.S. 1960].

1961 **Bulmer, K.** *The changeling worlds.* Brown, Watson, 156p.
Interplanetary travel and adventure. [U.S. 1959]

1961 **Bulmer, K.** *City under the sea.* Brown, Watson, 160p.
Adventures in the sea-cities of the future. [U.S. 1957]

1961 **Bulmer, K.** *Of Earth foretold.* Digit Books, 160p.
The Prophets of Earth, android missionaries, are sent to take the Word of Man through space.

1961 **Bulmer, K.** *Secret of ZI.* Digit Books, 156p.
Fight against the invaders of Earth. [U.S. 1958]

1961 **Castle, J. (Payner, R. C. and Garrod, J. W.)** *The seventh fury.* Souvenir Press, 238p.
As East and West move towards a new summit meeting, the loss of a tubule containing a deadly virus endangers the peace and the health of the world.

1961 **Clark, L.** *More than Moon.* Centaur Press, 227p.
Adventure on the Moon.

1961 **Clarke, A. C.** *A fall of moondust.* V. Gollancz, 224p.
Space adventure story about the rescue of a dust-cruiser buried in the Sea of Thirst. [U.S.1961]

1961 **Clarke, A. C.** *The other side of the sky.* V. Gollancz, viii, 245p.
Fourteen stories; bibliographic note by author. [U.S. 1958]

1961 **Clement, H. (Stubbs, H. C.)** *Needle.* V. Gollancz, 222p.
A symbiotic creature from outer space selects a young boy as a suitable organism to inhabit during his search on earth. [U.S. 1950]

1961 **Conklin, G.** *(ed.) 4 for the future.* Consul Books, 174p.
Four stories, [U.S. 1949].

1961 **Crispin, E. (Montgomery, R. B.)** *(ed.) Best SF four.* Faber & Faber, 224p.
Ten stories.

1961 **Derleth, A.** *(ed.) The time of infinity.* Consul Books, 205p.
Last nine stories from original seventeen in the U.S. 1951 edition, *The outer reaches*

1961 **Dick, P. K.** *Time out of joint.* Science Fiction Book Club, 221p.
Fantasy of life in the future – space travel and world government. [U.S. 1959]

1961 **Gillon, D. and Gillon, M.** *The unsleep.* Barrie & Rockliff, 240p.
The Psycho-mentors keep the citizens of the future happy with television, pleasure, and personality adjustment.

1961   **Gordon, R. (Hough, S. B.)** *The worlds of Eclos.* Consul, 160p.
Space flight misses Mars and speeds on through the galaxy. First published U.S. 1959 as *First to the stars.*

1961   **Heinlein, R.** *Starship troopers.* Four Square, 222p.
Heroic adventures with the Mobile Infantry in the planetary wars of the future. [U.S. 1959].

1961   **Hesky, O. L.** *The purple armchair.* H. Blond, 232p.
A whimsical tale of London in the days when the population is half-a-million and everyone lives underground.

1961   **Hough, S. B.** *Beyond the eleventh hour.* Hodder & Stoughton, 192p.
World war and the search for universal peace.

1961   **Johnson, L. P. V. (Le Roy, P. V.)** *In the time of the Thetans.* Macmillan, 274p.
Earth fights off an invasion from Mars.

1961   **Keene, D. and Pruyn, L.** *World without women.* Muller, 148p.
An epidemic kills off most of the women in the world, and then the battles begin. [U.S. 1960].

1961   **Knight, D.** *A for anything.* Four Square, 160p.
Adventures in the future when a special device makes it possible to reproduce any object. First published U.S. 1959 as *The people maker.*

1961   **Lymington, J. (Chance, J. N.)** *The coming of the strangers.* Hodder & Stoughton, 190p.
Mysterious invisible creatures from space invade an English seaside town.

1961   **McIntosh, J. T. (MacGregor, J. M.)** *The fittest.* Corgi, 220p.
The animal world makes war on mankind. [U.S. 1955]

1961   **Maine, C. E. (MacIlwain, D.)** *The man who owned the world.* Hodder & Stoughton, 190p.
The Martians seek to use a man who has survived for eight thousand years as a means of controlling Earth. Published U.S. 1960 as *He owned the world.*

1961   **Matheson, R.** *Third from the Sun.* Corgi, 190p.
First published U.K. 1956 as *Born of man and woman.*

1961   **Moore, C. L.** *Shambleau.* Consul Books, 174p.
The erotic adventures of North West Smith on Mars.

1961   **Pape, R.** *And so ends the world.* Elek Books, 222p.
An explosion on the Moon threatens all life on Earth.

1961   **Pohl, F.** *Drunkard's Walk.* V. Gollancz, 176p.
Suicide hysteria sweeps a university campus. [U.S. 1960]

1961   **Rafcam, N.** *The troglodytes.* Stockwell, 296p.
A race of diminutive beings is discovered in Antarctica.

1961   **Russell, E. F.** *Far stars.* D. Dobson, 191p.
Six stories.

1961   **Simak, C. D.** *Aliens for neighbours.* Faber & Faber, 255p.
Nine stories. First published U.S. 1960 as *The worlds of Clifford Simak.*

1961   **Slaughter, F. G.** *Epidemic!* Hutchinson, 255p.
The Black Death rages again in Manhattan. [U.S. 1961]

1961   **Szilard, Dr. L.** *The voice of the dolphins.* V. Gollancz, 176p.
Short stories. The principal stories describe what might happen if
dolphins were able to communicate; if the Russians won the third world
war and stage their own Nurenberg; if a self-induced coma could keep
us alive but unconscious for centuries. [U.S. 1959]

1961   **Van Vogt, A. E.** *The war against the Rull.* Panther, 156p.
Space adventure and interplanetary warfare. [U.S. 1959]

1961   **Ward, H. L.** *The green suns.* Translated from the French by Alan
Neame. Sidgwick & Jackson, 206p.
A far-fetched tale of Atlantaeans and ypsionic rays. First published 1956 as *Les
Soleils verts.*

1961   **White, J.** *The secret visitors.* Brown, Watson, 160p.
Interplanetary warfare.

1961   **Williamson, J.** *After world's end.* Brown, Watson, 155p.
The struggle to survive on Earth. [U.S. 1954]ı

1961   **Williamson, J.** *The Legion of Time.* Digit Books, ? p.
Space warfare. [U.S. 1953]ı

1961   **Wilson, A. (Johnstone, F.)** *The old men at the Zoo.* Secker &
Warburg, 352p.
Within the setting of a war between Western powers the story examines the
central themes of political authority and the instinctual life.

[1961]   **Wright, L.** *A man called Destiny.* Digit Books, 160p.
One man intervenes in the struggle between Earth and the Interstellar Traders.
[U.S. 1958].

[1961]   **Wright, L.** *Who speaks of conquest?* Digit Books, 156p.
The Commander of the United Terran Space Fleet takes on the galaxy. [U.S.
1957]

1961   **Wyndham, J. (Harris, J. B.)** *Consider her ways.* M. Joseph, 223p.
Six stories.

1962   **Ainsbury, R. (Verrill, A. H.)** *When the Moon ran wild*. Consul Books, 158p.
A ten-thousand megaton bomb, exploded in the upper atmosphere, changes the orbit of the Moon.

1962   **Aldiss, B.** *(ed.) Best fantasy stories*. Faber & Faber, 208p.
Ten stories; editorial introduction.

1962   **Aldiss, B.** *Hothouse*. Faber & Faber, 253p.
The Earth has ceased to rotate and the plants have crowded out the animals. Published U.S. 1962 as *The long afternoon of Earth*.

1962   **Amis, K. W. and Conquest, G.** *(eds.) Spectrum II*. V. Gollancz, 271p.
An anthology of exceptional merit.

1962   **Anderson, P.** *Twilight world*. V. Gollancz, 181p.
An after-the-disaster story; mankind begins to colonise Mars. [U.S. 1961]

1962   **Asimov, I.** *Foundation and Empire*. Panther, 172p.
Second in the *Foundation* trilogy. [U.S. 1952]

1962   **Bahnson, A. H.** *The stars are too high*. Science Fiction Book Club, 252p.
American spaceship, operated by reversed gravity, brings peace to the world [U.S. 1959]

1962
[1963]   **Ballard, J. G.** *The drowned world*. V. Gollancz, 175p.
Tropical swamps and lagoons cover what used to be the British Isles. A survey party from Greenland comes south to discover what can be reclaimed in Europe.

1962   **Barron, D. G.** *The Zilov bombs*. A. Deutsch, 173p.
The British resistance plots to throw off Russian rule.

1962   **Bone, J. F.** *The Lani People*. Transworld, 152p.
A romantic tale of the Lani, humanoids who are female,beautiful and entirely submissive. [U.S. 1962]

1962   **Booth, P.** *Long night among the stars*. Collins, 191p.
The life story and experiences of the first Englishman in space.

1962   **Brackett, L. (Hamilton, E. L.)** *The long tomorrow*. Mayflower, 223p.
Life in the oppressive world after the atomic war. [U.S. 1955]

1962   **Bradbury, R.** *The small assassin*. New English Library, 144p.
Thirteen stories. Not published U.S.

1962   **Brinton, H.** *Purple-6*. Hutchinson, 208p.
A Russian space-probe falls on Dartmoor and the world faces the possibility of an atomic war.

1962   **Brunner, J.** *No future in it*. V. Gollancz, 192p.
Eleven stories.

1962   **Budrys, A.** *The unexpected dimension.* V. Gollancz, 159p.
Seven stories. [U.S. 1960]

1962   **Budrys, A.** *Who?* V. Gollancz, 176p.
The story opens when the Russians return a kidnapped American physicist, injured in a laboratory explosion. Who is he? [U.S. 1958]

1962   **Bulmer, H. K.** *No man's world.* Digit Books, 160p.
Adventure on a forbidden planet. [U.S. 1961]

1962   **Bulmer, H. K.** *The wind of liberty.* Digit Books, 160p.
The Freedom Fighters strike out for planetary liberty.

1962   **Burgess, A. (Wilson, J. B.)** *A clockwork orange.* W. Heinemann, 208p.
An original and powerful story of the rootless, violent young in a regimented world of the future.

1962   **Burgess, A. (Wilson, J. B.)** *The wanting seed.* W. Heinemann, 285p.
The misery of life in Enspun, one of the three great power blocks – enormous cities, a Ministry of Infertility, famine and cannibalism.

1962   **Buzzati, D.** *Larger than life.* Translated from the Italian by Henry Reed. Secker & Warburg, 154p.
A philosophical tale about the creation of a huge electronic machine which can reproduce the functions of the human brain. First published 1960 as *Il grande ritratto.*

1962   **Christopher, J. (Youd, C. S.)** *The world in winter.* Eyre & Spottiswoode, 253p.
Europe frozen in a new Ice Age whilst Nigeria enjoys a Mediterranean climate.

1962   **Clarke, A. C.** *Reach for tomorrow.* V. Gollancz, 166p.
Twelve stories. [U.S. 1956]

1962   **Clifton, M.** *Eight keys to Eden.* V. Gollancz, 187p.
An unusual story of a scientist sent to investigate the disappearance of an Earth colony on the planet Eden; he finds an answer in terms of a new form of knowledge. [U.S. 1960]

1962   **Conklin, G.** *(ed.) Enemies in space.* Brown, Watson, 160p.
First published U.K. 1953 as *Invaders of Earth.*

1962   **Conklin, G.** *(ed.) Great science fiction by scientists.* Collier Books, 313p.
Sixteen stories. [U.S. 1962]

1962   **Cranford, R.** *Leave them their pride.* Jarrolds, 200p.
The African States attack the Republic of South Africa.

1962   **Creasey, J.** *The terror.* Hodder & Stoughton, 191p.
A megalomaniac tries to hold the world to ransom.

1962   **Dagmar, P.** *Alien skies.* Digit Books, 160p.
[1963]   Alien spaceships threaten Earth.

1962   **Danvers, J. (Caseleyr, C. A.)** *The end of it all.* W. Heinemann, 231p.
         The last days of the human race after a nuclear war.

1962   **Fast, H. M.** *The edge of tomorrow.* Corgi.
         Seven stories. [U.S. 1961]

1962   **Galouye, D. F.** *Dark universe.* V. Gollancz, 188p.
         Survivors from a nuclear war live underground in perpetual darkness until the day
         when they go back to light and life on the surface. [U.S. 1961]

1962   **Gordon, D. (Payne, D. G.)** *Star-raker.* Hodder & Stoughton, 256p.
         A tale of adventure and supersonic flight.

1962   **Hailey, A.** *In high places.* M. Joseph, 397p.
         Blackmail and intrigue follows proposed Act of Union between Canada and the
         United States.

1962   **Harrison, H. S. B.** *The catacombs.* Chatto & Windus, 223p.
         In the destroyed world of the future the people of the underground struggle
         against the Communes.

1962   **Heinlein, R.** *The day after tomorrow.* Mayflower, 160p.
         Heroic Americans repel a Chinese invasion. Originally published U.S. 1949 as
         Sixth Column.

1962   **Henderson, Z.** *Pilgrimage.* V. Gollancz, 239p.
         Descendants of earthmen return to the planet of their origin. [U.S. 1961]

1962   **Hoyle, F. and Elliot, J. H.** *A for Andromeda.* Souvenir Press, 206p.
         The story, based on a BBC television serial of the same name, begins with a
         series of signals from the Andromeda constellation – information of immense
         importance and deadly peril.

1962   **Jenkins, G.** *A grue of ice.* Collins, 319p.
         The fight for Thompson Island and its large deposits of caesium.

1962   **King, F. H.** *The inaugurator.* Holsum Publishing Company, (Southport),
         11p.
         The International Unit of Production System of World Trade leads to universal
         peace and prosperity.

1962   **Knight, D.** *Far out.* V. Gollancz, 282p.
         Thirteen stories; introduction by Anthony Boucher. [U.S. 1962]

1962   **Leach, D.** *The Garthians.* Arthur Stockwell (Ilfracombe), 168p.
         Love and adventure on the planet Gar.

1962   **Lloyd, R.** *The troubling of the city.* Allen & Unwin, 214p.
The powers of darkness attack the holy city of Winchester.

1962   **Lymington, J. (Chance, J. N.)** *A sword above the night.* Hodder &
Stoughton, 157p.
Mysterious spaceships invade earth.

1962   **McCutchan, P.** *Bluebolt One.* Harrap, 254p.
Commander Shaw saves the day in Africa.

1962   **MacTyre, P. (Adams, R. J.)** *Midge.* Hodder & Stoughton, 195p.
In the desolate days after World War 3, intelligent and telepathic midges assist
humanity.

1962   **Maine, C. E. (McIlwain, D.)** *The darkest of nights.* Hodder &
Stoughton, 254p.
Civil war and general chaos follow on the outbreak of a deadly epidemic.

1962   **Mills, R. P.** *(ed.) Best from fantasy & science fiction*, 9th series.
V. Gollancz, 256p.
Sixteen stories [U.S. 1960]

1962   **Mills, R. P.** *(ed.) A decade of fantasy & science fiction.* V. Gollancz,
404p.
Introduction, twenty-four stories. [U.S. 1960]

1962   **Mitchison, N.** *Memoirs of a spacewoman.* V. Gollancz, 176p.
The experiences of a woman communications expert in her work with the many
varieties of rational creatures in the planetary system.

1962   **Newman, B.** *The blue ants.* Robert Hale, 192p.
The protonic bomb puts an end to the Russo-Chinese war of 1970.

1962   **Nourse, A. E.** *Tiger by the tail.* D. Dobson, 184p.
Nine stories. [U.S. 1961]

1962   **Ranzetta, L.** *The uncharted planet.* Brown, Watson, 156p.
Space adventure.

1962   **Roshwald, M.** *A small Armageddon.* W. Heinemann, 211p.
A Polaris submarine turns pirate and extorts what it wants from the world.

1962   **Russell, E. F.** *Dark tides.* D. Dobson, 184p.
Introduction; twelve stories about strange events on Earth.

1962   **Russell, E. F.** *The great explosion.* D. Dobson, 203p.
The first expedition from Terra to the colonies founded in space by rebels against
the old terrestrial societies finds very odd people in the planets. [U.S. 1962]

1962   **Santesson, H. S.** *(ed.) Fantastic Universe omnibus.* Panther, 224p.
Short stories.

1962   **Sheckley, R.** *Shards of space.* Corgi, 152p.
Eleven stories. [U.S. 1962]

1962   **Simak, C.** *Time is the simplest thing.* V. Gollancz, 263p.
The adventures of a parapsychological hero, engaged in exploring the world by telepathic means, pursued both by his colleagues and by anti-parapsychological groups. [U.S. 1961]

1962   **Sissons, M.** *(ed.) Asleep in Armageddon.* Panther, 189p.
Ten stories.

1962   **Stuart, I. (MacLean, A.)** *The Satan Bug.* Collins, 256p.
The ultimate biological weapon is stolen from the Mordon Microbiological Research Establishment (i.e. Porton Down); all life on Earth in danger.

1962   **Van Greenaway, P.** *The crucified city.* New Authors, 220p.
London after the Bomb.

1962   **Verron, R.** *Moon killer.* Wright & Brown, 175p.
Moon rocket brings back a deadly dust to Earth.

1962   **Vonnegut, K.** *The sirens of Titan.* V. Gollancz, 319p.
An extraordinary tale that moves from the predicament of a space traveller caught in a chronolsynclastic infundibulum to the launching of a new religion of a God the Utterly Indifferent. [U.S. 1959]

1962   **Wade, T.** *The world of Theda.* Brown, Watson, 154p.
Horror story.

1962   **Wadey, V.** *A planet named Terra.* Digit Books, 160p.
Reincarnated human beings live in utopia on a remote planet.

1962   **Wadey, V.** *The united planets.* Digit Books, 160p.
Sequel to above.

1962   **Wallace, B. E.** *The device.* Hodder & Stoughton, 255p.
A broadcast device can be used to create panic.

1962   **Wood, W.** *The news from Karachi.* V. Gollancz, 124p.
A moral story about the Bomb. [U.S. 1962]

1962   **Zeigfreid, K. (Fanthorpe, R. L.)** *Atomic nemesis.* Badger Books, 158p.
Intrigue against the Empire in the days when Earth has colonized the galaxy.

1963   **Aldiss, B.** *The airs of Earth.* Faber & Faber, 256p.
Introduction; eight stories.

1963   **Aldiss, B.** *(ed.) More Penguin science fiction.* Penguin, 236p.
Introduction; twelve stories.

1963   **Amis, K. and Conquest, R.** *(eds.) Spectrum III.* V. Gollancz, 272p.
Introduction; eight stories.

1963   **Anderson, P.** *After Doomsday.* V. Gollancz, 159p.
Space battles in the days after the destruction of Earth. [U.S. 1961]

1963   **Asimov, I.** *(ed.) The Hugo Winners.* D. Dobson, 318p.
Introduction by Asimov: prize-winning short stories (1955 to 1961) by Walter M.
Miller, E. F. Russell, Murray Leinster, A. C. Clarke, Avram Davidson, Clifford D.
Simak, R. Bloch, Daniel Keyes, Poul Anderson. [U.S. 1962]

1963   **Asimov; I.** *Nine tomorrows.* D. Dobson, 236p.
Nine stories about the near future. [U.S. 1959]

1963   **Asimov, I. and Conklin, G.** *(eds.) Fifty short science fiction tales.*
Collier-Macmillan, 287p.
Introductions by Asimov and Conklin: fifty stories. [U.S. 1963]

1963   **Ballard, J. G.** *The four-dimensional nightmare.* V. Gollancz, 208p.
Eight stories – inner space, time, human destiny.

1963   **Bateman, R.** *When the whites went.* D. Dobson, 183p.
A tale of the days when the white nations have vanished from the world.

1963   **Blish, J.** *Year 2018.* Four Square, 160p.
First published as *They shall have stars,* U. K. 1956.

1963   **Blish, J.** *Titan's daughter.* Four Square Books, 142p.
Conflict between the tetraploids, giant men and women, and the rest of the
human race. [U.S. 1961]

1963   **Bloch, R.** *Atoms and evil.* Frederick Muller, 160p.
Thirteen stories. [U.S. 1962].

1963   **Blow, E. J.** *Appointment in space.* Consul Books, 221p.
Space journey to Mars.

1963   **Brunner, J.** *The dreaming Earth.* Pyramid Books, Thorpe & Porter,
159p.
New drug causes mysterious disappearances in the overpopulated world of the
future. [U.S. 1963].

1963   **Bulmer, K.** *Defiance.* Brown, Watson, 160p.
Adventures with the Terran Survey Corps.

1963   **Bulmer, K.** *Earth's long shadow.* Brown, Watson, 159p.
Space adventures.

1963   **Bulmer, K.** *The fatal fire.* Brown, Watson, 160p.
Adventures in space.

1963   **Burdick, E. and Wheeler, H.** *Fail-safe.* Hutchinson, 255p.
The world comes to the brink of a nuclear war when two American planes,
because of a technical failure, drop atomic bombs on Moscow. [U.S. 1962]

1963   **Casewit, C. W.** *The peacemakers.* Brown, Watson, 192p.
Two scientists work for the salvation of the world. [U.S. 1960]

1963   **Charbonneau, L.** *Corpus Earthling.* Digit Books, 160p.
Martians take over human bodies. [U.S. 1960]

1963   **Clarke, A.C.** *Dolphin Island.* V. Gollancz, 186p.
Submarine adventures in the great oceans.

1963   **Clarke, A. C.** *Tales of ten worlds.* V. Gollancz, 245p.
Fifteen stories. [U.S. 1962]

1963   **Clifton, M.** *When they come from space.* D. Dobson, 184p.
A satire upon Washington bureaucracy. [U.S. 1962]

1963   **Conklin, G.** *(ed.) 17 X infinity.* Mayflower, 272p.
Introduction, seventeen stories. [U.S. 1963]

1963   **Cooper, E.** *Tomorrow came.* Panther, 122p.
Twelve stories.

1963   **Creasey, J.** *The depths.* Hodder & Stoughton, 190p.
Menace from the ocean deeps.

1963   **Crispin E. (Montgomery, R. B.)** *(ed.) Best SF 5.* Faber & Faber, 256p.
Eleven stories.

1963   **Cunningham, E. V. (Fast, H. M.)** *Phyllis.* A. Deutsch, 214p.
High-minded Russian and American scientists threaten to explode a pair of nuclear bombs unless the politicians agree to ban the bomb. [U.S. 1962]

1963   **Dagmar, P.** *Once in time.* Digit Books, 160p.
Struggle for the autonomy of Man.

1963   **Dagmar, P.** *Sands of time.* Digit Books, 155p.
The men of the Galaxies rebel against rule by computer.

1963   **Dagmar, P.** *Spykos 4.* Digit Books, 154p.
The planet Doros faces extinction and looks to Earth for aid.

1963   **Danforth, M.** *From outer space.* Brown, Watson, 160p.
A delegation from Mars gives a warning to Earth.

1963   **Delius, A.** *The day Natal took off.* Pall Mall Press, 168p.
A satirical account of the secession of Natal from the Republic of South Africa.

1963   **Derleth, A.** *(ed.) The outer reaches.* Consul Books, 172p.
Introduction; first eight stories of original U.S. 1951 publication, *The outer reaches.*

1963   **Dickson, G. R.** *Necromancer.* Mayflower, 190p.
Superman tries to solve galactic problems. [U.S. 1962]

1963   **Gardner, A.** *The escalator.* Frederick Muller, 288p.
Polaris submarine, *Marco Polo*, is hijacked by nuclear disarmers.

1963   **Garrett, R.** *Unwise child.* Mayflower, 192p.
A robot becomes too dangerous to remain on Earth. [U.S. 1962]

1963   **George, P.** *Dr. Strangelove.* Corgi, 146p.
The book of a famous film directed by Stanley Kubrick, *Dr. Strangelove, or How I learned to Stop Worrying and Love the Bomb*, U.K. 1963. The film was based on the earlier story, *Two hours to doom* (1958) by Peter Bryant (i.e. Peter George). The author worked with Kubrick and Terry Southern in writing the script of the film.

[1963]   **Gordon, D. (Payne, D. G.)** *Flight of the Bat.* Hodder & Stoughton, 221p.
Heroic British pilot demonstrates that Russian defence system can be penetrated.

1963   **Gore, W.** *To the Keepers of the Slaughter-House.* Mitre Press, 88p.
Two stories "addressed to all those who think that fundamental problems may be settled, for once and for all, by the application of violence."

1963   **Grant, M.** *(pseud.) Hyper-drive.* Brown, Watson, 160p.
Warfare in space.

1963   **Grisewood, H.** *The recess.* Macdonald, 192p.
A parliamentary recess follows the news of a change in USA defence plans.

1963   **Gunn, J.** *The joy makers.* V. Gollancz, 191p.
A world of the future dedicated to pleasure and the realization of the desires that caused men to rebel. [U.S. 1961]

1963   **Haggard, W. (Clayton, R. H. M.)** *The high wire.* Cassell, 181p.
Espionage and a new, cheap, 'clean' atomic bomb.

1963   **Hamilton, E.** *Battle for the stars.* Mayflower, 192p.
Interplanetary adventures. [U.S. 1961]

1963   **Harrison, H. (Dempsey, H.)** *Death world.* Penguin, 160p.
Settlers on the planet Pyrrus fight against a hostile environment. [U.S. 1960]

1963   **Hay, G.** *(ed.) Hell hath Fury.* Neville Spearman, 240p.
Seven stories originally published in *Unknown Worlds*.

1963   **Heinlein, R. A.** *Methuselah's children.* V. Gollancz, 192p.
A tale of a long-lived group who penetrate interstellar space. [U.S. 1958]

1963   **Hoyle, F. and Hoyle, G.** *Fifth planet.* W. Heinemann, ix, 218p.
The Helios Centre at Harwell controls the first space journey to the planet Achilles.

1963   **Ingrey, D.** *Pig on a lead.* Faber & Faber, 252p.
Adventures in the days after the great catastrophe.

1963   **Knebel, F. and Bailey, C.** *Seven days in May.* Weidenfeld & Nicolson, 342p.
A military coup against the United States government. [U.S. 1962]

1963   **Knight, D.** *(ed.) A century of science fiction.* V. Gollancz, 352p.
Introduction – definitions of science fiction – twenty-six stories on themes of robots, time travel, space, other worlds, aliens, supermen, inventions. [U.S.'1962]

1963   **Kornbluth, C. M. and Pohl, F.** *Search the sky.* Brown, Watson, 158p.
The Wesley Effect makes possible contact with Earth colonists in the far planets. [U.S. 1954]

1963   **Kuttner, H.** *Bypass to otherness.* Consul Books, 155p.
Eight stories. [U.S. 1961]

1963   **Langart, D. T. (Garrett, R.)** *Anything you can do.* Mayflower, 190p.
An alien creature becomes the most feared criminal on Earth. [U.S. 1963]

1963   **Lukens, A. (Detzer, D.)** *Sons of the wolf.* World Distributors, 157p.
Werewolves and adventures in the future. [U.S. 1959]

1963   **Lymington, J. (Chance, J. N.)** *The screaming face.* Hodder & Stoughton, 160p.
Mankind waits for extinction.

1963   **Lymington, J. (Chance, J. N.)** *The sleep eaters.* Hodder & Stoughton, 220p.
Invasion threatens from other beings in space.

1963   **Magidoff, R.** *(ed.) Russian science fiction.* Translated by Doris Johnson. Allen & Unwin, 272p.
Ten short stories by modern Russian writers. [U.S. 1963]

1963   **Maine, C. E. (MacIlwain, D.)** *World without men.* Brown, Watson, 160p.
Experiences of the last man in a world of women.

1963   **Merril, J.** *(ed.) The best of Sci-fi 1.* Mayflower, 384p.
Short stories.

1963   **Miller, W. M.** *Conditionally human.* V. Gollancz, 192p.
Three novellas – robots, theatre, world epidemic.

1963   **Mills, R. P.** *(ed.) The best from Fantasy and Science Fiction*, 10th series. V. Gollancz, 258p.
Sixteen stories. [U.S. 1961]

1963   **Moorcock, M.** *The stealer of souls.* Neville Spearman, 215p.
Five stories about the adventures of Elric of Melniboné.

1963   **Padgett, L. (Kuttner, H.)** *The far reality.* Consul Books, 155p.
The Third World War is a game of Fairy-chess: the Castles are underground cities, the Knights are psychometricians, and the solution to Checkmate lies in the future. [U.S. 1951]

1963   **Padgett, L. (Kuttner, H.)** *Tomorrow & tomorrow.* Consul Books, 106p.
A guardian of Uranium Pile Number One has dreams that suggest he should let the pile explode. [U.S. 1951]

1963   **Paine, L.** *This time tomorrow.* Consul Books, 154p.
Adventures and anxieties on the eve of the Third World War.

1963   **Pohl, F.** *(ed.) The expert dreamers.* V. Gollancz, 228p.
Fifteen stories by scientists. [U.S. 1962]

1963   **Ranzetta, L.** *The Maru invasion.* Brown, Watson, 159p.
Earth endangered by invaders from space.

1963   **Ranzetta, L.** *The night of the death rain.* Brown, Watson, 157p.
Interplanetary disasters.

1963   **Roberts, C.** *Nuclear subtraction.* Brown, Watson, 159p.
An after-the-disaster tale of survival and endurance.

1963   **Sellings, A. (Ley, H.)** *The silent speakers.* D. Dobson, 184p.
Personal and political consequences follow when a man discovers he has telepathic powers. Published U.S. 1962 as *Telepath.*

1963   **Sheckley, R.** *Immortality Inc.* V. Gollancz, 152p.
Body-snatching in the days of transplants. First published U.S. 1958 as *Immortality delivered.*

1963   **Simak, C. D.** *They walked like men.* V. Gollancz, 224p.
Alien invasion of Earth. [U.S. 1962]

1963   **Tenn, W. (Klass, P.)** *Time in advance.* V. Gollancz, 153p.
Four stories. [U.S. 1958]

1963   **Van Vogt, A. E.** *Away and beyond.* Panther, 219p.
Eight stories. [U.S. 1952]

1963   **Vonnegut, K.** *Cat's cradle.* V. Gollancz, 231p.
An attack on the human capacity for self-deception. [U.S. 1963]

1963   **Wade, T.** *The voice from Baru.* Brown, Watson, 160p.
Spacemen fight to survive on a strange planet.

1963   **West, M.** *The shoes of the fisherman.* W. Heinemann, 302p.
A Russian refugee is elected Pope and sets out to work for world peace. [U.S. 1963]

1963   **Wibberley, L.** *The mouse on the Moon.* Frederick Muller, 190p.
The Duchy of Grand Fenwick enters the space race. [U.S. 1962]

1963   **Woodman, G.** *The heretic.* Shipyard Press (Whitstable), 11p.
An Orwellian tale of rebellion in a regimented future world.

[1963] **Wright, L.** *Assignment Luther.* Digit Books, 158p.
Colonial Board sends an agent to investigate a planet of the star Luther Four.
Based on stories published in *New Worlds Science Fiction* 1955 and 1957.

1963   **Zeigfreid, K. (Fanthorpe, R. L.)** *Android.* Brown, Watson, 160p.
A synthetic man does his utmost to make life miserable on Earth.

1964   **Aldiss, B.** *(ed.) The dark light years.* Faber & Faber, 190p.
A sardonic tale of the utods who are very different from human beings.

1964   **Aldiss, B.** *Greybeard.* Faber & Faber, 237p.
Travel and adventure in the sterile future when the old have inherited the earth.

1964   **Aldiss, B.** *(ed.) Introducing SF.* Faber & Faber, 224p.
Twelve stories; editorial introduction.

1964   **Aldiss, B.** *(ed.) Yet more Penguin Science Fiction.* Penguin, 208p.
Introduction; twelve stories.

1964   **Anderson, P.** *Strangers from Earth.* Mayflower, 190p.
Eight short stories. [U.S. 1961]

1964   **Anderson, P.** *Time and stars.* V. Gollancz, 206p.
Five stories – space travel, men and aliens. [U.S. 1964].

1964   **Asimov, I.** *The Martian way.* D. Dobson, 222p.
Four stories. [U.S. 1955].

1964   **Ball, B. N.** *(ed.) Tales of science fiction.* H. Hamilton, 158p.
Preface – 'Science fiction is about "ifs". It looks at the trends in scientific
progress and takes them a stage further" – nine stories.

1964   **Ballard, J. G.** *The terminal beach.* V. Gollancz, 224p.
Twelve stories – themes of space and time.

1964   **Barrett, W. E.** *The fools of time.* Heinemann, 309p.
A scientist perfects an anti-catabolic drug which halts the aging process. An age-
race between Russian and American scientists follows. [U.S. 1963]

1964   **Biggle, L.** *All the colours of darkness.* D. Dobson, 210p.
Complications follow after the invention of an instantaneous matter transmitter.
[U.S. 1963]

1964   **Blish, J.** *A life for the stars.* Faber & Faber, 148p.
Second in *Cities in Flight* series: the city of Scranton takes off into space. [U.S.
1962]

1964   **Boardman, T.** *(ed.) Connoisseur's SF.* Penguin, 233p.
[1965]   Introduction; ten stories.

1964   **Boulle, P.** *Monkey planet.* Translated from the French by Xan Fielding.
          Secker & Warburg, 223p.
          An allegorical tale about life on a planet in which the hunters are intelligent apes
          and the hunted are naked human beings. Originally published 1963 as *La
          Planète des singes,* and source of the film, *Planet of the Apes,* produced by 20th
          Century-Fox in 1967.

1964   **Bradbury, R.** *The machineries of joy.* R. Hart-Davis, 239p.
          Twenty stories. [U.S. 1964].

1964   **Braddon, R.** *The year of the angry rabbit.* W. Heinemann, 180p.
          Vicious rabbits threaten the safety of Australia and the world.

1964   **Brooke-Rose, C.** *Out.* M. Joseph, 196p.
          An inverted future world: the colourless are unreliable and the coloured of every
          shade are the dominant groups.

1964   **Bruckner, K. C.** *The hour of the robots.* Translated from the German
          by Frances Lobb. Burke, 187p.
          Two robots take part in the cold war between Russia and the United States.
          Published 1951 as *Nur zwei Roboter?*

1964   **Budrys, A.** *The furious future.* V. Gollancz, 192p.
          Nine stories. First published U.S. 1963 as *Budrys's Inferno.*

1964   **Budrys, A.** *Some will not die.* Mayflower-Dell, 159p.
          The rigours of life in the days after the Plague. [U.S. 1961]

1964   **Caidin, M.** *Marooned.* Hodder & Stoughton, 378p.
          The retro-rockets fail to fire and an astronaut stays in earth orbit. [U.S. 1964]

1964   **Carnell, J.** *(ed.) New writings in SF 1.* D. Dobson, 192p.
          Introduction; five stories.

1964   **Carnell, J.** *(ed.) New writings in SF 2.* D. Dobson, 191p.
          Introduction; eight stories.

1964   **Chandler, A. B.** *The deep reaches of space.* H. Jenkins, 190p.
          Shipwreck and adventures in deep space.

1964   **Chandler, A. B.** *Rendezvous on a lost world.* H. Jenkins, 190p.
          Spaceships crew have extraordinary adventures in one of the Rim worlds. [U.S.
          1961].

1964   **Charbonneau, L.** *The sentinel stars.* Transworld, 156p.
          TRH-247 leads the revolt against the oppressive and highly organized world state
          of the 22nd Century. [U.S. 1963]

1964   **Clement, H. (Stubbs, H. C.)** *Close to critical.* V. Gollancz, 190p.
          Communications established with the planet Tenebra. [U.S. 1964]

1964   **Clement, H. (Stubbs, H. C.)** *Cycle of fire.* V. Gollancz, 195p.
Adventure and discovery on the planet Abyormen. [U.S. 1957]

1964   **Cooper, E.** *Transit.* Faber & Faber, 232p.
Experimental investigations on the planet Achernar to decide the race most suited to control a galactic area.

[1964]   **Cooper, S.** *Mandrake.* Hodder & Stoughton, 253p.
Regimentation and terror in the days when a mysterious Minister of Planning directs the nation.

1964   **Creasey, J.** *The sleep.* Hodder & Stoughton, 192p.
Dr Palfrey to the rescue of a world that has gone to sleep.

1964   **Dobraczynski, J.** *To drain the sea.* Translated from the Polish by H. C. Stevens. Heinemann, 279p.
Most of Europe destroyed by a nuclear explosion; the survivors face a changed world. First published 1961 as *Wyczerpać morze.*

1964   **Donne, M.** *Claret, sandwiches and sin.* W. Heinemann, 200p.
An amusing tale of universal peace and how it is maintained in the happy world of the future.

1964   **The Editors** *The Saturday Evening Post Reader of fantasy and science fiction.* Selected by the Editors of the *Saturday Evening Post.* Souvenir Press, 311p.
Twenty stories. [U.S. 1964]

1964   **Farmer, P. J.** *Strange relations.* V. Gollancz, 189p.
Five stories. [U.S. 1960]

1964   **Galouye, D. F.** *Counterfeit world.* V. Gollancz, 159p.
Conflict between the real world and the simulated world of electromechanical models. [U.S. 1964]

1964   **Galouye, D. F.** *The last leap.* Corgi, 172p.
Seven stories on aspects of "the super-mind".

1964   **Gordon, R. (Hough, S. B.)** *The time factor.* Gibbs & Phillips, 125p.
A time machine enables traveller to make pictures of the future. First published U.S. 1962 as *First through time.*

1964   **Harness, C. L.** *The paradox men.* Faber & Faber, 256p.
An extravagant tale of time-travel and force-screens. First published U.S. 1953 as *Flight into yesterday.*

1964   **Harrison, H. (Dempsey, H.)** *The ethical engineer.* V. Gollancz, 176p.
The adventures of two castaways on a distant planet. [U.S. 1964]

1964   **Heinlein, R. A.** *The unpleasant profession of Jonathan Hoag.* D. Dobson, 256p.
Six stories. [U.S. 1969]

1964   **Hodder-Williams, C.** *The Main Experiment.* Hodder & Stoughton, 224p.
A scientist fights malevolent forces that threaten the world.

1964   **Hoyle, F. and Elliot, J.** *Andromeda breakthrough.* Souvenir Press, 192p.
Based on a BBC television serial: the nations of the world unite against a menace from outer space.

1964   **Judd, C. (Kornbluth, C. M. and Merril, J.)** *Gunner Cade.* V. Gollancz, 218p.
Heroic adventures of an Armsman in the service of the Emperor. [U.S. 1952]

1964   **Knight, D.** *Beyond the barrier.* V. Gollancz, 188p.
Time travel and time paradoxes. [U.S. 1964]

1964   **Knight, D.** *In deep.* V. Gollancz, 158p.
Seven stories. [U.S. 1963]

1964   **Kornbluth, C. M.** *The syndic.* Faber & Faber, 223p.
After World War III the United States is divided between Syndic rule on the East coast and the Mob who control the West. [U.S. 1953]

1964   **Lane, J. (Dakers, E.)** *A state of mind.* Frederick Muller, 204p.
The search for values in the rigorously controlled world of the future.

1964   **Long, F. B.** *It was the day of the robot.* D. Dobson, 141p.
Love and rebellion in the regimented world of the future. [U.S. 1963]

1964   **Lymington, J. (Chance, J. N.)** *The night spiders.* Corgi, 160p.
Twenty-eight stories.

1964   **Lymington, J. (Chance, J. N.)** *Froomb!* Hodder & Stoughton, 223p.
A man travels forward in time and sees his own future.

1964   **McCutchan, P.** *Bowering's breakwater.* Harrap, 248p.
The outbreak of a world war causes difficulties for a British liner.

1964   **McIntosh, J. T. (MacGregor, J. M.)** *The Noman Way.* Digit Books, 158p.
On the planet Noman the highly lethal Sports keep the population stable.

1964   **Merril, J.** *(ed.) The best of Sci-Fi 2.* Mayflower, 400p.
Short stories.

1964   **Mills, R. P.** *(ed.) The best from Fantasy and SF, 11th Series.* V. Gollancz, 255p.
Introduction – a poem by Walt Whitman – thirteen stories. [U.S. 1963]

1964   **Mills, R. P.** *(ed.) The worlds of science fiction.* V. Gollancz, 349p.
Sixteen stories. [U.S. 1963]

1964   **Nourse, A. E.** *Beyond infinity.* Corgi, 174p.
First published U.K. 1962 as *Tiger by the tail.*

1964   **Nourse, A.E.** *The counterfeit man*. D. Dobson, 192p.
Eleven stories. [U.S. 1963].

1964   **Randall, R.** *The shrouded planet*. Mayflower, 189p.
Space travel and adventurers.

1964   **Ranzetta, L.** *Yellow inferno*. Brown, Watson, 158p.
A demon scientist menaces the Western world.

1964   **Ray, R.** *No stars for us*. Brown, Watson, 158p.
Trouble at a rocket base.

1964   **Sellings, A. (Ley, A.)** *The uncensored man*. D. Dobson, 183p.
Themes of 'inner space'.

1964   **Sheckley, R.** *Journey beyond tomorrow*. V. Gollancz, 189p.
An ironic tale of life in the future. [U.S. 1962]

1964   **Simak, C.** *All the traps of Earth*. Four Square, 143p.
Four stories from original collection published U.S. 1962.

1964   **Simak, C.** *The night of the Puudly*. Four Square, 143p.
Five stories from U.S. original 1962 *All the traps of Earth*.

1964   **Simak, C.** *Way Station*. V. Gollancz, 224p.
Enoch Wallace maintains a galactic trans-shipment centre on Earth, unknown to all until a government agency begins investigations. [U.S. 1963]

1964   **Smith, T.** *The best of Sci-Fi 3*. Mayflower, 384p.
Introduction; thirty stories. [U.S. 1963]

1964   **Sutton, J.** *The missile lords*. Sidgwick & Jackson, 379p.
Moral, political and commercial interests involved in the launching of a new rocket. [U.S. 1963].

1964   **Tubb, E. C.** *Moon Base*. H. Jenkins, 175p.
Adventures at the British Moon Base.

1964   **Verron R.** *The day of the dust*. Wright & Brown, 190p.
A race of malevolent creatures threatens all life on Earth.

1964   **Wallis, D.** *Only lovers left alive*. Anthony Blond, 256p.
A moral tale about violence and viciousness in the days when the only citizens are teenagers.

1964   **Wilkinson, B.** *Night of the short knives*. Hodder & Stoughton, 280p.
Intrigue by Russians and French at SHAPE: i.e. SHAFE.

1964   **Wright, L.** *Space born*. H. Jenkins, 173p.
Space adventure and the fight for the safety of the world.

1964   **Wyndham, J.** *The John Wyndham omnibus*. M. Joseph, 532p.
Contains: *The day of the Triffids, The Kraken wakes, The Chrysalids*.

1965   **Aldiss, B.** *(ed.) Best science fiction stories of Brian Aldiss.* Faber & Faber, 253p.
Introduction; fourteen stories.

1965   **Aldiss, B.** *Earthworks.* Faber & Faber, 155p.
Adventures in Africa, the only place where the soil is still fertile.

1965   **Amis, K. & Conquest, R.** *(eds.) Spectrum IV.* V. Gollancz, 320p.
Opens with a discussion, "Unreal estates", between C. S. Lewis, Aldiss and Amis; fourteen stories.

1965   **Anderson, P.** *Shield.* D. Dobson, 158p.
Adventures of a man whom nothing can harm. [U.S. 1963]

1965   **Anderson, P.** *Trader to the stars.* V. Gollancz, 176p.
Three space adventure stories. [U.S. 1964].

1965   **Anderson, W. C.** *Adam M-1.* Alvin Redman, 255p.
The Americans construct an artificial man for space travel. [U.S. 1964]

1965   **Baldwin, B.** *The red dust.* Hale, 190p.
An explosion in Antarctica starts a devastating plague.

1965   **Ball, B. N.** *Sundog.* D. Dobson, 216p.
Space adventures on the run from the Moonbase to Pluto.

1965   **Ballard, J. G.** *The drought.* J. Cape, 252p.
In a desolate world, without rain, the survivors hoard water and struggle to keep alive. First published U.S. 1964 as *The burning world.*

1965   **Blackburn, J.** *A ring of roses.* Cape, 187p.
A bubonic plague carrier threatens the safety of the world.

1965   **Blacker, I. R.** *Chain of command.* Cassell, 186p.
A tale of espionage in the future when the Russians begin to mass troops along their frontiers.

1965   **Blish, J.** *Best science fiction stories of James Blish.* Faber & Faber, 224p.
A personal selection of seven stories by James Blish. U.K. only.

1965   **Boardman, T.** *(ed.) The unfriendly future.* Four Square, 178p.
Introduction; six stories.

1965   **Boulle, P.** *The garden on the Moon.* Translated from the French by Xan Fielding. Secker & Warburg, 315p.
Space race themes. Originally published 1964 as *Le Jardin de Kanashima.*

1965   **Bradbury, E. P. (Moorcock, M.)** *Barbarians of Mars.* Compact Books, 158p.
Third in the Michael Kane adventures: Mars saved from the Green Death.

1965   **Bradbury, E. P. (Moorcock, M.)** *Blades of Mars.* Compact Books, 156p.
Second in Michael Kane adventures: heroic and romantic exploits on Mars.

1965   **Bradbury, E. P. (Moorcock, M.)** *Warriors of Mars.* Compact Books, 157p.
Opens the Kane trilogy: Professor Michael Kane, conveyed by matter transmitter to Mars, becomes a planetary hero.

1965   **Brunner, J.** *The long result.* Faber & Faber, 204p.
The struggle for power begins when Earth discovers that it may be inferior to its own space colony.

1965   **Brunner, J.** *Now then.* Mayflower-Dell, 143p.
Three novellas.

1965   **Brunner, J.** *Telepathist.* Faber & Faber, 238p.
Experiences of a cripple who discovers he has telepathic powers. Originally published U.S. 1964 as *The whole man.*

1965   **Bulmer, H. K.** *The demons.* Roberts & Vinter, 190p.
War against the enemies of the Archon Empire. [U.S. 1964]

1965   **Burkett, W. R.** *Sleeping planet.* V. Gollancz, 297p.
Earth invaded by aliens from space. [U.S. 1965]

1965   **Burns, A.** *Europe after the rain.* Calder & Boyars, 128p.
A search and journey through a nightmare, devastated Europe of the future – a projection of contemporary disorder.

1965   **Campbell, J. W.** *(ed.) Analog Anthology.* D. Dobson, 797p.
Introduction by Campbell: twenty-six short stories of the 1950s. First published U.S. in *Prologue to Analog*, 1962, *Analog 1*, 1963, *Analog 2*, 1964.

1965   **Carnell, J.** *(ed.) Lambda One.* Penguin, 206p.
Eight stories. [U.S. 1964].

1965   **Carnell, J.** *(ed.) New writings in SF3.* D. Dobson, 189p.
Introduction; three stories.

1965   **Carnell, J.** *(ed.) New writings in SF4.* D. Dobson, 186p.
Introduction; seven stories.

1965   **Carnell, J.** *(ed.) New writings in SF5.* D. Dobson, 190p.
Introduction; seven stories.

1965   **Carnell, J** *(ed.) New writings in SF6.* D. Dobson, 190p.
Seven stories about mental powers.

[1965]   **Charbonneau, L. H.** *The Specials.* H. Jenkins, 191p.
A group of individuals with telepathic powers fight to liberate the world from the domination of a dangerous syndicate. [U.S. 1964]

1965   **Christopher, J. (Youd, C. S.)** *A wrinkle in the skin.* Hodder &
Stoughton, 220p.
Struggles of the survivors after gigantic earthquakes have devastated the world.

1965   **Clarke, A. C.** *An Arthur C. Clarke omnibus.* Sidgwick & Jackson,
508p.
Contains: *Childhood's end, Prelude to space, Expedition to Earth.*

1965   **Compton, D. G.** *The quality of mercy.* Hodder & Stoughton, 157p.
Life on an American base in the days when a mysterious disease is killing off
populations.

1965   **Daventry, L.** *A man of double deed.* V. Gollancz, 176p.
Telepathy and the composite mind in the twenty-first century.

1965   **Davidson, A.** *The best from "Fantasy and Science Fiction" 12th Series.*
V. Gollancz, 225p.
Fourteen stories. [U.S. 1963]

1965   **Davies, L. P.** *The artificial man.* H. Jenkins, 189p.
A problem of identity in the days when East threatens West.

1965   **Derleth, A.** *(ed.) Far boundaries.* Consul Books, 180p.
Twenty stories. [U.S. 1951]

1965   **Gardner, A. H.** *Assignment Tahiti.* F. Muller, 224p.
A romance of the revolt of Communist China.

1965   **George, P.** *Commander-1.* W. Heinemann, 253p.
Thermonuclear war and the great holocaust-to-come.

1965   **Gilliatt, P.** *One by one.* Secker & Warburg, 190p.
The horrors of the plague in London.

1965   **Gold, H. L.** *(ed.) The old die rich.* D. Dobson, 250p.
Twelve stories. [U.S. 1955].

1965   **Gold, H. L.** *(ed.) The weird ones.* D. Dobson, 173p.
Seven stories. [U.S. 1962]

1965   **Gray, A.** *(pseud.) The penetrators.* Souvenir Press, 314p.
The author states that the book "had to be written because ICBM warfare will
never be anything but racial suicide." [U.S. 1965].

1965   **Green, J.** *The loafers of Refuge.* V. Gollancz, 176p.
Earthmen learn to understand the differences between themselves and other
kinds of rational life. [U.S. 1965]

1965   **Griffiths, J.** *The survivors.* Collins, 159p.
An after-the-disaster story of the struggle to survive.

1965   **Hale, M.** *The Fourth Reich.* J. Cape, 189p.
Espionage and adventure in Central Africa.

1965   **Hamilton, E.** *The haunted stars.* H. Jenkins, 176p.
Machines from outer worlds discovered on the Moon. [U.S. 1960]

1965   **Harrison, H. (Dempsey, H.)** *Bill, the galactic hero.* V. Gollancz, 160p.
An ironic tale of savage wars in space. [U.S. 1965].

1965   **Harrison, H. (Dempsey, H.)** *Two tales and eight tomorrows.*
V. Gollancz, 191p.
Ten stories. [U.S. 1968].

1965   **Heinlein, R.** *Farnham's Freehold.* D. Dobson, 315p.
An American family survives the missiles, bombs, epidemics and other horrors of
the future. [U.S. 1964].

1965   **Heinlein, R.** *Glory road.* New English Library, 256p.
Strange foes and heroic adventures in space. [U.S. 1963]

1965   **Heinlein, R. A.** *Stranger in a strange land.* New English Library, 400p.
An ironic tale of life, religion and sexual relations in a brave new future world.
[U.S. 1961]

1965   **Hersey, J.** *White Lotus.* H. Hamilton, 615p.
Experiences of American slaves in a future time when the Chinese dominate the
world. [U.S. 1965]

1965   **High, P. E.** *The prodigal Sun.* Compact Books, 190p.
A man returns from space to threaten Earth. [U.S. 1964]

1965   **Irving, C.** *The 38th floor.* W. Heinemann, 317p.
International politics: American, Chinese, and Russian manoeuvres at the United
Nations. [U.S. 1965].

1965   **Knight, D.** *(ed.) A century of great short science fiction novels.*
V. Gollancz, 379p.
Six novels, from Stevenson to Heinlein, each with a note on the author. [U.S.
1964].

1965   **Knight, D.** *(ed.) Thirteen French science fiction stories.* Corgi, 166p.
Introduction, thirteen stories, Afterword on the authors. [U.S. 1965]

1965   **Knight, D.** *(ed.) Tomorrow x 4.* Gold Medal, 176p.
Introduction, four stories. [U.S. 1964]

1965   **Kuttner, H.** *The best of Kuttner, No. 1.* Mayflower, 286p.
Fifteen stories. [U.K. only]

1965   **Kuttner, H.** *Return to otherness.* Mayflower, 288p.
Eight stories. [U.S. 1962]

1965   **Leiber, F.** *The big time.* New English Library, 127p.
Group of people transported to the future in order to change the course of history. [U.S. 1961]

1965   **Lymington, J. (Chance, J. N.)** *The green drift.* Hodder & Stoughton, 191p.
A space invasion story.

1965   **Lymington, J. (Chance, J. N.)** *The Star Witches.* Hodder & Stoughton, 128p.
An alien world seeks to destroy Earth.

1965   **Merril, J.** *(ed.) The best of Sci-Fi 4.* Mayflower, 389p.
Twenty-eight stories. [U.S. 1963]

1965   **Miller, W. M.** *The view from the stars.* V. Gollancz, 192p.
Nine stories. [U.S. 1965]

1965   **Moorcock, M.** *The best of New Worlds.* Compact Books, 318p.
Selections from the magazine *New Worlds.*

1965   **Moorcock, M.** *The Fire clown.* Compact Books, 160p.
A mysterious being brings hope to Earth in the days of the Federation of Solar Planets.

1965   **Moorcock, M.** *Stormbringer.* H. Jenkins, 190p.
Elric of Melniboné defeats the Lords of Chaos and blows the Horn of Fate to herald the new world: five stories.

1965   **Moorcock, M.** *The sundered worlds.* Compact Books, 191p.
The human race is led to safety from a cosmic disaster.

1965   **Muller, R.** *The lost diaries of Albert Smith.* J. Cape, 352p.
An account of "The Movement", a political party that seeks to restore the greatness of the British people.

1965   **Pincher, C.** *Not with a bang.* Weidenfeld & Nicolson, 302p.
World catastrophe follows on the discovery of a drug that halts the onset of old age.

1965   **Pohl, F.** *(ed.) The seventh Galaxy reader.* V. Gollancz, 247p.
Introduction; fifteen stories. [U.S. 1964].

1965   **Pohl, F. and Williamson, J.** *The reefs of space.* D. Dobson, 192p.
The desire for freedom in the over-organized world of the future. [U.S. 1965]

1965   **Raphael, R.** *The thirst quenchers.* V. Gollancz, 174p.
Radiation engineers struggle to save the world from drought.

1965   **Reynolds, M.** *The Earth War.* Four Square, 141p.
In the twenty-first century it is forbidden to fight with weapons developed after 1900. [U.S. 1964]

1965 **Ross, J.** *A view of the island.* Hutchinson, 200p.
A post-atomic tale: the dead continue to exist after the holocaust.

1965 **Russell, E. F.** *Somewhere a voice.* D. Dobson, 184p.
Introduction; seven stories.

1965 **Simak, C. D.** *Worlds without end.* H. Jenkins, 176p.
Three stories. [U.S. 1956]

1965 **Sturgeon, T. (Waldo, E. H.)** *The joyous invasions.* V. Gollancz, 208p.
Three stories.

1965 **Vance, J.** *The dragon masters.* D. Dobson, 136p.
On the planet Aerlith the Utter Men fight their wars and seek their inheritance.
[U.S. 1962]

1965 **Wallace, I.** *The man.* Cassell, 760p.
Complications in the United States when the fourth President after John
Kennedy is a negro. [U.S. 1964]

1965 **White, J.** *Open prison.* Four Square, 158p.
Interplanetary conflict and escape adventures.

1965 **Wynd, O.** *Death the red flower.* Cassell, 224p.
Chinese plot to involve Britain in a total war.

1966 **Aldiss, B.** *The saliva tree.* Faber & Faber, 232p.
Ten stories: only three set in future.

1966 **Amis, K. & Conquest, R.** *(eds.) Spectrum 5.* V. Gollancz, 272p.
Introduction; eight stories.

1966 **Anderson, P.** *The corridors of time.* V. Gollancz, 209p.
Space and time adventures. [U.S. 1965]

1966 **Anderson, P.** *Planet of no return.* D. Dobson, 105p.
Interplanetary travel and adventure. [U.S. 1956]

1966 **Anderson, P.** *The Star Fox.* V. Gollancz, 288p.
The space ship, Star Fox, sets off for the great war between Earth and the
Aleriona. [U.S. 1965],

1966 **Anderson, P.** *Three worlds to conquer.* Mayflower, 142p.
Planetary adventures on Ganymede & Jupiter. [U.S. 1964]

1966 **Anderson, P.** *Virgin planet.* Mayflower, 156p.
A solitary male arrives on a planet inhabited by women. [U.S. 1959]

1966 **Asimov, I.** *An Isaac Asimov Omnibus.* Sidgwick & Jackson, 548p.
Contains: *Foundation, Foundation and Empire, Second Foundation.* [U.S. 1964]

1966   **Asimov, I.** *Fantastic voyage*. Based on the screenplay by Harry Kleiner, adapted by David Duncan from the original story by Otto Klement and Jay Lewis Bixby. D. Dobson, 211p.
A submarine, the size of a molecule, travels through the bloodstream of a man suffering from a clot of blood on the brain. [U.S. 1966]

1966   **Ballard, J. G.** *The crystal world*. J. Cape, 224p.
In a remote area of the African jungle all organic matter begins to crystallize.

1966   **Barren, C. and Abel, R.** *Trivana I*. Panther, 171p.
Colonization of Venus.

1966   **Barter, A. F. and Wilson, R.** *(eds.) Untravelled worlds*. MacMillan & St. Martin's Press, New York, viii, 168p.
Editor's introduction; twelve stories.

1966   **Biggle, L.** *The fury out of time*. D. Dobson, 257p.
Space travel and interplanetary communications. [U.S. 1965]

1966   **Boardman, T.** *(ed.) An ABC of SF*. Four Square, 205p.
Introduction; twenty-six stories.

1966   **Boulle, P.** *Time out of mind*. Selected and translated from the French by Xan Fielding. Secker & Warburg, 254p.
Nine stories.

1966   **Brown, J. G.** *(ed.) From Frankenstein to Andromeda*. Macmillan, viii, 150p.
Fifteen entries – short stories and extracts from book-length fiction.

1966   **Brunner, J.** *No other gods but me*. Roberts & Vintner, 159p.
Three novellas.

1966   **Bulmer, H. K.** *Behold the stars*. Mayflower, 126p.
Warfare in space as men from Earth begin to penetrate the galaxies. [U.S. 1965]

1966   **Burroughs, W.** *Nova Express*. J. Cape, 180p.
A well-known attack on the false and vicious in American life, on the corrupters of language and the dealers in lives – all projected into the running battle between the police and the partisans of all nations. [U.S. 1964]

1966   **Calisher, H.** *Journal from Ellipsia*. Secker & Warburg, 375p.
An odd tale about an envoy from the distant planet of Ellipsia. [U.S. 1965]

1966   **Campbell, J. W.** *(ed.) Analog 3*. D. Dobson, 269p.
Introduction; eight stories. [U.S. 1965]

1966   **Campbell, J. W.** *The thing from outer space*. Tandem Books, 220p.
First published U.K. 1952 as *The thing and other stories*.

1966   **Carnell, J.** *(ed.) New writings in SF7*. D. Dobson, 190p.
Introduction; seven stories.

1966   **Carnell, J.** *(ed.) New writings in SF8.* D. Dobson, 190p.
Introduction; seven stories.

1966   **Carnell, J.** *(ed.) New writings in SF9.* D. Dobson, 187p.
Seven stories about problems of over-population

1966   **Carter, M.** *Minutes of the night.* Heinemann, 304p.
Personal relationships and moral considerations as the world approaches a nuclear war.

1966   **Charbonneau, L.** *No place on earth.* H. Jenkins, 188p.
Revolt in the twenty-third century against the tyrannical Leader Party. [U.S. 1958]

1966   **Clark, W.** *Number 10.* W. Heinemann, 215p.
The author, formerly press secretary to Anthony Eden, writes about the dealings of a Prime Minister with an emergent African nation.

1966   **Colvin, J. (Moorcock, M.)** *The deep fix.* Compact Books, 160p.
Short stories.

1966   **Compton, D. C.** *Farewell, Earth's bliss.* Hodder & Stoughton, 192p.
Conflict on Mars, a convict settlement of the space age.

1966   **Cooper, E.** *All Fools' Day.* Hodder & Stoughton, 192p.
Mass suicide, brought on by solar radiation, almost destroys mankind.

1966   **Coppel, A.** *Dark December.* H. Jenkins, 176p.
A horror story of life in a devastated United States after a two-year nuclear war. [U.S. 1960]

1966   **Crispin, E.** *(ed.)* **Montgomery, R. B.)***Best SF Six.* Faber & Faber, 252p.
Fourteen stories.

1966   **Cummings, Ray** *Brigands of the Moon.* Consul Books, 192p.
Heroic adventures in space. [U.S. 1931]

1966   **Davidson, A.** *(ed.) The best from Fantasy and Science Fiction, Thirteenth Series.* V. Gollancz, 256p.
Introduction, thirteen stories. [U.S. 1964].

1966   **Davidson, A.** *(ed.) The best from Fantasy and Science Fiction, Fourteenth Series.* V. Gollancz, 251p.
Introduction; seventeen stories. [U.S. 1965]

1966   **De Camp, L. S.** *The floating continent.* Compact Books, 158p.
Hero rescues a princess from the pirates of planet Krishna. First published U.S. 1962 as *The search for Zei.*

1966   **De Camp, L. S.** *A planet called Krishna.* Compact Books, 160p.
Space adventures and romance on the banned planet of Krishna. First published
U.S. 1954 as *Cosmic manhunt.*

1966   **Dick, P. K.** *The three stigmata of Palmer Eldritch.* J. Cape, 278p.
Interplanetary traffic, drug peddlers, space colonists. [U.S. 1965]

1966   **Disch, T. M.** *102 H Bombs.* Compact, 192p.
Introduction; fourteen stories.

1966   **Evans, I. O.** *(ed.) Science fiction through the ages 1.* Panther, 156p.
Introduction, twelve stories, bibliography.

1966   **Evans, I. O.** *(ed.) Science fiction through the ages 2.* Panther, 174p.
Introduction, twelve stories, bibliography.

1966   **Galouye, D.** *The lost perception.* V. Gollancz, 190p.
Earth struggles to contain an alien invasion.

1966   **Gantz, F. K.** *Not in solitude.* D. Dobson, 240p.
Adventures on Mars. [U.S. 1959]

1966   **Godwin, F.** *The towers of pain.* Jarrolds, 207p.
A criminal conspiracy to seize control of the United Kingdom.

1966   **Gotlieb, P.** *Sunburst.* Coronet, 160p.
Children with supernormal powers, the consequence of a reactor explosion,
terrify their world.

1966   **Harker, K.** *The Symmetrians.* Compact, 160p.
After an atomic war, a cult of Absolute Symmetry becomes the world religion.

1966   **Harrison, H. (Dempsey, H.)** *Plague from space.* V. Gollancz, 218p.
An epidemic begins in New York when a space ship returns from Jupiter with an
unknown virus. [U.S. 1965]

1966   **Harrison, H. (Dempsey, H.)** *The Stainless Steel Rat.* New English
Library, 158p.
Slippery Jim di Griz, the most successful criminal in the galaxy, reforms and joins
the Special Corps. [U.S. 1961]

1966   **Heinlein, R. A.** *A Heinlein triad.* V. Gollancz, 426p.
The stories are: Puppet Master, Magic Inc., Waldo. [First published U.S. 1965 as
Three by Heinlein].

1966   **Heinlein, R. A.** *The menace from earth.* D. Dobson, 255p.
Eight stories. [U.S. 1959].

[1966]   **Heinlein, R. A.** *A Robert Heinlein Omnibus.* Sidgwick & Jackson,
644p.
Contains: *Beyond this horizon, The man who sold the Moon, The green hills of
Earth.* [U.S. 1959]

1966   **Henderson, Z.** *The anything box.* V. Gollancz, 205p.
Fourteen stories. [U.S. 1965]

1966   **Henderson, Z.** *The people: no different flesh.* V. Gollancz, 223p.
Six stories. [U.S. 1967]

1966   **Herbert, F.** *Dune.* V. Gollancz, 430p.
Paul Muad-Dib fights for his own against the House of Harkonnen and the
Padisha Emperor Shaddam IV. A classic of its kind. [U.S. 1965]

1966   **Hill, D.** *(ed.) Window on the future.* Hart-Davis, 159p.
Introduction; seven stories in which each author "isolates a feature of today's
world – speculates on its possible development and effects – and creates a future
in which those effects are realised".

1966   **Howard, H. (Ognall, L. H.)** *Counterfeit.* Collins, 192p.
Arabs plot to flood the world markets with counterfeit sterling.

1966   **Howard, I.** *(ed.) Things.* Mayflower, 172p.
Six stories. [U.S. 1963]

1966   **Hoyle, F.** *October the first is too late.* W. Heinemann, 200p.
Social and political problems follow when the England of 1966, the Europe of
1917, and the Greece of 425 B.C. begin to exist simultaneously.

1966   **Hunter, J.** *The flame.* Faber & Faber, 279p.
The New Vigour movement and the dangers of an authoritarian right-wing
political party.

1966   **Jenkins, G.** *Hunter-Killer.* Collins, 288p.
Submarine adventures.

1966   **Jones, D. F.** *Colossus.* R. Hart-Davis, 246p.
A highly advanced defence computer makes contact with its Russian counterpart.

1966   **Judd, C. (Kornbluth, C. M. and Merril, J.)** *Outpost Mars.* New
English Library, 192p.
Space adventures. [U.S. 1952]

1966   **Keyes, D.** *Flowers for Algernon.* Cassell, 274p.
Experiences of a moron used as a guinea pig by a team of scientists who have
developed a technique to increase intelligence.

1966   **Knight, D.** *(ed.) The dark side.* D. Dobson, 241p.
Introduction; twelve stories. [U.S. 1965]

1966   **Knight, D.** *(ed.) Orbit 1.* Whiting & Wheaton, 192p.
Introduction; nine previously unpublished stories. [U.S. 1966]

1966   **Knight, D.** *(ed.) The other foot.* Whiting & Wheaton, 159p.
An accidental exchange of minds brings extraordinary complications. First
published U.S. 1965 as *Mind switch.*

1966   **Kornbluth, C. M.** *(ed.) Science fiction showcase.* Whiting & Wheaton, 268p.
Twelve stories [U.S. 1959]

1966   **Kuttner, H.** *The best of Kuttner, No.2.* Mayflower, 287p.
Fourteen stories. [U.K. only]

1966   **Kuttner, H.** *The dark world.* Mayflower, 127p.
Adventures in a parallel world. [U.S. 1965]

1966   **Leiber, F.** *Gather, Darkness!* New English Library, 192p.
Events after the Second Atomic Age and the end of a false religion. [U.S. 1950]

1966   **Leiber, F.** *The silver eggheads.* Four Square, 192p.
Satirical vision of the revolt against the robot-censors and computer-word-machines of a future America. [U.S. 1961]

1966   **Long, F. B.** *This strange tomorrow.* Brown, Watson, 160p.
A romance – two persons lost in space. [U.S. 1966]

1966   **Maine, C. E.** *B.E.A.S.T.* Hodder & Stoughton, 190p.
Danger follows when things go wrong with the Biological Evolutionary Animal Simulation Test.

1966   **McCutchan, P.** *A time for survival.* Harrap, 208p.
An after-the-bomb story.

1966   **Mair, A.** *The Douglas Affair.* W. Heinemann, 244p.
A Scottish nationalist movement is ruthlessly suppressed by the government.

1966   **Mead, S.** *The carefully considered rape of the world.* Macdonald, 245p.
The old science fiction plot – the artificial insemination of the world's women by creatures from another planet. [U.S. 1966]

1966   **Merril, J.** *(ed.) The best of Sci-Fi: 5.* Mayflower, 317p.
Introduction; twenty-one stories. [U.S. 1956]

1966   **Moorcock, M.** *The twilight man.* Compact, 190p.
Fear and its consequences in the days when the earth no longer rotates.

1966   **Morgan, D.** *The richest corpse in show business.* Compact Books, 190p.
The entertainment industry of the future.

1966   **Moudy, W.** *No man on Earth.* Whiting & Wheaton, 176p.
A superman appears among a tribe of hill people on an isolated reservation. [U.S. 1965]

1966   **Nolan, W. F.** *(ed.) Almost human.* Souvenir Press, 227p.
Introduction by Van Vogt, editorial preface; fourteen stories about androids. First published U.S. 1965 as *The pseudo people.*

1966   **Pangborn, E.** *Davy*. D. Dobson, 267p.
In the fourth century "after the Deluge", a party of rebels against the Holy Murcan Church set off eastwards in search of the legendary lands across the great ocean. [U.S. 1964]

1966   **Petty, J.** *The last refuge*. Whiting & Wheaton, 204p.
A solitary, rebellious hero refuses to accept the regimented conditions of an authoritarian world.

1966   **Pohl, F.** *Alternating currents*. Penguin, 190p.
Ten stories. [U.S. 1956]

1966   **Pohl, F.** *The eighth Galaxy reader*. V. Gollancz, 248p.
Introduction; twelve stories. [U.S. 1965]

1966   **Pohl, F.** *The Frederik Pohl Omnibus*. V. Gollancz, 318p.
Thirteen stories from the 1950s.

1966   **Pohl, F.** *A plague of pythons*. V. Gollancz, 158p.
Body transfer and mind control in the days of the powerful Executive Committee. [U.S. 1965]

1966   **Pohl, F.** *(ed.) Star fourteen*. Whiting & Wheaton, 240p.
Introduction; fourteen stories selected from *Star Science Fiction Stories*. First published U.S. 1960 as *Star of stars*.

1966   **Pohl, F. and Williamson, J.** *Starchild*. D. Dobson, 191p.
Interplanetary adventure and conflict. [U.S. 1965]

1966   **Pohl, F. and Williamson, J.** *Undersea quest*. D. Dobson, 189p.
Submarine adventure and detective work. [U.S. 1954]

1966   **Quest, R.** *Countdown to Doomsday*. Harrap, 293p.
Nuclear submarine adventures.

1966   **Rankine, J. (Mason, D. R.)** *The blockade of Sinitron*. Nelson, 122p.
Space adventures.

1966   **Rankine, J. (Mason, D. R.)** *Interstellar two-five*. D. Dobson, 183p.
Space Service adventures with space ship *Interstellar two-five*.

1966   **Raphael, R.** *Code Three*. V. Gollancz, 252p.
Automania: throughways five miles wide and 600 mph cars.

1966   **Reynolds, M.** *Space pioneer*. New English Library, 160p.
Colonists and capitalists in conflict on the planet New Arizona. [U.S. 1965]

1966   **Reynolds, M.** *Time gladiator*. Four Square, 160p.
World Court decides that nine men will fight out the differences between West-world, Sov-world, and Common Europe. [U.S. 1964]

1966   **Roberts, K.** *The furies*. R. Hart-Davis, 254p.
After devastation caused by simultaneous explosion of American and Russian H-bombs, giant wasps attack the survivors.

1966   **Sellings, A. (Ley, A.)** *The Quy Effect*. D. Dobson, 141p.
An inventor discovers a new source of power.

1966   **Sheckley, R.** *Mindswap*. V. Gollancz, 216p.
Interplanetary adventures. [U.S. 1966]

1966   **Sheckley, R.** *The tenth victim*. Mayflower, 109p.
The world of the near future controls aggressive instincts in the population by means of The Big Hunt. [U.S. 1966]

1966   **Simak, C. D.** *All flesh is grass*. V. Gollancz, 260p.
A galactic intelligence seeks to impose peace and harmony on all people. [U.S. 1965]

1966   **Temple, W. F.** *Shoot at the Moon*. Whiting & Wheaton, 192p.
Space adventure. [U.S. 1966]

1966   **Toynbee, P.** *Leftovers*. Weidenfeld & Nicolson, 189p.
Experiences of ten persons after a poisonous cloud has wiped out the rest of mankind.

1966   **Tubb, E. C.** *Ten from tomorrow*. R. Hart-Davis, 187p.
Ten stories.

1966   **Vance, J.** *Star King*. D. Dobson, 158p.
Interplanetary adventure. [U.S. 1964]

1966   **Varshavsky, I. and others.** *Path into the unknown*. MacGibbon & Kee, 191p.
Selection of eight Russian short stories. The basic assumptions are optimistic – no fearful wars of the future; mankind united in the pursuit of the general good.

1966   **Wahloo, P.** *Murder on the 31st floor*. Translated from the Swedish by Joan Tate. M. Joseph, 190p.
An ironic tale of paternalistic state control presented as a criminal investigation. Published 1964 as *Mord på 31 : a Våningen*.

1966   **White, J.** *The watch below*. Whiting & Wheaton, 192p.
Underwater conflict between men and water-dwelling creatures from another planet.

1966   **Wilhelm, K.** *Andover and the android*. D. Dobson, 160p.
Eleven stories. [First published U.S. 1963 as *The mile-long spaceship*.]

1966   **Young, R. F.** *The world of Robert F. Young*. V. Gollancz, 224p.
Introduction by Avram Davidson, sixteen stories. [U.S. 1965]

1967   **Aldiss, B.** *An age.* Faber & Faber, 224p.
Time travel into the Devonian Era.

1967   **Aldiss, B.** *The primal urge.* Sphere, 190p.
Life and love in the near future when Emotional Registers signal sexual interest.
[U.S. 1961].

1967   **Aldiss, B. W. and Harrison, H. (Dempsey, H.)** *(eds.) Nebula Award
Stories 2.* V. Gollancz, 246p.
Introduction by editors; eleven stories. [U.S. 1967]

1967   **Anderson, P.** *The trouble twisters.* V. Gollancz, 191p.
Three stories – space travel and adventure. [U.S. 1966]

1967   **Asimov, I.** *The rest of the robots.* D. Dobson, 556p.
Ten stories about robots. [U.S. 1964]

1967   **Asimov, I.** *Through a glass clearly.* Four Square, 128p.
Four stories.

1967   **Balchin, N. M.** *Kings of infinite space.* Collins, 256p.
Lunar landings and training for space flights in 1969.

1967   **Ballard, J. G.** *The day of forever.* Panther, 141p.
Ten stories.

1967   **Ballard, J. G.** *The disaster area.* J. Cape, 192p.
Nine stories – themes of disaster and horror.

1967   **Ballard, J. G.** *The overloaded man.* Panther, 160p.
Ten stories: inner space, space travel, survival and sanity.

1967   **Ballard, J. G.** *The wind from nowhere.* Penguin, 192p.
A global wind scours the world at 300 mph and few survive. [U.S. 1966]

1967   **Barth, J.** *Giles Goat-Boy.* Secker & Warburg, 744p.
A vast, hilarious tale – allegory and satire – of a mad future world when computers
control everything. [U.S. 1962]

1967   **Bernard, R.** *The halo highway.* Corgi, 158p.
A story from *The Invaders* television series: the struggle against the aliens moves
to the United States.

1967   **Bester, A.** *An Alfred Bester Omnibus.* Sidgwick & Jackson, 710p.
Contains: *The demolished man, Tiger!, Tiger!, The dark side of the Earth.*

1967   **Blish, J.** *The seedling stars.* Faber & Faber, 185p.
After the Earth has ceased to be habitable, the human race survives by creating
mutants adapted to different planetary environments. [U.S. 1956]

1967   **Blish, J.** *Welcome to Mars.* Faber & Faber, 160p.
Adventures on the planet Mars. [U.S. 1967]

1967   **Borden, W.** *Superstoe.* V. Gollancz, 255p.
A comic tale of the attempt to reform the U.S. government.

1967   **Bourne, J.** *Computer takes all.* Cassell, 310p.
An admonitory tale about what would happen when the computer takes over.

1967   **Bradbury, R.** *(ed.) Timeless stories for today and tomorrow.* Bantam Books, 258p.
Introduction; twenty-six stories. [U.S. 1952]

1967   **Brown, R.** *A forest is a long time growing.* M. Joseph, 240p.
An admonitory thriller about co-operation between blacks and whites in Rhodesia after a murderous racial war.

1967   **Campbell, J. W.** *(ed.) Analog 1.* Panther, 176p.
Introduction; eight stories. [U.S. 1962]

1967   **Campbell, J. W.** *(ed.) Analog 2.* Panther, 224p.
Introduction; eight stories. [U.S. 1964]

1967   **Campbell, J. W.** *(ed.) Analog 4.* D. Dobson, 224p.
Introduction by Campbell: seven stories. [U.S. 1966]

1967   **Campbell, J. W.** *(ed.) Prologue to Analog.* Panther, 236p.
Introduction by Campbell: ten stories from the 1950s. [U.S. 1962]

1967   **Carnell, E. J.** *(ed.) New writings in SF 10.* D. Dobson, 189p.
Introduction; seven stories.

1967   **Carnell, E. J.** *(ed.) New writings in SF 11.* D. Dobson, 190p.
Introduction; nine stories.

1967   **Charbonneau, L.** *Antic Earth.* H. Jenkins, 221p.
Space adventures on an emergency landing station. Published U.S. 1967 as *Down to Earth.*

1967   **Chilton, I.** *Take away the flowers; Fuller's World.* W. Heinemann, 143p.
Two tales of space adventure.

1967   **Clarke, A. C.** *(ed.) Time probe.* V. Gollancz, 242p.
Introduction; eleven stories about aspects of science and technology. [U.S. 1966]

1967   **Clarke, A. C.** *Glide path.* Sidgwick & Jackson, 229p.
Scientists and flyers collaborate to perfect a talk-down system for aeroplanes. [U.S. 1963]

1967   **Compton, D. G.** *The silent multitude.* Hodder & Stoughton, 190p.
Cities crumble into dust when a new breed of microbe begins to feed on brick.

1967   **Conklin, G.** *(ed.) Seven come infinity.* Coronet Books, 288p.
Preface; seven stories. [U.S. 1966]

1967   **Conklin, G.** *(ed.) Thirteen great stories of science fiction.* Hodder & Stoughton, 192p.
Thirteen stories about inventions. [U.S. 1960]

1967   **Cooney, M.** *Doomsday England.* Cassell, 183p.
The Russians secretly plant a monster cobalt bomb somewhere in England.

1967   **Cooper, E.** *A far sunset.* Hodder & Stoughton. 189p.
Adventures of the sole survivor of a space-ship.

1967   **Cordell, A. (Graber, G. A.)** *The bright Cantonese,* V. Gollancz, 224p.
By accident an American nuclear destroyer devastates the province of Kwangtung. China retaliates by bombing all major U.S. coastal cities.

1967   **Cowper, R. (Murry, C. M.)** *Breakthrough.* D. Dobson, 214p.
Telepathy and parapsychology adventures.

1967   **Creasey, J.** *The famine.* Hodder & Stoughton, 188p.
Dr. Palfrey fights to save the world from famine.

1967   **Davies, L. P.** *Twilight journey.* H. Jenkins, 191p.
Dream control and personality formation in the twenty-second century.

1967   **Delany, S. R.** *Babel – 17.* V. Gollancz, 192p.
Space pirates, planetary warfare, and love affairs. [U.S. 1966]

1967   **Dick, P. K.** *The penultimate truth.* J. Cape, 254p.
Proles down below in nuclear shelters, and on the surface an aged dictator kept alive by transplants. [U.S. 1964]

1967   **Disch, T. M.** *The genocides.* Whiting & Wheaton, 192p.
End-of-the-world theme: vast plants cover the Earth; the cities are empty and mankind has dwindled to a few survivors. [U.S. 1965]

1967   **Duke, M.** *This business of Bomfog.* W. Heinemann, 197p.
A Huxleyan vision of the future.

1967   **Ferman, E. L.** *(ed.) The best from Fantasy & Science Fiction: 15th series.* V. Gollancz, 256p.
Introduction; thirteen stories. [U.S. 1966].

1967   **Friedberg, G.** *The revolving boy.* V. Gollancz, 191p.
A boy born in a space-ship is able to put astrophysicists in touch with other beings in space. [U.S. 1966]

1967   **Gordon, R. (Hough, S. B.)** *The paw of God.* Anthony Gibbs, 189p.
The spirit of adventure lives on in the new age of total comfort and security.

1967   **Gray, M. W.** *Minutes to impact.* Cassell, 163p.
A nuclear war thriller.

1967   **Haggard, W. (Clayton, R. H. M.)** *The conspirators.* Cassell, 192p.
Nuclear bomb recovered off the Devon coast; Security Executive investigates.

1967   **Harrison, H. (Dempsey, H.)** *Make room! Make room!* Penguin, 224p.
Hunt for a killer in the crowded, affluent and starving world of 1999. [U.S. 1966]

1967   **Harrison, H. (Dempsey, H.)** *Sense of obligation.* D. Dobson, 135p.
Struggle to save the planet Dis from annihilation. First published U.S. 1962 as
Planet of the damned.

1967   **Harrison, H. (Dempsey, H.)** *War with the robots.* D. Dobson, 158p.
Introduction; eight stories about robots and society. [U.S. 1962]

1967   **Heinlein, R.** *Beyond this horizon.* Panther, 206p.
Application of genetic science to life in the future. [U.S. 1952]

1967   **Heinlein, R.** *The door into summer.* V. Gollancz, 190p.
An amusing tale of an inventor who comes out of a deep freeze in the year 2000.
[U.S. 1957]

1967   **Heinlein, R.** *The Moon is a harsh mistress.* D. Dobson, 383p.
A computer takes part in a revolt on Luna in the 21st century. [U.S. 1966]

1967   **Herbert, F.** *Destination void.* Penguin, 220p.
Complications on the 200-year journey to Tau Ceti. [U.S. 1966]

1967   **Hill, D.** *(ed.) The devil his due.* R. Hart-Davis, 156p.
Introduction; eight stories that demonstrate the concept of evil in science fiction.

1967   **Hodder-Williams, C.** *The egg-shaped thing.* Hodder & Stoughton,
248p.
An ingenious tale of variations on the relativity principle.

1967   **Hunter, M.** *(pseud.) The Cambridgeshire disaster.* Collins, 192p.
Nuclear explosion at air force base.

1967   **Janifer, L. M.** *(ed.) Master's choice.* H. Jenkins, 328p.
Introduction, eighteen stories.
See: Janifer, L. M. 1969 [U.S. 1966]

1967   **Jensen, A.** *Epp.* Translated from the Norwegian by Oliver Stallybrass.
Chatto & Windus, 116p.
An ironic account of life in an organised future. Originally published 1965 as *Epp.*

1967   **Jones, D.F.** *Implosion.* R. Hart-Davis, 264p.
In a future Britain the few women not permanently sterile are sent to special
breeding centres.

1967   **Joseph, M. K.** *The hole in the zero.* V. Gollancz, 192p.
Space adventure and time travel.

1967   **Kavan, A. (Edmonds, H.)** *Ice.* Peter Owen, 158p.
An allegorical tale set in the future when the world is vanishing beneath vast fields of ice.

1967   **Knight, D.** *Analogue Men.* Sphere, 190p.
Life in a controlled society of the future. First published U.S. 1955 as *Hell's pavement.*

1967   **Knight, D.** *(ed.) Nebula Award stories 1.* V. Gollancz, 256p.
Eight prize-winning short stories for 1965; begins the series of annual awards made by the Science Fiction Writers of America. [U.S. 1966]

1967   **Knight, D.** *Three novels.* V. Gollancz, 189p.
Tales of future possibilities: *Rule Golden, Natural state, The dying man.* [U.S. 1967]

1967   **Knight, D.** *Turning on.* Gollancz, 160p.
Fourteen stories. [U.S. 1966]

1967   **Laumer, K.** *A plague of demons.* Penguin, 170p.
A solitary hero struggles to save mankind. [U.S. 1965]

1967   **Laumer, K.** *Worlds of the Imperium.* D. Dobson, 133p.
Discovery of an alternative world where history took a different direction. [U.S. 1962]

1967   **Leiber, F.** *The wanderer.* D. Dobson, 346p.
World alarm as a vast planet comes into the solar system. [U.S. 1964]

1967   **Leslie, T.** *Yu-Malu, The Dragon Princess.* Wright & Brown, 172p.
A Chinese secret society threatens the West.

1967   **Lymington, J. (Chance, J. N.)** *Ten million years to Friday.* Hodder & Stoughton, 191p.
Panic and violence follow when an archaic world intrudes upon the modern age.

1967   **McCaffrey, A.** *Restoree.* Rapp & Whiting, 236p.
Struggle for power in the world of Lothar. [U.S. 1967]

1967   **McIntosh, J. T. (MacGregor, J. M.)** *Time for a change.* M. Joseph, 183p.
Time travel and adventure.

1967   **Mackenzie, N.** *Adventure in space.* Wright & Brown, 174p.
Space adventure and world disaster.

1967   **Martin, D. S.** *No lack of space.* Stockwell, 182p.
Nineteen stories.

1967   **Merril, J.** *(ed.) The best of science fiction 9.* Mayflower, 381p.
Twenty-eight stories. [U.S. 1964]

1967   **Merril, J.** *(ed.) The best of science fiction 10.* Mayflower, 382p.
Thirty-three stories. [U.S. 1965]

1967   **Moorcock, M.** *(ed.) Best science fiction stories from New Worlds.*
Panther, 144p.
Introduction; seven stories.

1967   **Moskowitz, S.** *(ed.) A sense of wonder.* Sidgwick & Jackson, 198p.
Contains: Wyndham, J. *Exiles on Asperus*; Leinster, M. *The mole pirate*;
Williamson, J. *The Moon era.* First published U.S. 1967 as *Three stories.*

1967   **Muller, R.** *After all, this is England.* Penguin. 368p.
Originally published 1965 as *The lost diaries of Albert Smith.*

1967   **Nolan, W. F.** *(ed.) The pseudo-people.* Mayflower, 223p.
Originally published U.K. 1966 as *Almost human.*[U.S. 1965]

1967   **Norton, A.** *The X Factor.* V. Gollancz, 191p.
Space adventure, space pirates and ancient civilizations in distant galaxies.
[U.S. 1965]

1967   **Owen, M.** *The white mantle.* R. Hale, 192p.
As the Polar ice caps spread across the globe, the American and Chinese
governments decide on a plan to send selected citizens to Alpha Centauri.

1967   **Peters, L.** *Riot '71.* Hodder & Stoughton, 190p.
Violence, racialism and political extremism in a future Britain.

1967   **Pincher, C.** *The giantkiller.* Weidenfeld & Nicolson, 293p.
A wicked trade union leader founds a new political party and seeks to dominate
the nation.

1967   **Playboy.** *The Playboy Book of science fiction and fantasy.* Souvenir
Press, 402p.
Thirty-two stories. [U.S. 1966]

1967   **Pohl, F.** *(ed.) The ninth Galaxy Reader.* V. Gollancz, 203p.
Introduction; twelve stories. [U.S. 1966]

1967   **Pohl, F. and Kornbluth, C. M.** *(eds.) The wonder effect.* V. Gollancz,
160p.
Introduction by Pohl; nine stories. [U.S. 1962]

1967   **Purser, P.** *The twentymen.* Hodder & Stoughton, 254p.
Political thriller: Britain under a coalition government.

1967   **Reed, K.** *Mister da V and other stories.* Faber & Faber, 222p.
Thirteen stories.

1967   **Reeman, D.** *The deep silence.* Hutchinson, 303p.
Submarine rescue operations off the Korean coast.

1967   **Roberts, J. H. (Duncan, R. L.)** *The February plan*. A. Deutsch, 313p.
Powerful thriller of a terrifying plan rigged by a fanatical general to threaten the world. [U.S. 1967]

1967   **Santesson, H. S.** *(ed.) Gods for tomorrow*. Tandem, 208p.
Short stories.

1967   **Silverberg, R.** *Needle in a time-stack*. Sphere, 190p.
Ten stories – future visions as a parody on the present. [U.S. 1966]

1967   **Simak, C. D.** *The best science fiction stories of Clifford Simak*. Faber & Faber, 251p.
Seven stories.

1967   **Simak, C. D.** *Why call them back from heaven?* V. Gollancz, 160p.
Moral problems in the days when the Forever Centre stores millions of bodies for revival at a future date. [U.S. 1967]

1967   **Sutton, J.** *Beyond Apollo*. V. Gollancz, 223p.
Establishment of the first bases on the Moon. [U.S. 1966]

1967   **Taylor, R. W.** *Doomsday square*. V. Gollancz, 254p.
A new secret weapon leads to nuclear disarmament.

1967   **Thomas, L.** *Orange Wednesday*. Constable, 256p.
Intelligence prepares for *Orange Wednesday*, code-name for the re-unification of Germany.

1967   **Tubb, E. C.** *Death is a dream* R. Hart-Davis, 170p.
Three survivors from the twentieth century wake from suspended animation into a cruel cynical future epoch.

1967   **Vance, J.** *The killing machine*. D. Dobson, 158p.
Hero pursues a hormagaunt to the archaic world of Thamber. [U.S. 1964]

1967   **Van Vogt, A. E.** *Rogue ship*. D. Dobson, 213p.
Extraordinary adventures of the space ship "Hope of Man". [U.S. 1965]

1967   **Van Vogt, A. E.** *A Van Vogt Omnibus*. Sidgwick & Jackson, 490p.
Contains: *Planets for sale, The beast, The Book of Ptath*.

1967   **Van Vogt, A. E. and Mayne-Hull, E.** *The winged men*. Sidgwick & Jackson, 490p.
War in the remote future between birdmen and fishmen. [U.S. 1967]

1967   **Wadsworth, P. M.** *Overmind*. Sidgwick & Jackson, 294p.
The Venusians exhort the inhabitants of Earth to follow the One Law of God.

1967   **White, J.** *Hospital Station*. Corgi, 191p.
First in the *Chronicles of Sector General*, an immense hospital established on the edge of the galaxy to care for all cases and all creatures. [U.S. 1962]

1967   **White, J.** *Star surgeon.* Corgi, 156p.
Continues the *Chronicles of Sector General.*

1967   **Wilhelm, K.** *The killing thing.* Jenkins, 174p.
Experiences of a spaceman, marooned on an empty planet, alone with a
murderous robot. Also published U.S. 1967 as *The killer thing.*

1967   **Wilson, C.** *The mind parasites.* Arthur Barker, 222p.
Towards the end of the twentieth century it becomes evident that a mind-parasite
is preying on mankind.

1967   **Wilson, R.** *Time out for tomorrow.* Mayflower-Dell, 141p.
Twelve stories. [U.S. 1963]

1967   **Young, B. A.** *Cabinet Pudding.* H. Hamilton, 209p.
A comic tale of politics and politicians in the United Kingdom of 1996.

1967   **Zelazny, R.** *This immortal.* R. Hart-Davis, 187p.
A blue creature from Vega helps Earth after a nuclear war. [U.S. 1966]

1968   **Alban, A. (Thompson, A. A.)** *Catharsis Central.* D. Dobson, 192p.
Chaos and revolt in a robot-controlled future world.

1968   **Aldiss, B. & Harrison, H. (Dempsey, H.)** *Farewell, fantastic Venus!*
MacDonald, 293p.
History of the planet Venus with extracts from stories of the planet. Published
U.S. 1968 as *All about Venus.*

1968   **Arias, G.** *The Encartelados (The Poster People).* Translated from the
Spanish by Frank McDermott and Brian Featherstone. V. Gollancz,
159p.
A programme novel in which the author dedicates himself to persuading Marshal
Tranco, the self-styled saviour of his country, to call free elections for the office of
Head of State.

1968   **Asimov, I.** *Asimov's mysteries.* Rapp & Whiting, xi, 288p.
Introduction; fourteen stories – all mysteries. [U.S. 1968]

1968   **Ball, B.** *Timepiece.* D. Dobson, 144p.
Trouble with time in the twenty-ninth century.

1968   **Beeching, J.** *The Dakota Project.* J. Cape, 256p.
A British expatriate discovers the sinister secret of 'Produce X' in Dakota.

1968   **Bennett, M.** *The furious masters.* Eyre & Spottiswoode, 240p.
National troubles follow after a space craft lands on a Yorkshire moor.

1968   **Bester, A.** *Starburst.* Sphere, 158p.
Eleven stories. [U.S. 1958]

1968   **Biggle, L.** *The angry espers.* R. Hale, 192p.
Space adventure and intergalactic warfare. [U.S. 1961]

1968   **Biggle, L.** *Watchers of the dark.* Rapp & Whiting, 228p.
Mysterious forces threaten the world of the Primores Galaxy. [U.S. 1966]

1968   **Blish, J. & Knight, N. L.** *A torrent of faces.* Faber & Faber, 270p.
The chief of the Disaster Plans Board directs operations to save the world from an approaching meteor. [U.S.1967]

1968   **Boardman, T.** *(ed.) SF. Horizons-One.* D. Dobson, 189p.
Ten stories from the magazine *SF Horizons.*

1968   **Bradbury, R.** *R is for rocket.* R. Hart-Davis, 233p.
Seventeen stories [1962]

1968   **Bradbury, R.** *S is for space.* R. Hart-Davis, 238p.
Introduction, sixteen stories [U.S. 1966]

1968   **Bramwell, F.** *Voyage to the stars.* Nelson, 162p.
Interstellar travel and conflict with other peoples.

1968   **Brunner, J.** *Not before time.* New English Library, 128p.
Ten stories.

1968   **Brunner, J.** *Out of my mind.* New English Library, 128p.
Ten stories – past, present, and future.

1968   **Budrys, A.** *The iron thorn.* V. Gollancz, 189p.
A mystery story: opens with a warrior caste, living in a strange metallic building and engaged in a struggle with winged creatures from the desert [U.S. 1967]

1968   **Bulmer, H. K.** *The Doomsday men.* R. Hale, 191p.
Murder and detection in an apparently happy future world. [U.S. 1968]

1968   **Campbell, J. W.** *(ed.) Analog 5.* D. Dobson, ix, 242p.
Preface ('Scientists are stupid!'); nine short stories. [U.S. 1967]

1968   **Carnell, J.** *(ed.) New writings in SF 12.* D. Dobson, 190p.
Foreword; six stories.

1968   **Carnell, J.** *(ed.) New writings in SF 13.* D. Dobson, 190p.
Foreword; eight stories.

1968   **Chance, J.** *The light benders.* R. Hale, 159p.
Contamination comes to Earth from space.

1968   **Clark, L.** *A father of the nation.* Veracity Ventures, 256p.
Britain returns to constitutional government and the Mother of Parliaments is purified.

1968   **Clark, W.** *Special relationship.* W. Heinemann, 223p.
A political tale of Anglo-American relations and the search for common ground in the modern world.

1968 **Clarke, A. C.** *A second Arthur Clarke omnibus.* Sidgwick & Jackson, 283p.
Contains: *Earthlight, Fall of moondust, Sands of Mars.*

1968 **Clarke, A. C.** *2001: a space odyssey.* Based on the screenplay by Stanley Kubrick and Arthur C. Clarke. Hutchinson, 224p.
The book of the film [U.K. 1968] which was based on A. C. Clarke's short story, 'The Sentinel'. The story of the first manned spaceflight to Saturn and the passage through the Star Gate.

1968 **Compton, D. G.** *Synthajoy.* Hodder & Stoughton, 190p.
The synthajoy tape technique to heal the mentally sick, and the problems it causes.

1968 **Cooney, M.** *Ten days to oblivion.* Cassell, 167p.
Secret Service thriller – the fight against the Russian sabotage schemes.

1968 **Cooper, C.** *The thunder and lightning man.* Faber & Faber, 182p.
A tale of interplanetary communications and the coming of an alien space ship to Earth.

1968 **Cooper, E.** *Five to twelve.* Hodder & Stoughton, 187p.
By the end of the twenty-first century women outnumber men whom they have reduced to chattels.

1968 **Cooper, E.** *News from elsewhere.* Mayflower, 127p.
Eight stories.

1968 **Corey, P.** *The planet of the blind.* R. Hale, 192p.
Intrigue and adventure on a distant planet.

1968 **Corston, G.** *Aftermath.* R. Hale, 206p.
The struggle for survival in a calamitous future world.

1968 **Cowper, R.** *Phoenix.* D. Dobson, 183p.
A future dark age and renaissance: from slaves to the invention of steam power.

1968 **Craig, D. (Tucker, A. J.)** *The Alias man.* J. Cape, 224p.
A civil servant is assigned to espionage work with Parliamentary Investigations in the security conscious Britain of the 'seventies.

1968 **Creasey, J.** *The Blight.* Hodder & Stoughton, 192p.
A mysterious disease, which threatens the world timber supply, brings Dr Palfrey into action.

1968 **Crispin, E. (Montgomery, R. B.)** *The stars and under.* Faber & Faber, 174p.
Introduction ('What Science Fiction is'); nine stories.

1968 **Davidson, A.** *Rork!* Rapp & Whiting, 141p.
Mystery and adventure on the planet Pia 2. [U.S. 1965]

1968   **Davies, L. P.** *The alien.* Herbert Jenkins, 183p.
Mystery story about a man believed to have come from space.

1968   **Delany, S. R.** *The Einstein Intersection.* V. Gollancz, 159p.
Adventures in a mythical future when our world intersects another very different universe. [U.S. 1967]

1968   **Delany, S. R.** *The jewels of Aptor.* V. Gollancz, 189p.
Fantastic adventures in the forests and ruined cities of a future epoch. [U.S. 1962]

1968   **Delany, S. R.** *Out of the dead city.* Sphere, 143p.
The first in the *Fall of the Towers* trilogy: an epic story of war and adventure set in the Empire of Toromon in the remote future. First published U.S. 1963 as *Captives of the flame.*

1968   **Delany, S. R.** *The Towers of Toron.* Sphere, 140p.
Continues the *Fall of the Towers* trilogy. [U.S. 1964]

1968   **Dick, P. K.** *Counter-clock world.* Sphere, 160p.
Adventures and anxieties in a world where the dead rise again and time runs backward. [U.S. 1967]

1968   **Dick, P. K.** *The world Jones made.* Sidgwick & Jackson, 192p.
Jones can foresee the future – a power that affects his world. [U.S. 1956]

1968   **Disch, T. M.** *Camp Concentration.* R. Hart-Davis, 177p.
Personal freedom and secret military projects in the United States of the near future. [U.S. 1969]

1968   **Disch, T. M.** *Under compulsion.* R. Hart-Davis, 220p.
Seventeen stories. Later published U.S. 1971 as *Fun with your new head.*

1968   **Donnelly, D.** *The nearing storm.* Hutchinson, 216p.
An admonitory tale about Britain's political future.

1968   **Donson, C.** *Born in space.* R. Hale, 191p.
Struggle for freedom on the planet Ethra.

1968   **Drummond, J.** *The Gantry episode.* V. Gollancz, 224p.
Inspector Cope investigates the mystery of LSD in the Gantry reservoir.

1968   **Earnshaw, B.** *Planet in the eye of time.* Hodder & Stoughton, 191p.
Problems of religious belief, space and time adventure in a waning galaxy.

1968   **Ferman, E. L.** *(ed.) The best from Fantasy and Science Fiction: 16th Series.* V. Gollancz, 256p.
Thirteen stories, four poems, six drawings. [U.S. 1967]

1968   **Frayn, M.** *A very private life.* Collins, 192p.
A highly original fable – a little girl sets out to discover the world in a mechanised future.

1968   **Galouye, D. R.** *Project barrier.* V. Gollancz, 208p.
Five novellas.

1968   **Green, R.** *The great leap backward.* R. Hale, 190p.
An ironic tale of life in A.D. 2021 when the computers have taken over direction of human affairs.

1968   **Groves, J. W.** *Shellbreak.* R. Hale, 190p.
Adventure in the decadent future of 2505.

1968   **Gurney, D. (Bair, P.)** *The "F" Certificate.* Bernard Geis, 251p.
Violence and aggression in the immediate future.

1968   **Haining, P.** *(ed.) The future makers.* Sidgwick & Jackson, 191p.
Introduction; eight stories.

1968   **Harness, C. L.** *The Ring of Ritornel.* V. Gollancz, 221p.
Revenge and retribution in the days of galactic civilization. [U.S. 1968]

1968   **Harris, J.** *Right of reply.* Hutchinson, 232p.
A Suez-style crisis in the 1970s.

1968   **Harrison, H. (Dempsey, H.)** *(ed.) Backdrop of Stars.* D. Dobson, 224p.
Introduction; thirteen stories. Published U.S. 1968 as *SF. Author's Choice.*

1968   **Harrison, H. (Dempsey, H.)** *The technicolor time machine.* Faber & Faber, 190p.
Time machine transports cameramen to the distant past. [U.S. 1967]

1968   **Harrison, H. (Dempsey, H.) and Aldiss, B.** *(eds.) The year's best SF 1.* Sphere, 206p.
Introduction by Harrison, Afterword by Aldiss; fifteen stories.

1968   **Hart-Davis, D.** *The megacull.* Constable, 208p.
Operation Dewdrop is 'designed to reduce the population of the United Kingdom by half.'

1968   **Hay, J.** *The invasion.* Hodder & Stoughton, 192p.
Future war: Chinese invade Australia.

1968   **Herbert, F.** *The eyes of Heisenberg.* Sphere, 157p.
Genetic surgeons can manipulate the gametes of unborn children to produce a race of immortals. [U.S. 1969]

1968   **High, P. E.** *Invader on my back.* R. Hale, 176p.
Heroic adventure in the days when the criminals control the cities. [U.S. 1968]

1968   **High, P. E.** *Reality forbidden.* R. Hale, 192p.
Terror comes to the world after the invention of dream-machine. [U.S. 1967]

1968   **Hill, E.** *Pity about Earth*. R. Hale, 190p.
Journalism and interplanetary adventure.

1968   **Hodder-Williams, C.** *Fistful of digits*. Hodder & Stoughton, 288p.
A gigantic computer is used to condition human minds.

1968   **Hurd, D. and Osmond, A.** *Send him victorious*. Collins, 287p.
Intrigue and political upheaval in a future Britain.

1968   **Johannesson, O.** *The great computer*. Translated from the Swedish
by Naomi Walford. V. Gollancz, 128p.
Unusual scientific romance of the remote future, when civilisation is dominated
by computers. First published 1966 as *Sagan om den stora data maskinen*.

1968   **Jones, G.** *The dome*. Faber & Faber, 239p.
The oppressive world of the future – an adventure story about the man who
rebels against control by computer.

1968   **Jones, M.** *The day they put Humpty together again*. Collins, 224p.
An amusing tale of spare-part surgery and its consequences.

1968   **Knight, D.** *(ed.) Beyond tomorrow*. V. Gollancz, xi, 332p.
Ten stories. [U.S. 1965]

1968   **Knight, D.** *(ed.) Cities of Wonder*. D. Dobson, xi, 252p.
Eleven stories [U.S. 1966]

1968   **Knight, D.** *(ed.) Orbit 2*. Rapp & Whiting, 255p.
Ten stories [U.S. 1967]

1968   **Kornbluth, C. M.** *The best science fiction stories of C. M. Kornbluth*.
Faber & Faber, 277p.
Introduction by Edmund Crispin – twelve stories.

1968   **Lafferty, R. A.** *Past master*. Rapp & Whiting, 191p.
Thomas More brought back to life on the planet Astrolabe in order to solve the
problems of an ideal world. [U.S. 1968]

1968   **Laumer, K.** *Galactic odyssey*. D. Dobson, 160p.
Planetary romance and adventure. [U.S. 1967]

1968   **Laumer, K.** *The Monitors*. D. Dobson, 160p.
A mysterious race of controllers take over the direction of the world. [U.S. 1966]

1968   **Laumer, K.** *Nine by Laumer*. Faber & Faber, 222p.
Nine stories [U.S. 1967]

1968   **Laumer, K.** *The other side of time*. D. Dobson, 160p.
Adventures in a parallel world. [U.S. 1965]

1968   **Laumer, K.** *The other sky*. D. Dobson, 192p.
Four novellas. First published U.S. 1968 as *Greylorn*.

1968   **Laumer, K.** *A trace of memory.* Mayflower, 188p.
Adventures in time and space. [U.S. 1963].

1968   **Le Baron, A. (Laumer, K.)** *The meteor men.* Corgi, 127p.
A story from *The Invaders* television series: another battle against the alien Dorns. [U.S. 1967].

1968   **Leiber, F.** *The secret songs.* R. Hart-Davis, 229p.
Introduction, eleven stories.

1968   **Leinster, M. (Jenkins, W.F.)** *Invaders of space.* Tandem Books, 141p.
Piratical activities in space. [U.S. 1964]

1968   **Leinster, M. (Jenkins, W. F.)** *Miners in the sky.* Sphere, 125p.
Space adventure on the asteroids. [U.S. 1967]

1968   **Leinster, M. (Jenkins, W. F.)** *A Murray Leinster Omnibus.* Sidgwick & Jackson, 160 + 144 + 143p.
Contains: *Operation Terror, Invaders of Space, Checkpoint Lambda.*

1968   **Leinster, M. (Jenkins, W. F.)** *Operation terror.* Tandem Books, 160p.
Invasion from outer space. [U.S. 1962]

1968   **Leinster, M. (Jenkins, W. F.)** *Space gypsies.* Sphere, 127p.
Earthmen assist the humanoids. [U.S. 1967].

1968   **Leinster, M. (Jenkins, W. F.)** *The wailing asteroid.* Sphere, 142p.
Space adventure with a robot asteroid. [U.S. 1961].

1968   **Leslie, P.** *The night of the Trilobites.* Corgi, 128p.
From the television series, *The Invaders*: a Welsh village fights the invaders of Earth.

1968   **Levene, M.** *Carder's paradise.* R. Hart-Davis, 184p.
Life in a future regulated by the Pleasure Principle.

1968   **McCutchan, P.** *The Day of the Coastwatch.* Harrap, 207p.
Attempts to escape from the oppressive New Socialist State of the 1990s.

1968   **McIntosh, J. T. (MacGregor, J. M.)** *Six gates from Limbo.* M. Joseph, 174p.
Adventure and discovery on a perfect world.

1968   **Mackelworth, R. W.** *Fire mantle.* R. Hale, 188p.
A scientist devises a scheme to save the world from a mysterious enemy.

1968   **Mason, D. R.** *From Carthage then I came.* R. Hale, 191p.
The fight for individual values in a regimented future world.

1968   **Mason, D. R.** *Landfall is a state of mind.* R. Hale, 192p.
Adventure on the space-freighter, Zenobia.

1968   **Mason, D. R.** *Ring of violence.* Robert Hale, 190p.
In the tribal world of the twenty-fourth century a small group sets out to establish
a new community.

1968   **Mason, D. R.** *The Tower of Rizwan.* R. Hale, 189p.
Adventure on the planet Rizwan.

1968   **Masson, D. I.** *The caltraps of time.* Faber & Faber, 192p.
Seven stories originally published in *New Worlds SF.*

1968   **Merril, J.** *Daughters of Earth.* V. Gollancz, 256p.
Contains: *Project Nursemaid, Daughters of Earth, Home calling.*

1968   **Merril, J.** *(ed.) SF: The best of the best.* R. Hart-Davis, 438p.
Introduction – "Science fiction as a descriptive label has long since lost whatever
validity it might once have had" – twenty-nine stories.

1968   **Moorcock, M.** *(ed.) The best SF from New Worlds: No. 2.* Panther,
190p.
Introduction; eleven stories.

1968   **Moorcock, M.** *(ed.) The best SF from New Worlds: No. 3.* Panther,
160p.
Introduction; eleven stories.

1968   **Moorcock, M.** *(ed.) The traps of time.* Rapp & Whiting, 207p.
Introduction; ten stories, all speculations about the nature of time.

1968   **Morgan, D. and Kippax, J. (Hynam, J.)** *The neutral stars.*
Macdonald, 159p.
Third in *Venture Twelve* series: Commander Tom Bruce defends Earth against the
aliens.

1968   **Morgan, D. and Kippax, J. (Hynam, J.)** *Thunder of stars.* Macdonald,
159p.
Begins the *Venturer Twelve* series: Tom Bruce of the Solar System Patrol
investigates dangerous activities.

1968   **Niven, L.** *World of Ptavvs.* Macdonald, 160p.
Planetary adventure and the conquest of space. [U.S. 1967]

1968   **Nolan, W. F. and Johnson, G. C.** *Logan's run.* V. Gollancz, 134p.
A tale of escape from the oppressive world of the twenty-first century when life
ends by law at the age of twenty-one. [U.S. 1968]

1968   **Nourse, A. E.** *PSI High and others.* Faber & Faber, 182p.
Three novellas on themes of future adventure. [U.S. 1967]

1968   **Pangborn, E.** *The judgement of Eve.* Rapp & Whiting, 189p.
Trial and self-discovery in the primitive world after the holocaust. [U.S. 1966]

1968 **Patterson, J. E. W.** *The call of the planets.* A. J. Chapple, (Bala, North Wales) 90p.
The inhabitants of Jupiter have much to teach mankind.

1968 **Platt, C.** *The garbage world.* Panther, 144p.
An asteroid, rubbish dump for the planets, is in danger of disintegrating. [U.S. 1967]

1968 **Pohl, F.** *Digits and dastards.* D. Dobson, 192p.
Introduction – "I will confess in public to a long-standing desire to teach *something* to *somebody*" – six stories and two mathematical essays. [U.S. 1966]

1968 **Pohl, F.** *(ed.) 10th Galaxy reader.* V. Gollancz, 240p.
Eleven stories. [U.S. 1967]

1968 **Pohl, F. and Williamson, J.** *Undersea Fleet.* D. Dobson, 187p.
Submarine adventures. [U.S. 1956]

1968 **Rankine, J. (Mason, D. R.)** *Never the same door.* D. Dobson, 173p.
A struggle for existence on an undiscovered planet.

1968 **Rankine, J. (Mason, D. R.)** *One is one.* D. Dobson, 176p.
Love and adventure out in the galaxy.

1968 **Roberts, K.** *Pavane.* R. Hart-Davis, 224p.
Alternative history beginning with victory of Spanish Armada and a universal Catholic Church; ends, with fateful development of science, the division of the Church, and revolt of the new world colonies. [U.S. 1968]

1968 **Robeson, K.** *(pseud.).* The adventures of the American superman, Doc Savage, appeared in the United Kingdom from 1968 onwards in Corgi editions or in Bantam Books editions imported from the United States. See *Note* 11 for more details. The following appeared in 1968:
The Annihilist. Doc Savage discovers who was killing the criminals of New York.
Cold death. Doc Savage saves the world from Var, the faceless fiend.
The Czar of fear. Doc Savage in action against the terrors of the Green Bell.
Death in silver. Doc Savage saves America from the hooded assassins.
The devil's playground. Doc Savage puts paid to the Devil's Tomahawks.
The Flaming Falcons. Doc Savage discovers the lair of the Blood-birds of Indo-China.
Fortress of solitude. Doc Savage vanquishes a superman.
The Green Eagle. Doc Savage deals with the fainting sickness.

1968 **Ross, J.** *(ed.) Best of Amazing.* R. Hale, 224p.
Foreword – science fiction is "a natural fusion of the two cultures that should be one" – nine stories. [U.S. 1967]

1968 **Sellings, A. (Ley, A.)** *The long eureka.* D. Dobson, 184p.
Nine stories.

1968   **Sellings, A. (Ley, A.)** *The Power of X.* D. Dobson, 156p.
The power of duplication causes problems.

1968   **Serling, R. J.** *The President's plane is missing.* Cassell, 296p.
A world crisis starts when the plane on which the President of the United States
is flying suddenly disappears from the radar screens. [U.S. 1967]

1968   **Silverberg, R.** *The time hoppers.* Sidgwick & Jackson, 182p.
Time-travel adventures in the year 2490. [U.S. 1967]

1968   **Simak, C. D.** *The Werewolf Principle.* V. Gollancz, 216p.
Space travel, talking animals, telepathy, and friendly aliens. [U.S. 1967]

1968   **Sladek, J. T.** *The reproductive system.* V. Gollancz, 192p.
An ironic fantasy about commercialism, computers, the space race, East & West,
and a cellular reproducing system. [U.S. 1968]

1968   **Sturgeon, T. (Waldo, E. H.)** *Caviar.* Sidgwick & Jackson, 193p.
Eight stories. [U.S. 1955]

1968   **Sturgeon, T. (Waldo, E. H.)** *Starshine.* V. Gollancz, 158p.
Six stories. [U.S. 1966]

1968   **Taylor, G.** *Day of the republic.* Peter Davies, 183p.
The Black Guard takes over in Australia and repudiates all treaties.

1968   **Temple, W. F.** *The fleshpots of Sansato.* MacDonald, 188p.
The adventures of a special agent on the planet Montefor.

1968   **Thomas, T. L. and Wilhelm, K.** *The clone.* R. Hale, 189p.
A world disaster story: a vast clone overruns a city and threatens to destroy the
planet. [U.S. 1965]

1968   **Tronchin-James, N.** *Ministry of Procreation.* R. Hale, 144p.
An enterprising young man takes advantage of the Procreation Act in a future
Britain.

1968   **Tubb, E. C.** *Gath.* R. Hart-Davis, 143p.
The Earthman, Dumarest, survives all the perils of the planet Gath. [U.S. 1967]

1968   **Van Greenway, P.** *The man who held the Queen to ransom and sent
Parliament packing.* Weidenfeld & Nicolson, 256p.
A Cromwellian captain takes over the House of Commons, imprisons the Royal
family and rules the nation by decree.

1968   **Vance, J.** *The palace of love.* D. Dobson, 189p.
Interplanetary adventures. [U.S. 1967]

1968   **Vielle, E. E.** *No subway.* Collins, 191p.
Disaster could follow on the building of a Channel Tunnel.

1968   **Warner, D. (Currie, J. D. & Warner, E.)** *Death on a warm wind*. Rapp & Whiting, 158p.
Colston's Theory explains and predicts a series of devastating earthquakes.

1968   **Way, P.** *The Kretzmer Syndrome*. H. Jenkins, 186p.
Political struggles in the United Kingdom.

1968   **Wheeler, P.** *The friendly persuaders*. Hutchinson, 208p.
Visitors from the planet Tarax seek to take over Earth.

1968   **White, J.** *All judgement fled*. Rapp & Whiting, 190p.
In 1978 a vast space ship enters the Solar System and goes into orbit.

1968   **White, J.** *Deadly litter*. Corgi, 157p.
Four stories on space themes. [U.S. 1964]

1968   **Williams, E. C.** *The time injection*. R. Hale, 190p.
Life in a future Stone Age.

1968   **Wilson, R.** *The girls from Planet 5*. Hale, 22p.
Earth invaded by lovely girls from outer space. [U.S. 1955]

1968   **Wright, L.** *A planet called Pavanne*. H. Jenkins, 186p.
A tale of galactic mystery and adventure.

1968   **Zelazny, R.** *The dream master*. R. Hart-Davis, 157p.
A neuroparticipant enters the mind of a woman patient. [U.S. 1967]

1968   **Zelazny, R.** *Lord of light*. Faber & Faber, 257p.
In a world dominated by technocrats the ignorant masses believe that they are directed by gods. [U.S. 1967],

1968   **Zelazny, R.** *(ed.) Nebula Award Stories 3*. V. Gollancz, 256p.
Introduction and Afterword by Zelazny; winners and runners-up in the 1967 Nebula Award selected by the Science Fiction Writers of America; seven stories. [U.S. 1968]

1968   **Zerwick, C. and Brown, H.** *The Cassiopeia affair*. V. Gollancz, 235p.
As the world prepares for a nuclear war, a scientist picks up signals from another planetary civilization.

1969   **Ableman, P.** *The twilight of the Vilp*. V. Gollancz, 157p.
A comic tale of novel-writing and interplanetary communication.

1969   **Aldiss, B.** *Barefoot in the head*. Faber & Faber, 284p.
An elaborate and ambitious fantasy of Britain in the days after the Acid Head War.

1969   **Aldiss, B.** *A Brian Aldiss omnibus*. Sidgwick & Jackson, 590p.
Five stories.

1969 **Aldiss, B.** *Intangibles Inc.* Faber & Faber, 198p.
A collection of five novellas.

1969 **Aldiss, B. and others.** *The inner landscape.* Allison & Busby, 151p.
Contains: Aldiss, B. *Danger: Religion!;* Ballard, J. G. *The voices of time;* Peake, M. *Boy in darkness.*

1969 **Anderson, P.** *Let the spacemen beware!* D. Dobson, 224p.
[1970] Mystery and adventure on the planet Gwydion. [U.S. 1963]

1969 **Anderson, P.** *The makeshift rocket.* D. Dobson, 97p.
A comic tale of the first beer-powered spaceship in interplanetary history. [U.S. 1962]

1969 **Anderson, P.** *(ed.) Nebula Award Stories 4.* V. Gollancz, 240p.
Introduction – "Science fiction remains more interested in the glamour and mystery of existence" – essay on 'The science fiction novel in 1968'; six prize-winning stories.

1969 **Anthony, P. (Jacob, P. A.)** *Omnivore.* Faber & Faber, 221p.
Three travellers bring back deadly creatures to Earth. [U.S. 1968]

1969 **Anthony, P. (Jacob, P. A.) and Margroff, R. E.** *The Ring.* Macdonald, 254p.
Romantic adventures in the twenty-first century. [U.S. 1968]

1969 **Asimov, I.** *A second Isaac Asimov omnibus.* Sidgwick & Jackson, 516p.
Contains: *Currents of space, Pebble in the sky, Stars like dust.* Published U.S. 1961 as *Triangle.*

1969 **Baxter, J.** *The Pacific Book of science fiction.* Angus & Robertson, 180p.
Introduction; twelve stories by Australian writers. First published Sydney 1968 as *The Pacific Book of Australian SF.*

1969 **Bester, A.** *The dark side of the Earth.* Pan, 171p.
First published 1967 as part of *An Alfred Bester omnibus.* Contains seven short stories. [U.S. 1964]

1969 **Biggle, L.** *The still, small voice of trumpets.* Rapp & Whiting, 189p.
The Interplanetary Relations Bureau finds political problems on the planet Kurr. [U.S. 1968]

1969 **Blish, J.** *Black Easter.* Faber & Faber, 165p.
Necromancy and theology in a political power struggle. [U.S. 1968]

1969 **Bova, B.** *The weathermakers.* D. Dobson, 250p.
Military and scientists struggle to take over a new weather control technique. [U.S. 1967]

1969   **Boyd, J. (Upchurch, B.)** *The last starship from Earth.* V. Gollancz, 182p.
An ironic tale of choice and responsibility in the technological world of the future. [U.S. 1968]

1969   **Bradbury, R.** *I sing the Body Electric.* Hart-Davis, 305p.
Seventeen stories and one poem. [U.S. 1969]

1969   **Brunner, J.** *A plague on both your causes.* Hodder & Stoughton, 187p.
Political conflict in an imaginary African country.

1969   **Brunner, J.** *Quicksand.* Sidgwick & Jackson, 240p.
A mysterious visitor from the perfect world of Llanraw exposes the deficiencies of our time. [U.S. 1967]₁

1969   **Brunner, J.** *The squares of the city.* Penguin, 312p.
A thriller that poses questions about political government and the nature of society. [U.S. 1965]

1969   **Brunner, J.** *Stand on Zanzibar.* MacDonald, xvii, 507p.
A vigorous and effective study of the consequences of over-population in 2010 A.D. when the human race has passed the 7 billion mark. [U.S. 1968]

1969   **Bulmer, H. K.** *The patient dark.* R. Hale, 192p.
First published U.S. 1958 and U.K. 1961 as *Secret of ZI.*

1969   **Bulmer, K.** *The ulcer culture.* Macdonald, 160p.
A Huxleyan vision of the unhappy future.

1969   **Burke, J.** *Moon Zero Two.* Pan, 141p.
Adapted by John Burke from the story for the film by Gavin Lyall, Frank Hardman and Martin Davison. Amatory and astronautical adventures.

1969   **Caidin, M.** *The last fathom.* M. Joseph, 271p.
Adventure and espionage at the deepest underwater levels. [U.S. 1967]

1969   **Campbell, J. W.** *(ed.) Analog 6.* D. Dobson, xvii, 313p.
Introduction; fourteen short stories. [U.S. 1968]

1969   **Carnell, J.** *(ed.) New writings in SF 14.* D. Dobson, 234p.
Foreword; seven stories.

1969   **Carnell, J.** *(ed.) New writings in SF 15.* D. Dobson, 234p.
Foreword; six stories

1969   **Carnell, J.** *(ed.) New writings in SF 16.* D. Dobson, 190p
Foreword; six stories.

1969   **Carter, A.** *Heroes and villains.* W. Heinemann, 214p.
Post-catastrophe story about the girl who left safety and security for the dangerous world of the Barbarians.

1969   **Clement, H. (Stubbs, H. C.)** *Small changes.* R. Hale, 230p.
Nine stories [U.S. 1969]

1969   **Cole, B.** *The Funco File.* W. H. Allen, 283p.
Comic tale of the super-computer that examines four extraordinary persons. [U.S. 1969]

1969   **Conklin, G.** *(ed.) Science fiction oddities.* Rapp & Whiting, 156p.
Introduction; nine stories. [U.S. 1966]

1969   **Conklin, G.** *(ed.) Science fiction oddities: Second series.* Rapp & Whiting, 160p.
Ten stories. [U.S. 1966]

1969   **Conklin, G.** *(ed.) Seven trips through time and space.* Hodder & Stoughton, 256p.
Introduction, seven stories. [U.S. 1968]

1969   **Cooper, E.** *Sea-horse in the sky.* Hodder & Stoughton, 191p.
Sixteen people, transported to another world, discover new meanings in life.

1969   **Corley, E.** *Siege.* Michael Joseph, 319p.
Afro-American Army of Liberation seizes Manhattan Island: 'If the Negro has been driven to revolution, who drove him there?' [U.S. 1969]

1969   **Craig, D. (Tucker, A. J.)** *Message ends.* J. Cape, 188p.
Activities of the Parliamentary Investigations Committee, "appointed to scrutinize the functioning of any State or Government department".

1969   **Creasey, J.** *The oasis.* Hodder & Stoughton, 192p.
Fantastic yarn about an attempt at world domination by means of a strange new drug.

1969   **Crichton, M.** *The Andromeda Strain.* J. Cape, 295p.
Scientists struggle to save the world from a lethal epidemic. [U.S. 1969]

1969   **Daventry, L.** *Reflections in a mirage.* R. Hale, 192p.
Adventures on an unexplored planet. [U.S. 1969]

1969   **Davies, L. P.** *Dimension A.* H. Jenkins, 206p.
Adventure in parallel worlds.

1969   **Del Martia, A.** *(pseud.) One against time.* Mayflower, 140p.
Problems of a bank-clerk with a super-brain.

1969   **Delany, S.R.** *City of a thousand suns.* Sphere Books, 141p.
Concludes the *Fall of the Towers* trilogy [U.S. 1965]

1969   Delany, S. R. *Nova.* V. Gollancz, 280p.
Space adventure and interstellar rivalries in the thirty-first century. [U.S. 1968]

1969   Dick, P. K. *Do androids dream of electric sheep?* Rapp & Whiting, 210p.
Adventures in the days when Earth is desolate and androids are escaping from Mars. [U.S. 1968]

1969   Dick, P. K. *The game-players of Titan.* Sphere, 160p.
The Vugs of Titan play elaborate games for the possession of Earth. [U.S. 1963]

1969   Dick, P. K. *The variable man.* Sphere 220p.
One short novel and four novellas – interplanetary warfare, precognition, mutants. [U.S. 1963]

1969   Disch, T. M. *Echo round his bones.* R. Hart-Davis, 156p.
Matter transmitters, reduplication of human beings, and Earth removed from the solar system. [U.S. 1967]

1969   Donson, C. *The perspective process.* R. Hale, 191p.
Space-travellers help to restore harmony on Earth.

1969   Donson, C. *Tritonastra.* R. Hale, 192p.
Panic on Earth when the Tritonastrans dominate space.

1969   Dreyer, P. *A beast in view.* André Deutsch, 223p.
Political upheavals and criminal activities in the South Africa of the near future.

1969   Farmer, P. J. *Flesh.* Rapp & Whiting, 212p.
Rituals and orgies in honour of the Great White Mother in the world of the thirtieth century. [U.S. 1968]

1969   Fennerton, W. *The Lucifer cell.* Hodder & Stoughton, 306p.
A thriller about life in London under a Chinese occupation. [U.S. 1968]

1969   Garner, W. *The Us or Them War.* Collins 288p.
Americans and Russians discover simultaneously that another power has invented the ultimate non-nuclear weapon.

1969   Gaskell, J. (Lynch, J.) *A sweet sweet summer.* Hodder & Stoughton, 223p.
Fantastic adventures when the Aliens take over the British Isles.

1969   Green, J. *(pseud.) An affair with genius.* V. Gollancz, 190p.
Nine stories.

1969   Greenfield, I. A. *Waters of death.* Sidgwick & Jackson, 175p.
A plot against the sea-farmers of the Caribbean miscarries. [U.S. 1967]

1969   Greenlee, S. *The spook who sat by the door.* Allinson & Busby, 182p.
Simultaneous black guerilla uprisings in eight American cities: 'The most powerful nation in history stood on the brink of panic and chaos.' [U.S. 1969]

1969   **Groves, J. W.** *The heels of Achilles.* R. Hale, 192p.
A mad world in which the dead walk again.

1969   **Hale, J.** *The paradise man.* Rapp & Whiting, 221p.
A comedy about technology gone mad.

1969   **Harrison, H. (Dempsey, H.)** *Deathworld 3.* Faber & Faber, 251p.
The inhabitants of the planet Felicity are bred for the sole purpose of attacking and killing other life forms. [U.S. 1968]

1969   **Harrison, H. (Dempsey, H.)** *(ed.) Four for the future.* Macdonald, 188p.
Introduction; four stories on themes of sacrifice and redemption.

1969   **Harrison, H. (Dempsey, H.) and Aldiss, B.** *(eds.) The year's best SF. 2.* Sphere, 207p.
Introduction by Harrison – "Science fiction shambled to life in the crumbling yellow pages of the pulp magazines" – twelve stories, one poem, reviews of *2001; A space odyssey.* Afterword – "The house that Jules built" – by Aldiss.

1969   **Hartridge, J.** *Binary divine.* Macdonald, 172p.
A mystery of the Lost Month when disasters reduce the world population to a tenth of its former size.

1969   **Heinlein, R.** *Citizen of the galaxy.* V. Gollancz, 320p.
Space adventures. [U.S. 1957]

1969   **Heinlein, R.** *Podkayne of Mars.* New English Library, 159p.
Romantic adventure on Mars and Venus. [U.S. 1963]

1969   **High, P. E.** *These savage futurians.* D. Dobson, 134p.
Revolt against the Masters in the epoch after the collapse of world civilization. [U.S. 1967]

1969   **High, P. E.** *The time mercenaries.* D. Dobson, 118p.
World government brings back a long-dead submarine commander to assist in the war against the aliens.

1969   **High, P. E.** *Twin planets.* D. Dobson, 159p.
Earthman comes to the rescue of parallel world of Firma. [U.S. 1967]

1969   **Holm, S.** *Termush.* Translated from the Danish by Sylvia Clayton. Faber & Faber, 110p.
Experiences after an atomic war. First published 1967 as *Termush.*

1969   **Hoyle, F. and Hoyle, G.** *Rockets and Ursa Major.* W. Heinemann, 169p.
Danger threatens Earth as explorer ship DSP 15 returns from a mission to Ursa Major.

1969   **Hurd, D. and Osmond, A.** *The smile on the face of the tiger.* Collins, 268p.
International commotions when China asks for the return of Hong Kong.

1969   **Janifer, L. M.** *(ed.) Master's choice 1.* Universal-Tandem, 175p.
Ten stories from *Master's choice* first published U.S. 1966 and U.K.1968.

1969   **Janifer, L. M.** *(ed.) Master's choice 2.* Universal-Tandem, 160p.
Remaining eight stories from *Master's choice.*

1969   **Jones, L.** *(ed.) The new SF.* Hutchinson, 223p.
Preface by Moorcock, M. – "Some time ago most people gave up trying to say
what SF was" – thirteen stories, a discussion on J.G. Ballard, and George
MacBeth on "The new science fiction".

1969   **Kettle, P.** *The day of the women.* Leslie Frewin, 207p.
A women's political party gains power and takes over the government of the
United Kingdom.

1969   **Knebel, F.** *Trespass.* W. H. Allen, 313p.
Conflict between Black and White in the United States. [U.S. 1969]

1969   **Knight, D.** *Off Centre.* V. Gollancz, 192p.
Five stories. [U.S. 1965]

1969   **Knight, D.** *(ed.) One hundred years of science fiction.* V. Gollancz,
368p.
Introduction by Knight – twenty short stories from Ambrose Bierce and Kipling to
Budrys and A. C. Clarke. [U.S. 1968]

1969   **Knight, D.** *Orbit Three.* Rapp & Whiting, 224p.
Nine stories, each with an editorial commentary. [U.S. 1968]

1969   **Knight, D.** *(ed.) Worlds to come.* V. Gollancz, ix, 337p.
Introduction; nine stories. [U.S. 1967]

1969   **Lauder, G. D. (Dick-Lauder, Sir G.)** *Our man for Ganymede.*
D. Dobson. 190p.
A romance of war between Earth and the planet Ganymede.

1969   **Laumer, K.** *It's a mad, mad galaxy.* D. Dobson, 160p.
Five stories. [U.S. 1968]

1969   **Le Guin, U. K.** *The left hand of darkness.* Macdonald, 286p.
A most original and inventive tale of old and new, good and evil, which opens with
the arrival of an envoy from the Ekumen to the remote planet of Winter. [U.S.
1969]

1969   **Leiber, F.** *A spectre is haunting Texas.* V. Gollancz, 245p.
A satiric look at American values in the ruined world after a nuclear war. [U.S.
1969]

1969   **Leinster, M. (Jenkins, W. F.)** *The Listeners.* Sidgwick, & Jackson,
192p.
Enormous squid-like creatures are discovered at the bottom of the Luzon Deep.
First published U.S. 1961 as *Creatures of the abyss*

1969   **Leslie, P.** *The Autumn accelerator.* Corgi, 128p.
The fight against the Invaders who start the attack on Earth by destroying all the trees.

1969   **Lessing, D.** *The four-gated city.* MacGibbon & Kee, 710p.
Fifth and last part in *Children of Violence* stories. The final section moves into the future – the destruction of contemporary civilization.

1969   **Lymington, J. (Chance, J. N.)** *Give daddy the knife, darling.* Hodder & Stoughton, 191p.
A tale of unidentified flying objects and a danger to mankind.

1969   **Lymington, J. (Chance, J. N.)** *The nowhere place.* Hodder & Stoughton, 192p.
General alarm after part of an English village disappears.

1969   **McCaffrey, A.** *Dragonflight.* Rapp & Whiting, 310p.
Adventures with dragons and dragonmen on the planet Pern. [U.S. 1968]

1969   **McCutchan, P. D.** *The all-purpose bodies.* Harrap, 205p.
Mystery of brain surgery and compomen-assembled human spare parts.

1969   **McCutchan, P. D.** *The Bright Red Business Men.* Harrap, 224p.
Commander Shaw of 6D2 investigates a glue-like, plastic liquid that threatens to engulf the world.

1969   **Mannes, M. (Blow, Mrs. M.)** *They.* V. Gollancz, 215p.
A satire about the lack of values and silliness of the young. [U.S. 1968]

1969   **Mason, D. R.** *The Janus syndrome.* R. Hale, 190p.
Espionage and self-discovery on the planet Lados.

1969   **Merle, R.** *The day of the dolphin.* Translated from the French by Helen Weaver. Weidenfeld & Nicolson, 320p.
Experiment to communicate with dolphins who refuse to cooperate in military enterprises. First published 1967 as *Un animal doué de raison.*

1969   **Moorcock, M.** *Behold the Man.* Allison & Busby, 144p.
Karl Glogauer travels from the future by time machine to the Palestine of John the Baptist and there assumes the role of Christ.

1969   **Moorcock, M.** *(ed.) Best science fiction from New Worlds: No. 4.* Panther, 160p.
Introduction; eleven stories.

1969   **Moorcock, M.** *The black corridor.* Mayflower, 126p.
Ryan escapes from the terrors of Earth, with his family in the deep freeze of a space craft, to colonize a new and better world.

1969   **Moorcock, M.** *The final programme.* Illustrated by Malcolm Dean. Allison & Busby, 168p.
An elaborate fantasy of a comic strip hero who pursues every kind of experience. First in the Jerry Cornelius series. [U.S. 1968]

1969   **Moorcock, M.** *The ice schooner.* Sphere, 190p.
Voyage of discovery across the frozen wastes of the new ice age.

1969   **Moorcock, M.** *The Jewel in the Skull.* Mayflower, 156p.
Opens the *History of the Runestaff:* Dorian Hawkmoon faces the dark forces of
Granbretan.

1969   **Moorcock, M.** *The Mad God's Amulet.* Mayflower, 142p.
Part Two in the *History of the Runestaff:* the Dark Empire of Granbretan and its
sorcerer-scientists plot world conquest.

1969   **Moorcock, M.** *The Runestaff.* Mayflower, 143p.
Fourth in the *History of the Runestaff.* Hawkmoon defeats Baron Meliadus.

1969   **Moorcock, M.** *The sword of the dawn.* Mayflower, 144p.
Third in the *History of the Runestaff.* Hawksmoon continues the struggle against
the Dark Empire.

1969   **Moorcock, M.** *The time dweller.* R. Hart-Davis, 176p.
Nine stories – six on future themes.

1969   **Niven, L.** *A gift from earth.* Macdonald, 254p.
Space adventure. [U.S. 1968]

1969   **Niven, L.** *Neutron star.* Macdonald, 286p.
Ten stories. [U.S. 1968]

1969   **Panshin, A.** *Rite of passage.* Sidgwick & Jackson, 254p.
Survival and adventure in the space colonies after the destruction of Earth. [U.S.
1968]

1969   **Pohl, F.** *(ed.) Second If Reader.* Rapp & Whiting, 240p.
Introduction – science fiction "should not be judged by how accurately it portrays
the future, but by how lucidly and entertainingly it describes for you the possible
varieties of future that lie within your grasp." Ten stories. [U.S. 1963]

1969   **Pohl, F. and Williamson, J.** *Undersea city.* D. Dobson, 190p.
Adventures in and out of the submarine cities of the Sundra Strait. [U.S. 1958]

1969   **Rackham, J.** *Time to live.* D. Dobson, 141p.
Romantic time-adventure on the planet Kalmed. [U.S. 1966]

1969   **Rankine, J. (Mason, D. R.)** *Binary Z.* D. Dobson, 190p.
Discovery of an indestructible ovoid programmed to resist any attack.

1969   **Rankine, J. (Mason, D. R.)** *Moons of Triopus.* D. Dobson, 176p.
Moral and political problems on the planet Triopus.

1969   **Rankine, J. (Mason, D. R.)** *The Weisman experiment.* D. Dobson,
184p.
Adventure and self-discovery in an authoritarian future world.

1969   **Reed, K.** *Armed camps.* Faber & Faber, 176p.
Violence and non-violence in the barbaric world of 2001.

1969   **Robeson, K.** *(pseud.)* See remarks on Robeson (1968)
Dust of death. Bantam Books, 139p.
Doc Savage brings peace to South America.
Hex. Corgi, 120p.
Doc Savage subdues a master of crime.

1969   **Russ, J.** *Picnic on Paradise.* Macdonald, 157p.
Trans-Temporal Agent intervenes in the war on the planet Paradise. [U.S. 1968]

1969   **Ryder, J.** *Kark.* R. Hale, 190p.
One man rebels against the state system in a regimented Britain of the future.

1969   **Saberhagen, F.** *Brother berserker.* Macdonald, 167p.
The fight against the berserkers – vast machines programmed to destroy human
life throughout space. [U.S. 1967]

1969   **Sallis, J.** *(ed.) The war book.* R. Hart-Davis, 188p.
Introduction – "the technique of genre SF leads almost inevitably to a
preoccupation with war" – fourteen stories on themes of war and peace.

1969   **Schmitz, J. H.** *The demon breed.* Macdonald, 157p.
Longevity and regeneration research projects lead to conflict between the
Parahuans and the worlds of the Hub. First published 1968 in *Analog Science
Fiction/Science Fact* with the title of *The Tuvela.*

1969   **Seymour, A.** *The coming self-destruction of the United States of
America.* Souvenir Press, 314p.
Black and White conflicts lead to the destruction of the United States.

1969   **Shaw, B.** *The two-timers.* V. Gollancz, 174p.
Adventures in time and in parallel worlds. [U.S. 1968]

1969   **Sheckley, R.** *Citizen in space.* New English Library, 191p.
Twelve stories. [U.S. 1955]

1969   **Sheckley, R.** *Dimension of miracles.* V. Gollancz, 192p.
A comic tale about the man who wins a prize in the Intergalactic Sweepstakes.
[U.S. 1968]

1969   **Sheckley, R.** *The people trap.* V. Gollancz, 222p.
Fourteen stories. [U.S. 1968]

1969   **Silverberg, R.** *Anvil of time.* Sidgwick & Jackson, 192p.
Time travel adventures. First published U.S. 1968 as *Hawksbill Station.*

1969   **Silverberg, R.** *The man in the maze.* Sidgwick & Jackson, 192p.
Search for the one man who can understand the first alien race discovered by
mankind. [U.S. 1966]

1969   Silverberg, R. *Thorns.* Rapp & Whiting, 222p.
Two exceptional people seek their true identity – she the mother of a hundred children and he the starman transformed by surgery. [U.S. 1967]

1969   Silverberg, R. *To worlds beyond.* Sphere, 157p.
Introductions by Asimov and Silverberg; nine stories. [U.S. 1965]

1969   Simak, C. *The goblin reservation.* Rapp & Whiting, 192p.
Time travel and planetary adventure. [U.S. 1968]

1969   Smith, C. (Linebarger, P.) *Space lords.* Sidgwick & Jackson, 204p.
Five stories about space. [U.S. 1965]

1969   Stableford, B. *Cradle of the sun.* Sidgwick & Jackson, 210p.
The struggle to stop the mysterious decline of the human race.

1969   Sturgeon, T. (Waldo, E. H.) *Venus plus X.* V. Gollancz, 191p.
A tale of parallel worlds and the Ledom who watch over humanity. [U.S. 1960]

1969   Tubb, E. C. *Escape into space.* Sidgwick & Jackson, 188p.
Struggles of the first space colonists to survive on a hostile planet.

1969   Van Vogt, A. E. *The Book of Ptath.* Panther, 157p.
In the changed climates, societies and geographies of a future Earth the struggle for control goes on. First published U.K. in *A Van Vogt Omnibus*, 1967. [U.S. 1947]

1969   Van Vogt, A. E. *Moonbeast.* Panther, 187p.
A time machine transports people from Earth to an extraordinary society on the Moon. Published U.S. 1963 as *The Beast.*

1969   Van Vogt, A. E. *The world of Null-A.* D. Dobson, 248p.
Involved tale, claimed to be based on Korzybski's Theory of General Semantics, in which a superman goes through various existences and intervenes in the struggle for Sol. [U.S. 1948]

1969   Vonnegut, K. *Welcome to the Monkey house.* J. Cape, xv, 298p.
Preface – personal and literary; includes eight stories set in the future. [U.S. 1968]

1969   Weatherhead, J. *Transplant.* Harrap, 182p.
Social difficulties in the days when organ transplanting has become general.

1969   Wilhelm, K. *Let the fire fall.* Herbert Jenkins, 223p.
A degenerate cult sweeps the world after a spaceship comes to Earth. [U.S. 1969]

1969   Williams, E. C. *Monkman comes down.* R. Hale, 190p.
An astronaut finds himself on a planet of remarkable differences.

1969   Williams, E. C. *To end all telescopes.* R. Hale, 190p.
A new kind of telescope reveals other worlds and civilizations far off in space.

1969   **Williamson, J.** *Bright new universe.* Sidgwick & Jackson, 192p.
Space travel and adventure. [U.S. 1967]

1969   **Williamson, J.** *Seetee ship.* Mayflower, 191p.
Space adventure and interplanetary conflict. First published U.S. 1968 under the pseudonym of Will Stewart.

1969   **Williamson, J.** *Seetee shock.* Mayflower, 187p.
First published U.S. 1950 and U. K. 1954 under pseudonym of Will Stewart.

1969   **Wise, A.** *The day the Queen flew to Scotland for the grouse shooting.* Hodder & Stoughton, 189p.
Civil war between North and South in the United Kingdom.

1969   **Wollheim, D. A. and Carr, T.** *(eds.) World's best science fiction 1969. 1 & 2.* V. Gollancz, 320 + 320p.
Introduction; thirty-two stories. [U.S. 1969]

1969   **Zelazny, R.** *A rose for Ecclesiastes.* R. Hart-Davis, 207p.
Introduction by Theodore Sturgeon; four novellas.

1970   **Aldiss, B.** *The moment of eclipse.* Faber & Faber, 214p.
Fourteen stories.

1970   **Anderson, C.** *Magellan.* V. Gollancz, 189p.
Revolt in the regimented world of the future. [U.S. 1970]

1970   **Anderson, P.** *Beyond the beyond.* V. Gollancz,.224p.
Five stories. [U.S. 1969]

1970   **Anderson, P.** *Satan's world.* V. Gollancz, 204p.
Space adventures in far galaxies. [U.S. 1969]

1970   **Anderson, P.** *The War of Two Worlds.* D. Dobson, 108p.
The Martians take over the Earth after the twenty-year war between the two planets. [U.S. 1959]

1970   **Anthony, P. (Jacob, P. A.)** *Chthon.* Macdonald, 252p.
Extraordinary adventures in an archaic world.

1970   **Anthony, P. (Jacob, P.A.)** *Sos the Rope.* Faber & Faber, 157p.
First in trilogy; romantic adventures in the tribal world of America after the catastophe. [U.S. 1968]

1970   **Arrighi, M.** *An ordinary man.* Allan Wingate, 190p.
An ironic, didactic tale of consequences, designed to disprove the thesis that "America was morality. . . . The FBI was, as it always had been, an organisation staffed by sincere, dedicated, high-minded men." [U.S. 1970]

1970   **Asimov, I.** *Nightfall.* Rapp & Whiting, 343p.
Twenty stories. [U.S. 1969]

1970   **Atkinson, H.** *The most savage animal.* Cassell, 325p.
A president of the International Red Cross Committee tries to end the war in Vietnam.

1970   **Bair, P.** *The tribunal.* Macdonald, 294p.
In France the Aquitanians declare their independence; in Italy anarchists try to destroy the Leaning Tower.

1970   **Barjavel, R.** *The Ice People.* Translated from the French by Charles Lam Markmann. R. Hart-Davis, 205p.
Below the Antarctic ice scientists discover survivors from an ancient civilization. First published 1968 as *La Nuit des temps.*

1970   **Bearne, C. G.** *(ed.) Vortex: new Soviet science fiction.* Introduction by Ariadne Gromova. McGibbon & Kee, 224p.
Seven stories.

1970   **Bennett, D.** *Adam and Eve and Newbury.* Hodder & Stoughton, 191p.
A man struggles against the impersonal control of the Welfare State.

1970   **Blish, J.** *(ed.) Nebula Award Stories 5.* V. Gollancz, 216p.
Introduction; six stories and two essays on science fiction in 1969. [U.S. 1970]

1970   **Blum, R.** *The simultaneous man.* A. Deutsch, 240p.
A horrible future in which governments encourage experiments on human beings. [U.S. 1970]

1970   **Boucher, A. (White, W. A. P.)** *The compleat werewolf.* W. H. Allen, 256p.
Ten stories. [U.S. 1969]

1970   **Boyd, J.** *The pollinators of Eden.* V. Gollancz, 212p.
A fantasy of sentient plants on the planet Flora. [U.S. 1969]

1970   **Brunner, J.** *The jagged orbit.* Sidgwick & Jackson, 397p.
A view of the future United States – more technology, new weapons, more violence, growing insecurity. [U.S. 1969]

1970   **Buchard, R.** *Thirty seconds over New York.* Translated by J. Williams and R. Abrashkin. Collins, 224p.
Atom bomb threat to New York. First published 1969 as *Trente secondes sur New York.*

1970   **Bulmer, K.** *Quench the burning stars.* R. Hale, 191p.
The inhabitants of Earth face extermination from a race of unknown non-human aliens.

1970   **Bulmer, K.** *Star trove.* R. Hale, 192p.
Adventures of a private agent in the intergalactic world of the future.

1970   **Carnell, J.** *(ed.) New writings in SF 17.* D. Dobson, 190p.
Foreword; seven stories.

1970   **Clarke, A. C.** *The Lion of Commarre; Against the fall of night.*
V. Gollancz, 214p.
A reissue of two earlier works: both deal with themes of search and adventure in
future worlds. [U.S. 1968]

1970   **Clarke, A. C.** *(ed.) 3 for tomorrow.* V. Gollancz, 216p.
Foreword – "the more man 'conquers' *(sic)* Nature, the more prone he becomes to
artificial catastrophe." Contains three stories: Silverberg, R. *How it was when the
past went away*; Zelazny, R. *The Eve of Rumoko*; Blish, J. *We all die naked.*

1970   **Clement, H. (Stubbs, H. C.)** *Natives of space. Pan: Ballantine, 156p.*
Three stories on space topics. [U.S. 1965]

1970   **Compton, D. G.** *The electric crocodile.* Hodder & Stoughton, 222p.
Admonitory tale about the use of computers.

1970   **Conklin, G.** *(ed.) Science fiction Elsewhen.* Rapp & Whiting, 152p.
Introduction; four stories. [U.S. 1968]

1970   **Conklin, G.** *(ed.) Science fiction Elsewhere.* Rapp & Whiting, 166p.
Introduction – "In the world of science fiction, the Future and the Galaxy are the
two great oceans of the imagination" – five stories. [U.S. 1968]

1970   **Cook, R.** *A state of Denmark.* Hutchinson, 269p.
The population tamely accept a dictatorship.

1970   **Cooper, E.** *The last continent.* Hodder & Stoughton, 192p.
An expedition from Mars discovers survivors on Earth two thousand years after
the great catastrophe.

1970   **Cooper, E.** *Son of Kronk.* Hodder & Stoughton, 189p.
Hilarious adventures in the sex-struck world of the future.

1970   **Cooper, E.** *The square root of tomorrow.* R. Hale, 192p.
Foreword – "Science Fiction, whatever else it might be, is not a literature of
prophecy" – twelve stories.

1970   **Cooper, H.** *Sexmax.* New English Library, 127p.
Love upsets the guidance patterns in a computer-controlled world. [U.S. 1969]

1970   **Craig, D. (Tucker, A. H.)** *Contact lost.* J. Cape, 209p.
Strange adventures in the future, when Britain has become a satellite of Moscow.

1970   **Creasey, J.** *The smog.* Hodder & Stoughton, 192p.
Dr. Palfrey traces the source of a mysterious fog that menaces the world.

1970   **Crispin, E. (Montgomery, E. B.)** *(ed.) Best science fiction: 7.* Faber &
Faber, 212p.
Foreword – "Science fiction has gone out into the wide, wide literary world, and
has subjected itself to that world's standards" – twelve stories.

1970   **Daventry, L.** *The ticking is in your head.* R. Hale, 191p.
A struggle for power in the advanced world of the future.

1970   **Davis, B.** *(ed.) The old masters.* New English Library, 128p.
Editorial preface, Introduction by John Carnell; ten stories from the period
1945–55.

1970   **Dick, P.** *A Philip K. Dick Omnibus.* Sidgwick & Jackson, 428p.
Contains: *Dr. Futurity, Unteleported man, Eye in the sky.*

1970   **Dick, P.** *Ubik.* Rapp & Whiting, 202p.
Extrasensory perception and its uses in industrial espionage. [U.S. 1969]

1970   **Dickson, G. R.** *None but man.* Macdonald, 253p.
Interplanetary warfare. [U.S. 1969]

1970   **Dirac, H.** *The profit of doom.* Sidgwick & Jackson, 190p.
The future of medical transplants, when men can obtain eternal life, if they pay.

1970   **Egleton, C.** *A piece of resistance.* Hodder & Stoughton, 192p.
The British resistance fights the Russian invaders.

1970   **Elder, M.** *Paradise is not enough.* R. Hale, 190p.
When robots do all the work, men are left to eat, drink and be merry.

1970   **Fairman, P. W.** *The forgetful robot.* V. Gollancz, 163p.
Fifteen space yarns from a robot. [U.S. 1968]

1970   **Farmer, P. J.** *The alley god.* Sidgwick & Jackson, 176p.
Three stories on science fiction themes. [U.S. 1962]

1970   **Gordon, D. (Payne, D. G.)** *Leap in the dark.* Hodder & Stoughton,
224p.
Crews of a new supersonic airliner become impotent.

1970   **Hall, R.** *The open cage.* Collins, 286p.
Escaped convict returns to a chaotic world – vast floods, electric storms, nuclear
explosions.

1970   **Harker, K.** *The flowers of February.* R. Hale, 191p.
Killer spores arrive from outer space.

1970   **Harrison, H. (Dempsey, H.)** *Captive universe.* Faber & Faber, 185p.
Escape from an oppressive world into a nightmare future. [U.S. 1969]

1970   **Harrison, H. (Dempsey, H.)** *In our hands, the stars.* Faber & Faber,
190p.
International complications after an Israeli scientist discovers a cheap means of
space travel. First published U.S. 1970 as *The Daleth Effect.*

1970   **Harrison, H. (Dempsey, H.) and Aldiss, B.** *(eds.) The year's best SF 3.* Sphere, 206p.
Introduction by Harrison – '1969 was another good year for science fiction' – seventeen stories; Afterword by Aldiss.

1970   **Hartridge, J.** *Earthjacket.* Macdonald, 182p.
A nightmare world of the future in which the air supply is controlled.

1970   **Hay, G.** *(ed.) The disappearing future.* Panther, 158p.
Speculative forecasts about the future from the earliest, in 1763, to the most recent.

1970   **Hay, J. and Keshishian, J. M.** *Death of a Cosmonaut.* Dent, 242p.
Adventure story of the NASA flight missions. First published U.S. 1969 as *Autopsy for a cosmonaut.*

1970   **Heinlein, R.** *The worlds of Robert Heinlein.* New English Library, 127p.
Introduction ("Pandora's Box") by Heinlein: four stories. [U.S. 1966]

1970   **Herbert, F.** *The heaven makers.* New English Library, 141p.
Struggle against the Chem, a race of immensely powerful immortals who sport with mankind. [U.S. 1968]

1970   **Herbert, F.** *The Santaroga barrier.* Rapp & Whiting, 256p.
Psychology expert finds a surprising explanation for the exclusiveness of a small American community. [U.S. 1968]

1970   **Herbert, F.** *The worlds of Frank Herbert.* New English Library, 142p.
Eight stories – other worlds, different societies.

1970   **Hesse, H.** *The Glass Bead Game.* Translated by Richard & Clara Winston. Cape, 558p.
Another translation of *Das Glasperlenspiel* (1943) first published U.S. 1969. See Hesse, 1949.

1970   **High, P. E.** *Double illusion. D. Dobson, 142p.*
A solitary hero leads the revolt against the dangers of a computer-controlled society.

1970   **Hoffman, L.** *The Caves of Karst.* D. Dobson, 224p.
Adventures on the planet Karst in the days of the Earth Empire. [U.S. 1969]

1970   **Hoyle, F. and Hoyle, G.** *Seven steps to the sun.* W. Heinemann, 247p.
Time-travel adventures in ten-year leaps from 1979 to 2019. [U.S. 1970]

1970   **King, V.** *Light a last candle.* Rapp & Whiting, 217p.
A normal man fights for his freedom in a repressive world.

1970   **Knight, D.** *(ed.) Orbit 4.* Rapp & Whiting, 254p.
Nine original stories, each with an introduction. [U.S. 1968]

1970   **Knight, D.** *(ed.) Orbit 5.* Rapp & Whiting, 222p.
Twelve stories. [U.S. 1969]

1970   **Knight, D.** *(ed.) Towards infinity.* V. Gollancz, 319p.
Introduction; nine stories. [U.S. 1968]

1970   **Lafferty, R. A.** *The reefs of Earth.* D. Dobson, 144p.
Alien creatures threaten all life on Earth. [U.S. 1968]

1970   **Laumer, K.** *Catastrophe planet.* D. Dobson, 158p.
Adventures in the future after earthquakes have destroyed the cities of the world.
[U.S. 1966]

1970   **Levin, I.** *This perfect day.* Random House, 334p.
Dissidents in a computer-controlled world. [U.S. 1970]

1970   **Lindsay, D.** *(ed.) Blue moon.* Mayflower, 176p.
Eight stories.

1970   **McCaffrey, A.** *Decision at Doona.* Rapp & Whiting, 246p.
Colonists from over-crowded Earth meet intelligent aliens in a similar plight. [U.S.
1969]

1970   **McCutchan, P.** *Hartinger's Mouse.* Harrap, 222p.
Commander Shaw investigates a lethal disease that brings Britain to a standstill.

1970   **Mano, D. K.** *War is heaven.* Barrie & Jenkins, 226p.
[1971]   War in an imaginary South American country. [U.S. 1970]

1970   **Mariner, D. (Smith, D. M.)** *A Shackleton called Sheila.* R. Hale,
221p.
International conspiracy – assassination attempt foiled.

1970   **Merril, J.** *The best of Sci-Fi 12.* Mayflower, 364p.
Twenty-five stories [U.S. 1968]

1970   **Merril, J.** *(ed.) SF: the best of the best. Part One.* Mayflower, 203p.
Twelve of first thirteen stories in original U.S. 1967 edition. Omits –Henderson, Z.
The anything box.

1970   **Merril, J.** *(ed.) SF: the best of the best. Part Two.* Mayflower, 221p.
Last sixteen stories from original U.S. 1967 edition.

1970   **Miller, J.** *The big win.* J. Cape, 241p.
Adventures in the days when France is the only great power. [U.S. 1969]

1970   **Mitchell, A.** *The Bodyguard.* J. Cape, 188p.
Len Rossman dictates his recollections of life in the violent and vicious days of
the European Revolution.

1970   **Moorcock, M.** *(ed.) Best science fiction from New Worlds, No.5.*
Panther, 160p.
Introduction; eleven stories.

1970   **Moorcock, M.** *(ed.) Best science fiction from New Worlds, No.6.*
Panther, 160p.
Introduction; eleven stories.

1970   **Moorcock, M.** *The Blood Red Game.* Sphere, 154p.
First published in 1965 as *The sundered worlds.*

1970   **Moorcock, M.** *The Eternal Champion.* Mayflower, 159p.
Twentieth century hero called to the far future for the saving of humanity.

1970   **Moorcock, M.** *Phoenix in Obsidian.* Mayflower, 127p.
Continues the heroic adventures of the Eternal Champion.

1970   **Moorcock, M.** *The shores of death.* Sphere, 156p.
First published as *The twilight man,* 1966.

1970   **Moorcock, M.** *The singing citadel.* Mayflower, 125p.
Four stories of heroic adventure.

1970   **Moorcock, M.** *The winds of Limbo.* Sphere, 160p.
First published 1965 as *The Fireclown.*

1970   **Nolan, W. F.** *(ed.) A sea of space.* Bantam Books, 195p.
Fourteen stories on space themes. Published simultaneously in U.S. & Canada.

1970   **Nolan, W. F.** *(ed.) A wilderness of stars.* V. Gollancz, 288p.
Introduction by Shelly Lowenkopf; ten stories "around the theme of man in
conflict with the outer reaches of space". [U.S. 1969]

1970   **Paget, J.** *World well lost.* R. Hale, 206p.
War between the totalitarian state of Earth and the colonists of Alpha Centauri IV.

1970   **Pinchin, F. J.** *Mars 314.* Wingate-Baker, 144p.
The first manned space-craft goes to Mars.

1970   **Platt, C.** *The city dwellers.* Sidgwick & Jackson, 189p.
A sudden drop in population endangers the urban systems of the world.

1970   **Pohl, F.** *The age of the pussyfoot.* V. Gollancz, 191p.
Adventures in the very different world of 2527 A.D. [U.S. 1969]

1970   **Pincher, C.** *The Penthouse conspirators.* M. Joseph, 240p.
A British nuclear submarine is sunk – who sank it?

1970   **Poyer, J.** *North Cape.* V. Gollancz, 231p.
American reconnaissance plane shot down over Russia. [U.S. 1969]

1970   **Priest, C.** *Indoctrinaire.* Faber & Faber, 227p.
Unravelling of the mystery of the Advanced Technique Concentration.

1970   **Rackham J.** *Danger from Vega.* D. Dobson, 149p.
Interplanetary warfare and adventure. [U.S. 1966]

1970   **Rayner, C.** *The meddlers*. Cassell, 304p.
Scandal and sensation follow upon a successful experiment in artificial
innovulation.

1970   **Roberts, K.** *The inner wheel*. R. Hart-Davis, 203p.
Novel in three parts about appearance of the "Gestalt" mind with e.s.p. powers.
[U.S. 1970]

1970   **Ross, J.** *The god killers*. Sidgwick & Jackson, 190p.
A duel of champions helps to prevent interstellar war.

1970   **Saberhagen, F.** *Berserker*. Penguin, 224p.
Mankind defies and defeats the Berserkers. [U.S. 1967]

1970   *Science Fiction Special (1)*. Sidgwick & Jackson, 180 + 175 + 191p.
Contains three novels: Dick, P. K., *The world Jones made,* Dickson, G., *Space
swimmers,* Greenfield, I. A., *Waters of death.*

1970   *Science Fiction Special (2)* Sidgwick & Jackson, 192 + 192 + 188p.
Contains three novels: Leinster, M., *The Listeners,* Williamson, J., *Bright new
universe,* Tubb, E. C. *Escape into space.*

1970   **Sellings, A. (Ley, A.)** *Junk day*. D. Dobson, 192p.
Survival adventures in the days after civilization has been destroyed.

1970   **Shaw, B.** *Night Walk*. New English Library, 143p.
Security on Emm Luther try all means to prevent Sam Tallon bringing his secret
back to Earth [U.S. 1967]

1970   **Shaw, B.** *The palace of eternity*. V. Gollàncz, 192p.
Interplanetary conflict when mankind encounters an alien civilization. [U.S.
1969]

1970   **Shaw, B.** *Shadow of heaven*. New English Library, 125p.
Life in the disaster epoch after a nuclear war has made Earth sterile. [U.S. 1969]

1970   **Silverberg, R.** *Hawksbill Station*. New English Library, 192p.
First published U.S. 1968 (U.K. 1969) as *The Anvil of time.*

1970   **Silverberg, R.** *A Robert Silverberg omnibus*. Sidgwick & Jackson, 142
+ 144 + 182p.
Contains: *Invaders from Earth, Masters of life and death, The time hoppers.* [U.S.]

1970   **Silverberg, R.** *To open the sky*. Sphere, 203p.
Mass hysteria, cults and fads in the over-populated world of the third millennium.
[U.S. 1967],

1970   **Silverberg, R.** *Vornan – 19*. Sidgwick & Jackson, 252p.
Fears for the survival of the world at the end of the twentieth century. [U.S. 1968]

1970   **Slaughter, F. G.** *Countdown*. Hutchinson, 320p.
Investigation of an American rocket disaster. [U.S. 1970]

1970   **Smith, C. (Linebarger, P. M.)** *Under old Earth*. Panther, 188p.
Short stories.

1970   **Spinrad, N.** *Bug Jack Barron*. Macdonald, 327p.
The Foundation for Human Immortality preserves people in liquid helium – for a price. [U.S. 1969]

1970   **Stableford, B.** *The blind worm*. Sidgwick & Jackson, 192p.
The restoration of the human race when Earth is very old and the cities are passing away.

1970   **Sturgeon, T. (Waldo, E. H.)** *Sturgeon in orbit*. V. Gollancz, 192p.
Stories on science fiction and space travel themes. [U.S. 1964]

1970   **Tate, P.** *The thinking seat*. Faber & Faber, 225p.
Trouble comes when it is found that the effluent from the Saline Water Plant in California is changing sea and climate. [U.S. 1969]

1970   **Tucker, J. B.** *Not an earthly chance*. R. Hale, 160p.
Aliens from the Moon plan to take over the world.

1970   **Van Vogt, A. E.** *The pawns of Null-A*. D. Dobson.
Sequel to *The world of Null-A*: superman contends with the Follower for the safety of the universe. First published U.S. 1956 as *Players of $\overline{A}$*.

1970   **Van Vogt, A. E. and Mayne-Hull, E.** *The sea thing*. Sidgwick & Jackson, 222p.
Introduction by Van Vogt; seven stories. First published U.S. 1969 as *Out of the unknown*.

1970   **Wahloo, Peter.** *The steel spring*. Translated by Joan Tate. M. Joseph, 188p.
A moral tale about capitalism, centralised government and alienation. First published 1968 as *Stalsprånget*.

1970   **White, J.** *The aliens among us*. Corgi, 223p.
Seven stories about creatures of other worlds. [U.S. 1962]

1970   **Williams, R. M.** *Beachhead planet*. Sidgwick & Jackson, 190p.
Invasion of earth.

1970   **Williams, T. O.** *A month for mankind*. R. Hale, 191p.
Inhabitants of the planet Boran plan to take possession of Earth.

1970   **Wise, A.** *Leatherjacket*. Weidenfeld & Nicolson, 208p.
An underground movement plans to revive Nazism.

1970   **Wise, A.** *Who killed Enoch Powell?* Weidenfeld & Nicolson, 197p.
Not a political tract – a thriller.

1970   **Wollheim, D. A. and Carr, T.** *(eds.) World's best science fiction, 1970*. V. Gollancz.
Introduction; thirteen stories [U.S. 1970]

1970   **Zamyatin, Y.** *We*. Translated from the Russian by Bernard Guilbert Guerney, with introduction and bibliographical note by Michael Glenny. J. Cape, 285p.
A famous prophecy of life in a totalitarian state – a model for *1984* and *Brave New World*. Written in 1920 but not published in Russia.

1970   **Zelazny, R.** *Isle of the Dead*. Rapp & Whiting, 190p.
A citizen of the twentieth century lives on to be a powerful god of a remote future society. [U.S. 1969]

1971   **Abé, K.** *Inter Ice Age 4*. Translated from the Japanese by E. Dale Saunders. Cape, 228p. Illus.
In the twenty-first century, as the ice caps begin to melt, some scientists begin secret work on biological mutations. First published 1964 as *Dayion Kampyoki*. [U.S. 1970]

1971   **Adlard, M.** *Interface*. Sidgwick & Jackson, 191p.
Technology and trouble in the vast automated Stahlex works on Teeside.

1971   **Aldiss, B.** *The Best SF Stories of Brian Aldiss*. Faber & Faber, 260p.
Revised and enlarged edition of the 1965 book – "Six stories from the old collection banished into outer darkness and eight new recruits taking their place."

1971   **Aldiss, B.** *Omnibus 2*. Sidgwick & Jackson, 590p.
Contains: *Non-stop, Male response, Space, Time and Nathaniel*.

1971   **Allen, J.** *Date for your death*. Translated from the Danish by Marianne Helweg. Hogarth Press, 192p.
A new computer programme can predict the date of a man's death. First published 1970 as *Data for din dod*.

1971   **Amosoff, N. M.** *Notes from the future*. Translated from the Russian by George St. George. J. Cape, 384p.
Professor Prokhoroff conducts the first experiment in prolonged anabiosis and returns to consciousness in 1991. First published as *Zapiski iz budushchego*. [U.S. 1970]

1971   **Anderson, A.** *Wings of the morning*. R. Hale, 192p.
Patient wakes to life in 2020 after fifty years in the deep freeze. [U.S. 1970].

1971   **Anderson, P.** *Tau Zero*. V. Gollancz, 192p.
Continuous acceleration gives a time contraction that brings a spaceship to the end of the universe. [U.S. 1971]

1971   **Anthony, P. (Jacob, P. A.)** *Prostho plus*. V. Gollancz, 190p.
A comic tale of the adventures of a prosthodontist kidnapped by aliens. [U.S. 1971]

1971   **Ardies, T.** *Their man in the White House*. Macmillan, 190p.
Russian plot to place an agent in the family of a candidate for the Presidency. [U.S. 1971]

1971   **Asimov, I.** *Nightfall One*. Panther, 176p.
Contains first five stories from *Nightfall*, 1970.

1971   **Asimov, I.** *Nightfall Two*. Panther, 192p.
Contains remaining stories from *Nightfall*, 1970.

1971   **Ball, B.** *Timepit*. D. Dobson, 188p.
Follows on *Timepiece*, 1968: bizarre adventures with the Pivot of Time and the Zugbugs.

1971   **Baxter, J.** *(ed.) The second Pacific book of science fiction*. Angus & Robertson, x, 149p.
Introduction – "These fine stories are equal to anything done in the world today" – thirteen stories by Australian authors. Also published Australia 1971.

1971   **Berk, H.** *The Sun grows cold*. V. Gollancz, 245p.
After World War III life begins again in an underground centre where memories are wiped out and new personalities created. [U.S. 1971]

1971   **Bertin, J.** *The Pyramids from space*. John Gresham, 192p.
Sinister cosmic traps transport the unwary through time-space. [U.S. 1970]

1971   **Bevis, H. U.** *Space stadium*. John Gresham, 192p.
Instead of vast armies picked teams make war in deep space. [U.S. 1970]

1971   **Blish, J.** *Anywhen*. Faber & Faber, 185p.
Eight stories. [U.S. 1970]

1971   **Bodelsen, A.** *Freezing point*. Translated from the Swedish by Joan Tate. Michael Joseph, 175p.
A grotesque, frightening tale of the choice that has to be made between natural death and artificial life in a "frozen down" condition. First published as *Frysepunktet*, 1969.

1971   **Boyd, J.** *The rakehells of heaven*. V. Gollancz, 192p.
A comic tale of the Mandon Space Academy mission to the distant planet of Harlech. [U.S. 1969]

1971   **Caidin, M.** *The Mendelov Conspiracy*. W. H. Allen, 274p.
A scientist prepares a drastic cure for the madness of atomic warfare. [U.S. 1969].

1971   **Carnell, J.** *(ed.) The best from New Writings in SF*. D. Dobson, 253p.
Foreword, eleven stories.

1971   **Carnell, J.** *(ed.) New Writings in SF 18*. D. Dobson, 188p.
Foreword; seven stories.

1971   **Carnell, J.** *(ed.) New Writings in SF 19*. D. Dobson, 190p.
Foreword; seven stories.

1971   **Casini, T.** *The last mass of Paul VI*. Translated from the Italian by Scott McCallum. Britons Publishing Company, 183p.
Theological views on the contemporary role of the Catholic Church, set in the context of a flight by Paul VI to China. First published 1970 as *L'ultima messa di Paolo VI*.

1971   **Cheetham, A.** *Science against man*. Macdonald, 221p.
Eleven stories about science and society. [U.S. 1970].

1971   **Compton, D. G.** *Hot wireless sets, aspirin tablets, the sandpaper sides of used matchboxes, and something that might have been castor oil*. M. Joseph, 212p.
An original and mordant comedy of a secret research establishment at work on plans for a time-travel device.

1971   **Cooper, E.** *The Overman Culture*. Hodder & Stoughton, 190p.
A group of children discover their true identity and solve the mystery of their society.

1971   **Cooper, E.** *Unborn tomorrow*. R. Hale, 223p.
Foreword – "I have written several novels and a large number of short stories, and I still do not know what science fiction is." – nine stories.

1971   **Coughlin, W. J.** *The destruction committee*. Harrap, 278p.
A tale of future violence and political struggle in the United States.

1971   **Craig, W.** *The Tashkent Crisis*. Hodder & Stoughton, 279p.
The Russians demand the unconditional surrender of the United States, and then . . . [U.S. 1971].

1971   **Creasey, J.** *The unbegotten*. Hodder & Stoughton, 189p.
Dr. Palfrey fights the menace of world-wide sterility.

1971   **Darrington, H.** *Gravitor*. Sidgwick & Jackson, 203p.
Scientists plot to change Earth's gravity and save the world from tyranny.

1971   **Daventry, L.** *Terminus*. R. Hale, 192p.
Life in the regimented world of 1980.

1971   **Delany, S. R.** *The fall of the Towers*. Sphere, 416p.
One-volume edition of the *Empire of Toromon* trilogy.

1971   **Dick, P. K.** *Eye in the sky*. Arrow, 256p.
An accident to the Proton Beam Deflector has an extraordinary effect on individual lives. [U.S. 1957].

1971   **Dick, P. K.** *The galactic pot-healer*. V. Gollancz, 191p.
In a repressive, inflation-ridden world the hero agrees to raise the ancient cathedral of Heldscalla from the sea-bed of Mare Nostrum. [U.S. 1969]

1971   **Dick, P. K.** *The preserving machine*. V. Gollancz, 252p.
Fourteen stories, of which Dick wrote in an unpublished foreword that they "are a

series of events. Crisis is the key to story-writing, a sort of brinkmanship mires his characters in happenings so sticky as to seem impossible of solution." [U.S. 1969]

1971   **Dick, P. K. and Nelson, R.** *The Ganymede takeover*. Arrow, 192p.
Extraordinary consequences follow on the use of illusion machines. [U.S. 1967]

1971   **Disch, T. M.** *White Fango goes dingo*. Arrow, 192p.
First published U.K. 1966 as *102 H-bombs*.

1971   **Drury, A.** *Throne of Saturn*. M. Joseph, xii, 588p.
Trials and tribulations of the preparations for the first American expedition to Mars. [U.S. 1970]

1971   **Edmondson, G. C.** *The ship that sailed the time stream*. Arrow, 192p.
Adventures of a US Navy ship that finds itself switched back to the Viking period. [U.S. 1965]

1971   **Egleton, C.** *Last post for a partisan*. Hodder & Stoughton, 224p.
Continues the story of the Russian occupation of Great Britain, begun in *A piece of resistance*.

1971   **Elder, M.** *The alien Earth*. R. Hale, 188p.
The Planetary Council sends a spaceship to investigate the forgotten planet of Earth.

1971   **Ellison, H.** *(ed.) Dangerous visions 1*. David Bruce & Watson, 359p.
Foreword by Isaac Asimov, Introduction by Harlan Ellison, and Introduction to the British edition by Harlan Ellison: fourteen original stories, each with an introduction by the editor, from the original U.S. 1967 one-volume edition.

1971   **Ellison, H.** *(ed.) Dangerous visions 2*. David Bruce & Watson, 293p.
Forewords by Asimov and Ellison: nineteen stories from the 1967 edition.

1971   **Frame, J.** *Intensive care*. W. H. Allen, 342p.
Fantasy of the National Sleep Days which were intended to eliminate unrest and disorder. [U.S. 1970]

1971   **Geen, E.** *Tolstoy lives at 12N B9*. Weidenfeld & Nicolson, 224p.
An ironic account of life in the organized, supervised, computerised future.

1971   **Geston, M. S.** *Lords of the starship*. M Joseph, 158p.
In a time of warring nations the Caroline Republic plans to build a vast starship. [U.S. 1967]

1971   **Gibson, C.** *The Pepper Leaf*. Chatto & Windus, 240p.
Four people from the Decontamination Farms Society are cut off from their community by an earthquake.

1971   **Gordon, S.** *Time story*. New English Library, 144p.
Criminal from the present escapes into the future.

1971   **Goulart, R.** *Gadget man.* New English Library, 111p.
A sergeant from the Social Wing of the Police Corps seeks a rebel in the
Republic of Southern California. [U.S. 1971]

1971   **Green, J.** *Gold the man.* V. Gollancz, 221p.
Hero visits the planet of the giant Hilt-Sil to discover why they are attacking
Earth.

1971   **Grinnell, D.** *To Venus! To Venus!* R. Hale, 189p.
Americans go to the rescue of Russians on Venus. [U.S. 1970]

1971   **Harrison, H. (Dempsey, H.)** *The Stainless Steel Rat's revenge.* Faber
& Faber, 185p.
Slippery Jim intervenes with spectacular effect in Cliandian affairs. [U.S. 1970]

1971   **Harrison, H. (Dempsey, H.)** *The year 2000.* Faber & Faber, 288p.
Introduction by Harrison: thirteen stories about life in the future. [U.S. 1970]

1971   **Harrison, H. (Dempsey, H.) and Aldiss, B.** *(eds.) The year's best SF
4.* Sphere, 221p.
Introduction by Harrison, Afterword by Aldiss: fourteen stories.

1971   **Harrison, M. J.** *The committed men.* New Authors Ltd., 184p.
A post-catastrophe story: the future belongs to the mutants who are immune from
the lethal effects of radiation. [U.S. 1971]

1971   **Harrison, M. J.** *The Pastel City.* New English Library, 144p.
On a desolate Earth the Lord of Methven fights for the young Queen.

1971   **Hassler, K. W.** *Destination Terra.* John Gresham, 192p.
Trouble with the Intergalactic Council when a Centavian is brought to Terra. [U.S.
1970]

1971   **Hassler, K. W.** *A message from Earth.* John Gresham, 192p.
One man saves Earth from destruction by the might of the planet Kraaken. [U.S.
1970]

1971   **Heinlein, R.** *I will fear no evil.* New English Library, 414p.
Brain of old man transplanted into body of young female. [U.S. 1970]

1971   **Heinlein, R.** *The star beast.* New English Library, 173p.
Adventures of Lummox, a domesticated creature from space. [U.S. 1954]

1971   **Herbert, F.** *Dune Messiah.* V. Gollancz, 256p.
Second in the *Dune* cycle: Paul Muad-Dib fights the Bene Gesserit sisterhood.
[U.S. 1969]

1971   **High, P. E.** *Butterfly Planet.* R. Hale, 160p.
A secret struggle for the safety of the world.

1971   **Hill, E.** *The G. C. Radiation.* R. Hale, 159p.
A handful of Americans and Russians survive a universal disaster.

1971 **Hoyle, F. and Hoyle, G.** *The molecule men; and, the Monster of Loch Ness*. Heinemann, 255p.
First novella is a variant on the space invasion story; second novella concerns a creature of immense power discovered on the bed of Loch Ness.

1971 **Hughes, J.** *Ends*. Secker & Warburg, 227p.
When the government announces the date of Cessation the Starvies, the Lifers and the Fail-goners refuse to accept the edict. [U.S. 1971]

1971 **Hunter, E. (Lombino, S. A.)** *Nobody knew they were there*. Constable, 249p.
Anxieties and assassinations on the campus in 1974. [U.S. 1971]

1971 **Hurd, D. and Osmond, A.** *Scotch on the Rocks*. Collins, 225p.
The Scottish Liberation Army raises the standard of revolt.

1971 **Hyams, E.** *The death lottery*. Longman, 224p.
A lottery on the deaths of political leaders promises millions to the winners.

1971 **Jensen, N.** *The galactic colonizers*. R. Hale, 192p.
Space explorers meet a new kind of rational being.

1971 **Jones, D. F.** *Don't pick the flowers*. Panther, 237p.
Drilling operations in the Pacific release nitrogen into the atmosphere with catastrophic results.

1971 **King, V.** *Candy man*. V. Gollancz, 191p.
Android discovers the purpose of his existence.

1971 **Lange, O.** *Vandenberg*. Peter Davies, 333p.
Life under the Soviet Military Government of the United States. [U.S. 1971]

1971 **Le Guin, U.** *City of illusions*. V. Gollancz, 192p.
A first-class tale of a search for identity in the distant future when Earth is a world of forest people, wandering tribes and the mysterious Shing. [U.S. 1967]

1971 **Lem, S.** *Solaris*. Translated from the Polish by Joanna Kilmartin and Steve Cox. Faber & Faber, 204p.
An original and highly inventive story: the attempt to understand the planet Solaris, apparently a single living organism. First published 1961 as *Solaris*. [U.S. 1970]

1971 **Levy, D.** *The gods of Foxcroft*. New English Library, 240p.
Moral tale of the waste of natural resources, annihilating wars, pollution – and the hope of regeneration. [U.S. 1970]

1971 **Lippincott, D.** *E pluribus bang!* M. Joseph, 221p.
Comic tale of the 39th President of the United States, believed to have committed murder. [U.S. 1970]

1971 **Long, F. B.** *Monster from out of time*. R. Hale, 176p.
Time travel and space adventures.

1971   **Ludwig, E. W.** *The mask of Jon Culon.* J. Gresham, 192p.
Sleeper awakes in the strange world dominated by the Brothers of New Earth.
[U.S. 1970]

1971   **McCaffrey, A.** *The ship who sang.* Rapp & Whiting, 349p.
A human brain is encapsulated as the controlling mechanism of a spaceship.
[U.S. 1969]

1971   **McCutchan, P.** *This Drakotny.* Harrap, 222p.
Commander Shaw takes a hand in the power struggle in Czechoslovakia.

1971   **Mackelworth, R. W.** *Tiltangle.* R. Hale, 190p.
Struggle to survive in a new ice age.

1971   **Maine, C. E. (McIlwain, D.)** *The Random factor.* Hodder & Stoughton, 240p.
Investigation of the Yope, a complex piece of extra-terrestrial engineering that can project people into other times.

1971   **Maitland, D.** *T minus Tower.* MacGibbon & Kee, 191p.
A complicated and comic tale of the plan to send the Post Office Tower into space.

1971   **Mason, D. R.** *Matrix.* R. Hale, 191p.
Revolt against the androids and computers of Paradise City. [U.S. 1970]

1971   **Mason D. R.** *Satellite 54-Zero.* Ballantine: Pan, 185p.
Space satellite makes contact with a source of power on Jupiter. [U.S. 1971]

1971   **Melling, L.** *First man on Mars.* Torch Publishing Co., 151p.
Heroic adventures on the fertile planet of Mars.

1971   **Meyers, R.** *Destiny and the dolphins.* R. Hale, , 192p.
Submarine adventures: ends with the obliteration of the human race by a plague.

1971   **Montano, P.** *Godhead.* Arlington Books, 208p.
Pope Valentine works in his own way for church unity and world peace.

1971   **Moorcock, M.** *(ed.) Best SF from New Worlds 7.* Panther, 175p. Illus.
Short stories

1971   **Moorcock, M.** *City of the Beast.* New English Library, 127p.
First published in 1965 as *Warriors of Mars* under the pseudonym of Edward P. Bradbury.

1971   **Moorcock, M.** *A cure for cancer.* Illustrated by Malcolm Dean. Allison & Busby, 256p.
The exotic and erotic adventures, exploits and extravagances of Jerry Cornelius. Second in the series.

1971   **Moorcock, M.** *The Knight of the swords.* Mayflower, 143p.
First in *The Books of Corum.*

1971   **Moorcock, M.** *Lord of the spiders.* New English Library, 126p.
First published 1968 as *Blades of Mars* under the pseudonym of Edward P. Bradbury.

1971   **Moorcock, M.** *Masters of the pit.* New English Library, 128p.
First published 1965 as *Barbarians of Mars* under the pseudonym of Edward P. Bradbury.

1971   **Moorcock, M.** *(ed.) New Worlds 1.* Sphere, 176p. Illus.
Stories by six authors.

1971   **Moorcock, M.** *(ed.) New Worlds 2.* Sphere, 192p.
Fourteen stories.

1971   **Moorcock, M.** *The Queen of the Swords.* Mayflower, 144p.
Second in the *Books of Corum:* Prince Corum defeats the mighty powers of Queen Xiombarg.

1971   **Moorcock, M.** *The rituals of infinity.* Arrow, 192p.
Professor Faustaff builds bridges between subspace worlds.

1971   **Moorcock, M.** *The sleeping sorceress.* New English Library, 140p.
Elric of Melniboné continues the war against the Lords of Chaos.

1971   **Moorcock, M. and Jones, L.** *(eds.) The nature of the catastrophe.* Hutchinson, viii, 213p.
Introduction by James Colvin; sixteen conjectures by various authors and one comic strip on Jerry Cornelius themes.

1971   **Morgan, D.** *Inside.* Corgi, 158p.
Survivors from the devastation of Earth learn how they can restore the world.

1971   **Nolan, W. F.** *(ed.) 3 to the highest power.* Corgi, 139p.
Three stories – Ray Bradbury, Theodore Sturgeon, Chad Oliver – each with an editorial introduction. [U.S. 1968]

1971   **Oliver, C.** *The shores of another sea.* V. Gollancz, 192p
Invasion by alien intelligence. [U.S. 1970]

1971   **Percy, W.** *Love in the ruins.* Eyre & Spottiswoode, 403p.
In a divided, crumbling United States Dr. Thomas More, a descendant of the saint, finds a way to diagnose the maladies of his countrymen. [U.S. 1971]

1971   **Pohl, F.** *Day million.* V. Gollancz, 188p.
Introduction by Pohl; ten stories. [U.S. 1970]

1971   **Pohl, F.** *(ed.) The 11th Galaxy Reader.* R. Hale, 254p.
Introduction, 10 stories. [U.S. 1969]

1971   *Pollution! Omnibus.* Sidgwick & Jackson, 256p.
Contains: Harrison, H. *Make room!*; Kornbluth, C. M. *Shark ship*; Simak, C. *City*.

971   **Purser, P.** *The Holy Father's navy.* Hodder & Stoughton, 191p.
Papal aircraft carrier is the instrument of a modern crusade.

971   **Quigley, J.** *The last checkpoint.* Collins, 222p.
Tragedy of an idealist, Chief of State in the German Democratic Republic, whom the Russians cannot tolerate and the West cannot undestand.

1971   **Rankine, J. (Mason, D. R.)** *The Plantos Affair.* D. Dobson, 150p.
Problems of reality and illusion on the planet Plantos Three.

1971   **Roth, P.** *Our gang.* Cape, 200p.
Satire on the life, works, death and descent into Hell of Richard Nixon.
[U.S 1971]

1971   **Rowe, H.** *(pseud.) The power box.* Cassell, 339p.
Conflict of interests in the development of a new television company.

1971   **Sale, D.** *Come to mother.* W. H. Allen, 208p
A young wife returns to living after fifty years in the deep freeze.

1971   **Salinger, P.** *For the eyes of the President only.* Collins, 349p.
Admonitory tale about American intervention in Southern American affairs. [U.S 1971]

1971   *Science Fiction Special 3.* Sidgwick & Jackson, 294 + 193 + 182p.
Contains: Wadsworth, P. M., *Overmind*; Sturgeon, T., *Caviar*; Silverberg, R., *The time-hoppers.*

1971   *Science fiction Special 4.* Sidgwick & Jackson, 190 + 191 + 192p.
Contains: Van Vogt, A. E., *The winged man* (with Edna Mayne Hull); Harness, C. L., *The rose*; Silverberg, R., *The man in the maze.*

1971   *Science Fiction Special 5.* Sidgwick & Jackson, 254 + 210 + 178p.
Contains: Panshin, A., Rite of passage; Stableford, B., *Cradle of the sun*; Haining, P., *The future makers.*

1971   **Scott, A.** *Project Dracula.* Sphere, 319p.
Explosion in a biological research station releases deadly anthrax spores.

1971   **Shaw, B.** *1 million tomorrows.* V. Gollancz, 246p.
By 2176 A.D. all men can halt the ageing process if they are prepared to become sterile and impotent.[U.S. 1970]

1971   **Shipway, G.** *The Chilian Club.* Peter Davies, 246p.
Plans to save Britain from chaos and from the Communist-dominated trades unions.

1971   **Silverberg, R.** *(ed.) Alpha One.* Ballantine-Pan, 288p.
Introduction; fourteen stories. [U.S. 1970]

1971   **Silverberg, R.** *(ed.) Dark stars.* Ballantine-Pan, x, 309p.
Introduction – "a book of dark dreams for a dark time" – sixteen stories chosen to "demonstrate why science fiction is uniquely suited to be the vehicle of modern myth". [U.S. 1969]

1971   **Silverberg, R.** *(ed.) Great short novels of science fiction.* Ballantine: Pan, vii, 373p.
Editor's introduction; six stories. [U.S. 1970]

1971   **Silverberg, R.** *(ed.) The mirror of infinity.* Sidgwick & Jackson, xi 248p.
Introduction gives brief history of science fiction; thirteen stories, each with a critical introduction. [U.S. 1970]

1971   **Silverberg, R.** *(ed.) Science fiction Hall of Fame, Volume One.* V. Gollancz, xi, 558p.
Introduction – "This is as nearly definitive an anthology of modern science fiction writers as il likely to be compiled for quite some time" – twenty-six stories chosen by the members of the Science Fiction Writers of America. [U.S. 1970]

1971   **Simak, C. D.** *(ed.) Nebula Award stories 6.* V. Gollancz, 220p.
Introduction by Simak, foreword by Thomas D. Clareson; seven stories. [U.S. 1971]

1971   **Smith, E. E.** *Galactic Patrol.* W. H. Allen, 255p.
Third in the *Lensman Series:* Kimball Kinnison fights the Boskonians. [U.S. 1950]

1971   **Smith, E. E.** *Grey Lensman.* W. H. Allen, 256p.
Fourth in *Lensman Series:* Now it was up to Lensman Kinnison using his fantastic mental powers, to infiltrate the Boskonian strongholds." [U.S. 1951]

1971   **Spinrad, N.** *The last hurrah of the Golden Horde.* MacDonald, 215p.
Eighteen stories. [U.S. 1970]

1971   **Stone, L. F.** *Out of the Void.* R. Hale, 192p.
A tale of the first space journey and of the men from Mars who came back thirty years later.

1971   **Story, J. T.** *Little dog's day.* Allison & Busby, 174p.
Anti-bureaucratic activities in the highly efficient United Europe of the future.

1971   **Stout, M.** *W.H.A.M.* Sphere, 157p.
The movement, We Hate all Males, finishes off the men – almost.

1971   **Sutton, H. (Slavitt, D.)** *Vector.* Hodder & Stoughton, 354p.
When the President bans the manufacture of biological weapons, the research institutes look for other methods. [U.S. 1970]

1971   **Swerling, A.** *The Cambridge Plague.* Trinity Lane Press, Cambridge, 135p. Illus.
Fantasia on the social and sexual consequences of a plague in Cambridge.

1971   **Tate, P.** *Gardens 12345.* Faber & Faber, 207p.
The Agency for Temperate Environmental Control works for "the study and analysis of behaviours in amiable natural surroundings."

1971   **Tenn, W. (Klass, P.)** *The human angle.* Ballantine-Pan, 221p.
Seven stories – space, politics, art [U.S. 1956]

1971   **Tenn, W. (Klass, P.)** *Of men and monsters.* Ballantine: Pan, 251p.
Ironic account of indomitable mankind in the fight against the Monster Lords of Earth [U.S. 1968]

1971   **Tenn, W. (Klass, P.)** *The square root of man.* Ballantinte: Pan, 221p.
Author's note; nine stories. [U.S. 1968]

1971   **Tenn, W. (Klass, P.)** *The wooden star.* Ballantine: Pan, 251p.
Author's note; eleven stories – "social satires, thinly disguised as science fiction". [U.S. 1968]

1971   **Tucker, W.** *The Year of the Quiet Sun.* R. Hale, 221p.
The Time Displacement Vehicle is designed to take a team of trained investigators into the future. [U.S. 1970]

1971   **Van Vogt, A. E.** *Quest for the future.* Sidgwick & Jackson, 253p.
Time-travel between different worlds and different times. [U.S. 1970]

1971   **Van Vogt, A. E.** *Van Vogt Omnibus 2.* Sidgwick & Jackson, 512p.
Contains: *The mind cage*; *Slan*, *The winged man* (with E. Mayne Hull).

1971   **Warren, A.** *This time next October.* Dent, 147p
United Kingdom torn between rival factions – the Neutralists and the Thirteen Club.

1971   **White, J.** *Tomorrow is too far.* M. Joseph, 174p.
Experiments in time travel.

1971   **Williams, E. C.** *The call of Utopia.* R. Hale, 192p.
A prisoner from the submarine cages plans his revenge.

1971   **Williams, R. M.** *Now comes tomorrow.* Sidgwick & Jackson, 160p.
Leukemia Seven ravages the world.

1971   **Winton, G.** *The fighting Téméraire.* M. Joseph, 239p.
British submarine sinks Russian destroyer in the Black Sea.

1971   **Wollheim, D. A. and Carr, T.** *(eds.) World's best science fiction 1971.*
V. Gollancz, 320p.
Editor's introduction; 15 stories. [U.S. 1971]

1971   **Zelzany, R.** *Damnation alley.* Faber & Faber.
Heroic expolits in the devastated United States after the Big Raid. [U.S. 1969]

1972   **Adlard, M.** *Volteface.* Sidgwick & Jackson, 210p.
Continues the themes of *Interface*, 1971: executives of Stahlex deal with the dangers and problems of a great industrial complex.

1972   **Anderson, P.** *The Byworlder.* V. Gollancz, 190p.
Problems and permutations of human-alien communication after the Sigman appears. [U.S. 1971]

1972   **Anderson, P.** *The enemy stars.* Coronet Books, 141p.
A spaceship journeys for centuries to Alpha Crucis. [U.S. 1959]

1972   **Anderson, P.** *The rebel worlds.* Coronet Books, 144p.
Starship Commander Flandry once again saves the Terran Empire. [U.S. 1969]

1972   **Anderson, P.** *Un-Man and other novellas.* D. Dobson, 158p.
Three novellas: supermen v. potential world dictators; a commercial war;
interplanetary peace-keeping. [U.S. 1962]

1972   **Anthony, P. (Jacob, P. A.)** *Macroscope.* Sphere, 347p.
A new viewing device shows mankind the depths of space. [U.S. 1969]

1972   **Anthony, P. (Jacob, P. A.)** *Var the Stick.* Faber & Faber, 191p.
Continues the story begun in *Sos the Rope:* more romantic adventures in the
archaic future. [U.S. 1970]

1972   **Ardies, T.** *This suitcase is going to explode.* Macmillan, 234p.
Who is planting nuclear bombs in cities? [U.S. 1972]

1972   **Asimov, I.** *The gods themselves.* V. Gollancz, 288p.
A new source of power, the Inter-Universe Electron Pump, threatens to blow up
the sun. [U.S. 1972]

1972   **Ball, B. N.** *Night of the robots.* Sidgwick & Jackson, 235p.
Mankind struggles against the robots.

1972   **Ball, J.** *The first team.* M. Joseph, 416p.
A resurgent United States recovers its liberty from the occupying power.
[U.S. 1971]

1972   **Bee, D.** *The victims.* Macmillan, 232p.
Virulent influenza in Africa becomes a world danger.

1972   **Bertin, J.** *The interplanetary adventurers.* R. Hale, 190p.
Treasure-hunting and insurrection on Mars. [U.S. 1970]

1972   **Bevis, H. V.** *The time winder.* John Gresham, 192p.
Scientist escapes the robots of the Central Authority by travelling back in time.
[U.S. 1970]

1972   **Biggle, L.** *(ed.) Nebula Award Stories 7.* V. Gollancz, 320p.
Introduction by Damon Knight; observations on science fiction by Poul Anderson
('The Science') and Theodore Sturgeon ('The Fiction'): eleven stories. [U.S. 1972]

1972   **Binder, P. and Ordish, G.** *Ladies only.* D. Dobson, 241p.
Comic tale of fertility drugs, the Multibirth Pill, and then the perfecting of
parthenogenetic techniques.

1972   **Blackburn, J.** *Devil Daddy.* Cape, 191p.
The powers of evil threaten the world with the Satan Germ.

1972   **Blish, J.** *And all the stars a stage.* Faber & Faber, 206p.
The survivors of mankind voyage through space to find a new world. [U.S. 1971]

1972   **Blish, J.** *The day after Judgement.* Faber & Faber, 166p.
Sequel to *Black Easter;* Strategic Air Command joins in the battle against the forces of evil. [U.S. 1972]

1972   **Blish, J.** *Star Trek 1.* Corgi Books, 136p.
Seven episodes adapted by James Blish from the *Star Trek* television series which were created by Gene Roddenbury, Paramount Picture Corporation. For information on the *Star Trek* publications see *Note 12.*

1972   **Bova, B.** *Star watchman.* D. Dobson, 223p.
Soldiers of the Star Watch, the interstellar army of the Terran Empire, fight the rebels of Shinar. [U.S. 1944]

1972   **Brunner, J.** *Timescoop.* Sidgwick & Jackson, 156p.
A world-emperor plunders the past in order to gain absolute power. [U.S. 1969]

1972   **Burke, J.** *Expo 80.* Cassell, 298p.
International plots and sabotage in 1980.

1972   **Burroughs, E. R.** *The Moon maid.* Tom Stacey Reprints, 412p.
Contains three stories: two on lunar adventure themes – *The Moon maid, The Moon men* – and one on the future of Earth – *The Red Hawk.* [U.S. 1926]

1972   **Burroughs, W. S.** *The Wild Boys.* Calder & Boyars, 184p.
Underground armies operate in the great cities of a suppressive future police state. [U.S. 1971]

1972   **Calvin, H. (Hanley, C.)** *Take two popes.* Hutchinson, 208p.
The Pope and his double are kidnapped on a visit to a banana republic.

1972   **Carnell, J.** *(ed.) New writings in SF20.* Corgi, 192p.
Foreword; six stories about the macabre.

1972   **Carnell, J.** *(ed.) New writings in SF21.* Sidgwick & Jackson, 192p.
Foreword by Diane Lloyd; seven stories.

1972   **Carter, L.** *Giant of world's end.* Fivestar (Manchester), 141p.
Heroic adventures seven hundred million years in the future. [U.S. 1969]

1972   **Cheetham, A.** *(ed.) Bug-eyed monsters.* Sidgwick & Jackson, 280p.
Ten stories about variations in organic and intelligent life forms.

1972   **Clarke, A. C.** *The lost worlds of 2001.* Sidgwick & Jackson, 240p.
Various versions of the script for the Stanley Kubrik film *Space Odyssey 2001.* [U.S. 1972]

1972   **Clarke, A. C.** *Tales from the White Hart.* Sidgwick & Jackson, 179p.
Preface; fifteen stories written between 1953 and 1956. [U.S. 1957]

1972   **Clarke, A. C.** *The wind from the Sun.* V. Gollancz, 193p.
Eighteen short stories, all written in the 'sixties'. [U.S. 1972]

1972   **Conklin, G.** *(ed.) Possible tomorrows.* Sidgwick & Jackson, 188p.
Five stories, originally published U.S. 1964 as *Five-odd.*

1972   **Cooper, E.** *Kronk.* Coronet, 189p.
First published 1970 as *Son of Kronk.*

1972   **Cooper, E.** *Who needs men?* Hodder & Stoughton, 192p.
Men are no longer necessary in a world where women can reproduce by cloning or parthenogenesis; but there are still those men in the Highlands.

1972   **Cowper, R. (Murry, C. M.)** *Clone.* V. Gollancz, 190p.
An amusing and ironical tale about the adventures of four identical laboratory-produced creatures.

1972   **Cowper, R. (Murry, C. M.)** *Kuldesak.* V. Gollancz, 187p.
After 2,000 years of underground existence men rediscover the wonders of life on the surface.

1972   **Dallas, I.** *The Book of Strangers.* V. Gollancz, 151p.
A journey across deserts and mountains in search of the true Islamic faith.

1972   **Daventry, L.** *Degree XII.* R. Hale, 190p.
An alien comes to destroy Earth.

1972   **Daventy, L.** *Twenty-One billionth paradox.* R. Hale, 204p.
Five criminals are condemned to voyage to the edge of the universe. [U.S. 1971]

1972   **Davies, L. P.** *Ground Star Conspiracy.* Sphere, 160p.
New edition of *The Alien,* 1968.

1972   **Davies, L. P.** *What did I do tomorrow?* Barrie & Jenkins, 192p.
A school boy suddenly finds himself in the future and suspected of murder.

1972   **Dick, P. K.** *A maze of death.*V. Gollancz, 216p.
Mysterious murders on planet Delmak-O. [U.S. 1970]

1972   **Dick, P. K.** *Solar Lottery.* Arrow Books, 192p.
First published U.K. 1956 as *World of chance.* [U.S. 1955]

1972   **Dick-Lauder, G.** *A skull and two cyrstals.* D. Dobson, 192p.
Space adventure – a mysterious girl and a heroic spaceman.

1972   **Disch, T. M. 34.** MacGibbon & Kee, 201p. Illus.
Six stories on themes of human behaviour.

1972   **Du Maurier, D.** *Rule Britannia.* V. Gollancz, 318p.
Economic disasters follow on British withdrawal from Common Market; and American troops arrive to consolidate USUK – the union of the United Kingdom with the United States.

1972 **Egleton, C.** *The Judas mandate.* Hodder & Stoughton, 224p.
Last of the trilogy that began with *A piece of resistance:* the British underground movement continues the struggle against the Russians.

1972 **Elder, M.** *Nowhere on earth.* R. Hale, 191p.
A tale of freedom-fighters, Thought Police and over-population in the Britain of 2173.

1972 **Farmer, P. J.** *Night of light.* Penguin, 176p.
An Earthman takes part in the struggle between good and evil on the planet Kareen. [U.S. 1966]

1972 **Forrest, D.** *After me, the Deluge.* Hodder & Stoughton, 189p.
Extraordinary goings-on after God tells Father Benoir the end of the world is at hand.

1972 **Gale, J .E.** *Like an evening gone.* Janay Publishing Company, 200p.
Space travel, planetary colonization, and the prospects for a resited Earth.

1972 **Garfield, B.** *Deep cover.* Hodder & Stoughton, 356p.
Espionage operations as USA and USSR come to the brink of war. [U.S. 1971]

1972 **Geston, M. S.** *Out of the mouth of the Dragon.* M. Joseph, 156p.
Final wars and desolate kingdoms. [U.S. 1959]

1972 **Glanville, B.** *The financiers.* Secker & Warburg, 226p.
Young man seeks to establish massive 'Megafund' for his 'Creative Capitalism' movement in order to reform society.

1972 **Gordon, R.** *The yellow fraction.* D. Dobson, 160p.
Account of the rocket project on the Earth-type world of Arcon. [U.S. 1969]

1972 **Goulart, R.** *Broke down engine.* Collier-Macmillan, 192p.
Foreword – "This is a book about us and machines" – thirteen stories. [U.S. 1971]

1972 **Goulart, R.** *What's become of Screwloose?* Sidgwick & Jackson, 184p.
Ten stories – androids, mechanical dogs, space adventure. [U.S. 1971]

1972 **Graham, J. M.** *Voice from Earth.* R. Hale, 192p.
Spaceship revisits Earth, an empty planet, and then runs into relativity problems.

1972 **Green, J.** *Conscience interplanetary.* V. Gollancz, 221p.
Space colonization – problems, difficulties and struggles all solved by the Conscience Man.

1972 **Hanks, K.** *Falk.* Cassell, 285p.
A leader appears after the nation-wide conflict that led to The Devastation of Britain.

1972 **Harris, W.** *The mistress of Downing Street.* M. Joseph, 191p.
A nymphomaniac Prime Minister conducts her diplomacy in bed.

1972   **Harrison, H. (Dempsey, H.)** *The Jupiter Legacy.* Sphere, 154p.
First published U.K. 1966 as *The plague from space.* [U.S. 1965]

1972   **Harrison, H. (Dempsey, H.)** *One step from Earth.* Faber & Faber, xi, 210p.
Introduction; nine stories on themes of matter transmission. [U.S. 1970]

1972   **Harrison, H. (Dempsey, H.)** *A Transatlantic Tunnel, Hurrah!* Faber & Faber, 192p.
In the parallel world of Alpha One a different history has the Americans still loyal subjects of the British monarchy; Augustine Washington fights to defend the Atlantic Tunnel. Published U.S. 1972 as *Tunnel through the deeps.*

1972   **Harrison, H. and Aldiss, B.** *The year's best SF5.* Sphere, 239p.
Introduction by Harrison – "Like the Hong Kong flu, science fiction seems to be everywhere these days" – three poems, one joke, fourteen stories; Afterword by Aldiss, "A day in the life-style of . . ."

1972   **Hassler, K. W.** *The glass cage.* D. Dobson, 192p.
Life in a computer-controlled city after the great biological war. [U.S. 1969]

1972   **Heim, M.** *The waters of Aswan.* Translated by J. Maxwell Brownjohn. Collins, 255p.
Faults in the Aswan Dam threaten to flood Egypt. Originally published 1971 as *Assuan: Wenn der Damm bricht.*

1972   **Henderson, Z.** *Holding wonder.* V. Gollancz, 302p.
Twenty stories. [U.S. 1971]

1972   **Herbert, F.** *The god makers.* New English Library, 190p.
A space investigator becomes a "god" on a remote planet. [U.S. 1972]

1972   **Herbert, F.** *Whipping star.* New English Library, 222p.
The Calebans, mysterious telepathic and invisible creatures, help in the struggle to save the galaxy. [U.S. 1970]

1972   **Hitchcock, R.** *Venus 13.* W. H. Allen, 160p.
Hilarious tale of the first space lovers.

1972   **Kapp, C.** *The patterns of Chaos.* V. Gollancz, 222p.
Interstellar operations as the planetary powers move towards a union of all federations. [U.S. 1970]

1972   **Kavanagh, P.** *The triumph of evil.* Hodder & Stoughton, 126p.
Plot to destroy democracy in the United States. [U.S. 1971]

1972   **King, V.** *Another end.* Five Star, 186p.
Space exploration in the far future.

1972   **Knight, D.** *(ed.) Elsewhere x 3.* V. Gollancz, 192p.
Contains: McKenna, R., *Fiddler's Green*; Aldiss, B., *The saliva Tree*; Asimov, I., *Ugly little boy.* [U.S. 1970]. See Knight, *Dimension X*, 1974.

1972   **Knight, D.** *(ed.) One hundred years of science fiction, vols. 1 & 2.* Pan, 240 + 192.p.
Two-volume edition of the U.S. 1968 and U.K. 1969 publications. [U.S. 1970]

1972   **Knight, D.** *(ed.) Orbit 6.* Rapp & Whiting, 245p.
Fifteen stories.

1972   **Knight, D.** *(ed.) A pocketful of stars.* V. Gollancz, xz, 294p.
Nineteen stories. [U.S. 1971]

1972   **Laumer, K.** *Assignment in nowhere.* D. Dobson, 143p.
Third in *Worlds of the Imperium* series: space adventures. [U.S. 1968]

1972   **Laumer, K.** *Envoy to new worlds.* D. Dobson, 140p.
Six stories. [U.S. 1963]

1972   **Le Guin, U.K.** *The lathe of heaven.* V. Gollancz, 192p.
Dilemma of a man whose dreams can change reality. [U.S. 1971]

1972   **Le Guin, U. K.** *Planet of exile.* Tandem, 126p.
Remnants of an Earth colony on Gamma Draconis III join with the humanoid hilfs against the barbarian Gaal invaders. [U.S. 1966]

1972   **Le Guin, U. K.** *Rocannon's world.* Tandem, 122p.
Rocannon, sole survivor of the expedition to Fomalhaut II, leads the struggle to save the planet from alien invaders. [U.S. 1966]

1972   **Lewin, L. C.** *Triage.* Macdonald, 215p.
The chairman of the Special Commission on National Priorities works secretly for "a more explicit public understanding of how things stand in our world today." [U.S. 1972]

1972   **Locke, G.** *(ed.) Worlds apart.* Cornmarket Reprints, 180p. Illus.
Tales of space travel first published in illustrated magazines between 1888 and 1912.

1972   **Lymington, J. (Chance, J. N.)** *The Year Dot.* Hodder & Stoughton, 192p.
The worst of science and control in the days before the machines stopped.

1972   **McIntosh, J. T. (MacGregor, J. M.)** *The cosmic spies.* R. Hale, 192p.
Space invasion by the beauteous Adamites.

1972   **McIntosh, J. T. (McGregor, J. M.)** *The space sorcerers.* R. Hale, 183p.
Heroic spaceman comes to the aid of the planet Shan.

1972   **Martin-Fehr, J.** *The end of his tether.* Janay Publishing Company, 294p.
An old man recalls the collapse of civilization after the atomic war.

1972   **Merril, J.** *(ed.) The Space-Time Journal.* Panther, 206p.
Twenty-one stories selected from *England swings SF.* [U.S. 1968]

1972   **Moorcock, M.** *An alien heat.* MacGibbon & Kee, 158p.
First part of trilogy, *The Dancers at the end of time:* adventurous exploits of
Jherek Carnelian in the days when Earth "was nearing its end and the human
race had at last ceased to take itself seriously."

1972   **Moorcock, M.** *Breakfast in the ruins.* New English Library, 176p.
Sequel to *Behold the Man,* 1969.

1972   **Moorcock, M.** *Elric of Melniboné.* Hutchinson, 191p.
"This is the tale of when Elric was a King, the commander of dragons, fleets and
all the folk of that half-human race which had ruled the world for ten thousand
years."

1972   **Moorcock, M.** *The English assassin.* Allison & Busby, 254p. Illus.
Third in Jerry Cornelius series – eight different futures, each in the form of "The
Alternative Apocalypse."

1972   **Moorcock, M.** *(ed.) King of the swords.* Mayflower, 141p.
Third of *The Books of Corum.*

1972   **Moorcock, M.** *(ed.) New Worlds 3.* Sphere, 208p.
Fourteen stories. Introduction by Moorcock.

1972   **Moorcock, M.** *(ed.) New Worlds 4.* Sphere, 240p.
Stories by eight authors.

1972   **Moore, B.** *Catholics.* J. Cape, 102p.
Ironic tale of the consequences of ecumenical practices: a Vatican envoy tries to
persuade an Irish monastic community to abandon old habits and ideas.

1972   **Mullally, F.** *The Malta Conspiracy.* R. Hart-Davis, 183p.
Undercover operations begin after a Maltese government offers the Soviet navy a
base.

1972   **Niven, L.** *Ringworld.* V. Gollancz, 288p.
Adventures on Ringworld, an extraordinary world that encircles the sun. [U.S.
1971]

1972   **Nuetzel, C.** *Last call for the stars.* John Gresham, 192p.
Old man is restored to youth and immortality by deep-freeze techniques. [U.S.
1971]

1972   **Pedler, K. & Davis, G.** *Mutant 59.* Souvenir Press, 295p.
All the plastic in the world breaks down, and then . . . Also published [U.S. 1972]

1972   **Pohl, F. & Williamson, J.** *Rogue star.* D. Dobson, 213p.
A love affair in space with a symbiotic creature. [U.S. 1969]

1972   **Priest, C.** *Fugue for a darkening island.* Faber & Faber, 147p.
A catastrophe story: refugees from a devastated Africa arrive in Britain as a civil war begins.

1972   **Rackham, J.** *Ipomoea.* D. Dobson, 128p.
Psychedelic drug endangers world safety. [U.S. 1969]

1972   **Rankine, J. (Mason, D. R.)** *The Ring of Garamas.* D. Dobson, 186p.
Commander Fletcher of the Inter-Galactic Organization faces the danger from Garamas.

1972   **Rosse, I.** *(pseud.) The Droop.* New English Library, 158p.
A virus infection leaves impotent all but a fraction of the male population.

1972   **Savarin, J. J.** *Waiters on the dance.* Aslington Books, 221p.
First in *Lemmus: A time trilogy:* history of the Galactic Organization and Dominions to the annihilation of life on Terra.

1972   *A second Pollution Omnibus.* Sidgwick & Jackson, 516p.
Contains: Kornbluth, C. M. and Pohl, F., *The space merchants*; Aldiss, B., *Total environment*; Disch, T. M., *The genocides.*

1972   **Shaw, B.** *Other days, other eyes.* V. Gollancz, 160p.
A new kind of glass is found to have properties that affect the whole of society. [U.S. 1972]

1972   **Sheckley, R.** *Can you feel anything when I do this?* V. Gollancz, 191p.
Sixteen stories – foibles, eccentricities, desires. [U.S. 1971]

1972   **Silverberg, R.** *Nightwings.* Sidgwick & Jackson, 190p.
The Watcher presides over the renewal of Earth . [U.S. 1970]

1972   **Silverberg, R.** *(ed.) Science fiction Hall of Fame: 1 & 2.* Sphere, 349 & 352p.
Two-volume edition of the U.S. 1970 and U.K. 1971 publication.

1972   **Simak, C. D.** *Destiny doll.* Sidgwick & Jackson, 189p.
Interplanetary search for a lost space-explorer leads to self-discovery on a distant planet. [U.S. 1971]

1972   **Smith, E. E.** *Children of the Lens.* W. H. Allen, 255p.
Sixth in *Lensman Series:* the Galactic Patrol in action again for the safety of the Solar system. [U.S. 1964]

1972   **Smith, E. E.** *Masters of the Vortex.* W. H. Allen, 192p.
Seventh in *Lensman series;* the search for the nuclear vortices. First published U.S. 1960 as *The Vortex Blaster.*

1972   **Smith, E. E.** *Second Stage Lensman.* W. H. Allen, 254p.
Fifth in the *Lensman* series: Kim Kinnison penetrates the Boskonian defences. [U.S. 1953]

1972   **Spinrad, N.** *The men in the jungle.* Sphere, 285p.
Heroic exploits on the savage planet of Sangre. [U.S. 1967]

1972   **Trevor, E. (Dudley-Smith, T.)** *The Domesday story.* Remploy, 256p.
First published 1952 under the name of Warwick Scott.

1972   **Van Vogt, A. E.** *The battle of forever.* Sidgwick & Jackson, 191p.
Evolution takes new direction in the remote future. [U.S. 1971]

1972   **Van Vogt, A. E.** *Children of tomorrow.* Sidgwick & Jackson, 256p.
Struggle between the generations in the world of the future. [U.S. 1970]

1972   **Vance, J.** *The dying Earth.* Mayflower, 140p.
Romance in a distant future world of monsters and magicians. [U.S. 1950]

1972   **Vance, J.** *The eyes of the overworld.* Mayflower, 174p.
Hero sets off on a quest in the desolate, dangerous world of the distant future.
[U.S. 1966]

1972   **Walker, D.** *The Lord's pink ocean.* Collins, 158p.
Two families survive a world disaster. [U.S. 1972]

1972   **Wallace, I.** *Deathstar Voyage.* D. Dobson, 192p.
Adventures of a charming female officer of the Galactic Police. [U.S. 1969].

1972   **White, J.** *Dark inferno.* M. Joseph, 158p.
Disaster and rescue in deep space.

1972   **Williams, C.** *Flash.* R. Hale, 158p.
Migrants from another galaxy endanger the human race.

1972   **Wollheim, D.** *(ed.) Trilogy of the future.* Sidgwick & Jackson, 251p.
Introduction, three stories – Simak, C. D., *The trouble with Tycho;* Vance, J., *The last castle;* Delany, S. R., *Empire star.* First published U.S. 1971 as *Ace science fiction reader.*

1972   **Wollheim, D. A. and Saha, A. W.** *(eds.) The 1972 annual world's best SF.* V. Gollancz, 301p. Illus.
Introduction by Wollheim; fourteen stories. [U.S. 1972]

1972   **Wyndham, J. (Harris, J. B.)** *The secret people.* Coronet, 192p.
First published 1935 by John Wyndham writing as John Beynon.

1972   **Wyndham, J. (Harris, J. B.)** *Stowaway to Mars.* Coronet, 189p.
First published in 1936 as *Planet plane* by John Wyndham writing as John Beynon.

1973   **Aarons, E. S.** *Assignment Black Viking.* Gold Lion, 160p.
Special agent tries to find out who is changing the weather. [U.S. 1967]

1973   **Aldiss, B.** *The comic inferno.* New English Library, 159p.
Introduction; nine stories. [U.S. 1972]

1973 **Aldiss, B.** *Cryptozoic*. Sphere, 192p.
Originally published 1967 as *An Age*. [U.S. 1968]

1973 **Aldiss, B.** *Frankenstein unbound*. J. Cape, 184p.
A time-slip switches a twenty-first century citizen to the Switzerland of 1816, where the time-traveller meets Mary Shelley and Frankenstein.

1973 **Aldiss, B.** *The Penguin Science Fiction Omnibus*. Penguin, 616p.
One-volume edition of *Penguin Science Fiction* (1961),*More Penguin Science Fiction* (1963), *Yet More Penguin Science Fiction* (1964).

1973 **Asimov, I.** *The Early Asimov, or eleven years of trying*. V. Gollancz, 540p.
Introduction by Asimov; twenty-seven stories not published in earlier collections, selected from period 1940-1950. [U.S. 1972]

1973 **Asimov, I.** *The Early Asimov. Vols. 1,2,3*. Panther, 188, 237, 192p.
These contain respectively the first eight, next twelve, and last seven stories of the one-volume edition.

1973 **Asimov, I.** *(ed.) The Hugo Winners. Vols. 1 & 2*. Sphere, 363, 365p.
These contain respectively the first five and last eight prize-winners of *Hugo Winners Two*. [U.S. 1971]

1973 **Asimov, I.** *(ed.) Nebula Award stories 8*. V. Gollancz, 287p.
Introduction by Asimov; eight stories selected by the Science Fiction Writers of America . [U.S. 1973]

1973 **Asimov, I.** *(ed.) Where do we go from here?* Michael Joseph, 414p.
Seventeen stories selected to show that "science fiction has potential as an inspiring and useful teaching device." [U.S. 1971]

1973 **Ball, B. N.** *The probability man*. Sidgwick & Jackson, 175p.
Adventures with the Frames, historical dramas played by planetary populations. [U.S. 1972]

1973 **Ballard, J. G.** *Crash*. J. Cape, 224p.
A near-future world in which "the marriage of sex and technology" reaches frequent and extraordinary climaxes.

1973 **Ballard, J. G.** *Vermilion Sands*. J. Cape, 208p.
Ballard writes: "*Vermilion Sands* is my guess at what the future will actually be like." Nine short stories of which "The singing statues" is additional to the original U.S. edition of 1971.

1973 **Barrett, G. J.** *The brain of Graphicon*. R. Hale, 192p.
Investigation of the spaceships vanished off Graphicon.

1973 **Binder, E.** *The night of the saucers*. Five Star.
No information available.

1973   **Blish, J.** *Best science fiction stories of James Blish.* Faber & Faber, 216p.
Revised version of the 1965 edition; omits "There shall be no darkness" and adds two new stories.

1973   **Blish, J.** *Midsummer century.* Faber & Faber, 106p.
A scientist, projected by accident into A.D. 25000, seeks to save the savage tribesmen of the future from the menace of the Birds. [U.S. 1972]

1973   **Bova, B.** *(ed.) The Science Fiction Hall of Fame. Vol. 2.* V. Gollancz, ix, 422p.
Introduction; ten stories selected by members of the Science Fiction Writers of America. [U.S. 1973]

1973   **Brett, L.** *The alien ones.* Five Star.
No information available.

1973   **Brunner, J.** *Age of miracles.* Sidgwick & Jackson, 190p.
Invasion of Earth has a moral lesson for mankind.

1973   **Brunner, J.** *Bedlam planet.* Sidgwick & Jackson, 159p.
Problems of planetary colonization: can human beings adapt to life on Sigma Draconis? [U.S. 1968]

1973   **Burgess, E. and Friggens, A.** *Anti-Zota.* R. Hale, 189p.
Conflict between the long-lifers and the short-lifers in the distant future.

1973   **Burgess, E. and Friggens, A.** *Mortorio.* R. Hale, 192p.
Mysterious forces protect the planet Mortorio from exploitation by Earth.

1973   **Caidin, M.** *Cyborg.* W. H. Allen, 282p.
Adventures of an astronaut, badly injured, who is transformed into a cybernetic organism. [U.S. 1972]

1973   **Caldwell, T.** *Your sins and mine.* White Lion, 181p.
Universal famine brings peace and brotherhood to mankind. [U.S. 1955]

1973   **Cameron, I. (Payne, D. G.)** *The mountains at the bottom of the world.* Hodder & Stoughton, 190p.
The Missing Link is discovered in Chile. [U.S. 1972]

1973   **Cameron, J.** *The astrologer.* Bodley Head, 309p.
An international astrological agency, Interzod, advises governments on the potential of their future citizens. [U.S. 1972]

1973   **Cameron, L.** *Cybernia.* Coronet, 174p.
Computer begins to take control of life in the automated community of Cybernia. [U.S. 1972]

1973   **Campbell, J. W.** *The best of John W. Campbell.* Sidgwick & Jackson, 378p.
Foreword by James Blish; five short stories.

1973   **Canning, V.** *The finger of Saturn*. Heinemann, 271p.
A secret group of families, supposed to have come from space, plan for their return.

1973   **Carim, E.** *A dream deferred*. Allen Lane, 206p.
Black militants stage uprisings in South African cities in order to obtain the release of political prisoners.

1973   **Carpentier, C.** *Flight One*. Eyre Methuen, 315p.
Alarms and excitement on the flight of the first American supersonic transport plane. [U.S. 1972]

1973   **Carrel, M.** *Bannister's Z-Matter*. R. Hale, 159p.
A scientist discovers the link between X-matter and Z-matter.

1973   **Carter, L.** *The man who loved Mars*. White Lion, 157p.
Two Earthmen seek the treasures of Ilionis. [U.S. 1973]

1973   **Clarke, A. C.** *Rendezvous with Rama*. V. Gollancz, 256p.
Astronauts investigate a mysterious arrival in our solar system.

1973   **Coney, M. G.** *Mirror Image*. V. Gollancz, 223p.
Problems of the colonists on Manlyn. [U.S.1972]

1973   **Coney, M. G.** *Syzygy*. Elmfield Press, 166p.
Once every fifty-two years the six moons of the planet Arcadia cause havoc. [U.S. 1973]

1973   **Conquest, R.** *(ed.)* *The Robert Sheckley Omnibus*. Edited and introduced by Robert Conquest. V. Gollancz, 320p.
Contains *Immortality Inc* and twelve stories.

1973   **Cooper, E.** *The cloud walker*. Hodder & Stoughton, 223p.
Kieron the Cloud Walker dreams of flying in the post-catastrophe epoch.

1973   **Cooper, E.** *The tenth planet*. Hodder & Stoughton, 192p.
The last spaceship takes off from a dying Earth, and some survivors arrive in the distant future.

1973   **Cordell, A. (Graber, G. A.)** *If you believe the soldiers*. Hodder & Stoughton, 224p.
Heroic civil servant helps to overthrow a military junta in the United Kingdom.

1973   **Courtier, S. H.** *Into the silence*. R. Hale, 175p.
Suddenly the world becomes soundless and the inhabitants become speechless.

1973   **Cowper, R. (Murry, C. M.)** *Time out of mind*. V. Gollancz, 159p.
Assassination thriller set in the near future.

1973   **Creasey, J.** *The voiceless ones*. Hodder & Stoughton, 190p.
Dr. Palfrey once again saves the world.

1973   **Davidson, A.** *Mutiny in space.* White Lion, 159p.
Mutiny and marooning on Valentine's Planet. [U.S. 1964]

1973   **Del Rey, L.** *(ed.) Best science fiction stories of the year 1.* Kaye & Ward, 246p.
Introduction; fifteen stories. [U.S. 1972]

1973   **Dickinson, P.** *The green gene.* Hodder & Stoughton, 192p.
A divided Britain: the Irish, Scots and Welsh have green skins.

1973   **Dickson, G. R.** *The alien way.* Corgi, 184p.
One man saves Earth from invasion by his knowledge of the alien Ruml. [U.S. 1965]

1973   **Dickson, G. R.** *The Outposter.* R. Hale, 214p.
The colonists on Garnera VI fight the raiders from space. [U.S. 1972]

1973   **Dickson, G. R.** *Sleepwalker's world.* R. Hale, 203p.
A powerful, malign entity seeks to dominate Earth. [U.S. 1971]

1973   **Disch, T. M.** *Getting into death.* Hart-Davis, MacGibbon, 206p.
[1974]   Thirty-six stories, from very short to short – fantasy, science fiction, the macabre.

1973   **Disch, T. M.** *The ruins of Earth.* Hutchinson, 349p.
Introduction ("the theme of this book is ecological catastrophe . . ."), sixteen stories about the worst of all possible worlds. [U.S. 1971]

1973   **Edmondson, G. C.** *Chapayaca.* R. Hale, 163p.
An anthropologist discovers an alien creature living among the Yaqui Indians. [U.S. 1971]

1973   **Elder, M.** *Down to Earth.* R. Hale, 190p.
The spaceship *Silver Bird* returns to an empty world.

1973   **Elder, M.** *The perfumed planet.* R. Hale, 192p.
A rescue team is marooned on Roker II.

1973   **Ellison, H.** *All the sounds of fear.* Panther, 158p.
Introduction; eight stories "in which the theme of alienation dominates". First half of original U.S. 1971 publication, *Alone against tomorrow.*

1973   **Elwood, R.** *(ed.) Flame Tree Planet. An anthology of religious science fantasy.* Concordia Publishing House, 159p.
Introduction by Roger Lovin; ten stories. [U.S. 1973]

1973   **Erdmann, P.** *The billion dollar killing.* Hutchinson, 255p.
World crisis follows when the Mafia, Soviet bankers, Arab and Swiss financiers seek to profit from American plan to raise the price of gold.

1973   **Farmer, P. J.** *Timestop.* Quartet Books, 151p.
The Cold War Corps plans to free Earth from the tyrants of the Haijae Union. [U.S. 1975]

1973   **Farmer, P. J.** *The wind whales of Ishmael.* Quartet Books, 130p.
In the far-off future the oceans have vanished, fishes fly through the air and men hunt the flying whales across the sky. [U.S. 1971]

1973   **Farren, M.** *The Texts of Festival.* Hart-Davis, MacGibbon, 206p.
[1974]   In a desolate Britain of primitive tribes and forgotten technologies the pop heroes of the twentieth century are remembered in new rituals.

1973   **Fearn, J. R.** *Conquest of the Amazon.* Philip Harbottle (Wallsend), 34p. Illus.
Superwoman struggles to save the Solar System from disintegration.

1973   **Garnett, D. S.** *Mirror in the sky.* R. Hale, 160p.
War with the Creeps who come from the depths of space. [U.S. 1969]

1973   **Gary, R.** *The gasp.* Weidenfeld & Nicolson, 253p.
French physicist builds an atomic device that will trigger off all other nuclear weapons.

1973   **Gerrold, D.** *The man who folded himself.* Faber & Faber, 148p.
A time-traveller meets versions of himself in the future. [U.S. 1973]

1973   **Goulart, R.** *The Chameleon Corps.* Collier-Macmillan, 216p.
Foreword; eleven stories which "use the mechanisms of science fiction and fantasy to examine some of the basic questions about identity and self." [U.S. 1972]

1973   **Goulart, R.** *Hawkshaw.* R. Hale, 162p.
Murder and mystery in the thirteen colonies of a future United States. [U.S. 1972]

1973   **Guin, W.** *Beyond Bedlam.* Sphere, 206p.
Eight short stories, originally published U.S. 1967 as *Living way out.*

1973   **Gutteridge, L.** *Killer pine.* J. Cape, 205p.
Three miniaturised investigators track down the cause of a tree disease that is destroying the Canadian forests.

1973   **Harrison, H. (Dempsey, H.)** *Deathworld 1.* Sphere, 157p.
First published as *Death world*, 1963.

1973   **Harrison, H. (Dempsey, H.)** *Deathworld 2.* Sphere, 160p.
First published U.K. 1964 as *The Ethical Engineer.*

1973   **Harrison, H. (Dempsey, H.)** *The Stainless Steel Rat saves the world.* Faber & Faber, 191p.
James Bolivar di Griz zooms back from the future in order to stop the enemy meddling with the course of time. [U.S. 1972]

1973   **Harrison, H. (Dempsey, H.) and Aldiss, B.** *(eds.) The Astounding-Analog Reader: 1 & 2.* Sphere, 316, 320p.
Two-volume edition of the original U.S. 1972 publication.

1973   **Harrison, H. (Dempsey, H.) and Aldiss, B.** *(eds.) The year's best science fiction No. 6.* Sphere, 235p.
Introduction by Harrison and afterword by Aldiss; twelve stories, five poems, four graphics.

1973   **Herbert, F.** *The Green Brain.* New English Library, 158p.
Intelligent insects fight with humanity for the safety of Earth. [U.S. 1968]

1973   **High, P. E.** *Come, hunt an Earthman.* R. Hale, 176p.
Aliens have their reasons for raiding Earth.

1973   **High, P. E.** *Sold – for a spaceship.* R. Hale, 175p.
On a devastated Earth mankind creates a new life.

1973   **Hjorstberg, W.** *Gray matters.* V. Gollancz, 160p.
By the twenty-fifth century human beings have become Cerebromorphs – brains stored in Depositories, wired to computers and memory files. [U.S. 1971]

1973   **Hodder-Williams, C.** *Panic o'clock.* United Writers, 327p.
The virus Virulent Panic threatens the safety of the world.

1973   **Howard, T.** *The kernel of death.* R. Hale, 192p.
Doctor discovers how to prevent death.

1973   **Hoyle, F. and Hoyle, G.** *The inferno.* Heinemann, 210p.
A supernova threatens the galaxy. Also published U.S. 1973.

1973   **Hurwood, B. J.** *The Invisibles.* R. Hale, 190p,
Research worker discovers extraordinary parapsychological powers. [U.S. 1971]

1973   **Hyams, E.** *The final agenda.* Allen Lane, 176p.
The New Anarchists struggle to build the just society.

1973   **Jorgensen, I.** *Whom the gods say.* Five Star.
No information available.

1973   **Juniper, L. M.** *A piece of Martin Cann.* Five Star.
No information available.

1973   **Kelley, L. P.** *Mindmix.* Coronet Books, 176p.
Experiment with brain transplants in the days when Virus Y ravages Earth. [U.S. 1972]

1973   **Knebel, F.** *Dark horse.* Hodder & Stoughton, 367p.
An American candidate for the presidency refuses to follow the party machine and goes his own original way. [U.S. 1972]

1973   **Knight, D.** *(ed.) Orbit 7.* Rapp & Whiting, 217p.
Twelve short stories. [U.S. 1970],

1973   **Knight, D.** *(ed.) A science fiction argosy.* V. Gollancz, 828p.
Contains two novels (Bester, A., *The Demolished Man*; Sturgeon, T., *More than human*), two novellas and twenty-two stories, from Asimov, Sheckley, Tenn, Wyndham, etc. [U.S. 1972]

1973 **Laumer, K.** *Dinosaur Beach.* R. Hale, 191p.
Agent from the remote future travels back in time to undo the tamperings with the time stream. [U.S. 1971]

1973 **Laumer, K.** *The house in November.* Sidgwick & Jackson, 192p.
Mysterious forces transform the condition of human life. [U.S. 1970]

1973 **Lees, D.** *Rape of a quiet town.* Constable, 200p.
Mercenaries attack Scarborough.

1973 **Leland, J.** *Lirri.* V. Gollancz, 271p.
Student protest and the search for a personal identity set in the near future.

1973 **Lem, S.** *The Invincible.* Translated from the Polish. Sidgwick & Jackson, 221p.
A space cruiser investigates the loss of the *Condor* on the mysterious and desolate planet, Regis Three. First published 1964 as title story in *Niezwyciężony i inne opowiadania.*

1973 **Long, F. B.** *Lest Earth be conquered.* Five Star.
No information available.

1973 **Long, P.** *Heil Britannia.* Everest Books, 192p.
Special Agent defeats plan for a totalitarian Britain.

1973 **McCaffrey, A.** *Dragonquest.* Rapp & Whiting, 302p.
Sequel to *Dragonflight*: the inhabitants of the planet Pern continue their tribal adventures. [U.S. 1971]

1973 **McGivern, W.** *Caprifoil.* Collins, 254p.
Espionage adventures and nuclear blackmail. [U.S. 1972]

1973 **McIntosh, J. T. (MacGregor, J. M.)** *Flight from rebirth.* R. Hale, 191p.
Rebirth Institutes offer immortality to some.

1973 **McIntosh, J. T. (MacGregor, J. M.)** *Galactic takeover bid.* R. Hale, 190p.
Terran ambition hesitates when the Men of Crock appear.

1973 **Malzberg, B.** *Phase IV.* Pan Books, 127p.
A new species of ant begins to take over the world; from the original screenplay by Mayo Simon. [U.S. 1973],

1973 **Mannheim, K.** *Vampires of Venus.* Five Star, 128p.
In the remote future human survivors on Venus seek their inheritance from Earth.

1973 **Mannheim, K.** *When the Earth died.* Five Star.
No information available.

1973 **Marshall, B.** *Urban the Ninth.* Constable, 191p.
An English cardinal is elected Pope, and sets out to restore the Church to orthodoxy and austerity. First in a trilogy.

1973   **Mason, C.** *Hostage.* Macmillan, 221p.
Beginning of World War III – Cairo destroyed by nuclear weapons; rival fleets put to sea.

1973   **Moorcock, M.** *The Bull and the Spear.* Allison & Busby, 168p.
First in *The Chronicle of Prince Corum:* the heroic prince defeats the forces of the Cold Folk.

1973   **Moorcock, M.** *The Champion of Garathorm.* Mayflower, 126p.
Second part of *The Chronicles of Count Brass:* Dorian Hawkmoon journeys through time and space with the Regent of Ukrania.

1973   **Moorcock, M.** *Count Brass.* Mayflower, 140p.
First part of *The Chronicles of Count Brass*: romance and heroic adventure during the struggle against the Dark Empire.

1973   **Moorcock, M.** *(ed.) New Worlds 5.* Sphere, 280p.
Introduction by Moorcock; twenty-two stories.

1973   **Moorcock, M.** *The Oak and the Ram.* Allison & Busby, 170p.
Sequel to *The Bull and the Spear.*

1973   **Morland, D.** *Heart Clock.* Faber & Faber, 213p.
The United Party governs Great Britain; it has an ingenious solution for the population problem.

1973   **Mullally, F.** *Venus afflicted.* Hart-Davis, MacGibbon, 286p.
Astrologer claims to have discovered a new planet.

1973   **Niven, L.** *Inconstant Moon.* V. Gollancz, 251p.
Twelve stories.

1973   **Pereira, W. D.** *Aftermath 15.* R. Hale, 183p.
After a disastrous war the United States becomes a savage and rigid society.

1973   **Pohl, F.** *The gold at the starbow's end.* V. Gollancz, 187p.
Four novellas and a short story. [U.S. 1972]

1973   **Rankine, J. (Mason, D. R.)** *The Fingalnan conspiracy.* Sidgwick & Jackson, 190p.
Commander York saves our universe from conquest by extra-galactic powers.

1973   **Reynolds, M.** *The cosmic eye.* Five Star.
No information available.

1973   **Roberts, K.** *Machines and men.* Hutchinson, 288p.
Five stories about machines and five about men.

1973   **Rogers, M.** *Mindfogger.* Allen Lane, 199p.
Electronics expert discovers a means of mind control. [U.S. 1973]

1973   **Rolls, B.** *Something in mind.* R. Hale, 190p.
New drug sends experimenters on trips in time and space.

1973   **Romano, D.** *Flight from Time One.* Sidgwick & Jackson, 251p.
Plot and counter-plot on the astral plane. [U.S. 1972]

1973   **Rowland, D. S.** *Despot in space.* R. Hale, 190p.
Professor Condor outwits the World Master with his matter transmitter.

1973   **Saberhagen, F.** *The Black Mountains.* Tandem, 174p.
Technology versus demonology in the far future. [U.S. 1971]

1973   **Saberhagen, F.** *The Broken Lands.* Tandem, 190p.
A champion leads the Free People against the despots of Earth. [U.S. 1968]

1973   *Science Fiction Special 6.* Sidgwick & Jackson, 254 + 160p.
Contains: Van Vogt, A. E., *Children of tomorrow*; Williams, R. M., *Now comes tomorrow.*

1973   *Science Fiction Special 7.* Sidgwick & Jackson, 477 + 428p.
Contains: *A Murray Leinster Omnibus*, 1968 and *A Philip K. Dick Omnibus*, 1970.

1973   **Shaw, B.** *Tomorrow lies in ambush.* V. Gollancz, 204p.
Eleven stories.

1973   **Silverberg, R.** *(ed.) Beyond control.* Sidgwick & Jackson, 219p.
Seven stories. [U.S. 1972]

1973   **Silverberg, R.** *Parsecs and parables.* R. Hale, 203p.
Ten stories. [U.S. 1970]

1973   **Silverberg, R.** *A time of changes.* V. Gollancz, 221p.
A prince of the planet Borthan tells of his attempt to open out his closed society. [U.S. 1971]

1973   **Simak, C.** *A choice of gods.* Sidgwick & Jackson, 190p.
Survivors of mankind will not permit the return of Earth colonists. [U.S. 1972]

1973   **Simpson, M.** *Sorry, wrong number.* A. Deutsch, 256p.
Problems of a young doctor in a regimented society; he gives drop-outs a place in the National Number System.

1973   **Sims, D. N.** *A plenteous seed.* R. Hale, 160p.
Revolt in a rigid, hierarchical society.

1973   **Sinclair, M.** *The dollar covenant.* V. Gollancz, 205p.
A multi-national company plots to secure control of a bankrupt, independent Scotland.

1973   **Smith, W. J.** *The Grand Voyage.* R. Hale, 175p.
Time-travel adventures.

1973   **Starr, R.** *Operation Omina.* R. Hale, 192p.
Dangers and difficulties of a two-year space journey. [U.S. 1970]

1973 **Sturgeon, T.** *To here and the easel.* V. Gollancz, 255p.
Contains five stories from *The worlds of Theodore Sturgeon*, first published U.S. 1972, and the title story.

1973 **Tennant, E.** *Time of the Crack.* J. Cape, 142p.
New groups and associations spring up in London after the Earth has split in two.

1973 **Tubb, E. C.** *Derai.* Arrow Books, 189p.
Adventures on the feudal world of Hive and a contest for immortality on the planet Folgone. Second in the *Dumarest Saga*. [U.S. 1968]

1973 **Tubb, E. C.** *Kalin.* Arrow Books, 192p.
Planetary adventures in company with a foreseer of the future. Fourth in the *Dumarest Saga*. [U.S. 1969]

1973 **Tubb, E. C.** *Toyman.* Arrow Books, 192p.
The Earthman Dumarest has to fight in the games for knowledge of Earth. Third in the *Dumarest Saga*.

1973 **Tubb, E. C.** *The winds of Gath.* Arrow Books, 192p.
First published 1968 as *Gath*. First in the *Dumarest Saga*.

1973 **Tucker, W.** *The time masters.* V. Gollancz, 186p.
Investigation of Gilbert Nash leads to unexpected results. [U.S. 1971]

1973 **Van Vogt, A. E.** *The far out worlds of A. E. Van Vogt.* Sidgwick & Jackson, 223p.
Twelve stories. [U.S. 1973]

1973 **Van Vogt, A. E.** *The Silkie.* New English Library, 156p.
An immensely powerful being comes to Earth. [U.S. 1969]

1973 **Van Vogt, A. E.** *The three eyes of evil; and Earth's last fortress.* Sidgwick & Jackson, 218p.
Two stories: the first published U.S. 1959 as *Siege of the unseen*, and the second originally published U.S. 1970.

1973 **Walker, P. L.** *The ice sunset.* Mitre Press, 155p.
Experiments with an energy-storage device causes the Antarctic ice to melt.

1973 **Watson, I.** *The embedding.* V. Gollancz, 254p.
A communications expert, studying an Amazon tribe, finds he is required when aliens land on Earth.

1973 **Wells, A.** *(ed.) The best of Isaac Asimov.* Sidgwick & Jackson, 336p.
Introduction by Asimov: twelve short stories; bibliography.

1973 **Wells, A.** *(ed.) The best of Arthur C. Clarke.* Sidgwick & Jackson, 336p.
Introduction by Clarke – biographical information. Eighteen stories; bibliography.

1973 **Wells, A.** *(ed.) The best of Robert Heinlein.* Sidgwick & Jackson, 348p.
Introduction by Peter Weston; eight stories, bibliography.

1973   **Wells, A.** *(ed.) The best of John Wyndham.* Sphere, 318p.
Introduction by Leslie Flood; twelve stories and bibliography.

1973   **West, P.** *Colonel Mint.* Calder & Boyars, 188p.
An American astronaut causes alarm when he reports that he has sighted an angel in space. [U.S. 1972]

1973   **Williams, E. C.** *Project: Renaissance.* R. Hale, 176p.
In the twenty-first century hopes of a renaissance of the arts are realised in an unexpected way.

1973   **Wolfe, G.** *The fifth head of Cerberus.* V. Gollancz, 244p.
Three novellas deal with the cruelties, peculiarities and originalities of life on the twin planets of Sainte Anne and Sainte Croix. [U.S. 1972]

1973   **Wollheim, D. A.** *(ed.* with Arthur W. Saha*) The 1973 Annual World's best SF.* V. Gollancz, 255p.
Editor's introduction; ten stories., [U.S. 1973]

1973   **Woolfolk, W.** *The Overlords.* W. H. Allen, 278p.
Organized criminals join with the wealthy to subvert the constitution of the United States.

1973   **Wyndham, J. (Harris, J. B.)** *Sleepers of Mars.* Coronet, 155p.
Introduction by Walter Gillings; five stories.

1973   **Wyndham, J. (Harris, J. B.)** *Wanderers of time.* Coronet, 158p.
Coronet, 158p.
Introduction by Walter Gillings; six stories.

1973   **Zelazny, R.** *The doors of his face, the lamps of his mouth.* Faber & Faber, 229p.
Fifteen short stories about mankind in the future. [U.S. 1971]

1974   **Aldiss, B.** *The eighty-minute hour: a space opera.* J. Cape, 286p.
An after-the-war entertainment: turbulences in time and space disperse the survivors through many worlds, as the nations take up their positions in the Capitalist-Communist League or in the League of Dissident Nations. Also published U.S. 1974.

1974   **Aldiss, B.** *(ed.) Space odysseys.* Weidenfeld Nicolson, 324p.
Editor's introduction; fifteen stories.

1974   **Aldiss, B.** *(ed.) Space Opera.* Weidenfeld & Nicolson, 324p.
Selection of sixteen representative stories (1900–1972) on themes of space travel and interplanetary adventure, with commentaries by Brian Aldiss.

1974   **Anderson, J.** *The abolition of death.* Constable, 232p.
Immortality drug discovered; government plot to secure control.

1974   **Anderson, P.** *Orbit unlimited.* Sidgwick & Jackson, 158p.
During the oppressive period of the Guardians the Constitutionalists (i.e. the middle-classes) take off for a new home in space. [U.S. 1961]

1974   **Anthony, P. (Jacob, P. A.)** *Race against time.* Sidgwick & Jackson, 179p.
Fourteen stories. [U.S. 1973]

1974   **Ardies, T.** *Pandemic.* Angus & Robertson, 240p.
Millionaire plans to destroy mankind. [U.S. 1973]

1974   **Ashley, M.** *(ed.) The history of the Science Fiction magazine, 1926–1935.* New English Library, 239p.
Preface, Introduction ('An Amazing Experiment'); ten stories, and checklists.

1974   **Asimov, I.** *Before the Golden Age.* Robson Books, xix, 986p.
Introduction – "That Golden Age began in 1938, when John Campbell became editor of *Astounding Stories*" – twenty-six stories from the 1930s. [U.S. 1974]

1974   **Asimov, I.** *(ed.) Tomorrow's children.* Futura Publications, 431p.
Editor's preface, eighteen stories about children of the future. [U.S. 1966]

1974   **Avallone, M.** *Beneath the Planet of the Apes.* Bantam, 134p.
Continues the film story *Planet of the Apes*; the eternal problems of war and peace are still there in the distant future. [U.S. 1970]

1974   **Bailey, H. and Platt, C.** *(eds.) New Worlds 7.* Sphere, 216p.
Twenty stories, of which some twelve are about the future.

1974   **Ball, B. N.** *Planet Probability.* Sidgwick & Jackson, 188p.
In the thirtieth century whole populations move to new worlds of experience. [U.S. 1973]

1974   **Ball, B. N.** *Singularity Station.* Sidgwick & Jackson, 176p.
Search for the passengers of a spaceship lost in the time-space continuum. [U.S. 1973]

1974   **Bannon, M.** *The Assimilator.* R. Hale, 191p.
Aliens from Tagor seek to control human minds.

1974   **Bannon, M.** *The wayward robot.* R. Hale, 188p.
A mad robot terrorises a community.

1974   **Barclay, E.** *Of Earth and fire.* R.. Hale, 175p.
The Outer Space Defence Service meets and alien race at the frontiers of our Solar System.

1974   **Barr, D.** *Space relations.* Millington, 248p
The Tannhäuser story retold in an erotic and planetary setting. [U.S. 1973]

1974   **Barrett, G. J.** *The lost fleet of Astranides.* R. Hale, 188p.
The Grandmaster leads the Astranidean invasion of Earth.

1974   **Barrett, G. J.** *The tomorrow stairs.* R. Hale, 183p.
Nightmare journey in the world of dreams.

1974   **Bayley, B. J.** *Empire of two worlds.* R. Hale, 157p.
Struggle for personal survival on planet Killibol. [U.S. 1974]

1974   **Bayley, B. J.** *The soul of the robot.* Allison & Busby, 206p.
Adventures of Jasperodus, the almost human robot.

1974   **Berger, T.** *Regiment of women,* Eyre Methuen, 349p.
In the twenty-first century the women rule the world, but there are rebels ready to
risk all. [U.S. 1973]

1974   **Biggle, L, Jr.** *The World Menders.* Elmfield Press, 205p.
Cultural Survey intervenes in the affairs of the *olz* and the *rascz* on the planet
Branoff IV. [U.S. 1971]

1974   **Blackden, P.** *Adam and Eve 2020 A.D.* Everest Books, 123p.
A solitary couple survive the devastation of the world.

1974   **Boland, J.** *Holocaust.* Futura Publications, 192p.
East and West in struggle for source of infinite energy.

1974   **Boorman, J. with Stair, B.** *Zardoz.* Pan, 130p.
Novel of the film *Zardoz* (Twentieth Century-Fox, 1973) in which Zed explores the
world of Vortex.

1974   **Bova, B.** *(ed.) The Science Fiction Hall of Fame. Vol. 3.* V. Gollancz, viii,
440p.
Introduction; ten stories selected by the Science Fiction Writers of America
[U.S. 1973]

1974   **Brent, J.** *The plastic man.* New English Library, 128p.
Computerised man runs amok; a cruel cult devoted to him springs up.

1974   **Brockley, F.** *Star quest.* R. Hale, 189p.
Search for the missing starship *Explorer.*

1974   **Brunner, J.** *The dramaturges of Yan.* New English Library, 160p.
Gregory Chart, dramatist to the galaxy, does not foresee the effect of his
methods on the people of Yan. [U.S. 1972]

1974   **Brunner, J.** *The sheep look up.* Dent, 461p.
Twelve months in future history: pollution, industrial upheavals and political
factions threaten the world. [U.S. 1972]

1974   **Brunner, J.** *Times without number.* Elmfield Press, 233p.
A mistake in the mechanics of time travel changes the history of Spain.
[U.S. 1962]

1974   **Bulmer, H. K.** *(ed.) New writings in SF 22.* Sidgwick & Jackson, 189p.
Foreword; eleven stories.

1974   **Bulmer, H. K.** *(ed.) New writings in SF 23.* Sidgwick & Jackson, 191p.
Foreword; nine stories.

1974   **Bulmer, H. K.** *(ed.) New writings in SF 24.* Sidgwick & Jackson, 190p.
Foreword; nine stories.

1974   **Caidin, M.** *Operation Nuke.* W. H. Allen, 240p.
Cyborg superman defeats plot to destroy U.S. cities. [U.S. 1973]

1974   **Chapdelaine, P. A.** *Swampworld West.* Elmfield Press, 156p.
Emigrants from Trippert's Plant come to terms with the different conditions and
alien life-forms on Swampworld.

1974   **Cleary, J.** *Peter's Pence.* Collins, 288p.
The progressive Pope, Martin VI, is kidnapped by the I.R.A.

1974   **Compton, D. G.** *The continuous Katherine Mortenhoe.* V. Gollancz,
256p.
The last days of the heroine filmed for television at a time when death from
disease is almost unknown. Published U.S. as *The unsleeping eye.*

1974   **Coney, M. G.** *Friends come in boxes.* V. Gollancz, 224p.
Memoirs of a Transfer Surgeon in the days when immortality is the norm.
[U.S. 1973]

1974   **Coney, M. G.** *The hero of Downways.* Futura Publications, 188p.
A subterranean people discover their inheritance on the surface of their planet.
[U.S. 1973]

1974   **Coney, M. G.** *Winter's children.* V. Gollancz, 192p.
Small community struggles to survive in a world buried under snow.

1974   **Conrad, P.** *Ex Minus.* R. Hale, 191p.
Disaster follows on an experiment to create human life.

1974   **Cooper, E.** *Prisoner of fire.* Hodder & Stoughton, 192p.
The heroine, endowed with great paranormal powers, rebels against the misuse
of telepathy by the state.

1974   **Cowper, R. (Murray, C. M.)** *The twilight of Briareus.* V. Gollancz,
255p.
Supernova changes world climate – cyclones, floods, Polar frosts – and changes
the perceptions of some human beings.

1974   **Cowper, R. (Murray, C. M.)** *Worlds apart.* V. Gollancz, 158p.
Entertaining experiences in the Csnarsian galaxy in parallel with less delightful
experiences on Earth.

1974   **Davidson, A.** *Masters of the Maze.* White Lion, 156p.
A man from Earth is chosen to penetrate the pathways of space and
time.[U.S. 1965]

1974   **De Camp, L. S.** *The Continent Makers.* Remploy, xvi, 255p.
Introduction by Isaac Asimov: stories about the Brazilian exploration of space.
[U.S. 1971]

1974   **De Camp, L. S.** *A Gun for Dinosaur.* Remploy, 319p.
Fourteen stories. [U.S. 1963]

1974   **Del Rey, L.** *(ed.) Best science fiction stories of the year. Second Annual Collection.* Kaye & Ward, 244p.
Introduction; fifteen stories. [U.S. 1973]

1974   **Del Rey, L.** *The sky is falling.* New English Library, 109p.
A resurrected man saves the world. [U.S. 1973]

1974   **Dick, P. K.** *Flow my tears, the policeman said.* V. Gollancz, 231p.
An unperson experiences the worst in a police state of the near future.
[U.S. 1974]

1974   **Dickson, G. R.** *Alien art.* R. Hale, 162p.
An intelligent otter helps to decide the future of the the planet Arcadia.
[U.S. 1973]

1974   **Disch, T. M.** *(ed.) Bad Moon rising.* Hutchinson, 315p.
Introduction ("On the road to 1984"): "The single theme unifying these stories (and poems) is a concern for the present political scene". Eighteen stories.
[U.S. 1973]

1974   **Dolinsky, M.** *Mind One.* Futura Publications, 240p.
A new drug makes total telepathy possible – disastrous consequences.
[U.S. 1972]

1974   **Drury, A.** *Come Nineveh, come Tyre.* M. Joseph, xiii, 481p.
Political assassination and national corruption lead to total disaster in United States. [U.S. 1973]

1974   **Effinger, G. A.** *Escape to tomorrow.* Universal-Tandem, 158p.
Second in the *Planet of the Apes* television series. [U.S. 1975]

1974   **Elder, M.** *The seeds of frenzy.* R. Hale, 188p.
The water plant, *Aquaflora Insania*, is responsible for extraordinary behaviour in the planet Haven.

1974   **Ellison, H.** *The time of the eye.* Panther, 156p.
Introduction – "I see the subtlest theme as one of Humanity's triumph over loneliness" – twelve stories which are the second half of original U.S. 1971 publication, *Alone against tomorrow.*

1974   **Elwood, R.** *(ed.) Frontiers 1: Tomorrow's alternatives.* Collier-Macmillan, 198p.
Author's preface, introduction by Frank Herbert, twelve stories about life in the future [U.S. 1973]

1974   **Elwood, R.** *(ed.) Frontiers 2: The new mind.* Collier-Macmillan, vi, 180p.
Introduction, preface by Frederik Pohl, nine stories about the possibilities of the mind. [U.S. 1973]

1974   **Ernsting, W. and Mahr, K.** *Perry Rhodan 4: Invasion from space.*
Futura Publications, 187p.
Perry Rhodan leads the Mutant Corps against the invading Mind Snatchers.
[U.S. 1970] see *Note 12.*

1974   **Farmer, P. J.** *Dare.* Quartet Books, 154p.
Earthman finds humanity in the inhabitants of the planet Dare. [U.S. 1965]

1974   **Garfield, B.** *Line of succession.* Hodder & Stoughton, 339p.
Bombs in the House of Representatives. President-elect of the United States
kidnapped. [U.S. 1972]

1974   **Garner, G.** *Space Probe.* R. Hale, 182p.
Piracy adventure in deep space.

1974   **Garnett, D. S.** *Time in eclipse.* R. Hale, 176p.
Fantasy of the watchers and Guardians in a time when MACHINE knows all.

1974   **Gerrold, D.** *Yesterday's children.* Faber & Faber, 211p.
Captain and First Officer struggle for command of the starship *Robert Burlingham*
during a pursuit through the galaxy. [U.S. 1974]

1974   **Gibbard, T. S. J.** *Vandals of eternity.* R. Hale, 191p.
The mysterious Eldrin send human beings on trips through time and space.

1974   **Gordon, S.** *One-Eye.* Sidgwick & Jackson, 256p.
Romantic tale of the far-off time after the Great Forgetting – monsters, mutants,
magic, and the hope of a new beginning. First in a series. [U.S. 1973]

1974   **Griffith, G.** *The raid of "Le Vengeur".* With a critical biography by Sam
Moskowitz, additional notes and bibliography by George Locke. Ferret
Fantasy. 144p illus.
Seven stories by George Griffith not previously published in book form. Valuable
biography and bibliography.

1974   **Haining, P.** *The hero.* New English Library, 237p.
A hero is sent into China for the purpose of preventing a nuclear confrontation.

1974   **Harrison, H. (Dempsey, H.)** *(ed.) The John, W. Campbell Memorial
Anthology.* Sidgwick & Jackson, 297p.
Introduction by Asimov and short stories by Poul Anderson, Asimov, Bester, Hal
Clement and others. [U.S. 1973]

1974   **Harrison, H. (Dempsey, H.)** *Star smashers of the Galaxy Rangers.*
Faber & Faber, 212p.
Two pals whizz through the galaxy from planet to planet. [U.S. 1973]

1974   **Hay, G.** *(ed.) Stopwatch.* New English Library, 224p.
Introduction; thirteen stories.

1974   **Heinlein, R.** *Time enough for love.* New English Library, 607p.
Lazarus Long recalls the experiences of a long, long life of intergalactic
adventure. [U.S. 1973]

1974   **Herbert, F.** *Hellstrom's hive.* New English Library, 278p.
Discovery of a new breed of human beings presents problems for U.S. security.
[U.S. 1972]

1974   **Herbert, J.** *The rats.* New English Library, 175p.
Huge man-eating rats terrorise London.

1974   **Herzog, A.** *The Swarm.* Heinemann, 256p. Illus.
Species of African bee threatens to exterminate human beings in the United
States. [U.S. 1974]

1974   **High, P. E.** *Speaking of dinosaurs.* R. Hale, 192p.
An alien group attempts to take part in human development.

1974   **Hitchcock, R.** *Percy's progress.* Sphere, 123p.
Based on the screenplay by Sid Colin and Ian la Frenais about the one fertile
man in the world.

1974   **Hoch, E.** *The transvection machine.* R. Hale, 176p.
Inventor of transvection machine promises instantaneous transportation for all.
[U.S. 1971]

1974   **Howell, S.** *Menace from Magor.* R. Hale, 190p.
Alien invasion of Earth.

1974   **James, L.** *Simon Rack: Earth lies sleeping.* Sphere, 169p.
Commander Simon Rack of the Galactic Security Service investigates matters
on Sol Three.

1974   **James, L.** *Simon Rack: Starcross.* Sphere, 155p.
Simon Rack keeps the intergalactic peace.

1974   **Kelley, L. P.** *The Coins of Murph.* Coronet Books, 191p.
In a savage future chance decides the issues of life and death in Ireland.
[U.S. 1971]

1974   **Kelley, L. P.** *The Earth Tripper.* Coronet Books, 159p.
Visitor from the planet Eleison causes havoc on Earth. [U.S. 1973]

1974   **Kelley, L. P.** *The man from maybe.* Coronet Books, 175p.
Escape from the deadly Marsman and various simulacra. Originally published
U.S. 1972 as *Time 110100.*

1974   **Kelley, L. P.** *Mythmaster.* Coronet Books, 157p.
The Patrol tracks down the dealers in human life. [U.S. 1973]

1974   **Kesteven, G. R.** *The Pale Invaders.* Chatto & Windus, 140p.
Post-catastrophe story: a primitive community has to face an invasion.

1974   **Keyes, I. F.** *The battle of Disneyland.* W. H. Allen, 190p.
Fantasies of insurrection, secession and destruction in the United States.

1974   **King, A.** *Stage Two.* R. Hale, 190p.
One man rebels against the memory machines.

1974   **King, C.** *Operation Mora.* R. Hale, 191p.
An investigator from the Bureau of Interplanetary Warfare tracks down a
murderer on Mora.

1974   **King, S.** *Carrie.* New English Library, 224p.
Young girl develops exceptional powers of matter control. [U.S. 1974]

1974   **Knight, D.** *(ed.) Dimension X.* Coronet, 156p.
Originally published in one volume with the stories in *Elsewhere x 3,* U.S. 1970
and U.K. 1972. Contains: Heinlein, R. A. *The man who sold the Moon* and
Kornbluth, C. M. *The marching morons.*

1974   **Knight, D.** *(ed.) Orbit 8.* Rapp & Whiting, 219p.
Sixteen stories. [U.S. 1970]

1974   **Knight, D.** *(ed.) Tomorrow and tomorrow.* V. Gollancz, 251p.
Foreword: ten stories chosen to illustrate "science Fiction's overriding concern to
show that change is the only permanent thing." [U.S. 1973]

1974   **Knight, D.** *Two novels.* V. Gollancz, 223p
Contains *The Earth Quarter*, published U.S. 1961 as *The Sun saboteurs*, a tale of
the refugees from impoverished Earth; *Double meaning* (U.S. 1965) a tale of an
alien life-form come to earth. [U.S. 1974]

1974   **Laumer, K.** *The glory game.* R. Hale, 186p.
Space hero outwits the Hukk and prevents a galactic war. [U.S. 1973]

1974   **Laumer, K.** *The Star Treasure.* Sidgwick & Jackson, 176p.
Lieutenant Tarleton fights the omnipotent Lord Imbolo for the freedom of the
world. [U.S. 1971]

1974   **Lee, D.** *Destiny past.* R. Hale, 157p.
Reporter searches for the reality behind the dead dictator of a conquered planet.

1974   **Lees, D.** *Elizabeth R.I.P.* Constable, 184p.
Plot to foist a pretender on the British throne.

1974   **Le Guin, U. K.** *The dispossessed.* V. Gollancz, 319p.
An outstanding story of human relationships, the pursuit of knowledge, capitalism
and socialism, revealed in the contrasting ways of life on two planets.
[U.S. 1974]

1974   **Leiber, F.** *Night monsters.* V. Gollancz, 190p.
Seven stories on themes of fear.

1974   **Leinster, M. (Jenkins, W. F.)** *Four from Planet 5.* White Lion, 160p.
Four children from space terrify the world with their mind-reading powers.
[U.S. 1959]

1974   **Lessing, D.** *The memoirs of a survivor.* Octagon Press, 182p.
For no apparent reason civilization collapses. A survivor discovers the truths of selfhood and existence.

1974   **Lightner, A. M. (Hopf, A. L.)** *Star Dog.* Faber & Faber, 179p.
Six-legged, telepathic dog arrives from space and sires telepathic offspring.

1974   **Lymington, J. (Chance, J. N.)** *The hole in the World.* Hodder & Stoughton, 224p.
Alien beings invade Earth through a gap in time.

1974   **Macey, P.** *Stationary orbit.* D. Dobson, 184p.
The Department of Interstellar Communication makes contact with aliens.

1974   **Mahr, K. and Shols, W. W.** *Perry Rhodan 3: Galactic Alarm.* Future Publications, 187p.
Perry Rhodan intervenes between Earth and the Arkonide Empire. [U.S. 1969] See *Note* 12.

1974   **Malzberg, B. N.** *Beyond Apollo.* Faber & Faber, 138p.
In 1981 the first expedition to Venus returns without its commander. What went wrong? [U.S. 1972]

1974   **Mason, D. R.** *The Phaeton Condition.* R. Hale, 192p.
Hero fights for the safety of the world. [U.S. 1973]

1974   **Merle, R.** *Malevil.* Translated from the French by Derek Coltmann. Michael Joseph, 575p.
Post-catastrophe story: the sole survivors live on in a castle in rural France. First published 1972 as *Malevil.*

1974   **Moorcock, M.** *(ed.) Best science fiction stories from New Worlds:* 8. Panther, 204p.
Nine stories and an essay, "Salvador Dali", by J. G. Ballard.

1974   **Moorcock, M.** *The Sword and the Stallion.* Allison & Busby, 166p.
Concludes *The Chronicle of Prince Corum;* the heroic Champion Eternal faces the evil Gods of Limbo.

1974   **Moorcock, M. and Platt, C.** *(eds.) New Worlds 6.* Sphere, 272p.
Introduction by Moorcock; twenty-six stories and 'Introduction to New Readers' by Platt.

1974   **Morgan, D. and Kippax, J. (Hynam, J.)** *Seed of stars.* Pan, 210p.
Second in *Venture Twelve* series: Commander Tom Bruce strives to defend Kepler III.

1974   **Morland, D.** *Albion! Albion!* Faber & Faber, 213p.
England at the end of the century, when the nation is divided into four violently opposed factions – City, United, Wanderers, Athletic – derived from the football fanatics of today.

1974   **Morris, E.** *A happy day.* Scorpio Press, 96p.
Brief, admonitory account of human survival in a disastrous future.

1974   **Muller, P.** *The man from Ger.* R. Hale, 191p.
Down the road there is a man from another planet.

1974   **Niven, L.** *Protector.* Futura Publications, 218p.
Brennan from the Belt Worlds meets an alien being in deep space. [U.S. 1973]

1974   **Page, T.** *The Hephaestus Plague.* Talmy, Franklin, 194p.
The new species of beetle, *Hephaestus Parmiter*, threatens the entire world.
[U.S. 1973]

1974   **Peck, R.** *Final solution.* R. Hale, 189p.
Sleeper wakes from suspended animation to find a vastly changed world.
[U.S. 1973]

1974   **Pedler, K. & Davis, G.** *Brainrack.* Souvenir Press, 285p.
Admonitory tale designed to show that the internal combustion engine "may well
have changed the whole of human evolution."

1974   **Peters, L. T.** *The Eleventh Plague.* Secker & Warburg, 192p.
Arab terrorists plan to use microbiological weapons against the United States.
[U.S. 1973]

1974   **Piserchia, D.** *Star rider.* Bantam Books, 219p.
Heroic girl sets out to save her people. [U.S. 1971]

1974   **Pohl, C. and Pohl, F.** *(eds.) Science fiction: the great years.*
V. Gollancz, 319p.
Introductions by Frederick and Carol Pohl: seven stories. [U.S. 1973]

1974   **Priest, C.** *Inverted world.* Faber & Faber, 256p.
Elaborate and interesting tale of the survival of a community in the period after
the Crash.

1974   **Priest, C.** *Real-time world.* New English Library, 158p.
Introduction, ten stories.

1974   **Random, A.** *Star Cluster Seven.* R. Hale, 192p.
Interplanetary adventures.

1974   **Rankine, J. (Mason, D. R.)** *Operation Umanaq.* Sidgwick & Jackson,
188p.
Wicked scientist plans to start a new ice age. [U.S. 1973]

1974   **Reynolds, M.** *Commune 2000 A.D.* Bantam Books, 183p.
Flight from the ideal world of the future reveals the flaws in the perfect society.
[U.S. 1974]

1974   **Roberts, K.** *The Chalk Giants.* Hutchinson, 271p.
Vision of the collapse of civilization, the coming of new societies, and the hope
for a better future.

1974   **Rowland, D.** *Master of space.* R. Hale, 178p.
Professor Condor uses his matter transporter to arrive on the planet Crana.

1974   **Saberhagen, F.** *Changeling Earth.* Tandem, 187p.
Continues the struggle between the Old Technology and the New Demonology.
[U.S. 1973]

1974   **Scheer, K-H and Ernsting, W.** *Perry Rhodan 1: Enterprise Stardust.*
Futura Publications, 189p.
First in the *Perry Rhodan* series: hero meets the highly advanced Arkonides and
with their help stops World War III. [U.S. 1969]. *See Note 12.*

1974   **Scheer, K-H and Ernsting, W.** *Perry Rhodan 2: The Radiant Dome.*
Futura Publications, 188p.
Perry Rhodan brings peace to Earth. [U.S. 1969]

1974   **Schmitz, J. H.** *The eternal frontiers.* Sidgwick & Jackson, 190p.
Space colonists fight for survival against gigantic bipeds. [U.S. 1973]

1974   *Science Fiction Special 8.* Sidgwick & Jackson, 156 + 253 + 190p.
Brunner, J., *Timescoop*; Van Vogt, A. E., *Quest for the future*; Dirac, H., *The profit
of doom.*

1974   *Science Fiction Special 9.* Sidgwick & Jackson, 188 + 257p.
Contains: Conklin, G., *Possible tomorrows*; Wollheim, D., *Trilogy of the future.*

1974   *Science Fiction Special 10.* Sidgwick & Jackson, 190 + 189 + 159p.
Contains: Silverberg, R., *Nightwings*; Simak, C. D., *Destiny doll*; Brunner, J., *The
dreaming Earth.*

1974   *Science Fiction Special 11.* Sidgwick & Jackson, 140 + 191 + 280p.
Contains: Leinster, M., *Time tunnel*; Van Vogt, A. E., *The battle of forever*;
Cheetham, A. *(ed.), Bug-eyed monsters.*

1974   **Silverberg, R.** *Dying inside.* Sidgwick & Jackson, 248p.
The disappointed middle age of a telepath. [U.S. 1972]

1974   **Silverberg, R.** *Recalled to life.* V. Gollancz, 184p.
National commotion in the United States when a scientist announced a
reanimation process. [U.S. 1958]

1974   **Sheckley, R.** *The same to you doubled.* Pan, 172p.
First published U.S. 1971 and U.K. 1972 as *Can you feel anything when I do this?*

1974   **Smith, E. E.** *Skylark Duquesne.* Panther, 256p.
Fourth and final volume in the *Skylark* series. [U.S. 1948]

1974   **Smith, E. E.** *Skylark of Valeron.* Panther, 224p.
Third in *Skylark* series – more space travel adventures. [U.S. 1949]

1974   **Smith, E. E.** *Skylark Three.* Sphere, 207p.
Second in the *Skylark* series: journey to the planet Osborne continues.
[U.S. 1948]

1974   **Smith, E. E.** *Spacehounds of IPC.* Panther, 224p.
Adventures with the Interplanetary Corporation. [U.S. 1947]

1974   **Spinrad, N.** *The Iron Dream.* Panther, 255p.
Suppose the Nazi movement had failed and Adolf Hitler had emigrated to the
United States where he became a reputable science fiction writer? [U.S. 1973]

1974   **Stableford, B. M.** *Day of wrath.* Quartet Books, 156p.
Third volume in *Dies Irae* trilogy: the war between the Humans and the Beasts
continues through the distortions in time. [U.S. 1971]

1974   **Stableford, B.** *Halcyon Drift.* J. M. Dent, 182p.
The *Hooded Swan* searches the Halcyon Drift for a missing spaceship. First in
Star Pilot Granger series. [U.S. 1972]

1974   **Stableford, B.** *In the Kingdom of the beasts.* Quartet Books, 170p.
Second in the *Dies Irae* series: Mark Chaos travels back through time gaps and
hyperspace to the planet Aquila.

1974   **Starr, R.** *Omina Uncharted.* R. Hale, 189p.
Exploration team from Earth faces incalculable problems on the planet Omina.

1974   **Stasheff, C.** *The Warlock in spite of himself.* Mayflower, 284p.
Earther agent arrives on lost planet of Gramarye – witches, warlocks, elves, and
minxes. [U.S. 1969]

1974   **Stasheff, C.** *King Kobold.* Mayflower, 266p.
Continues above story – battle against the supreme warlock goes on. [U.S. 1971]

1974   **Sturgeon, T. (Waldo, E. H.)** *Case and the dreamer.* Pan, 155p.
Three stories, all on themes of loving. [U.S. 1974]

1974   **Vance, J.** *City of the Chasch.* Mayflower Books, 172p.
Adventures on the planet Tschai with the Green Chasch, Blue Chasch, Dirdirmen
and the rest. First in *Planet of Adventure* series. [U.S. 1968]

1974   **Vance, J.** *Son of the Tree.* Mayflower Books, 128p.
A vast tree, twelve miles high and five miles in diameter, dominates all life on the
planet Kyril. [U.S. 1958]

1974   **Van Greenaway, P.** *Take the war to Washington.* V. Gollancz, 286p.
Combat group sails from Vietnam to attack the American government.

1974   **Vance, J.** *The Houses of Iszm.* Mayflower Books, 126p.
A botanist from Earth becomes involved in plots to obtain seeds of the tree-
houses of the planet Iszm. [U.S. 1964]

1974   **Vance, J.** *The languages of Pao.* Mayflower Books, 157p.
Beran, heir to the throne of the planet Pao, seeks to unite his people against
alien domination. [U.S. 1958]

1974   **Van Vogt, A. E.** *The darkness on Diamondia.* Sidgwick & Jackson, 254p.
Planetary conflict on the planet Diamondia. [U.S. 1972]

1974   **Van Vogt, A. E.** *Van Vogt Omnibus 3.* Sidgwick & Jackson, 437p.
Contains: *The Universe maker, The changeling, More than superhuman.*

1974   **W. W. (Bloom, W.)** *Taming power.* Mayflower, 189p.
First in the *Qhe* series – adventures of a superman.

1974   **W. W. (Bloom, W.)** *White fire.* Mayflower, 204p.
Second in the *Qhe* series: superman saves the world once again.

1974   **Watkins, W. J.** *The God Machine.* Angus & Robertson, 208p.
In an oppressive Fascist United States, a secret group helps the pursued to escape the Rehabs. [U.S. 1973]

1974   **Weekley, I.** *The moving snow.* John Murray, 182p.
Natural disaster story – snow & glaciers cover all Britain up to the Wash.

1974   **Wells, A.** *(ed.) The best of Fritz Leiber.* Sidgwick & Jackson, 368p.
Introduction by Leiber – "All I ever try to write is a good story with a measure of strangeness in it". Twenty-two stories, bibliography.

1974   **Wells, A.** *(ed.) The best of A. E. Van Vogt.* Sidgwick & Jackson, 437p.
Introduction by Van Vogt, thirteen stories, bibliography.

1974   **Wells, R.** *The Parasaurians.* Sidgwick & Jackson, 190p.
Hunting exploits and survival tactics in the twenty-second century. [U.S. 1969]

1974   **Wessex, M.** *The slowing down process.* R. Hale, 183p.
A space capsule returns to Earth with a dead astronaut and the germs of a deadly plague.

1974   **White, J.** *The Dream Millennium.* M. Joseph, 222p.
Problems of the Cold Sleepers as they voyage through space in search of a new home for mankind.

1974   **Wilhelm, K.** *(ed.) Nebula Award Stories 9.* V. Gollancz, 287p.
Introduction; winners and runners-up of the 1973 Award selected by the Science Fiction Writers of America: eight stories and two essays.

1974   **Willis, T.** *Death may surprise us.* Macmillan, 288p.
Jack Stoddart, a future Prime Minister, is kidnapped.

1974   **Zebrowski, G.** *The Omega Point.* New English Library, 155p.
A survivor from the destroyed Herculean Empire seeks revenge on the Earth Federation. [U.S. 1972]

1974   **Zetford, T.** *Hook: Whirlpool of stars.* New English Library, 128p.
Opens the *Hook* series – all devoted to the extraordinary achievements of a superman.

1974   **Zetford, T.** *Hook: the Boosted Man*. New English Library, 110p.
Second in the *Hook* series: superman reaches supreme levels of achievement.

1974   **Zetford, T.** *Hook: Star City*. New English Library, 127p.
Third in *Hook* series.

1975   **Adlard, M.** *Multiface*. Sidgwick & Jackson, 184p.
Third in the *Mark Tcity* trilogy: an experiment by the Executives has surprising results.

1975   **Aldiss, B. & Harrison, H. (Dempsey, H.)** *(eds.)* *Decade: the 1940s*. Macmillan, 213p.
Eight representative stories selected from *Astounding Science Fiction* issues of the 1940s.

1975   **Aldiss, B.** *(ed.)* *Evil Earths*. Weidenfeld & Nicolson, 322p.
Introduction: "The idea of this series is to do a job of archaeology among the strata of ancient SF magazines"– fourteen stories from nine magazines.

1975   **Aldiss, B.** *(ed.)* *The Gollancz/Sunday Times Best SF Stories*. V. Gollancz, 317p.
Winning entries in the Gollancz/Sunday Times SF competition of 1974.

1975   **Anderson, P.** *The long way home*. Panther, 188p.
A spaceship returns after an absence of six thousand years to find a vastly changed Earth. [U.S. 1955]

1975   **Anderson, P.** *World without stars*. D. Dobson, 125p.
Space-wrecked Earthmen fight for survival against a god-race. First serialised in *Analog* 1966 under title of *The ancient gods*. [U.S. 1974]

1975   **Anthony, P. (Jacob, P. A.)** *Neq the Sword*. Corgi, 191p.
Third in trilogy: heroic struggle to save the Empire continues.

1975   **Anthony, P. (Jacob, P. A.)** *Rings of ice*. Millington, 191p.
A world-wide flood wipes out all civilized life on Earth. [U.S. 1974]

1975   **Anthony, P. (Jacob, P. A.)** *Triple Détente*. Sphere, 175p.
Mankind struggles with the invaders from the planet Jazo. [U.S. 1974]

1975   **Ashe, G.** *Finger and the Moon*. Panther.
No information available.

1975   **Ashley, M.** *(ed.)* *The history of the Science Fiction magazine, Part 2*. New English Library, 298p.
Preface; Introduction to history of science fiction magazines (pp.11-76); ten stories from period 1936–45; appendices and checklists.

1975   **Asimov, I.** *(ed.)* *Before the Golden Age*. Vols. 1-3. Futura Publications, 240 + 240 + 288p.
First three parts of four-volume edition of the one-volume original publication, U.S. and U.K. 1974.

1975   **Avery, R. (Cooper, E.)** *The Deathworms of Kratos*. Coronet Books, 142p.
First in *The Expendables* series: heroic spacemen explore the dangers of Kratos. [U.S. 1975]

1975   **Avery, R. (Cooper, E.)** *The Rings of Tantalus*. Coronet Books, 157p.
Second in *The Expendables* series: Commander Conrad explores the planet Tantalus for the United Nations. [U.S. 1975]

1975   **Avery, R. (Cooper, E.)** *The War Games of Zelos*. Coronet Books, 192p.
Third in *The Expendables* series: Commander Conrad risks all in the annual War Games of the planet Zelos. [U.S. 1975]

1975   **Bagnall, R. D.** *The Fourth Connection*. D. Dobson, 160p.
Fourth Dimension discovered and instantaneous matter transmission made possible.

1975   **Bailey, H.** *(ed.) New Worlds 8*. Sphere, 224p.
Nine stories, of which six are about the future.

1975   **Bailey, H.** *New Worlds 9*. Corgi, 219p. Illus.
A varied collection of stories, illustrations and criticisms.

1975   **Ball, B.** *The Space Guardians*. D. Dobson, 142p.
Third in *Space: 1999* series: the Moon continues on its headlong course through space. [U.S. 1975]

1975   **Bannon, M.** *The Tomorrow Station*. R. Hale, 175p.
Strange creatures from time investigate an Earthman.

1975   **Barker, D. A.** *A matter of evolution*. R. Hale, 188p.
A mutant race on Earth imports female humanoids for research.

1975   **Barrett, G. J.** *City of the First Time*. R. Hale, 173p.
A leader brings his people out of the Nuclear War Survival Complex to a subterranean world.

1975   **Barrett, G. J.** *Overself*. R. Hale, 192p.
Evil powers take control of a professor.

1975   **Barrett, G. J.** *The Paradise Zone*. R. Hale, 191p.
The Galactic Police pursue drug-runners to a mysterious planet.

1975   **Bass, T. J. (Bassler, T. J.)** *The Godwhale*. Eyre Methuen, 206p.
After centuries of sterility the sea is alive again; the battle between the sea-dwellers and the landfolk begins. [U.S. 1974]

1975   **Beevor, A.** *The violent brink*. Murray, 211p.
Conflict between left and right factions threatens the stability of the United Kingdom.

1975   **Bester, A.** *Extro*. Eyre Methuen, 218p.
An Immortal tries to take over the world computer system but is taken over by the system. Also published U.S. 1975 as *The computer connection*.

1975   **Biggle, L., Jr.** *The light that never was*. Elmfield Press, 240p.
Adventures and discoveries about non-human intelligence on a planet devoted to artists. [U.S. 1972]

1975   **Biggle, L. Jr.** *Monument*. New English Library, 185p.
The people of the planet Langri oppose the take-over plans of a wicked billionaire. [U.S. 1974]

1975   **Blish, J.** *The quincunx of time*. Faber & Faber, 112p.
Earth Security discovers that someone is interfering with the Dirac instantaneous transmission system. [U.S. 1973]

1975   **Bova, B.** *(ed.) Science Fiction Hall of Fame. Vol. 2, Parts 1, 2, 3.* Sphere, 192 + 192 + 192p.
Three-volume edition of the original U.K. and U.S. 1973 publication.

1975   **Boyce, C.** *Catchworld*. V. Gollancz, 256p.
Starship on the way to planet Altair is involved in a struggle with its own computer.

1975   **Brown, F.** *Paradox lost*. R. Hale, ix, 210p.
Thirteen short stories. [U.S. 1973]

1975   **Brunner, J.** *The Shockwave Rider*. Dent, 288p.
A hero fights for liberty and privacy in the days when one computer network has information about everyone in North America. Also published U.S. 1975.

1975   **Brunner, J.** *Total eclipse*. Weidenfeld & Nicolson, 187p.
On Sigma Draconis space explorers discover that the city-sites of an extinct civilization have a lesson for mankind. [U.S. 1975]

1975   **Brunner, J.** *The wrong end of time*. Eyre Methuen, 185p.
To the isolationist, overpopulated and polluted United States the news comes that an alien spaceship threatens the world. [U.S. 1971]

1975   **Bulmer, H. K.** *(ed.) New writings in SF 25*. Sidgwick & Jackson, 189p.
Foreword; nine stories.

1975   **Bulmer, H. K.** *(ed.) New Writings in SF 26*. Sidgwick & Jackson, 191p.
Foreword; nine stories.

1975   **Bulmer, H. K.** *(ed.) New writings in SF 27*. Sidgwick & Jackson, 207p.
Foreword; ten stories.

1975   **Bulmer, H. K.** *To outrun Doomsday*. New Englsih Library, 157p.
Spaceman stranded on the planet Perim proves a saviour to the inhabitants. [U.S. 1967]

975 **Bulmer, H. K. and Carnell, J.** *(eds.) New writings in SF Special 1.*
Sidgwick & Jackson, 189 + 189 + 191p.
Contains vols. 21, 22, 23 of *New writings in SF.*

975 **Burgess, E. and Friggens, A.** *Mortorio Two.* R. Hale, 192p.
Inhabitants of Mortorio oppose the dictator of Earth.

975 **Campbell, J. W.** *(ed.) Analog 7.* D. Dobson, 352p.
Eleven stories. [U.S. 1970]

975 **Campbell, J. W.** *The Moon is hell.* New English Library, 128p.
Experiences of the first men on the moon. [U.S. 1951]

975 **Carlton, R.** *Beyond tomorrow.* R. Hale, 189p.
Test pilot takes the first starship into space and through forty-two years in time.

975 **Carlton, R.** *Star Arrow.* R. Hale, 192p.
Hero goes out into deep space to end the menace to Earth.

975 **Carr, J. L.** *How Steeple Sinderby Wanderers won the F.A. Cup.*
London Magazine Editions, 124p.
Sidney Swift leads a minor football team to the victory of victories.

975 **Carr, T.** *(ed.) The best science fiction of the year 4.* V. Gollancz, 272p.
Introduction; ten stories. [U.S. 1975]

975 **Carr, T.** *(ed.) Universe 1.* Illustrated by Alicia Austin. D. Dobson, 249p.
Introduction; twelve original stories. [U.S. 1971]

975 **Chandler, A.** *The broken cycle.* R. Hale, 158p.
Adventures with the Interstellar Federation Survey Service.

975 **Chetwynd-Hayes, R.** *(ed.) Tales of terror from outer space.* Fontana,
190p.
Introduction; fourteen stories, all but one "deal with invaders that either menace
or disconcert the inhabitants of this already agitated planet.'

975 **Christian, J.** *Five gates to Armageddon.* Harwood-Smart, Lewes,
224p.
Israeli fanatics plan to use an atomic bomb against the Aswan Dam.

975 **Clarke, A. C.** *Imperial Earth.* V. Gollancz, 287p.
Journeys and adventures from the moons of Saturn to old Terra in the advanced
era of 2276.

975 **Compton, D. G.** *The missionaries.* R. Hale, 222p.
Visitors from space come to convert mankind to the religion of Ustiliath. [U.S.
1973]

975 **Coney, M. G.** *Charisma.* V. Gollancz, 224p.
Research station discovers the existence of parallel worlds.

1975   **Coney, M. G.** *The girl with a symphony in her fingers.* Elmfield Press, 199p.
Nightmare world in which criminals are used as bonded labourers or for spare-part surgery.

1975   **Coney, M. G.** *Hello summer, goodbye.* V. Gollancz, 220p.
Love and war on a distant planet.

1975   **Conrad, P.** *Last man on Kluth.* R. Hale, 192p.
Reappearance of a vanished planet endangers a spaceship.

1975   **Conrad, P.** *The slave bug.* R. Hale, 189p.
The Ungerians try to take control of Earth.

1975   **Cooper, E.** *The slaves of heaven.* Hodder & Stoughton, 191p.
Raiders from space attack the Earth tribes in the post-nuclear age. [U.S. 1974]

1975   **Corlett, W.** *Return to the Gate.* H. Hamilton, 166p.
Recollections of a long life – from the beginning of the Civilian Army and its effect on a small community.

1975   **Courtier, S. H.** *The smiling trip.* R. Hale, 192p.
Diabolical plot to dominate human minds.

1975   **Dann, J.** *(ed.) Wandering stars.* Woburn Press, 239p.
Anthology of Jewish fantasy and science fiction : Introduction by Isaac Asimov, thirteen stories. [U.S. 1974]

1975   **Darlton, C.** *Perry Rhodan 6: The secret of the time vault.* Futura Publications , 115p.
Continues the story of *Perry Rhodan 5*. [U.S. 1971]. See *Note* 12.

1975   **Darlton, C.** *Perry Rhodan 8: The galactic riddle.* Futura Publications, 128p.
The Peacelord investigates the planet of eternal life. [U.S. 1971]

1975   **Delany, S. R.** *Dhalgren.* Bantam Books, 879p.
In the last days of Earth violence and social disintegration are universal. [U.S. 1974]

1975   **Del Rey, L.** *Best science fiction stories of the year. Third annual collection.* Kaye & Ward, 245p.
Foreword, fifteen stories to exhibit "the challenge of changing times." [U.S. 1974]

1975   **Dermott, V.** *Planet finders.* Remploy, 192p.
Space explorer fights to stake his claim to a new planet. [U.S. 1971]

1975   **Dick, P. K.** *Clans of the Alphane Moon.* Panther, 205p.
CIA agent meets a telepathic Ganymedean and is involved in an interplanetary spy ring. [U.S. 1964]

1975   **Dick, P. K.** *Now wait for last year*. Panther, 224p.
Time-travel in the days when Gino Molinari leads Earth in an interplanetary war.
[U.S. 1966]

1975   **Dick, P. K.** *The Zap Gun*. Panther, 190p.
Slavers from outer space, disappearing cities, and the race to save the world.
First serialized in *Worlds of Tomorrow*, November 1965 to January 1966 as
Operation Plowshare.

1975   **Dickson, G. R.** *Dorsai!* Sphere, 176p.
Third in the *Dorsai!* trilogy: Donal Graeme, strategist of space warfare, brings
peace to the galaxy. [U.S. 1960]

1975   **Dickson, G. R.** *The R-Master*. R. Hale, 216p.
A drug turns an individual into a genius who begins to question the activities of
the World Economic Council. [U.S. 1973]

1975   **Dickson, G. R.** *Soldier, ask not*. Sphere, 216p.
Second in *Dorsai* trilogy: Tam Olyn seeks vengeance throughout the planets.
[U.S. 1967]

1975   **Dickson, G. R.** *The star road*. R. Hale, 229p.
Nine stories – space travel themes. [U.S. 1973]

1975   **Dickson, G. R.** *Tactics of mistake*. Sphere, 238p.
First in *Dorsai* trilogy: Cletus Grahame develops a new kind of planetary warfare
on the planet Kultis. [U.S. 1971]

1975   **Dixon, R.** *Noah II*. Harwood-Smart, 240p.
A latter-day Noah leads his people away from a decadent Earth. First in *The
Quest* series.

1975   **Drennan, P.** *Wooden Centauri*. Elmfield Press, 224p.
After extraordinary experiences in space the voyagers return to a world
transformed.

1975   **Drury, A.** *The promise of joy*. M. Joseph, 446p.
Sequel to *Come Nineveh, come Tyre*, 1974. [U.S. 1974]

1975   **Effinger, G. A.** *Planet of the Apes: Man the fugitive*. Universal-
Tandam, 172p.
Excerpt from the CBS-TV series. [U.S. 1974]

1975   **Elder, M.** *Centaurian quest*. R. Hale, 189p.
Centaurs suddenly appear on Earth.

1975   **Elder, M.** *The Island of the Dead*. R. Hale, 183p.
Telepath investigates the crab-like inhabitants of a distant planet.

1975   **Elwood, R.** *(ed.)* *Continuum 1*. W. H. Allen, 190p.
Introduction; eight original stories about imaginary worlds. [U.S. 1974]

1975   **Faircloth, C. E.** *The midget planet.* A. H. Stockwell, 138p.
Space travel and war against the invaders of planet Tha.

1975   **Farmer, P. J.** *Traitor to the living.* Panther, 203p.
A machine, it is claimed, can help the living to communicate with the dead. [U.S. 1973]

1975   **Fast, H.** *A touch of infinity.* Hodder & Stoughton, 182p.
Thirteen stories. [U.S. 1973]

1975   **Ferman, E. L.** *The best from Fantasy & Science Fiction.* Robson Books, 322p.
Anthology of six stories – Anderson, Asimov, Blish, Bradbury, Leiber, Sturgeon – each with a critical essay and booklist. These originally appeared in 'one-author' issues of *The Magazine of Fantasy & Science Fiction.* [U.S. 1974]

1975   **Fitzgibbon, C.** *The Golden Age.* Hart-Davis, 189p.
In the third age of human history, after the Monster had divided the world into two separate histories, another Orpheus lives through the ancient myths. [U.S. 1975]

1975   **Garden, D. J.** *Dawn chorus.* R. Hale, 175p.
A cyberneticist decides the fate of mankind.

1975   **Garner, G.** *Starfall Muta.* R. Hale, 184p.
Spacemen face the terrifying inhabitants of the planet Muta.

1975   **Garnett, D. S.** *The forgotten dimension.* R. Hale, 182p.
A man, conditioned to kill, comes to assassinate the President of Earth.

1975   **Garnett, D. S.** *The star seekers.* R. Hale, 192p.
The world's richest man takes off for deep space. [U.S. 1971]

1975   **Gerrold, D. and Niven, L.** *The flying sorcerers.* Corgi, 316p.
Spaceman has to come to terms with the supreme witch-doctor on a primitive planet. [U.S. 1971]

1975   **Gibson, F.** *The manufactured people.* R. Hale, 192p.
Medical reconditioning and criminal activities.

1975   **Gibson, F.** *Shadow of Gastor.* R. Hale, 182p.
Mysterious alien is responsible for the disappearance of young people.

1975   **Gilchrist, J.** |*Birdbrain.* R. Hale, 176p.
Adventure in the Soviet-occupied Britain of 1991.

1975   **Gilchrist, J.** *Out North.* R. Hale, 191p.
Promise of space travel by the moon rocket service attracts would-be astronauts.

1975   **Gordon, S.** *Two-Eyes.* Sidgwick & Jackson, 240p.
Continues the romantic adventures begun in *One-eye.* [U.S. 1974]

1975   **Goulart, R.** *After things fell apart.* Arrow, 139p.
Adventures in the divided decadent United States of the future. [U.S. 1970]

1975   **Greenhough, T.** *Time and Timothy Grenville.* New English Library, 221p.
Adventure starts when the aliens arrive.

1975   **Gunn, J.** *The Immortals.* Panther, 173p.
The Immortals live in hiding from all who exploit their rare gifts. [U.S. 1962]

1975   **Gunn, J.** *(ed.) Nebula Award Stories 10.* V. Gollancz, 255p.
Introduction; six prize-winning stories with brief notes on the authors. [U.S. 1975]

1975   **Gutteridge, L.** *Fratricide is a gas.* J. Cape, 192p.
An ironic tale of espionage: a microman investigates a company involved in illicit bacteriological work.

1975   **Haldeman, J.** *The forever war.* Weidenfeld & Nicolson, 236p.
Clones, nova bombs, women soldiers, tachyon torpedos etc. in a vast interstellar war. [U.S. 1974]

1975   **Hamilton, A.** *The host man.* D. Dobson, 207p.
Conflict of interests in the first brain transplant.

1975   **Harding, L.** *The world of shadows.* R. Hale, 160p.
Mysterious aliens seek to use a spaceman's mind.

1975   **Harrison, H. (Dempsey, H.** *(ed.) Nova 1.* Sphere, ix, 240p.
Introduction; fifteen stories. [U.S. 1970]

1975   **Harrison, H. (Dempsey, H.)** *(ed.) Nova 2.* Sphere, 224p.
Introduction; fourteen stories. [U.S. 1971]

1975   **Harrison, H. (Dempsey, H.)** *(ed.) Nova 3.* Sphere, 192p.
Introduction; thirteen stories. [U.S. 1972]

1975   **Harrison, H. (Dempsey, H.)** *Prime number.* Sphere, 191p.
Nineteen stories. [U.S. 1970]

1975   **Harrison, H. (Dempsey, H.) and Aldiss, B.** *(eds.) The year's best science fiction No. 7.* Sphere, 174p.
Introduction by Harrison; twelve stories.

1975   **Harrison, M. J.** *The Centauri device.* Panther, 205p.
Adventures in deep space lead to the destruction of Earth. [U.S. 1974]

1975   **Harrison, M. J.** *The machine in shaft ten.* Panther, 1975.
Ten stories.

1975   **Harrison, W.** *Thirteen selected stories.* Futura Publications, 189p.
This collection first published U.S. 1974 as *Rollerball murder.*

1975   **Hawkey, R. and Bingham, R.** *Wild Card*. Cape, 248p.
An American president invents a cosmic menace in order to unite the nation.
[U.S. 1974]

1975   **Herbert, J.** *The fog*. New English Library, 301p.
A mysterious gas in Wiltshire threatens all England.

1975   **Hersey, J.** *My petition for more space*. H. Hamilton, 182p.
In a crowded world dissent is the worst crime. [U.S. 1974]

1975   **Household, G.** *The cats to come*. M. Joseph, 63p. Illus.
An engaging fantasy of a future world in which the cats rule.

1975   **Howell, S.** *Passage to oblivion*. R. Hale, 192p.
Inhabitants of a dying planet send a spaceship to Earth.

1975   **Hoyle, F. and Hoyle, G.** *Into deepest space*. Heinemann, vi, 215p.
Voyage into deep space to discover the fate of Earth.

1975   **Hyams, E.** *Morrow's Ants*. Allen Lane, 188p.
Perverted genius manipulates the obedient workers in a vast underground city.

1975   **James, L.** *Simon Rack: Backflash*. Sphere, 143p.
Third in series: heroic adventures on Zoachtl.

1975   **James, L.** *Simon Rack: new life for old*. Sphere, 142p.
Fifth in series: Galactic Security look for the secret formula that could mean the
extinction of mankind.

1975   **Jeppson, J. O.** *The Second Experiment*. Panther, 208p.
On the planet Roiissa the Elders concentrate on the Second Experiment, and
then the Earthmen arrive.

1975   **Kippax, J. (Hynam, J.)** *Where no stars guide*. Pan, 154p.
Fourth in *Venture Twelve* series: Commander Bruce to the rescue of Earth.

1975   **Knight, D.** *Natural State*. Pan, 189p.
First published U.K. 1967 as *Three novels*.

1975   **Kranz, E. K.** *The clouded mirror*. Remploy, 192p.
Adventures on the planet Nelsonia, thanks to teleportation. [U.S. 1971]

1975   **Lacey, A.** *The love warrior*. New English Library, 128p.
Heroic exploits in the days of the Second Empire of New Earth.

1975   **Lafferty, R. A.** *Nine hundred grandmothers*. D. Dobson, 319p.
Twenty-one stories. [U.S. 1970]

1975   **Lanier, S. E.** *Hiero's journey*. Sidgwick & Jackson, 348p.
The quest for the ancient knowledge in a monstrous North America five millennia
after the Death. [U.S. 1973]

1975   **Laumer, K.** *Once there was a giant.* R. Hale, 252p.
Six stories. [U.S. 1971]

1975   **Laumer, K.** *Retief's Ransom.* D. Dobson, 159p.
Comic adventures in aid of interplanetary peace. [U.S. 1971]

1975   **Lem, St.** *The Cyberiad.* Translated from the Polish by Michael Kandel,
Secker & Warburg, 295p. Illus.
A cycle of tales in which Irurl and Klapaucius invent ingenious machines. First
published as *Cyberiada*, 1972. [U.S. 1974]

1975   **Lem, S.** *The Futurological Congress.* Secker & Warburg, 149p.
Hilarious account of the disruption of the eighth World Futurological Congress.
First published 1971 as *Ze Wspomnień Ijona Tichego. Kongres Futurologiczny in
Bezsenność.* [U.S. 1974]

1975   **Lewis, C.** *The Cain Factor.* Harwood-Smart, 174p.
The imminent destruction of Earth compels humanity to unite in the search for
another habitable world.

1975   **Logan, C.** *Shipwreck.* V. Gollancz, 192p.
Prize-winning novel in Gollancz-Sunday Times 1974 Competition: a most
imaginative story of survival in deep space.

1975   **Lopez, A.** *Second Coming.* New English Library, 128p.
As America vanishes in earthquakes and floods, the brutal forces of the New
Messiah take control.

1975   **Lundwall, S. J.** *Alice's World.* Arrow Books, 112p.
The spaceships of the Confederation return to a changed Earth. [U.S. 1971]

1975   **Lymington, J. (Chance, J. N.)** *A spider in the bath.* Hodder &
Stoughton, 190p.
An invasion of enormous spiders threatens the town of Dormouth.

1975   **McCaffrey, A.** *To ride Pegasus.* Dent, 243p.
Four linked stories about precognition. [U.S. 1973]

1975   **Macey, P.** *Distant relations.* D. Dobson, 175p.
A tale of cloning, romantic attachments, and preparations for the space journey
to planet Eden.

1975   **Mackelworth, R. W.** *The year of the painted world.* R. Hale, 176p.
Space probe returns from Mars with a deadly virus.

1975   **Malzberg, B. N.** *The destruction of the temple.* New English Library,
143p.
Re-enactment of the death of President Kennedy in the ruins of New York. [U.S.
1974]

1975   **Malzberg, B. N.** *The falling astronauts.* Arrow Books, 191p.
Space pilot endangers world safety. [U.S. 1971]

1975   **Malzberg, B. N.** *Overlay.* New English Library, 141p.
The Galactic Bureau decides to take a hand in terrestrial affairs. [U.S. 1972]

1975   **Marden, W.** *The exile of Ellendon.* R. Hale, 186p.
Arrival of unicorns in Florida begins battle for liberty of another world. [U.S. 1974]

1975   **Marshall, B.** *Marx the First.* Constable, 181p.
Continues trilogy begun with *Urban the Ninth*: a future Pope allows the clergy to
marry – a policy that leads to war between Spain and Britain.

1975   **Mason, D. R.** *The end bringers.* R. Hale, 208p.
A trouble-maker has effect on a trouble-free world. [U.S. 1973]

1975   **Mitchison, N.** *Solution Three.* D. Dobson 160p.
In a well-organized society some misfits question the value of a sexual
reproduction.

1975   **Mohs, M.** *(ed.) Other worlds, Other gods.* New English Library, 264p.
Introduction ('Science fiction and the world of religion'), thirteen stories on
religious themes. [U.S. 1971]

1975   **Moorcock, M.** *(ed.) Before Armageddon. Volume 1.* W. H. Allen, 180p.
Introduction by Moorcock on history of imaginary war fiction: five stories.

1975   **Moorcock, M.** *The hollow lands.* Hart-Davis, MacGibbon, 180p.
Second in *Dancers at the end of time* series: Jherek Carnelian continues his time-
travelling adventures. [U.S. 1974]

1975   **Moorcock, M.** *The quest for Tanelorn.* Mayflower, 126p.
Third in the *Chronicles of Castle Brass*.

1975   **Moorcock, M. and James, P.** *The distant suns.* Illustrated by Jim
Cawthorn. Unicorn, 45p.
Jerry Cornelius pilots *The Hope of Man* through various adventures in deep
space.

1975   **Morgan, D.** *The country of the mind.* Corgi, 189p.
Idealist uses his Psi powers in the interest of peace and justice.

1975   **Morgan, D.** *High destiny.* Millington, 192p.
Haldor, Emperor of the Thirteen Worlds, stands firm for peace with honour. [U.S.
1973]

1975   **Morgan, D.** *Reiver.* R. Hale, 192p.
The Mercenary Guilds provide an outlet for the aggressive young in an era of
planetary peace.

1975   **Muller, P.** *Brother Gib.* R. Hale, 192p.
One man stands out against a robot-controlled, centralized world.

1975   **Niven, L.** *The flight of the horse.* Orbit, 212p.
Seven stories – mostly about Svetz of the Institute for Temporal Research. [U.S.
1974]

1975   **Niven, L.** *A hole in space.* Orbit, 196p.
Short stories – teleportation, suspended animation, alien visitors. [U.S. 1974]

1975   **Niven, L. and Pournelle, J.** *The Mote in God's Eye.* Weidenfeld & Nicolson, 537p.
In the 30th Century the Imperial Space Navy makes the first contact with intelligent nonhuman beings. [U.S. 1974]

1975   **Norman, B.** *End product.* Quartet, 248p.
Admonitory tale of cannibalism in the near future.

1975   **Parker, E. F.** *Girl in trouble.* Utopian Publications, 36p.
Space-Patrolman Kelly pursues the space-ship thieves.

1975   **Pearce, B.** *Kidnapped into space.* D. Dobson, 192p.
First contact made with creatures from another planet.

1975   **Pearson, P.** *Postscript for Malpas.* Macmillan, 159p.
Plot to disrupt British nuclear programme..

1975   **Pedler, K. & Davis, G.** *The Dynostar menace.* Souvenir Press, 271p.
When the fossil fuels are exhausted, work starts on a vast nuclear reactor in space.

1975   **Penny, D. G.** *Starchant.* R. Hale, 187p.
Three people, refugees from a planetary empire, search for a permanent home.

1975   **Penny, D. G.** *The sunset people.* R. Hale, 172p.
Catastrophe-story – the remnants of mankind look for salvation.

1975   **Pereira, W. D.** *The Charon Tapes.* R. Hale, 184p.
Adventures on a mysterious planet.

1975   **Powe, B.** *The last days of the American Empire.* Macdonald (Printed USA), 326p.
Satirical tale of the African invasion of a decadent and corrupt United States. Also published U.S. 1975.

1975   **Rackham, J. (Phillifent, J. T.)** *Alien sea.* D. Dobson, 154p.
Earth and Venus move towards a possible conflict. [U.S. 1968]

1975   **Random, A.** *Cradle of stars.* R. Hale, 192p.
Space criminal holds heroine to ransom.

1975   **Random, A.** *Dark Constellation.* R. Hale, 189p.
The Trans-Solar Defence faces the invaders from planet Deorca.

1975   **Rankine, J. (Mason, D. R.)** *Astral quest.* D. Dobson, 157p.
Sixth in *Space: 1999* series: Moon Base Alpha faces mutants from deep space.

1975   **Rankine, J. (Mason, D. R.)** *Lunar attack.* D. Dobson, 141p.
Fifth in *Space 1999* series: Moon Base Alpha faces alien spaceships.

1975 **Rankine, J. (Mason, D. R.)** *Moon Odyssey.* D. Dobson, 145p.
Second in *Space: 1999* series: Moon Base Alpha fights to survive.

1975 **Reeves, L. P.** *The Nairn Syndrome.* R. Hale, 172p.
A new drug causes the population to disappear.

1975 **Robeson, K.** *(pseud.) Meteor menace.* Corgi, 140p.
Doc Savage intervenes in Tibet. [U.S. 1933]. See *Note* 10.

1975 **Robeson, K.** *(pseud.) The thousand-headed man.* Corgi Books, 150p.
Doc Savage faces the monster in Indo-China. [U.S. 1934]

1975 **Russell, E. F.** *Like nothing on Earth.* D. Dobson, 155p.
Six stories selected from issues of *Astounding* in the 1950s.

1975 **Saberhagen, F.** *Berserkeer's planet.* Futura Publications, 165p.
The Interstellar Authority continues the struggle against the galactic menace of the berserkers. [U.S. 1975]

1975 **Sacks, J.** *(ed.) Best of "Science Fiction Monthly".* New English Library, 189p.
Introduction; sixteen stories selected from *Science Fiction Monthly*.

1975 **Scheer, K. H.** *Perry Rhodan 7: Fortress of the Six Moons.* Futura, 124p.
The Peace Lord finishes off the invading fleet of Topides. [U.S. 1971]

1975 **Scheer, K. H. and Mahr, K.** *Perry Rhodan 5: The Vega Sector.* Futura Publications, 189p.
Perry Rhodan defends Earth from the Topide reptiles. [U.S. 1970]

1975 **Schutz, J. W.** *People of the Rings.* R. Hale, 192p.
The mystery of Saturn's rings explained.

1975 *Science Fiction Special 12.* Sidgwick & Jackson, 210 + 235 + 192p.
Contains: Adlard, M., *Volteface;* Ball, B., *Night of the robots;* Silverberg, R., *The anvil of time.*

1975 *Science Fiction Special 13.* Sidgwick & Jackson, 175 + 190 + 190p.
Contains: Ball, B., *The probability man;* Brunner, J., *Age of miracles;* Simak, C. D., *A choice of gods.*

1975 *Science Fiction Special 14.* Sidgwick & Jackson, 185 + 221 + 219p.
Contains: Laumer, K., *The world shuffler;* Lem, S., *The Invincible;* Silverberg, R., *Beyond control.*

1975 *Science Fiction Special 15.* Sidgwick & Jackson, 297 + 192 + 223p.
Contains: Harrison, H., *The best of John, W. Campbell;* Van Vogt, A. E., *The farout worlds of A. E. Van Vogt;* Williamson, J., *Bright new universe.*

1975 **Scortia, T. N.** *Earthwreck.* Coronet Books, 224p.
Only two space stations – one Russian, the other American – survive the nuclear holocaust of Earth. [U.S. 1974]

1975   **Sharland, M.** *Nervestorm*. Aidan Ellis, 255 p.
C-in-C Northern Ireland helps right-wing group to plan military take-over in Britain.

1975   **Shaw, B.** *Orbitsville*. V. Gollancz, 224 p.
A fugitive space captain discovers a Dyson sphere.

1975   **Shear, D.** *Cloning*. R. Hale, 162 p.
Problems of androids and clones. [U.S. 1972]

1975   **Silent, W. T.** *Lord of the Red Sun*. R. Hale, 189 p.
Adventure and romance in the days of the Galactic Empire. [U.S. 1972]

1975   **Silverberg, R.** *Born with the dead*. V. Gollancz, 267 p.
Three novellas: the dead restored to life; a sign for a faithless world; suicide as an end.

1975   **Silverberg, R.** *(ed.) New Dimensions 5*. V. Gollancz, 234 p.
Fifteen original stories, one poem; brief note on each author. [U.S. 1975]

1975   **Silverberg, R.** *The silent invaders*. D. Dobson, 152 p.
Alien fights for the security of Earth. [U.S. 1963]

1975   **Silverberg, R.** *Sundance and other science fiction stories*. Abelard, 192 p.
Nine stories. [U.S. 1974]

1975   **Silverberg, R.** *(ed.) Threads of time*. Millington, 219 p.
Introduction – 'one of science fiction's unique virtues is its capacity to create a vision of a detailed and richly inventive imaginary universe'. Three novellas: Benford, G., *Threads of time;* Simak, C. D., *The Marathon Photograph;* Spinrad, N., *Riding the torch.*

1975   **Silverberg, R.** *To live again*. Sidgwick & Jackson, 231 p.
Plot to transplant the mind of an immensely wealthy man. [U.S. 1969]

1975   **Silverberg, R.** *Unfamiliar territory*. V. Gollancz, 212 p.
Thirteen stories; two of them additional to the original U.S. edition of 1973.

1975   **Silverberg, R.** *Up the line*. Sphere, 207 p.
Romantic adventures with the Time Service. [U.S. 1969]

1975   **Simak, C. D.** *Cemetery World*. Sidgwick & Jackson, 191 p.
In the distant future Earth has become the burial place of the galaxy. [U.S. 1973]

1975   **Simak, C. D.** *Our children's children*. Sidgwick & Jackson, 186 p.
Time-tunnels allow the children of the future to escape from trouble into the modern world. [U.S. 1974]

1975   **Sims, D. N.** *The past-time of eternity*. R. Hale, 190 p.
The Stellar Council sends an envoy to unravel the mysteries of the planet Midori.

1975   **Siodmak, C.** *City in the sky*. Barrie & Jenkins, 218p.
International Space City in earth orbit has a tiny satellite – a prison for the
dissident of Earth. [U.S. 1974]

1975   **Smith, C.** *The planet buyer*. Sphere, 156p.
Problems for the purchaser of Old Earth. A shorter version appeared in *Galaxy
Science Fiction*, April 1964, with the title of *The boy who bought Old Earth*.

1975   **Smith, C.** *Underpeople*. Sphere, 142p.
Deep below Old Earth a race of mutants labours for mankind. [U.S. 1968]

1975   **Smith, E. E.** *The best of E. E. 'Doc' Smith*. Futura Publications, 285p.
Preface by Philip Harbottle; Foreword by Walter Gillings; Afterword and
Bibliography. Eight stories.

1975   **Smith, E. E.** *The Galaxy Primes*. Panther, 188p.
Space adventure with the first starship from Earth. [U.S. 1965]

1975   **Smith, E. E.** *Subspace explorers*. Panther, 237p.
Warfare on Earth and in deep space. [U.S. 1965]

1975   **Stableford, B.** *Promised Land*. J. M. Dent, 160p.
Third in *Star Pilot Grainger* series: Earth colonists have to deal with the forest
people of Chao Phrya. [U.S. 1974]

1975   **Stableford, B.** *Rhapsody in black*. Dent, 160p.
Second in *Star Pilot Grainger* series: subterranean adventures on the planet
Rhapsody. [U.S. 1973]

1975   **Starr, R.** *Time factor*. R. Hale, 189p.
Time-travel adventures in the twenty-ninth century.

1975   **Stewart, F. M.** *Star Child*. W. H. Allen, 239p.
Time-traveller from the far future seeks to control human minds. [U.S. 1974]

1975   **Strick, P.** *(ed.)* *Antigrav*. Hutchinson, 184p.
Introduction; fifteen stories.

1975   **Suffling, M.** *Project Oceanus*. R. Hale, 189p.
Sea-farming and Marine Agriculture are the only means of saving the world.

1975   **Suffling, M.** *Space crusader*. R. Hale, 189p.
A Starfleet Captain ends piracy in the spaceways.

1975   **Sullivan, S.** *Summer rising*. Weidenfeld & Nicolson, 260p.
In the desolate, tribal world of the twenty-first century the Irish lead the way to
recovery.

1975   **Tilley, P.** *Fade-out*. Hodder & Stoughton, 369p.
A spacecraft from another star-system causes radio and radar blackout on Earth.
[U.S. 1975]

1975   **Tiptree, Jnr, J. (Sheldon, A.)** *Ten thousand light years from home.*
Eyre Methuen, 320p.
Introduction by Harry Harrison; twelve whimsical short stories that reverse
common assumptions. [U.S. 1973]

1975   **Tubb, E. C.** *Breakaway.* Futura Publications, 144p.
First in series based on the scripts of the ATV television programmes, *Space:
1999.* Atomic disaster threatens Moon Base Alpha.

1975   **Tubb, E. C.** *Century of the Manikin.* Millington, 142p.
The Chief of Propaganda and Emotional Control learns of the latent violence in a
perfect world`.[U.S. 1972]

1975   **Tubb, E. C.** *Collision Course.* Futura Publications, 143p.
Fourth in the ATV television series *Space: 1999*; asteroid threatens safety of the
Moon.

1975   **Tucker, W.** *Ice and iron.* V. Gollancz, 181p.
The survivors work to establish a new life as another Ice Age closes in on North
America. [U.S. 1974]

1975   **Van Vogt, A. E.** *Empire of the atom.* New English Library, 155p.
Out of a desolate Earth come new imperial ambitions. [U.S. 1956]

1975   **Van Vogt, A. E.** *The man with a thousand names.* Sidgwick &
Jackson, 224p.
Space adventure – force fields, body exchanges, alien entities. [U.S. 1974]

1975   **Van Vogt, A. E.** *More than superhuman.* New English Library, 220p.
Six stories. [U.S. 1971]

1975   **Van Vogt, A. E.** *The Secret Galactics.* Sidgwick & Jackson, 215p.
A time-jump facilitates alien plan to seize control of Earth. [U.S. 1974]

1975   **Van Vogt, A. E.** *The Wizard of Linn.* New English Library, 180p.
Sequel to *Empire of the Atom*; the ruler of Earth prepares to fight the invaders
from space. [U.S. 1968]

1975   **Vance, J.** *The Anome.* Coronet Books, 206p.
First in the *Durdane* trilogy: Gastel Etzwane acts against the power of the
Faceless Man. [U.S. 1973]

1975   **Vance, J.** *The Asutra.* Coronet Books, 187p.
Concludes the *Durdane* trilogy: the hero fights the parasitic Asutra. [U.S. 1974]

1975   **Vance, J.** *The Brains of Earth.* D. Dobson, 108p.
Man struggles for the safety of the world. [U.S. 1966]

1975   **Vance, J.** *The Brave Free Men.* Coronet, 224p.
Second in the *Durdane* trilogy. Defeat of the Rogushkoi, invaders of the Land of
Shant in the world of Durdane. [U.S. 1973]

1975   **Vance, J.** *The Dirdir*. D. Dobson, 150p.
Third in the *Planet of Adventure* series: adventures with the off-world race of the Dirdirmen. [U.S. 1969]

1975   **Vance, J.** *The Pnume*. D. Dobson, 156p.
Fourth in the *Planet of Adventure* series: adventures with the subterranean Pnume. [U.S. 1970]

1975   **Vance, J.** *Servants of the Wankh*. D. Dobson, 158p.
Second in the *Planet of Adventure* series, and even more exotic than the first. [U.S. 1969]

1975   **W. W.** *Qhe!* Mayflower, 157p.
Qhe, who is Cosmic Bond and Superlover, deals with the danger from space.

1975   **Watson, I.** *The Jonah Kit*. V. Gollancz, 221p.
As the astronomers discover that the Universe is not what it seems, the whales of Earth help to save mankind.

1975   **Wells, A.** *(ed.) The best of Frank-Herbert*. Sidgwick & Jackson, 302p.
Introduction by Herbert (" . . . the fact that we write about any future at all, even an *interesting* one, assumes that future will come to pass"); thirteen stories, bibliography.

1975   **Wells, A.** *(ed.) The best of Clifford. D. Simak*. Sidgwick & Jackson, 253p.
Introduction by Simak "A respect for life and a tolerance of viewpoint probably sum up the background of my work"; ten stories and a bibliography.

1975   **White, J.** *Comet*. H. Hamilton, 222p.
In the desolate age of New Earth, as a comet approaches, some seek knowledge from the forbidden books.

1975   **Wollheim, D.** *(ed. with A. W. Saha). The World's best SF short stories No. 1*. Elmfield Press, 280p.
Introduction by Wollheim – "Science fiction is a literature of prophecy, of prediction, of investigation into the worlds of if"–ten stories. First published US 1974 as *The 1974 Annual World's best SF*.

1975   **Wyatt, P.** *Irish rose*. M. Joseph, 213p.
A beautiful young woman threatens the hierarchical society of the time after the Great Fall.

1975   **Wylie, P.** *The end of the dream*. Elmfield Press, 273p.
End of the world story – earthquakes devastate the cities, rising seas cover the land, and deadly toxins poison mankind. [U.S. 1972]

1975   **Wyndham, J. (Harris, J. B.)** *The man from beyond*. M. Joseph, 283p.
Twelve stories.

1975   **Yolen, J.** *(ed.) Zoo 2000*. V. Gollancz, 224p.
Introduction; twelve stories about men and animals in the future. [U.S. 1973]

1975   **Zelazny, R.** *Today we choose faces*. Millington, 174p.
One man seeks to liberate humanity from the close, corporate life that followed on the disaster. [U.S. 1973]

1975   **Zelazny, R.** *To die in Italbar*. Faber & Faber, 183p.
Search for a saviour when a mysterious epidemic threatens the galaxy. [U.S. 1973]

1975   **Zetford, T.** *Hook: Virility gene*. New English Library, 111p.
Fourth·in *Hook* series: superman searches for the source of the virility gene.

1976   **Aldiss, B.** *(ed.) Galactic empires. Volume 1*. Weidenfeld & Nicolson xii, 338p.
Introduction, fifteen stories selected to "tell us a story adorned with alien creatures, swordplay, fascination gadgets, and – for preference – beautiful princesses."

1976   **Aldiss, B.** *(ed.) Galactic empires. Volume 2*. Weidenfeld & Nicolson viii, 296p.
Introduction – "A galactic empire is ramshackle and anachronistic, full of miscegenous worlds, leaky spaceships, and naked slaves working by torchlight in uranium mines" – twelve stories.

1976   **Aldiss, B. & Harrison, H. (Dempsey, H.)** *(eds.) Decade: the 1950s*. Macmillan, 219p.
Introduction by Harrison; twelve stories representative of the period.

1976   **Anderson, P.** *Ensign Flandry*. Coronet, 217p.
Heroic adventures with the Imperial Space Navy, as the young Dominic Flandry fights the Merseians. [U.S. 1966]

1976   **Anderson, P.** *Flandry of Terra*. Coronet, 220p.
Three linked stories – Captain Sir Dominic Flandry operates against the Merseians. [U.S. 1965]

1976   **Anderson, P.** *War of the Wing-Men*. Sphere, 160p.
Three terrestrials receive help from the inhabitants of planet Diomedes. [U.S. 1958]

1976   **Anderson, P.** *We claim these stars*. D. Dobson, 125p.
Dominic Flandry of Terran Intelligence saves the Imperium once again. [U.S. 1959]

1976   **Anthony, P. (Jacob, P. A.)** *Steppe*. Millington, 158p.
A nomad is projected into an extraordinary future world. [U.S. 1975]

1976   **Anvil, C.** *Strangers in Paradise*. H. Jenkins, 170p.
Men from the Space Patrol face the worst possible horrors on planet Paradise. [U.S. 1969]

1976   **Ashe, G. (Creasey, J.)** *A plague of demons*. J. Long, 185p.
Commissioner Dawlish deals with a major menace to law and order.

1976   **Ashley, M.** *(ed.) The history of the Science Fiction magazine, Part 3.* New English Library, 349p.
Preface; Introduction on history of science fiction magazines (pp.13-109); ten stories from period 1946–55; appendices and checklists.

1976   **Asimov, I.** *(ed.) Before the Golden Age: 4.* Futura Publications, 256p.
Completes the four-part edition of *Before the Golden Age*, first published in one volume in 1974.

1976   **Asimov, I.** *Buy Jupiter and other stories.* V. Gollancz, 206p.
Collection of twenty-four previously uncollected short stories from period 1950–73, each with a short note. [U.S. 1975]

1976   **Avery, R. (Cooper, E.)** *The venom of Argus.* Coronet, 160p.
Fourth in *The Expendables* series: heroic spacemen encounter the perils of planet Argus.

1976   **Axton, D.** *Prison of ice.* W. H. Allen, 219p.
World-wide drought – ice towed south from Arctic.

1976   **Bailey, H.** *(ed.) New Worlds 10.* Corgi, 238p. Illus.
Short stories, poems, criticism, and notes on the contributors.

1976   **Ballard, J. G.** *Low-flying aircraft.* J. Cape, 191p.
Nine stories including the novella *The ultimate city*.

1976   **Barclay, A,** *The City and the desert.* R. Hale, 190p
A leader unites the desert people of a desolate planet.

1976   **Barclay, A.** *No magic carpet.* R. Hale, 171p
Adventures with faster-than-light space travel.

1976   **Barclay, B.** *(pseud.) The empty palace.* A. Barker, 187p.
Scotland rich and independent, England poor and in decline, and all because "people just let the politicians do what they liked."

1976   **Barrett, G. J.** *The Bodysnatchers of Lethe.* R. Hale, 174p.
Hero defeats plot to control a galaxy.

1976   **Barrett, G. J.** *The nighjt of the deathship.* R. Hale, 195p.
Terrifying aliens emerge from a crashed spaceship.

1976   **Barrett, G. J.** *Slaver from the stars.* R. Hale, 192p.
Man and woman kidnapped from Earth to a planet of giants.

1976   **Barrett, G. J.** *Timeship to Thebes.* R. Hale, 188p.
Time travel to the days of Ancient Egypt.

1976   **Bax, M.** *The hospital ship.* Cape, 223p.
A hospital ship voyages the oceans, picking up the victims of twentieth-century madness.

1976   **Blackburn, J.** *The face of the Lion.* J. Cape, 159p.
Mutation of the Spanish influenza virus has catastrophic effects; mad Scottish laird plots to hold UK to ransom.

1976   **Brackett, L. (Hamilton, L.B.)** *The ginger star.* Sphere, 186p.
Adventures of Eric John Stark on the desperate planet of Skaith. [U.S. 1974]

1976   **Brackett, L. (Hamilton, L. B.)** *The hounds of Skaith.* Sphere, 190p.
Continues the heroic adventures of Eric John Stark on the planet Skaith. [U.S. 1974]

1976   **Brett, D.** *Black Folder.* Harrap, 160p.
Near future – Britain close to collapse.

1976   **Brown, C. N.** *(ed.) Alien worlds.* Mews Books, 144p.
Foreword; three novellas.

1976   **Brown, C. N.** *(ed.) Far travellers.* Mews Books, 143p.
Three novellas on space travel themes.

1976   **Brunner, J.** *The stone that never came down.* New English Library, 206p.
A new synthetic replicant has extraordinary effects on human behaviour. [U.S. 1973]

1976   **Bulmer, H. K.** *(ed.) New Writings in SF 28.* Sidgwick & Jackson, 187p.
Foreword; ten stories

1976   **Bulmer, H. K.** *(ed.) New Writings in SF 29.* Sidgwick & Jackson, 187p.
Foreword; eight stories.

1976   **Bulmer, H. K.** *Stained glass world.* New English Library, 160p.
First published as *The ulcer culture*, 1969.

1976   **Campbell, J. W.** *(ed.) Analog 8.* D. Dobson, 227p.
Nine stories. [U.S. 1970]

1976   **Canning, V.** *The Doomsday carrier.* Heinemann, 212p.
National commotion over escaped chipanzee, injected with a lethal plague bacillus.

1976   **Carr, T.** *(ed.) The best science fiction of the year 5.* V. Gollancz, 296p.
Introduction; twelve stories. [U.S. 1976]

1976   **Carr, T.** *(ed.) Universe Two.* D. Dobson, 255p. Illus.
Thirteen stories. [U.S. 1972]

1976   **Chandler, A. B.** *The way back.* R. Hale, 149p.
Space adventures – lost in space and time.

1976   **Clement, H. (Stubbs, H. C.)** *Ocean on top.* Sphere, 159p.
Agents of the Power Board discover a submarine society. [U.S. 1973]

1976   **Cole, A.** *Madness emerging.* R. Hale, 189p.
A deadly alien life form emerges from a Cornish mine.

1976   **Compton, D. G.** *Chronicules.* Arrow Books, 206p.
First published 1971 as *Hot wireless sets, Aspirin Tablets . . . and something that might have been Castor Oil.*

1976   **Coney, M.** *Brontomek!* V. Gollancz, 253p.
The Hetherington Organisation takes control of the planet Arcadia to the dismay of the colonists.

1976   **Corley, J.** *Benedict's planet.* Elmfield Press, 170p.
Planetary prospector discovers rare minerals and meets an unknown planetary people.

1976   **Cowper, R. (Murry, C. M.)** *The custodians.* V. Gollancz, 191p.
Four stories.

1976   **Creasey, J.** *The thunder maker.* Hodder & Stoughton, 189p.
Dr. Palfrey saves the world once again.

1976   **Cullingworth, N. J.** *Dodos of Einstein.* R. Hale, 191p.
A man investigates the workings of the world computer.

1976   **Darlton, C.** *Perry Rhodan 9: Quest through time and space.* Futura, 128p.
Perry Rhodan continues the search for the secret of eternal life. [U.S. 1972]

1976   **Darlton, C.** *Perry Rhodan 12: The rebels of Tuglan.* Futura, 128p.
Alien life form exerts its powers on crew of spaceship Stardust. [U.S. 1972]

1976   **Darlton, C.** *Perry Rhodan 15: Escape to Venus.* Futura, 116p.
The Peace Lord pursues the beauteous Thora to Venus. [U.S. 1972]

1976   **Davidson, A.** *Or all the seas with oysters.* White Lion, 176p.
Sixteen stories. [U.S. 1962]

1976   **Davis, B.** *(ed.) The best of Murray Leinster.* Corgi, 174p.
Introduction, ten stories written between 1945 & 1956.

1976   **Del Rey, L.** *Badge of Infamy.* D. Dobson, 121p.
A doctor escapes women and his profession by going to Mars where he joins in the fight for freedom. [U.S. 1963]

1976   **Del Rey, L.** *(ed.) Best science fiction stories of the year. Fourth annual collection.* Kaye & Ward, 248p.
Foreword – science fiction "should excite a sense of wonder, of something beyond the ordinary" – fifteen stories [U.S. 1975]

1976   **Dick, P. K.** *Dr. Futurity.* Methuen, 157p.
Doctor involved in a time-travel plot to change the course of American history. Originally published U.K. 1970 in *A Philip K. Dick Omnibus.* [U.S. 1960]

1976   **Dick, P. K.** *Martian time-slip.* New English Library, 240p.
Introduction by Brian Aldiss: a complex story of schizold personalities and of
Martian primitives in the long neglected Earth colony of Mars. [U.S. 1964]

1976   **Dick, P. K.** *Our friends from Frolix 8.* Panther, 211p.
Problems of the Old Men in the days when the New Men and Unusuals rule on
Earth. [U.S. 1970]

1976   **Dick, P. K.** *The turning wheel.* Coronet, 190p.
Nine stories – nuclear catastrophes, industrial competition, the system of the
universe. First published U.S. 1973 as *The Book of Philip K. Dick.*

1976   **Dick, P. K.** *The unteleported man.* Methuen, 124p.
In the days of matter transmission one man decides to find out what is happening
to the space colonists. Originally published U.K. 1970 in *A Philip K. Dick
Omnibus. [U.S. 1966]*

1976   **Dick, P. K.** *Vulcan's.hammer.* Arrow, 154p.
Revolt against the master computer in a time of universal unity. [U.S. 1960]

1976   **Disch, T. M.** *(ed.) The new improved Sun.* Hutchinson, 192p.
Introduction; twelve stories on utopian themes. [U.S. 1975]

1976   **Doyle, R.** *Deluge.* Arlington Books, 310p.
A sudden flood submerges London.

1976   **Dunn, S.** *The coming of Steeleye.* Coronet, 146p.
First part of an epic tale of the nine-foot superman whose eyes can blast his
enemies.

1976   **Dunn, S.** *Steeleye – The Wideways.* Coronet, 159p.
Second part of the Steeleye series – the hero continues the fight for the Eumigs.

1976   **Dunn, S.** *Steeleye – Waterspace.* Coronet, 144p.
Third part of the *Steeleye* series: the hero fights Komast the killer.

1976   **Edwards, P.** *Terminus.* Macmillan, 336p.
A sinister secret society plans to secure power in Eurafrica, the one surviving
area after two nuclear wars. [U.S. 1976]

1976   **Egleton, C.** *State visit.* Hodder & Stoughton, 224p.
Plot to kill the Queen in order to prevent signing of a German reunification treaty.

1976   **Elder, M.** *Double time.* R. Hale, 184p.
Over-crowding in the 21st century as pace of life accelerates.

1976   **Ellern, W. B.** *New Lensman.* Futura Publications, 191p.
Sequel to the original *Lensman* series.

1976   **Ellison, H.** *(ed.) Again, Dangerous Visions.* Millington, xvii, 760p. Illus.
Original stories by 42 writers, including Le Guin, Vonnegut, Bradbury, Blish and
others. [U.S. 1972]

1976   **Ellison, H.** *Approaching oblivion*. Millington, 164p.
Foreword by Michael Crichton, Introduction by Harlan Ellison, eleven stories.
[U.S. 1974]

1976   **Ellison, H.** *The beast that shouted love at the heart of the world*.
Millington, 215p.
Introduction; twelve stories. [U.S. 1974]

1976   **Elwood, R.** *(ed.) Continuum 2*. W. H. Allen, 191p.
Introduction; eight original stories. [U.S. 1974]

1976   **Elwood, R.** *(ed.) Dystopian visions*. R. Hale, vii, 197p.
Introduction; thirteen stories by young American writers on themes of violence,
prejudice, old age, sex, culture shock etc. [U.S. 1975]

1976   **Elwood, R.** *(ed.) Future city*. Sphere, 236p.
Introduction; foreword by Simak and afterword by Pohl; twenty-two stories about
the urban future. [U.S. 1973]

1976   **Farmer, P. J.** *The book of Philip José Farmer*. Elmfield Press, vi,
239p.
Foreword, sixteen stories. [U.S. 1973]

1976   **Farmer, P. J.** *The green odyssey*. Sphere, 157p.
Adventures of a crashed spaceman on an unknown planet. [U.S. 1957]

1976   **Farmer, P. J.** *The stone god awakens*. Panther, 205p.
Scientist from 1985 returns to consciousness in the remote future only to
discover a world of non-human beings. [U.S. 1970]

1976   **Farmer, P. J.** *Time's last gift*. Panther, 173p.
Time-travellers wander through the Europe of 12,000 B.C. [U.S. 1972]

1976   **Farren, M.** *The quest of the DNA cowboys*. Mayflower, 223p.
First in trilogy: journey through a fantastic world.

1976   **Farren, M.** *Synoptic manhunt*. Mayflower, 252p.
Continues trilogy: a killer-priest has orders to remove a potential menace to the
world's future.

1976   **Ferman, E. L. & Malzberg, B.** *(eds.) Arena: Sports SF*. Robson
Books, xi, 223p.
Introduction by Ferman; eleven stories about sport, and Afterword by Malzberg.
[U.S. 1976]

1976   **Finney, C. G.** *The unholy city*. Panther, 125p.
Narrator arrives in a strange land where everything is an ironic commentary on
American life. [U.S. 1937]

1976   **Follett, J.** *The Doomsday Ultimatum*. Weidenfeld & Nicolson, 224p.
A terrorist group provides the opportunity for a Prime Minister to seize absolute
power.

1976   **Foreman, R.** *The Ringway Virus*. Millington, 294 p.
New influenza virus wipes out entire human race save for one couple.

1976   **Foster, A. D.** *Icerigger*. New English Library, 313 p.
Space kidnapping and adventures on a frozen planet. [U.S. 1974]

1976   **François, Y. R.** *The CTZ paradigm*. R. Hale, 189 p.
The Krits prepare to take over the Interstellar Confederation. [U.S. 1975]

1976   **Freemantle, B.** *The November man*. J. Cape, 240 p.
Intrigue complicates disarmament negotations between the U.S.A. and the U.S.S.R.

1976   **Garner, G.** *Rifts of time*. R. Hale, 181 p.
Volunteer from the Space Force explores unknown dimensions in time.

1976   **Garnett, D. S.** *Cosmic carousel*. R. Hale, 192 p.
Seven stories.

1976   **Ghidalia, V. and Elwood, R.** *The Venus factor*. New English Library, 189 p.
Eight stories. The book was withdrawn for copyright reasons that related to 'The last seance' by Agatha Christie. [U.S. 1972]

1976   **Gilchrist, J.** *The English Corridor*. R. Hale, 190 p.
Vicissitudes and excitements of the Russian onslaught in Western Europe.

1976   **Gilchrist, J.** *Lifeline*. R. Hale, 176 p.
Revisionism in the British appendage of the Russian-dominated United States of Europe.

1976   **Gordon, S.** *Three-Eyes*. Sidgwick & Jackson, 268 p.
Third in the *One-Eye* trilogy. [U.S. 1975]

1976   **Goulart, R.** *The Hellhound Project*. R. Hale, 156 p.
Secret agent works to uncover plan for the ultimate weapon in A.D. 2030. [U.S. 1975]

1976   **Goulart, R.** *Nutzenbolts and more troubles with machines*. R. Hale, 182 p.
Foreword, eleven stories devoted to "juxtaposing future man with future gadgets". [U.S. 1975]

1976   **Goulart, R.** *Odd Job 101 and other future crimes and intrigues*. R. Hale, 166 p.
Seven stories – androids, lizard men, and others. [U.S. 1975]

1976   **Green, J.** *Star probe*. Millington, 162 p.
Unmanned space vehicle approaches Earth; preparations begin to intercept.

1976   **Greenhough, T.** *The wandering worlds*. New English Library, 172 p.
Exploration ships of Far Search move onwards through space.

1976   **Harrison, H. (Dempsey, H.)** *The best of Harry Harrison.* Futura
[1977]   Publications, 315p.

Twenty-one stories, published between 1961 and 1973, each with an
introduction by Harrison.

1976   **Harrison, H., Dempsey, H.** *(ed.) Nova 4.* Sphere, 221p.

Afterword; thirteen stories. [U.S. 1974]

1976   **Harrison, H. (Dempsey, H.)** *Planet of the damned.* Futura
Publications, 176p.

First published U.K. 1967 as *Sense of obligation.* [U.S. 1962]

1976   **Harrison, H. (Dempsey, H.)** *Skyfall.* Faber & Faber, 270p.

A vast spaceship, carrying a lethal radioactive fuel, is in decaying orbit around
Earth.

1976   **Harrison, H. (Dempsey, H.) and Aldiss, B.** *(eds.) The year's best
SF 8.* Sphere, 251p.

Introduction by Harrison and Bruce McAllister; five poems, special feature on
"1984 Revisited", twelve stories; Afterword by Aldiss, "The galaxy begins at
home".

1976   **Harrison, H. (Dempsey, H.) and Aldiss, B.** *(eds.) The year's best
SF 9.* Weidenfeld & Nicolson, 206p.

Introduction by Harrison, nine stories and two poems; Afterword by Aldiss,
"Science fiction on the Titanic".

1976   **Hay, G.** *(ed.) The Edward De Bono science fiction collection.* Elmfield
Press, 217p.

Commentary on science fiction by De Bono; twelve stories.

1976   **Heine, W. C.** *The Last Canadian.* R. Hale, 224p.

After a devastating plague one of the last surviving Canadians plays a crucial part
in a confrontation between Russia, Britain and the United Staftes. First published
Canada 1974.

1976   **Herbert, F.** *Children of Dune.* V. Gollancz, 444p.

Third in the *Dune* cycle: the children of Paul Muad-Dib take up the challenge of
their destinies. [U.S. 1976]

1976   **Hippolito, J. and McNelly, W.** *(eds.) The Book of Mars.* Sphere, xviii,
322p.

Editorial Foreword – 'It is our hope that this collection will show the chronological
growth of the dream of Mars and Martians over the last hundred years.'
Introduction by Isaac Asimov; twenty stories, two reports, one article. First
published U.S. 1971 as *Mars, we love you.*

1976   **Hoch, E. D.** *The Fellowship of the Hand.* R. Hale, 198p.

Earl Jazine of the Computer Cops investigates revolutionary activities.
[U.S. 1973]

1976   **Hoch, E. D.** *The Frankenstein factory.* R. Hale, 190p.

Investigation of the International Cryogenics Institute – whole men out of frozen
bodies. [U.S. 1975]

1976   **Hodder-William, C.** *The Prayer Machine.* Weidenfeld & Nicolson, 205p.
Nightmare vision of genetic engineering and of a regimented Britain.

1976   **Holdstock, R.** *Eye among the blind.* Faber & Faber, 219p.
Biologist investigates a mysterious disease in the colonized worlds of the galaxy; and on Ree'hdworld he finds the life-forms are going through an evolutionary change.

1976   **Holland, C.** *Floating worlds.* V. Gollancz, 465p.
Paula Mendoza, anarchist and rebel, finds she has a conspicuous part to play in the relationships between Earth, Empire and Middle Planets. [U.S. 1976]

1976   **Jackson, B.** *Epicenter.* R. Hale, 234p.
Nuclear power plant leakage threatens all life in Toronto. [U.S. 1971]

1976   **Jackson, B.** *Supersonic.* R. Hale, 234p.
Faster-than-sound air transport in trouble over the Atlantic. [U.S. 1975]

1976   **Jakober, M.** *The mind gods.* Macmillan, 165p.
Planetary warfare between the colonists of Vilna and the Confederacy of Janus.

1976   **Kern, G.** *F.A.T.E.1: Galaxy of the lost.* Mews Books, 110p.
Captain Kennedy, a Free Acting Terran Envoy, seals the crack in the universe. [U.S. 1973]

1976   **Kern, G.** *F.A.T.E 2: Slave ship from Sergan.* Mews Books, 110p.
Captain Kennedy fights the reptile creatures of Sergan. [U.S. 1973]

1976   **Kern, G.** *F.A.T.E 3: Monster of Metalaze.* Mews Books, 112p.
More heroic planetary adventures. [U.S. 1973]

1976   **Kern, G.** *F.A.T.E 4: Enemy within the skull.* Mews Books, 112p.
Captain Kennedy risks all for Earth. [U.S. 1974]

1976   **Kern, G.** *F.A.T.E 5: Jewel of Jarhen.* Mews Books, 111p.
Rescue of Captain Kennedy from a menace in the distant past. [U.S. 1974].

1976   **Ker, G.** *F.A.T.E 6: Seetee Alert!* Mews Books, 111p.
Peril to the Solar System averted. [U.S. 1974]

1976   **King, C.** *The world of Jonah Klee.* R. Hale, 174p.
Jonah Klee can move anything at will.

1976   **King, J. R.** *Bruno Lipshitz and the Disciples of Dogma.* V. Gollancz, 159p.
Spaceship arrives with missionaries – all of the species *Fido supersapiens* – who preach the new religion of the dog-god, creator of the universe.

1976   **Kotzwinkle, W.** *Doctor Rat.* A. Ellis, 244p.
Animals of the world rise against mankind. Also published U.S. 1976 as *Rebellion of the animals.*

1976   **Lafferty, R. A.** *Space Chantey*. D. Dobson, 123p. Illus.
Epic adventures in the Homeric style – from the pleasures of planet Lotophage to the final return. [U.S. 1968]

1976   **Laumer, K.** *The big show*. R. Hale, 153p.
Six stories. [U.S. 1972]

1976   **Laumer, K.** *The long twilight*. R. Hale, 222p.
Two beings from another world struggle for the future of Earth. [U.S. 1969]

1976   **Laumer, K.** *Time trap*. R. Hale, 160p.
Adventures in time and space. [U.S. 1970]

1976   **Le Guin, U. K.** *(ed.) Nebula Award Stories 11*. V. Gollancz, 255p.
Winners and runners-up of the 1975 Award selected by the Science Fiction Writers of America: Introduction, seven stories, two essays. [U.S. 1975]

1976   **Le Guin, U. K.** *The wind's twelve quarters*. V. Gollancz, viii, 303p.
Foreword; seventeen stories each with a brief note. [U.S. 1975]

1976   **Leiber, F.** *The Night of the Wolf*. Sphere, 221p.
Four novellas about the destruction of civilization and the new society promoted by the League of Sanity. [U.S. 1966]

1976   **Lem, S.** *The Star Diaries*. Translated from the Polish by Michael Kandel with line drawings by Lem. Secker & Warburg, x, 275p.
Continues the exploits of Ijon Tichy, hero of *The Futurological Congress*, who is the subject for a series of satirical, comical, and philosophical observations on eternal man in the space age. Originally published 1971 as *Dzienniki gwiazdowe*.

1976   **Lester, A.** *The thrice-born*. New English Library, 158p.
Love affair between a Borean hermaphrodite and an Earth woman gives the universe a lesson in equality.

1976   **Léourier, C.** *The Mountains of the Sun*. Translated from the French. Millington Books, 176p.
A universal flood reduces humanity to a tribal existence, and a hero leads his people to better things. First published 1972 as *Les Montagnes du soleil*. This translation first published U.S. 1973.

1976   **Lord, G.** *God and all His angels*. H. Hamilton, 217p.
Political machinations in an increasingly anarchistic United Kingdom.

1976   **Lundwall, S. J.** *2018 A.D., or the King Kong Blues*. Star, 158p.
Satire on big business, industry, advertising and the media. First published Sweden 1974.

1976   **McCaffrey, A.** *Dragonsong*. Sidgwick & Jackson, 202p.
Continues the saga of Pern and the dragon-riders of that mythical land begun in *Dragonflight*. [U.S. 1976]

1976   **McIntyre, V.** *The exile waiting*. V. Gollancz, 255p.
Extraordinary adventures on a desolate Earth of the distant future, when two pseudo-sibs arrive from space.

1976   **Mackelworth, R. W.** *Starflight 3000*. New English Library, 155p.
Vast spaceship is designed in order to escape from the tyranny of Milcon. [U.S. 1972]

1976   **MacLean, A.** *The Golden Gate*. Collins, 248p.
The President, oil sheikhs and oil ministers hi-jacked on the Golden Gate Bridge.

1976   **Mahr, K.** *Perry Rhodan 10: The Ghosts of Gol*. Futura Publications, 128p.
Perry Rhodan explores a giant planet of the Vega System. [U.S. 1975]

1976   **Mahr, K.** *Perry Rhodan 11: The Planet of the Dying Sun*. Futura Publications, 128p.
More adventures with energy eaters on Gol. [U.S. 1975]

1976   **Mahr, K.** *Perry Rhodan 14: Venus in danger*. Futura Publications, 128p.
The Peace Lord descends on the primitive planet of Venus. [U.S. 1975]

1976   **Mahr, K.** *Perry Rhodan 17: The Venus trap*. Futura Publications, 128p.
The Peace Lord speeds to the rescue of the Queen of Arkon. [U.S. 1975]

1976   **Mahr, K.** *Perry Rhodan 18: The menace of the Mutant Master*. Futura Publications, 128p.
The Peace Lord deals with yet another danger to the galaxy. [U.S. 1976]

1976   **Malzberg, B. N.** *Herovit's world*. Arrow, 209p.
Struggle for the mind of a science fiction writer. [U.S. 1973]

1976   **Malzberg, B. N.** *In the enclosure*. R. Hale, 190p.
A strange imprisonment which is a means of therapy and information. [U.S. 1973]

1976   **Malzberg, B. N.** *The men inside*. Arrow, 175p.
Plot to murder the head of the immensely powerful Hulm Institute. [U.S. 1973]

1976   **Marshall, B.** *Peter the Second*. Constable, 183p.
Last of the trilogy: in the days of the *Pax Sovietica Romana* the Papacy tries to deal with the dissident Church of Utrecht.

1976   **Mason, D. R.** *The Omega Worm*. R. Hale, 192p.
Commander Savage of European Space Security deals with a psychopathic scientist. [U.S. 1975]

1976   **Moorcock, M.** *The adventures of Una Persson and Catherine Cornelius in the twentieth century*. Quartet, 216p.
Una Persson continues the time travels begun in *The Land Leviathan* – this time in a twentieth century vastly different from recorded history.

1976   **Moorcock, M.** *The end of all songs*. Hart-Davis, MacGibbon, 336p.
Concludes *The Dancers at the End of Time* trilogy. Jherek Carnelian and company continue their time-travel adventures from a mishap in the Palaeozic to wedding bells at the end of time.

1976   **Moorcock, M.** *Legends from the End of Time.* With decorations by Jill Riches. W. H. Allen, 182p.
More experiences of the Iron Orchid, the Duke of Queens, Lord Jagged, Bishop Castle and others.

1976   **Moorcock, M.** *The lives and times of Jerry Cornelius.* Illustrated by Mal Dean, Richard Glyn Jones and Harry Douthwaite. Allison & Busby, 176p.
Fourth in the Jerry Cornelius series: he continues to move between present and future, from China to the Vatican.

1976   **Moorcock, M.** *Moorcock's Book of Martyrs.* Quartet Books, 176p.
Five stories.

1976   **Moorcock, M.** *The sailor on the seas of fate.* Quartet, 170p.
First section retells part of *The Quest for Tanelorn*; second part is a new Elric adventure; third part retells *The Jade Man's Eyes*.

1976   **Moorcock, M. and Butterworth, M.** *The Time of the Hawklords.* Aidan Ellis, 255p.
Electronic music frees the world from pain and the battle for Earth begins.

1976   **Morgan, D.** *The concrete horizon.* Millington Books, 227p.
Sociopathic Readjustment, Euthanasia Option, Carnival Weeks – these are the principal means of social control in the urban concentration of the future.

1976   **Morgan, D.** *Genetic Two.* R. Hale, 175p.
A struggle for survival on Zetzer IV.

1976   **Nation, T.** *Survivors.* Weidenfeld & Nicolson, 205p.
Epidemic wipes out all but a handful of survivors; they make south for the Mediterranean.

1976   **Neeper, C.** *A place beyond man.* Millington, 270p.
A human being makes direct contact with non-human beings. [U.S. 1975]

1976   **Norton, A.** *The Sioux spaceman.* R. Hale, 158p.
Red Indian seeks to free the slave people of Klor. [U.S. 1960]

1976   **Nowlan, P. F.** *Armageddon 2419 A.D.* Panther, 160p.
Sleeper awakes in 2419 A.D. to discover that the Mongolians rule the world. He leads the American uprising against the conquerors. This book, first published U.S. 1928, provided the initial ideas for the famous Buck Rogers comic strips. This edition U.S. 1962.

1976   **October, J.** *The Anarchy Pedlars.* R. Hale, 189p.
The Ismaili Assassin Sect plans to rule the world.

1976   **Pangborn, E.** *The Company of Glory.* Star, 174p.
A story-teller, who remembers the days before the Twenty-Minute War, proves a danger to the government. [U.S. 1975]

1976   **Pereira, W. D.** *Another Eden*. R. Hale, 189p.
Aliens attack Earth emigrants on planet Domus.

1976   **Pincher, C.** *The eye of the tornado*. M. Joseph, 208p.
An IRA and Russian plan to blackmail Britain with stolen nuclear bombs.

1976   **Pitts, D.** *Target Manhattan*. Hodder & Stoughton, 294p.
Red Indian terrorists try to hold New York to ransom. First published U.S. 1975
as *This city is ours*.

1976   **Pohl, F.** *The best of Frederick Pohl*. Futura Publications, xvi, 363p.
Introduction by Del Rey. Seventeen stories selected from the years between
1954 and 1967. Afterword by Frederick Pohl.

1976   **Pohl, F.** *In the problem pit*. Corgi, 194p.
Introduction ('Science Fiction Games') and Afterword on "SF: The Game-playing
Literature"; ten stories and two essays. [U.S. 1976]

1976   **Pohl, F.** *Man plus*. V. Gollancz, 215p.
A race of cyborgs is created for the colonization of Mars. [U.S. 1976]

1976   **Pohl, F. and Williamson, J.** *Farthest star*. Pan, 189p.
Crew of Ground Station One investigate the mysterious world of Cuckoo. [U.S.
1975]

1976   **Pratchett, T.** *Dark side of the Sun*. C. Smythe, Gerrards Cross, 158p.
Fantasies of variant life-forms and of the races classed as Human under the
Humanity Act.

1976   **Rankine, J. (Mason, D. R.)** *Android Planet*. A. Barker, 140p.
Eighth in *Space 1999* series: adventure on planet Pelorus.

1976   **Rankine, J. (Mason, D. R.)** *The Bromius Phenomenon*. D. Dobson,
207p.
Dag Fletcher investigates the loss of a starship.

1976   **Ray, R.** *Metamorphosis*. R. Hale, 190p.
Spaceman accepted as a god on a humanoid planet.

1976   **Reed, K.** *The killer mice*. V. Gollancz, 191p.
Fifteen stories.

1976   **Reeves, L. P.** *The last days of the peacemaker*. R. Hale, 192p.
A dream of London destroyed by a nuclear bomb.

1976   **Reeves, L. P.** *Time search*. R. Hale, 175p.
Time traveller returns to the period of the Second World War to find out what
happened to his granny.

1976   **Reynolds, M.** *Looking backward from the Year 2000*. Elmfield Press,
237p.
The author writes that he "has been doing social science fiction, extrapolating in

the field of socio-economics"; and he here gives his view of future society. [U.S. 1973]

1976   **Reynolds, M.** *Tomorrow might be different*. Sphere, 140p.
An ingenious solution to the Russian commercial onslaught on the world. [U.S. 1975]

1976   **Roberts, K.** *The Grain Kings*. Hutchinson, 208p.
Six stories.

1976   **Rotsler, W.** *Patron of the Arts*. Elmfield Press, 210p.
The art form of the future is the sensatron cube which produces three-dimensional images, capable of movement and emotion. [U.S. 1974]

1976   **Rowland, D. S.** *Nightmare planet*. R. Hale, 190p.
Space explorer navigates uncharted planetary system.

1976   **Rowland, D. S.** *Space Venturer*. R. Hale, 191p.
Struggles with the fearful robots of planet Crana.

1976   **Ryder, J.** *Vicious spiral*. R. Hale, 189p.
Man returns from the twelfth millenium to kill Adolf Hitler.

1976   **Ryman, R.** *The Quadrant War*. R. Hale, 173p.
Journey through space in the time of the war between the Mercenary Empires and the Earth Colonial Empire.

1976   **Savarin, J. J.** *Beyond the Outer Mirr*. Corgi, 253p.
Second in the *Lemmus* trilogy: the end comes for mankind.

1976   **Scheer, K. H.** *Perry Rhodan 13: The Immortal unknown*. Futura, 128p.
The Peace Lord to the rescue of Ferrol, as Vega goes nova. [U.S. 1975]

1976   **Schmitz, J. H.** *The Lion Game*. Sidgwick & Jackson, 157p.
Telzey Amberdon plays mental chess with formidable planetary opponents. [U.S. 1973]

1976   **Schmitz, J. H.** *The Telzey Toy*. Sidgwick & Jackson, 175p.
Four stories about Telzey Amberdon, mentalist extraordinary. [U.S. 1973]

1976   **Schutz, J. W.** *The Moon Microbe*. J. W. Schutz, 175p.
The germ from space may put an end to war.

1976   *Science Fiction Special 16*. Sidgwick & Jackson, 159 + 190 + 218p.
Contains: Brunner, J., *Bedlam Planet;* Rankine, J., *The Fingalnan Conspiracy;* Van Vogt, A. E., *The three eyes of evil.*

1976   *Science Fiction Special 17*. Sidgwick & Jackson, 251 + 245 + 254p.
Contains: Romano, D., *Flight from Time One;* Silverberg, R., *Dying Inside;* Van Vogt, A. E., *The darkness on Diamondia.*

1976   **Science Fiction Special 18.** Sidgwick & Jackson, 192 + 188 + 190p.
Contains: Laumer, K., *The house in November;* Ball, B. N., *Planet probability;* Schmitz, J. H., *The eternal frontiers.*

1976   *Science Fiction Special 19.* Sidgwick & Jackson, 190 + 176+ 188p.
Contains: Wells, R., *The Parasaurians;* Laumer, K. *The star treasure;* Rankine, J. *Operation Umanaq.*

1976   **Scortia, T. N. and Robinson, F. M.** *The Prometheus Crisis.* Hodder & Stoughton, xiv, 321p.
Catastrophe at a nuclear reactor. [U.S. 1975]

1976   **Shaw, B.** *Cosmic Kaleidoscope.* V. Gollancz, 188p.
Nine stories.

1976   **Shaw, B.** *Ground Zero Man.* Corgi, 160p.
Man discovers he has the power to detonate all the atomic bombs in the world. [U.S. 1971]

1976   **Shaw, B.** *A wreath of stars.* V. Gollancz, 189p.
An anti-neutrino planet comes close to Earth.

1976   **Sheckley, R.** *The status civilization.* V. Gollancz, 158p.
On a distant planet, a penal colony run by criminals, the hero conquers all before him. First published U.S. 1960 as *Omega.*

1976   **Shepherd, M.** *(pseud.) The road to Gandolfo.* Hart-Davis, MacGibbon, 319p.
Plot to kidnap the Pope has an unanticipated outcome. [U.S. 1975]

1976   **Sherwood, M.** *Maxwell's demon.* New English Library, 127p.
New life form takes over human personalities.

1976   **Shols, W. W.** *Perry Rhodan 16: Secret Barrier X.* Futura, 128p.
The Peace Lord to the rescue of the beauteous Thora on Venus. [U.S. 1975]

1976   **Silverberg, R.** *(ed.) Deep space.* Abelard-Schumann, 223p.
Introduction – "Not only technological progress but the growth of scientific understanding deprives science-fictionists of their cherished themes" –eight stories. [U.S. 1973]

1976   **Silverberg, R.** *The Feast of St. Dionysus.* V. Gollancz, 255p.
Five stories – space travel, the end of differences, time travel etc. [U.S. 1975]

1976   **Silverberg, R.** *Mutants.* Abelard-Schumann, 224p.
Introduction, eleven stories about mutants and genetic changes. [U.S. 1974]

1976   **Silverberg, R.** *(ed.) New Dimensions 6.* V. Gollancz, 247p.
Twelve original stories, each with a brief note. [U.S. 1975]

1976   **Silverberg, R.** *The stochastic man.* V. Gollancz, 229p.
The stochastic man guesses at the future; the clairvoyant sees the future. [U.S. 1975]

1976   **Silverberg, R.** *(ed.) Threads of time.* Millington, 219p.
Introduction, three original novellas by Gregory Benford, Clifford D. Simak, Norman Spinrad.

1976   **Silverberg, R.** *Tower of glass.* Pamther, 206p.
The androids struggle for their rights, as a vast communications tower is built to answer pulses from space. [U.S. 1970]

1976   **Smith, E. E. with Goldin, S.** *The Imperial Stars.* Panther, 155p.
First in *The Family d'Alembert* Series: the best agents in Empire of Earth fight the planetary menace. [U.S. 1976]

1976   **Smith, G. O.** *Venus Equilateral. Volume One.* Futura Publications, 240p.
Introduction by John, W. Campbell: six linked stories devoted to the experiences of Dr. Channing and his engineers in maintaining the interplanerary communicattion space station, Venus Equilateral. [U.S. 1947]

1976   **Smith, G. O.** *Venus Equilateral. Volume Two.* Futura Publications, 237p.
Foreword by Arthur C. Clarke: seven stories of the Channing saga. [U.S. 1947]

1976   **Smith, G. N.** *The night of the crabs.* New English Library, 144p.
Giant crabs appear on the Welsh coast.

1976   **Spinrad, N.** *No direction home.* Pillington, 238p.
Eleven stories. [U.S. 1975]

1976   **Stableford, B.** *The face of heaven.* Quartet Books, 151p.
First in *The Realms of Tartarus* series: mankind, now living on a gigantic platform that encircles Earth, discovers the menace of mutated life-forms. [U.S. 1971]

1976   **Starr, R.** *Return from Omina.* R. Hale, 191p.
Strange encounters and mysteries in deep space.

1976   **Stockbridge, G.** *Death reign of the Vampire King.* Mews Books, 146p.
Superman saves mankind from vampire bats: first in *The Spider* Series
[U.S. 1935]

1976   **Stockbridge, G.** *Hordes of the Red Butcher.* Mews Books, 144p.
And now Superman defeats the subhuman killers. Second in *The Spider* series.
[U.S. 1935]

1976   **Stockbridge, G.** *The city destroyer.* Mews Books, 142p.
Superman to the rescue of the world. Third in *The Spider* series. [U.S. 1942]

1976   **Stockbridge, G.** *Death and the Spider.* Mews Books, 126p.
Superman defeats the mind-controllers. Fourth in *The Spider* series. [U.S. 1942]

1976   **Storr, C.** *Unusual fathers.* Quartet, 153p.
Comic tale of the discovery of a way to make men pregnant.

1976   **Summers, D.** *A madness from Mars.* R. Hale, 173p.
Truffles from Mars have a curious effect on British ministers.

1976   **Summers, D.** *Stalker of the worlds.* R. Hale, 184p.
Search for missing hunters on the violent world of Terra Two.

1976   *Supernova 1: SF Introduction.* Faber & Faber, xii, 225p.
Biographical notes on the six authors; twelve stories.

1976   **Tevis, W. S.** *The man who fell to Earth.* Pan, 170p.
Alien being comes to Earth and tries every means of returning to his own planet.
[U.S. 1963]

1976   **Trout, K. (Farmer, P. J.)** *Venus on the half-shell.* Star, 207p.
A parody of Kurt Vonnegut's writings is a means of looking into the obsessions,
absurdities and inadequacies of human existence. [U.S. 1974]

1976   **Tracy, H.** *Death in reserve.* V. Gollancz, 190p.
A million in gold – or else someone will release deadly bacteria throughout
Britain.

1976   **Trew, A.** *Ultimatum* Collins, 223p.
Palestinian terrorists threaten to destroy London with a nuclear device.

1976   **Tubb, E. C.** *Alien seed.* A. Barker, 138p.
Seventh in *Space 1999* adventures – encounter with a new life form. Also
published U.S. 1976.

1976   **Tubb, E. C.** *A scatter of stardust.* D. Dobson, 119p.
Eight stories: space travel, a suicidal scientist, a mad spaceman and other
themes. [U.S. 1972]

1976   **Vance, J.** *The Gray Prince.* Coronet Books, 173p.
Conflict – social and colonial – on planet Koryphon. [U.S. 1974]

1976   **Vance, J.** *The Moon Moth.* D. Dobson, 125p.
Five stories. Originally published U.S. 1965 as *The world between.*

1976   **Vance, J.** *To live forever.* Sphere, 189p.
An Immortal seeks to escape the consequences of a crime of murder.
[U.S. 1956]

1976   **Van Vogt, A. E.** *Future glitter.* Sidgwick & Jackson, 216p.
Scientists plot to subvert the world dictatorship. [U.S. 1973]

1976   **Van Vogt, A. E.** *The undercover aliens.* Panther, 173p.
First published U.S. 1950 and U.K. 1953 as *The house that stood still.*

1976   **Van Vogt, A. E.** *The universe maker and the proxy intelligence.*
Title story (U.S. 1953) relates a series of time adventures. Second story (U.S.
1968) deals with space travel.

1976   **Vonnegut, K.** *Slapstick, or lonesome no more.* J. Cape, 243p.
Vonnegut writes "grotesque situational poetry" about twins brought up on an asteroid – Wilbur becomes President and Eliza dies on Mars. Also published U.S. 1976.

1976   **W. W. (Bloom, W.)** *The prophets of evil.* W. H. Allen, 174p.
Qhe, ruler of light, struggles with the wicked Prophets of the Prophet.

1976   **Wallace, J.** *A man for tomorrow.* R. Hale, 176p.
Earthman is sent on a special mission to meet the alien Lexians.

1976   **Wallace, J.** *The Plague of the Golden Rat.* R. Hale, 183p.
Spaceship brings back a deadly virus to Earth.

1976   **Warren, C.** *Alien heaven.* R. Hale, 175p.
Two refugees find happiness on a strange planet far away from overpopulated Earth.

1976   **Wells, A.** *(ed.) The best of Frank Herbert, 1952–64; 1965–70.* Sphere, 156, 170p.
Two-volume edition of the 1975 publication.

1976   **Wells, R.** *Candle in the Sun.* Sidgwick & Jackson, 158p.
The last man in the world meets the mysterious Arcadians. [U.S. 1971]

1976   **Wessex, M.** *The chain reaction.* R. Hale, 189p.
Freedox drug threatens human fertility.

1976   **Weston, P.** *(ed.) Andromeda 1.* Futura Publications, 206p.
Introduction; ten original stories.

1976   **White, T.** *(ed.) The best from Amazing.* R. Hale, 192p.
Eight stories selected from the *Amazing* magazine. [U.S. 1973]

1976   **White, T.** *(ed.) The best from Fantastic.* R. Hale, 192p.
Foreword, ten stories selected from *Fantastic* magazine. [U.S. 1973]

1976   **Williamson, J.** *The Moon children.* Elmfield Press, 190p.
The Venusians send a task force to Earth. [U.S. 1972]

1976   **Wilson, R. H.** *Ring of rings.* R. Hale, 189p.
A fatal attempt to change the course of history.

1976   **Wilson, S.** *The lost traveller.* Macmillan, 245p.
Post-catastrophe adventure yarn.

1976   **Wolf, G. K.** *Killerbowl.* Sphere, 155p.
Murderous football games in the twenty-first century. [U.S. 1975]

1976   **Wollheim, D. A.** *(ed.) The world's best SF short stories.* Elmfield Press, 269p.
Introduction, ten stories. First published U.S. 1975 as *The 1975 annual world's best SF.*

PART 2   SHORT-TITLE INDEX

Note: This index lists in alphabetical order the short titles of all entries made in *Part 1*. The surname or pseudonym of the author appears after each title; and the articles *A, An, The* – are omitted from the beginning of all entries.

Almost human (Nolan), 1965
Alpha One (Silverberg), 1971
Already walks tomorrow (Street), 1938
Alternating currents (Pohl), 1966
Amateurs in alchemy (Deegan), 1952
Amazing revolution (Anon), 1909
Amazon strikes again (Fearn), 1954
Amazon's diamond quest (Fearn), 1953
America fallen! (Walker), 1915
American emperor (Tracy), 1897
Amid the strife (Hookham), 1909
Amphibians (Wright), 1925
Analog anthology (Campbell, 1965
Analog 1 (Campbell), 1967
Analog 2 (Campbell), 1967
Analog 3 (Campbell), 1966
Analog 4 (Campbell), 1967
Analog 5 (Campbell), 1968
Analog 6 (Campbell), 1969
Analog 7 (Campbell), 1974
Analog 8 (Campbell), 1976
Analog, Prologue to (Campbell), 1967
Analogue men (Knight), 1967
Anarchy pedlars (October), 1976
And a new Earth (Jacomb), 1926
And all the stars a stage (Blish), 1972
Andover and the android (Wilhelm), 1966
Android (Ziegfried), 1963
Android planet (Rankine), 1976
Andromeda breakthrough (Hoyle & Elliot), 1964
Andromeda 1 (Weston), 1976
Andromeda Strain (Crichton), 1969
And so ends the world (Pape), 1961
And the stars remain (Berry), 1952
And wars shall cease (Marsh), 1939
Angel and the idiot (Anon), 1890
Angel of Pity (Stuart), 1935
Angel of the revolution (Griffith), 1893
Angel in the mist (Speaight), 1936
Angels and spaceships (Brown, F.), 1955
Angelo's moon (Brown, A.), 1955
Angry espers (Biggle), 1968
Angry planet (Cross), 1945
Anna Perenna (Sims), 1930
Annals of the twenty-ninth century (Blair), 1874
Annihilation (Statten), 1950
Annihilist (Robeson), 1968
Anno Domini 1963 (Finigan), 1943
Anno Domini 3867 (Wykehamicus), 1867
Anno Domini 2000 (Vogel), 1889
Anno Domini 2071 (Dioscorides), 1871
Anome (Vance), 1975
Another Eden (Pereira), 1976
Another end (King), 1972
Another kind (West), 1951

Another space, another time (Campbell), 1953
Another tree in Eden (Duncan), 1956
Anthem (Rand), 1938
Antic Earth (Charbonneau), 1967
Anticipation (Anon), 1781
Anticipation . . . of the King's speech (Anon), 1778
Antigrav (Strick), 1975
Anti-Zota (Burgess & Friggens), 1973
Antro (Deegan), 1953
Anvil of time (Silverberg), 1969
Anymoon (Bleackley), 1919
Anything box (Henderson), 1966
Anything you can do (Langart), 1963
Anywhen (Blish), 1971
Ape and essence (Huxley), 1949
Ape of London (Crisp), 1959
Apostle of the cylinder (Rousseau), 1918
Appointment in space (Blow), 1963
Approaching oblivion (Ellison), 1976
Approaching storm (Tillyard), 1932
Artic submarine (Mars), 1955
Arena: Sports SF (Ferman & Malzberg), 1976
Armageddon, 190– (Seestern), 1907
Armageddon 2419 A.D. (Nowlan), 1976
Armed camps (Reed), 1969
Armistice or total victory? (Kent), 1943
Armoured doves (Newman), 1931
Arrival of Master Jinks (Chappell), 1949
Arrogant history of White Ben (Dane), 1939
Arthur C. Clarke Omnibus (Clarke), 1965
Artificial man (Davies), 1965
As easy as A.B.C. (Kipling), 1917
Asimov's mysteries (Asimov), 1968
Asleep in Armageddon (Sissons), 1962
Asses in clover (O'Duffy), 1933
Assignment Black Viking (Aarons), 1973
Assignment in eternity (Heinlein), 1955
Assignment in nowhereee (Laumer), 1972.
Assignment Luther (Wright), 1963
Assignment Tahiti (Gardner), 1965
Assimilator (Bannon), 1974
Aster disaster (Young, A. M.), 1959
Astounding-Analog Reader 1 & 2 Harrison & Aldiss), 1973
Astralea's return (Anon), 1797
Astral quest (Rankine), 1975
Astrologer (Cameron), 1973
Asutra (Vance), 1975
Atom at Spithead (Divine), 1953
Atom wars on Mars (Tubb), 1952
Atomic nemesis (Zeigfreid), 1962
Atomic submarine (Mars), 1957
Atoms (Wignall & Knox), 1923
Atoms and evil (Bloch), 1976

Cure for death (Valentine), 1960
Currents of space (Asimov), 1955
Custodians (Cowper), 1976
Cuttings from 'The Times' of 1900 (N., J.), 1873
Cyberiad (Lem), 1975
Cybernetic controller (Clarke & Bulmer), 1952
Cybernia (Cameron), 1973
Cyborg (Caidin), 1973
Cycle of fire (Clement), 1964
Czar of fear (Robeson), 1968

Dakota Project (Beeching), 1968
Damnation alley (Zelazny), 1971
Danger! (Doyle), 1918
Danger from Vega (Rackman), 1970
Dangerous visions 1 (Ellison), 1971
Dangerous visions 2 (Ellison), 1974
Dangerous waters (Williams), 1952
Dare (Farmer), 1974
Dark Andromeda (Merak), 1954
Dark boundaries (Lorraine), 1953
Dark Constellation (Random), 1975
Dark December (Coppel), 1966
Dark dominion (Duncan), 1955
Dark frontier (Ambler), 1936
Dark horse (Knebel), 1973
Dark inferno (White), 1972
Dark light years (Aldiss), 1964
Dark side (Knight), 1966
Dark side of Earth (Bester), 1969
Dark side of the Moon (Corlett), 1976
Dark side of the Sun (Pratchett), 1976
Dark stars (Silvberberg), 1971
Dark tides (Russell), 1962
Dark world (Kuttner), 1966
Dark universe (Galouye), 1962
Darkest of nights (Maine), 1962
Darkness and dawn (anon), 1884
Darkness and light (Stapledon), 1942
Darkness on Diamondia (Van Vogt), 1974
Date for your death (Allen), 1971
Daughters of Earth (Merril), 1971
David go back (Connell), 1935
Davy (Pangborn), 1966
Dawn (Wright), 1930
Dawn chorus (Garden), 1975
Dawn of all (Benson), 1911
Dawn of civilization (Spence), 1897
Dawn of the twentieth century (Anon), 1882
Dawn of the twentieth century (Anon), 1888
Dawn's delay (Kingsmill), 1924
Day after Judgement (Blish), 1972
Day after tomorrow (Minnett), 1911

Day after tomorrow (Heinlein), 1962
Day in the life (Dozois), 1972
Day it rained forever (Bradbury), 1959
Day million (Pohl) 1971
Day Natal took off (Delius), 1963
Day of forever (Ballard), 1967
Day of judgement (Mackenzie), 1956
Day of misjudgement (MacLaren), 1957
Day of prosperity (Devinne), 1902
Day of the Coastwatch (McCutchan), 1968
Day of the dolphin (Merle), 1969
Day of the dust (Verron), 1964
Day of the republic (Taylor), 1968
Day of the Triffids (Wyndham), 1951
Day of the women (Kettle), 1969
Day of uniting (Wallace), 1926
Day of wrath (O'Neill), 1936
Day of wrath (Stableford), 1974
Day that changed the world (Anon), 1912
Day the Queen flew to Scotland (Wise), 1969
Day the world ended (Rohmer), 1930
Day they burned Miss Termag (Balsdon), 1961
Day they put Humpty together again (Jones, M.), 1968
Deadline to Pluto (Statten), 1951
Deadly image (Cooper), 1959
Deadly litter (White), 1968
Death and the Spider (Stockbridge), 1976
Deathbox (Tolstoi), 1936
Death guard (Chadwick), 1939
Death in reserve (Tracy), 1976
Death in silver (Robeson), 1968
Death is a dream (Tubb), 1967
Death lottery (Hyams), 1971
Death may surprise us (Willis), 1974
Death of a cosmonaut (Hay & Keshishian), 1970
Death of a world (Farjeon), 1948
Death of grass (Christopher), 1956
Death on a warm wind (Warner), 1968
Death rattle (Gobsch), 1932
Death reign of the Vampire King (Stockbridge), 1976
Death star (Bridges), 1940
Deathstar voyage (Wallace), 1972
Death the red flower (Wynd), 1965
Death trap (Cole), 1907
Death world (Harrison), 1963
Deathworld 1 (Harrison), 1973
Deathworld 2 (Harrison), 1973
Deathworld 3 (Harrison), 1969
Deathworms of Kratos (Avery), 1975
De Bracy's drug (Gridban), 1953
Decade: the 1940s (Aldiss & Harrison), 1975

Giant stumbles (Lymington), 1960
Gift from Earth (Niven), 1969
Giles Goat-Boy (Barth), 1967
Ginger star (Brackett), 1976
Girl in the Moon (Harbou), 1930
Girl in trouble (Parker), 1975
Girls from Planet 5 (Wilson), 1968
Girl with a symphony on her fingers (Coney), 1975
Give Daddy the knife, darling (Lymington), 1969
Gladiator-at-law (Pohl & Kornbluth)
Glass bead game (Hesse), 1970
Glass cage (Hassler), 1972
Glass centipede (Painter & Laing), 1936
Glide path (Clarke), 1967
Gloriana (Dixie), 1890
Glory (Stuart), 1933
Glory game (Laumer), 1974
Glory road (Heinlein), 1965
Goblin reservation (Simak), 1969
God and all his angels (Lord), 1976
Godhead (Montano), 1971
God killers (Ross), 1970
God machine (Watkins), 1974
God makers (Herbert), 1972
God of this world (Middleton), 1905
Godwhale (Bass), 1975
Gods divide (Howell Smith), 1936
Gods for tomorrow (Santesson), 1967
Gods of Foxcroft (Levy), 1971
Gods themselves (Asimov), 1972
G.O.G. 666 (Taine), 1955
Gold at the starbow's end (Pohl), 1973
Gold the man (Green), 1971
Golden Age (Fitzgibbon), 1975
Golden Amazon (Fearn), 1944
Golden Amazon returns (Fearn), 1948
Golden Amazon's triumph (Fearn), 1953
Golden apples of the sun (Bradbury), 1953
Golden bottle (Donnelly), 1892
Golden gate (MacLean), 1976
Golden star (Noel), 1935
Golf in the year 2000 (J.A.C.K.), 1892
Gollancz/Sunday Times best SF stories (Aldiss), 1975
Gone to ground (White), 1935
Gortschakoff and Bismarck (Anon), 1878
Goslings (Beresford), 1913
Governor Hardy (Blair), 1931
Grain Kings (Roberts), 1976
Grand Canyon (Sackville- West), 1942
Grand Voyage (Smith), 1973
Gravitor (Darrington), 1971
Gray matters (Hjorstberg), 1973
Gray Prince (Vance), 1976
Great Anglo-American war (Anson), 1896
Great beyond A.D. 2500 (Melling), 1955

Great bread riots (S.L.S.), 1885
Great Britain in 1841 (Anon), 1831
Great calamity (Kearney), 1948
Great computer (Johannesson), 1968
Great explosion (Russell), 1962
Great gesture (Blair), 1931
Great image (Pan), 1921
Great Irish rebellion (Anon), 1886
Great Irish "Wake" (Anon), 1888
Great leap backward (Green), 1968
Great miracle (Vanewords), 1914
Great Naval War of 1887 (Clowes), 1887
Great Ones (Deegan), 1953
Great Pacific War (Bywater), 1925
Great peril (Hawker), 1937
Great pirate syndicate (Griffith), 1899
Great raid (Williams), 1909
Great revolution of 1905 (Hayes), 1893
Great Russian invasion of India (Dekhnewallah), 1879
Great science fiction by scientists (Conklin), 1962
Great secret (Nisbet), 1895
Great short novels of science fiction (Silverberg), 1971
Great stone of Sardis (Stockton), 1898
Great stories of science fiction (Leinster), 1953
Great War in England (Le Queux), 1894
Great War of 189 – (Colomb), 1893
Great war syndicate (Stockton), 1889
Great was the fall (Naval Officer), 1912
Great weather syndicate (Griffith), 1906
Green Brain (Herbert), 1973
Green drift (Lymington), 1965
Green Eagle (Robeson), 1968
Green gone (Dickinson), 1973
Green hills of Earth (Heinlein), 1954
Green millennium (Leiber), 1960
Green mouse (Chambers), 1912
Green odyssey (Farmer), 1976
Green plantations (Elton), 1955
Green ray (Lindsay), 1937
Green suns (Ward), 1961
Greener than you think (Moore), 1949
Greybeard (Aldiss), 1964
Grey Lensman (Smith), 1971
Grey ones (Lymington), 1960
Grim tomorrow (Richmond), 1953
Ground star conspiracy (Davies), 1972
Ground Zero man (Shaw), 1976
Grue of ice (Jenkins), 1962
Guardians of time (Anderson), 1961
Gun for a Dinosaur (De Camp), 1974
Gunner Cade (Judd), 1964

Hadrian the Seventh (Rolfe), 1904
Halcyon Drift (Stableford), 1974

Last man on Kluth (Conrad), 1975
Last Martian (Statten), 1952
Last mass of Paul VI (Casini), 1971
Last men in London (Stapledon), 1932
Last millionaire (Campbell), 1923
Last miracle (Shiel), 1906
Last of my race (Tayler), 1924
Last peer (Anon), 1851
Last persecution (Sedgwick), 1909
Last post for a partisan (Egleton), 1971
Last refuge (Petty), 1966
Last revolution (Dunsany), 1951
Last shot (Palmer), 1914
Last space ship (Leinster), 1952
Last starship from Earth (Boyd), 1969
Last white man (Gandon), 1948
Last woman (Beresford), 1922
Late final (Gibbs), 1951
Lathe of heaven (Le Guin), 1972
Laughter in space (Statten), 1952
Leaders of the blind (Bannerman), 1921
Leaf from the future history of England
    (Anon), 1831
Leap in the dark (Gordon), 1970
Leatherjacket (Wise), 1970
Leave them their pride (Cranford),
    1962
Left hand of darkness (Le Guin), 1969
Leftovers (Toynbee), 1966
Legends from the End of Time
    (Moorcock), 1976
Legion of time (Williamson), 1961
Lesbia Newman (Dalton), 1889
Lest Earth be conquered (Long), 1973
Lest ye die (Hamilton), 1928
Let the fire fall (Wilhelm), 1969
Let the spacemen beware! (Anderson),
    1969
Level 7 (Roshwald), 1959
Life begins tomorrow (Parkman), 1948
Life for the stars (Blish), 1964
Lifeline (Gilchrist), 1976
Life the jade (Potter), 1912
Light a last candle (King), 1970
Light benders (Chance), 1968
Light of Mars (Chapkin), 1959
Light that never was (Biggle), 1975
Like an evening gone (Gale), 1972
Like nothing on Earth (Russell), 1975
Limbo '90 (Wolfe), 1953
Line of succession (Garfield), 1974
Liners of time (Fearn), 1947
Lion Game (Schmitz), 1976
Lion of Commarre (Clarke), 1970
Lion's hold (Lepper), 1929
Lirri (Leland), 1973
Listeners (Leinster), 1969
Little dog's day (Story), 1971
Lives and times of Jerry Cornelius
    (Moorcock), 1976

Loafers of Refuge (Green), 1965
Locust horde (Shaw), 1925
Lodestar (Branley), 1952
Logan's run (Nolan & Johnson), 1968
London's burning (Wootton), 1936
London's peril (Allen), 1900
London's transformation (Tems Dyvirta),
    1906
London under the Bolsheviks (Cournos),
    1920
Lonely astronomer (Gridban), 1954
Long eureka (Sellings), 1968
Long loud silence (Tucker), 1953
Long twilight (Laumer), 1976
Long night among the stars (Booth),
    1962
Long result (Brunner), 1965
Long tomorrow (Brackett), 1962
Long way back (Bennett), 1954
Long way home (Anderson), 1975
Looking ahead (Anon), 1891
Looking ahead (Mendes), 1899
Looking backward (Bellamy), 1889
Looking backward (Reynolds), 1976
Looking beyond (Geissler), 1895
Looking forward (Thiusen), 1890
Looking forward (Lesser), 1955
Lord of labour (Griffith), 1911
Lord of life (Bell), 1933
Lord of light (Zelazny), 1968
Lord of the flies (Golding), 1954
Lord of the Red Sun (Silent), 1975
Lord of the sea (Shiel), 1901
Lord of the spiders (Moorcock), 1971
Lord of the world (Benson), 1907
Lord Roastem's Campaign (Pollock) 1911
Lords of the starship (Geston), 1971
Lord's pink ocean (Walker), 1972
Loss of Eden (Brown & Serpell), 1940
Lost diaries of Albert Smith (Muller),
    1965
Lost fleet of Astranides (Barrett), 1974
Lost legacy (Heinlein), 1960
Lost perception (Galouye), 1966
Lost provinces (Tracy), 1898
Lost traveller (Wilson), 1976
Lost world (Shaw), 1953
Lost worlds of 2001 (Clarke), 1972
Love among the ruins (Waugh), 1953
Love in the ruins (Percy), 1971
Love warrior (Lacey), 1975
Low-flying aircraft (Ballard), 1976
Lucifer cell (Fennerton), 1968
Lunar attack (Rankine), 1975
Lunar flight (Fear), 1958
Lunatic republic (Mackenzie), 1959

Machine in Shaft Ten (Harrison), 1975

New writings in SF 11 (Carnell), 1967
New writings in SF 12 (Carnell), 1968
New writings in SF 13 (Carnell), 1968
New writings in SF 14 (Carnell), 1969
New writings in SF 15 (Carnell), 1969
New writings in SF 16 (Carnell), 1969
New writings in SF 17 (Carnell), 1970
New writings in SF 18 (Carnell), 1971
New writings in SF 19 (Carnell), 1971
New writings in SF 20 (Carnell), 1972
New writings in SF 21 (Carnell), 1972
New writings in SF 22 (Bulmer), 1974
New writings in SF 23 (Bulmer), 1974
New writings in SF 24 (Bulmer), 1974
New writings in SF 25 (Bulmer), 1975
New writings in SF 26 (Bulmer), 1975
New writings in SF 27 (Bulmer), 1975
New writings in SF 28 (Bulmer), 1976
New writings in SF 29 (Bulmer), 1976
New writings in SF: Special One (Bulmer
    & Carnell), 1975
New York to Brest (Laurie), 1890
News from elsewhere (Cooper), 1968
News from Karachi (Wood), 1962
News from nowhere (Morris), 1891
Next chapter (Maurois), 1927
Next crusade (Cromie), 1896
Next crusade (Anon), 1910
Next generation (Maguire), 1871
Next naval war (Eardley-Wilmot), 1894
Next 'Ninety-three' (Watlock), 1886
Next of kin (Russell), 1959
Night in Babylon (Wellard), 1953
Night journey (Guerard), 1951
Night land (Hodgson), 1912
Night monsters (Leiber), 1974
Night journey (Guerard), 1951
Night land (Hodgson), 1912
Night monsters (Leiber), 1974
Night of the big heat (Lymington), 1959
Night of the crabs (Smith), 1976
Night of the death rain (Ranzetta), 1963
Night of the deathship (Barrett), 1976
Night of light (Farmer), 1972
Night of the Puudly (Simak), 1964
Night of the robots (Ball), 1972
Night of the short knives (Wilkinson), 1964
Night of the Trilobites (Leslie), 1968
Night of the Wolf (Leiber), 1976
Nightfall (Asimov), 1970
Nightfall One (Asimov), 1971
Nightfall Two (Asimov), 1971
Nightmare planet (Rowland), 1976
Night spiders (Lymington), 1964
Night walk (Shaw), 1970
Nightwings (Silverberg), 1972
Nine by Laumer (Laumer), 1968
Nine hundred grandmothers (Lafferty).
    1975

Nine tales of space and time (Healy),
    1955
Nineteen eight-four (Orwell), 1949
1957 (Blair), 1930
1945; a vision (Anon), 1845
1944 (Halsbury), 1926
1946 MS. (Maugham), 1943
Nineteen hundred? (Farningham), 1892
1975 (Anon), 1876
1972 Annual World's Best SF
    (Wollheim), 1972
1973 Annual World's Best SF
    (Wollheim), 1973
Nineteenth century (Ellis), 1900
1938 (Kingsmill & Muggeridge), 1937
Nine tomorrows (Asimov), 1963
"1925" (Wallace), 1915
Ninth Galaxy Reader (Pohl), 1967
Ninya (Fagan), 1956
Noah, II (Dixon), 1975
Nobody knew they were there (Hunter), 1971
No dawn (Merak), 1959
No direction home (Spinrad), 1976
No future in it (Brunner), 1962
No lack of space (Martin), 1967
No magic carpet (Barclay, A.), 1976
No Man Friday (Gordon), 1956
No man on earth (Moudy), 1966
No man's world (Bulmer), 1962
Noman way (McIntosh), 1964
No more war (Stead), 1917
Non-stop (Aldiss), 1958
None but man (Dickson), 1970
None so blind (Baker), 1946
No other gods but me (Brunner), 1966
No place like Earth (Carnell), 1952
No place on Earth (Charbonneau),
    1966
No rates and taxes (Pinkerton), 1902
Nordenholt's million (Connington), 1923
North afire (Newton), 1914
North Cape (Poyer), 1970
North Sea bubble (Oldmeadow), 1906
North Sea monster (Spencer &
    Randerson), 1934
No stars for us (Ray), 1964
No subway (Vielle), 1968
No traveller returns (Collier), 1931
Not an earthly chance (Tucker), 1970
Not before time (Brunner), 1968
Not in our stars (Maurice), 1923
Not in our stars (Eton), 1937
Not in solitude (Gantz), 1966
Not since Genesis (Clouston), 1938
Not with a bang (Pincher), 1965
Notes from the future (Amosoff), 1971
Nova (Delany), 1969
Nova 1 (Harrison), 1975

Our man for Ganymede (Lauder), 1969
Our man in Havana (Greene), 1958
Our own Pompeii (Anon), 1887
Our stranger (Meredith), 1936
Out (Brooke-Rose), 1964
Outer reaches (Derleth), 1963
Outlaws of the air (Griffith), 1895
Out North (Gilchrist), 1975
Out of my mind (Brunner), 1968
Out of the dead city (Delany), 1968
Out of the mouth of the Dragon
    (Geston), 1972
Out of the silence (Cox), 1925
Out of the void (Stone), 1971
Out of this world (Barzman), 1960
Outpost Mars (Judd), 1966
Outposter (Dickson), 1973
Outward urge (Lea), 1944
Overlay (Malzberg), 1975
Overloaded man (Ballard), 1967
Overlord New York (Elliot), 1953
Overlords (Woolfolk), 1973
Overlords of Andromeda (Falkner), 1955
Overman Culture (Cooper), 1971
Overmind (Wadsworth), 1967
Overself (Barrett), 1975
Overture to Cambridge (Macleod), 1936
Owl of Athene (Philpotts), 1936
Oxford in 1888 (R. P.), 1838

Pacific Book of science fiction (Baxter),
    1969
Pacific Book of science fiction, No. 2
    (Baxter), 1971
Palace of eternity (Shaw), 1970
Palace of love (Vance), 1968
Pale invaders (Kesteven), 1974
Palingenesia (Anon), 1884
Pandemic (Ardies), 1974
Panic o'clock (Hodder-Williams), 1973
Paradise is not enough (Elder), 1970
Paradise man (Hale), 1969
Paradise Zone (Barrett), 1975
Paradox lost (Brown), 1975
Paradox men (Harness), 1964
Parallel case (Anon), 1876
Parasaurians (Wells), 1974
Paris prelude (Howard), 1932
Parsecs and parables (Silverberg), 1973
Passage to oblivion (Howell), 1975
Passing of Arthur (Hamilton), 1904
Passionate Calvary (Anthony), 1932
Past master (Lafferty), 1968
Pastel city (Harrison, M. J.), 1971
Past-time of eternity (Sims), 1975
Path into the unknown (Varshavsky),
    1966
Patient dark (Bulmer), 1969
Patron of the arts (Rotsler), 1976

Pattern for conquest (Smith), 1951
Pattern of shadows (Burke), 1954
Patterns of chaos (Kapp), 1972
Paul Rees (Augustinus), 1899
Pavane (Roberts), 1968
Paw of God (Gordon), 1967
Pawns in ice (Gibbs), 1948
Pawns of Null-A (Van Vogt), 1970
Peace in nobody's time (Borodin), 1944
Peace on Earth (Turner), 1905
Peace under Earth (Beaujon), 1938
Peaceful revolution (Gentle Joseph),
    1916
Peacemaker (Forester), 1934
Peacemaker (Remenham), 1947
Peacemakers (Casewit), 1963
Pebble in the sky (Asimov), 1958
Peggy the aeronaut (Carter), 1910
Pendulum of fate (Alexander), 1933
Penetrators (Gray), 1965
Penguin island (France), 1909
Penguin Science Fiction (Aldiss), 1961
Penguin Science Fiction Omnibus
    (Aldiss), 1973
Penthouse conspirators (Pincher), 1970
Penultimate truth (Dick), 1967
People: no different flesh (Henderson),
    1966
People of the Rings (Schutz), 1975
People of the ruins (Shanks), 1920
People trap (Sheckley), 1969
Pepper leaf (Gibson), 1971
Percy's progress (Hitchcock), 1974
Perfect world (Scrymsour), 1922
Perfumed planet (Elder), 1973
Peril of Pines Place (Blyth), 1912
Perry Rhodan 1 (Scheer & Ernsting),
    1974
Perry Rhodan 2 (Scheer & Ernsting),
    1974
Perry Rhodan 3 (Mahr & Shols), 1974
Perry Rhodan 4 (Ernsting & Mahr), 1974
Perry Rhodan 5 (Scheer & Mahr), 1975
Perry Rhodan 6 (Darlton), 1975
Perry Rhodan 7 (Scheer), 1975
Perry Rhodan 8 (Darlton), 1975
Perry Rhodan 9, (Darlton), 1975
Perry Rhodan 10 (Mahr), 1976
Perry Rhodan 11 (Mahr), 1976
Perry Rhodan 12 (Darlton), 1976
Perry Rhodan 13 (Scheer), 1976
Perry Rhodan 14 (Mahr), 1976
Perry Rhodan 15 (Darlton), 1976
Perry Rhodan 16 (Shols), 1976
Perry Rhodan 17 (Mahr), 1976
Perry Rhodan 18 (Mahr), 1976
Perspective process (Donson), 1969
Peter the Second (Marshall), 1976
Peter's Pence (Cleary), 1974
Petrified planet (Statten), 1951

Sirens of Titan (Vonnegut), 1962
S is for Space (Bradbury), 1968
Sister Earth (Brede), 1951
Six gates from Limbo (McIntosh), 1968
Sixth column (Heinlein), 1962
Sixty days to live (Wheatley), 1939
Sixty years hence (Henningsen), 1847
Skeleton man (Munn), 1919
Sketches of the future (Gorst), 1898
Skrine (Sully), 1960
Skull and two crystals (Dick-Lauder), 1972
Sky block (Frazee), 1955
Skyfall (Harrison), 1976
Sky is falling (Del Rey), 1974
Skylark Duquesne (Smith), 1974
Skylark of space (Smith), 1959
Skylark of Valeron (Smith), 1974
Skylark Three (Smith), 1974
Sky-raft (Clark), 1937
Sky wolves (Radcliffe), 1938
Slan (Van Vogt), 1953
Slapstick (Vonnegut), 1976
Slave bug (Conrad), 1975
Slaver from the stars (Barrett), 1976
Slave ship (Pohl), 1960
Slaves of heaven (Cooper), 1975
Sleep (Creasey), 1964
Sleep eaters (Lymington), 1963
Sleeper awakes (Wells), 1910
Sleepers of Mars (Wyndham), 1973
Sleeping planet (Burkett), 1965
Sleeping sorceress (Moorcock), 1971
Sleepwalker's world (Dickson), 1973
Slow burner (Haggard), 1958
Slowing down process (Wessex), 1974
Small Armageddon (Roshwald), 1962
Small assassin (Bradbury), 1962
Small changes (Clement), 1969
Smashed world (Slater), 1952
Smile on the face of the tiger (Hurd & Osmond), 1969
Smiling trip (Courtier), 1975
Smog (Creasey), 1970
Socialist revolution of 1888 (Anon), 1884
Solar lottery (Dick), 1972
Solaris (Lem), 1971
Sold – for a spaceship (High), 1973
Soldier, ask not (Dickson), 1975
Soldier of the future (Dawson), 1908
Solution Three (Mitchison), 1975
Solution T-25 (Du Bois), 1952
Something in mind (Rolls), 1973
Sometime never (Dahl), 1949
Somewhere a voice (Russell), 1965
Somewhere in Christendom (Sharp), 1919
Some will not die (Budrys), 1964

Some women of the University (Blayre), 1934
Son of Kronk (Cooper), 1970
Son of the Tree (Vance), 1974
Sons of the wolf (Lukens), 1963
Sorry, wrong number (Simpson), 1973
SOS from Mars (Cross), 1954
Sos the Rope (Anthony), 1970
Soul of the robot (Bayley), 1974
Sound of his horn (Sarban), 1952
Space-born (Wright), 1964
Space-borne (Fanthorpe), 1959
Space chantey (Lafferty), 1976
Space crusader (Suffling), 1975
Spaceflight Venus (Wilding), 1954
Space guardians (Ball), 1975
Space gypsies (Leinster), 1968
Spacehounds of IPC (Smith), 1974
Space hunger (Grey), 1953
Space lords (Smith), 1969
Space merchants (Pohl & Kornbluth), 1955
Space odysseys (Aldiss), 1974
Space on my hands (Brown), 1953
Space Opera (Aldiss), 1974
Space pioneer (Reynolds), 1966
Space probe (Garner), 1974
Space raiders (Beverley), 1936
Space relations (Barr), 1975
Space salvage (Bulmer), 1953
Space sorcerers (McIntosh), 1972
Space stadium (Bevis), 1971
Space, time and Nathaniel (Aldiss), 1957
Space-time Force (Yorke), 1953
Space-time journal (Merril), 1972
Space treason (Bulmer), 1952
Space venturer (Rowland), 1976
Space warp (Statten), 1952
Spaceways (Maihe), 1953
Speaking of dinosaurs (High), 1974
Special relationship (Clark, W.), 1968
Specials (Charbonneau), 1965
Spectre is haunting Texas (Leiber), 1969
Spectrum I (Amis & Conquest), 1961
Spectrum II (Amis & Conquest), 1962
Spectrum III (Amis & Conquest), 1963
Spectrum IV (Amis & Conquest), 1965
Spectrum 5 (Amis & Conquest), 1966
Spider in the bath (Lymington), 1975
Spires, bells and dreams! (Lazlo), 1928
Split image (De Rouen), 1955
Split worlds (Barr), 1959
Spook who sat by the door (Greenlee), 1969
Sprague de Camp's new anthology (Campbell), 1953
Spurious sun (Borodin), 1948
Spykos 4 (Dagmar), 1963
Square root of man (Tenn), 1971

Suggested invasion of England by the Germans (Anon), 1871
Suicide fleet (Desmond), 1959
Summer in three thousand (Martin), 1946
Summer rising (Sullivan), 1975
Sunburst (Gotlieb), 1966
Sundance (Silverberg), 1975
Sundered worlds (Moorcock), 1965
Sundial (Jackson), 1958
Sundog (Ball), 1965
Sun grows cold (Berk), 1971
Sun makers (Statten), 1950
Sun shall rise (Ward), 1935
Sunken world (Coblentz), 1951
Sunset (Morison), 1932
Sunset people (Penny), 1975
Supernova 1 (Supernova), 1976
Supersonic (Jackson), 1976
Superstoe (Borden), 1967
Superwoman (Sutter), 1937
Surprise of the Channel Tunnel (Forth), 1883
Survivors (Griffiths), 1965
Survivors (Nation), 1976
Survivors (Sibson), 1932
Swampworld West (Chapdelaine), 1974
Swarm (Herzog), 1974
Swastika night (Constantine), 1937
Sweet sweet summer (Gaskell), 1969
Swoop! (Wodehouse), 1909
Swoop of the eagles (V), 1889
Swoop of the vulture (Blyth), 1909
Swooping vengeance (Dorman), 1954
Sword above the night (Lymington), 1962
Sword and the Stallion (Moorcock), 1974
Sword of Rhiannon (Brackett), 1956
Sword of the dawn (Moorcock), 1969
Symmetrians (Harker), 1966
Synaptic manhunt (Farren), 1976
Syndic (Kornbluth), 1964
Synthajoy (Compton), 1968
Syren of the skies (Griffith), 1894
Syzygy (Coney), 1973

Tactics of mistake (Dickson), 1975
Take away the flowers (Chilton), 1967
Take the war to Washinton (Van Greenaway), 1974
Take two popes (Calvin), 1972
Taking of Dover (Lester), 1888
Tales from the White Hart (Clarke), 1972
Tales of science fiction (Ball), 1964
Tales of space and time (Wells), 1899
Tales of ten worlds (Clarke), 1963
Tales of terror from outer space (Chetwynd-Hayes), 1975

Taming power (W.W.), 1974
Target Manhattan (Pitts), 1976
Tashkent Crisis (Craig), 1971
Tau Zero (Anderson, P.), 1971
Technicolor time machine (Harrison), 1968
Teetotalitarian State (De Chair), 1947
Telepathist (Brunner), 1965
Television girl (Wentworth-James), 1928
Telzey Toy (Schmitz), 1976
Ten days to oblivion (Cooney), 1968
Ten days to the Moon (Mingston), 1955
Ten from tomorrow (Tubb), 1966
Ten million years to Friday (Lymington), 1967
Ten thousand light years from home (Tiptree), 1975
Ten year plan (Freese), 1932
Ten years hence? (Coron), 1925
10th Galaxy reader (Pohl), 1968
Tenth planet (Cooper), 1973
Tenth victim (Sheckley), 1966
Terminal beach (Ballard), 1964
Terminus (Daventry), 1971
Terminus (Edwards), 1976
Termush (Holm), 1969
Terrible awakening (Desmond), 1949
Terror (Creasey), 1962
Terror by night (Mattingley), 1913
Terror in the sky (Mackenzie), 1955
Terror of the air (Le Queux), 1920
Texts of Festival (Farren), 1973
That hideous strength (Lewis), 1945
That very Mab (Lang & Kendall), 1885
Their man in the White House (Ardies), 1971
Their winged destiny (Horner), 1912
Then we shall hear singing (Jameson), 1942
Theodore Savage (Hamilton), 1922
These savage futurians (High), 1969
They (Mannes), 1969
They blocked the Suez Canal (Divine), 1935
They shall have stars (Blish), 1956
They shall not die (Parkinson), 1939
They walked like men (Simak), 1963
They went on together (Nathan), 1941
Thing (Campbell), 1952
Thing from outer space (Campbell), 1966
Things (Howard), 1966
Thinking seat (Tate), 1970
Third from the Sun (Matheson), 1961
Third mutant (Elliot), 1953
Thirst quenchers (Raphael), 1965
Thirteen French science fiction stories (Knight), 1965
Thirteen great stories of science fiction (Conklin), 1967

World of Null-A (Van Vogt), 1969
World of Ptavvs (Niven), 1968
World of Jonah Klee (King), 1976
World of Robert F. Young (Young), 1966
World of shadows (Harding), 1975
World of Theda (Wade), 1962
World of women (Beresford), 1920
World out of mind (McIntosh), 1955
World peril of 1910 (Griffith), 1907
World set free (Wells), 1914
World stood still (Holt-White), 1912
World well lost (Paget), 1970
World without a child (Kernahan), 1905
World without end (Mackenzie), 1955
World without men (Maine), 1963
World without stars (Anderson), 1975
World without women (Keene and
    Pruyn), 1961
World wrecker (Bounds), 1956
Worlds apart (Locke), 1972
Worlds apart (Cowper), 1974
Worlds at war (Rayer), 1950
Worlds of Eclos (Gordon), 1961
Worlds of Frank Herbert (Herbert), 1970
Worlds of Robert Heinlein (Heinlein),
    1970
Worlds of the Imperium (Laumer), 1967
Worlds of science fiction (Mills), 1964
Worlds of tomorrow (Derleth), 1954
Worlds to come (Knight), 1969
Worlds to conquer (Statten), 1952
Worlds without end (Simak), 1965
World's awakening (Navarchus), 1908
World's beginning (Ardrey), 1945
World's best science fiction, 1969
    (Wollheim & Carr), 1969
World's best science fiction, 1970
    (Wollheim & Carr), 1971
World's best science fiction, 1971
    (Wollheim & Carr), 1971
World's best SF short stories 1
    (Wollheim), 1975
World's best SF short stories 2
    (Wollheim), 1976
Wotan's wedge (Gerard), 1938
Wrath of grapes (Wibberley), 1955
Wrath to come (Oppenheim), 1925
Wrath to come (Mackenzie), 1957
Wreath of stars (Shaw), 1976
Wreck of a world (Grove), 1889
Wreck of Westminster Abbey (Anon),
    1788
Wrecking ray (Wedlake), 1935
Wrinkle in th skin (Christopher), 1965
Writing on the wall (General Staff),
    1906
Wrong end of time (Brunner), 1975
Wrong side of the Moon (Ashton),
    1952

X Factor (Norton), 1967

Yankee Napoleon (Macpherson), 1907
Year Dot (Lymington), 1972
Year of miracle (Hume), 1891
Year of the Angry Rabbit (Braddon), 1964
Year of the comet (Christopher), 1955
Year of the painted world (Mackelworth),
    1975
Year of the Quiet Sun (Tucker), 1971
Year of the regeneration (Lawrence),
    1932
Year 2000 (Harrison), 1971
Year 2018 (Blish), 1963
Year's best SF1 (Harrison & Aldiss), 1968
Year's best SF2 (Harrison & Aldiss), 1969
Year's best SF3 (Harrison & Aldiss), 1970
Year's best SF4 (Harrison & Aldiss), 1971
Year's best SF5 (Harrison & Aldiss), 1972
Year's best SF6 (Harrison & Aldiss), 1973
Year's best SF7 (Harrison & Aldiss), 1975
Year's best SF8 (Harrison & Aldiss), 1976
Year's best SF9 (Harrison & Aldiss), 1976
Year's best science fiction novels
    (Bleiler & Dikty), 1953
Year's best science fiction novels
    (Bleiler & Dikty), 1955
Yellow danger (Shiel), 1898
Yellow fraction (Gordon), 1972
Yellow inferno (Ranzetta), 1964
Yellow Peril (Shiel), 1929
Yellow planet (Browne), 1954
Yellow wave (MacKay), 1895
Yesterday: a Tory FairyTale (Davey),
    1924
Yesterday's children (Gerrold), 1974
Yet more Penguin Science Fiction
    (Aldiss), 1964
Yorl of the Northmen (Strong'ith'arm),
    1892
You'll see (Larsen), 1957
Young Diana (Corelli), 1918
Young men are coming (Shiel), 1937
Your sins and mine (Caldwell), 1973
Yu-Malu, the Dragon Princess (Leslie),
    1967

Zalma (Ellis), 1895
Zap Gun (Dick), 1975
Zardoz (Boorman), 1974
Zenith-D (Lorraine), 1953
Zero hour (Statten), 1953
Z formations (Shaw), 1953
Zilov bombs (Barron), 1962
Zodiak (Eidlitz), 1931
Zoo 2000 (Yolen), 1975

PART 3   AUTHOR INDEX

Names of Authors

The forenames of authors, wherever known, are entered in full. Thus, authors who have always used their initials – P.G. Wodehouse and E.M. Forster, for instance – appear with their complete forenames – Pelham Grenville Wodehouse, Edward Morgan Forster; and the additional names, not normally used by authors, are given in full as: Aldous [Leonard] Huxley, [Richard Horatio] Edgar Wallace, Eric [Robert Russell] Linklater.

Anonymous Works

Anonymous works do not appear in this index; but, wherever the author's name has been established, then entry is made under that name.

Pseudonyms

Entry is made under the author's real name, wherever that is known, and a cross reference is made in the main entry under the pseudonym.

Aarons, Edward, S. *Assignment Black Viking*, 1973
Abdullah, Achmed *The red stain*, *1916*
Abé, Kobo *Inter Ice Age 4*, 1971
Ableman, Paul *The twilight of the Vilp*, 1969
Adam, Ruth *War on Saturday week*, 1937
Adams, J. See Kuppord, S. *(pseud.)*
Adams, Robert James See MacTyre, Paul *(pseud.)*
Adams, Walter Marsham See Macaulay, Clarendon *(pseud.)*
Adams, William [Wheen] Scovell *The Fourth Programme*, 1955
Adderley, [Hon.] James [Granville] *Behold the days come*, 1907
Addison, Hugh (Harry Collinson Owen) *The battle of London*, 1923
Adlard, Mark *Interface*, 1971
– *Multiface*, 1975
– *Volteface*, 1972
Agricola *(pseud.) How England was saved*, 1908
Ainsbury, Ray (A.H. Verrill) *When the moon ran wild*, 1962
Alban, Antony *Catharsis Central*, 1968
Aldiss, Brian Wilson *An age*, 1967
– *The airs of Earth*, 1963
– *Barefoot in the Head*, 1969
– (ed.) *Best Fantasy stories*, 1962
– (ed.) *Best SF stories*, 1965
– *Best SF stories of Brian Aldiss*, 1971
– *A Brian Aldiss Omnibus*, 1969
– *A Brian Aldiss Omnibus (2)*, 1971
– *The canopy of time*, 1959

– *The comic inferno*, 1973
– *Cryptozoic*, 1973
– *The dark light years*, 1964
– *Earthworks*, 1965
– *The eighty-minute hour*, 1974
– *Equator*, 1961
– (ed.) *Evil Earths*, 1975
– *Frankenstein unbound*, 1973
– (ed.) *Galactic empires 1*, 1976
– (ed.) *Galactic empires 2*, 1976
– (ed.) *The Gollancz/Sunday Times best SF stories*, 1974
– *Greybeard*, 1964
– *Hothouse*, 1962
– *Intangibles Inc.*, 1969
– *The Interpreter*, 1961
– (ed.) *Introducing SF*, 1964
– *The moment of eclipse*, 1970
– (ed.) *More Penguin Science Fiction*, 1963
– *Non-stop*, 1958
– *Omnibus 2*, 1971
– (ed.) *Penguin Science Fiction*, 1961
– *Penguin Science Fiction Omnibus*, 1973
– *The primal urge*, 1967
– *The saliva tree*, 1966
– (ed.) *Space odysseys*, 1974
– (ed.) *Space Opera*, 1974
– *Space, time and Nathaniel*, 1957
– (ed.) *Yet more Penguin Science Fiction*, 1964
– and others *The inner landscape*, 1969
See Harrison, Harry, joint editor
Aldiss, Brian Wilson and Harrison, Harry *(eds.) Decade: the 1940s*, 1975

Ashe, Gordon (John Creasey) *A plague of demons*, 1976
Ashley, Michael *The history of the science fiction magazine, Part 1*, 1974
- *The history of the science fiction magazine, Part 2*, 1975
- *The history of the science fiction magazine, Part 3*, 1976
Ashton, Francis and Ashton Stephen *Wrong side of the Moon*, 1952
Ashton, Winifred See Dane, Clemence *(pseud.)*
Asimov, Isaac *Asimov's mysteries*, 1968
- *(ed.) Before the Golden Age*, 1974
- *(ed.) Before the Golden Age 1–3*, 1975
- *(ed.) Before the Golden Age 4*, 1976
- *Buy Jupiter*, 1976
- *The caves of steel*, 1954
- *The currents of space*, 1955
- *The early Asimov*, 1973
- *Earth is room enough*, 1960
- *The end of eternity*, 1959
- *Fantastic voyage*, 1966
- *Foundation*, 1953
- *Foundation and Empire*, 1962
- *The gods themselves*, 1972
- *(ed.) The Hugo Winners*, 1963
- *(ed.) The Hugo Winners, 1963–67*, 1973
- *(ed.) The Hugo Winners, 1968–70*, 1973
- *I, robot*, 1952
- *An Isaac Asimov Omnibus*, 1966
- *The Martian way*, 1964
- *The naked sun*, 1958
- *(ed.) The Nebula Award Stories 8*, 1973
- *Nightfall*, 1970
- *Nightfall One*, 1971
- *Nightfall Two*, 1971
- *Nine tomorrows*, 1963
- *Pebble in the sky*, 1958
- *The rest of the robots*, 1967
- *Second Foundation*, 1958
- *A second Asimov Omnibus*, 1969
- *Stars like dust*, 1958
- *Through a glass clearly*, 1967
- *Tomorrow's children*, 1974
- *Where do we go from here?*, 1973
- and Conklin, G. *(eds.) Fifty short science fiction tales*, 1963
Askham, Francis (Julia Eileen Courtney Greenwood) *The heart consumed*, 1944
Asterley, Hugh Cecil *Escape to Berkshire*, 1961
Atholl, Justin *The man who tilted the Earth*, 1943

Atkins, John [Alfred] *Tomorrow revealed*, 1955
Atkinson, Hugh *The most savage animal*, 1970
Augustinus *(pseud.) Paul Rees*, 1899
- *Two brothers*, 1898
Austin, Frederick Britten *In Action; studies in war*, 1913
- *The war-god walks again*, 1926
Avallone, Michael *Beneath the Planet of the Apes*, 1974
Avery, Richard (Edmund Cooper) *Deathworms of Kratos*, 1975
- *The Rings of Tantalus*, 1975
- *The Venom of Argus*, 1976
- *The War Games of Zelos*, 1975
Axton, David *Prison of ice*, 1976

Bagnall, Robert David *The Fourth Connection*, 1975
Bahnson, Agnew H. *The Stars are too high*, 1962
Bailey, Andrew J. *The Martian Emperor-President*, 1932
Bailey, Hilary *(ed.) New Worlds 8*, 1975
- *New Worlds 9*, 1975
Bailey, Hilary & Platt, Charles *(eds.) New Worlds 7*, 1974
Bair, Patrick See Gurney, David *(pseud.) The tribunal*, 1970
Baker, Frank *The birds*, 1936
Baker, Gordon *None so blind*, 1946
Balchin, Nigel [Martin] *Kings of infinite space*, 1967
Baldwin, Bee *The red dust*, 1965
Baldwin, Oliver Ridsdale See Hussingtree, Martin *(pseud.)*
Ball, Brian Neville *Night of the robots*, 1972
- *Planet Probability*, 1974
- *The probability man*, 1973
- *Singularity Station*, 1974
- *The space guardians*, 1975
- *Sundog*, 1965
- *Tales of science fiction*, 1964
- *Timepiece*, 1968
- *Timepit*, 1971
Ball, Frank Norman *Metatopia*, 1961
Ball, John *The first team*, 1972
Ballard, James Graham *Crash*, 1973
- *The crystal world*, 1966
- *The day of forever*, 1967
- *The disaster area*, 1967
- *The drought*, 1965
- *The drowned world*, 1962
- *The four-dimensional nightmare*, 1963
- *Low-flying aircraft*, 1976

Bennett, Margot *The furious masters*, 1968
- *The long way back*, 1954
Benson, Robert Hugh *The dawn of all*, 1911
- *Lord of the world*, 1907
Bentley, Norman K *Drake's mantle*, 1928
Beresford, John Davys *A common Enemy*, 1941
- *Goslings*, 1913
- *Revolution*, 1921
- *What dreams may come*, 1941
- *A world of wumen*, 1920
- and Wynne-Tyson, Esme *The riddle of the tower*, 1944
Beresford, Leslie See Pan *(pseud.)*
- *The last woman*, 1922
- *The second rising*, 1910
Berger, Thomas *Regiment of women*, 1974
Berk, Howard *The sun grows cold*, 1971
Berkeley, Reginald [Cheyne] *Cassandra*, 1931
Bernard, John *The new race of devils*, 1921
Bernard, Rafe *The halo highway*, 1967
- *The wheel in the sky*, 1954
Berriàult, Gina *The descent*, 1961
Berry, Bryan See Garner, Rolf *(pseud.)*
- *And the stars remain*, 1952
- *Born in captivity*, 1952
- *Dread visitor*, 1952
- *From what far star*, 1953
- *Return to Earth*, 1952
- *The venom-seekers*, 1953
Bertin, Jack *The interplanetary adventurers*, 1972
- *The pyramids from space*, 1971
Besant, Sir Walter *The inner house*, 1888
- *The revolt of man*, 1882
Best, Herbert *The twenty-fifth hour*, 1940
Bester, Alfred *An Alfred Bester Omnibus*, 1967
- *The dark side of Earth*, 1969
- *The demolished man*, 1953
- *Extro*, 1975
- *The stars my destination*, 1959
- *Starburst*, 1968
- *Tiger! Tiger!*, 1956
Beverley, Barrington *The air devil*, 1934
- *The space raiders*, 1936
Bevis, H. U. *Space stadium*, 1971
- *The time winder*, 1972
Beynon, John (John Beynon Harris) *Planet plane*, 1936
- *The secret people*, 1935

Biggle, Lloyd *All the colours of darkness*, 1964
- *The angry espers*, 1968
- *The fury out of time*, 1966
- *The light that never was*, 1975
- *Monument*, 1975
- *(ed.) Nebula Award Stories 7*, 1972
- *The still, small voice of trumpets*, 1969
- *Watchers of the dark*, 1966
- *The world menders*, 1974
Binder, Pearl and Ordish, George *Ladies only*, 1972
Bingham, Frederick *The cap becomes a coronet*, 1894
Bishop, Morchard (Oliver Stonor) *The star called Wormwood*, 1941
Black, Dorothy *Candles in the dark*, 1954
Black, Ladbroke [Lionel Day] *The poison war*, 1933
Blackburn, John [Fenwick] *Devil daddy*, 1972
- *The face of the Lion*, 1976
- *A ring of roses*, 1965
- *A scent of new-mown hay*, 1958
Blackden, Paul *Adam and Eve 2020 A.D.*, 1974
Blacker, Irwin Robert *Chain of command*, 1965
Blair, Andrew *Annals of the twenty-ninth century*, 1874
Blair, Eric Arthur See Orwell, George *(pseud.)*
Blair, Hamish (Andrew James Fraser Blair) *Governor Hardy*, 1931
- *The great gesture*, 1931
- *1957*, 1930
Blair, Patrick See Gurney, David (pseud.)
Blake, Stacey *Beyond the blue*, 1920
Blakemore, Felix John *The coming hour (?),* 1927
Bland, Charles Ashwold *Independence: a retrospect*, 1891
Blayre, Christopher (Edward Heron Allen) *The Purple Sapphire*, 1921
- *Some women of the University*, 1934
- *The strange papers of Dr. Blayre*, 1932
Bleackley, Horace [William] *Anymoon*, 1919
Bleiler, Everett Franklin and Dikty, Thaddeus Eugene *(eds.) The best science fiction stories*, 1951
- *The best science fiction stories*, Second series, 1953
- *The best science fiction stories, Third series*, 1953
- *The best science fiction stories, Fourth series*, 1955
- *The best science fiction stories, Fifth series*, 1956

Buchard, R. *Thirty seconds over New York*, 1970

Buckle, Richard *John Innocent at Oxford* ,1939

Budge *(pseud.) The Eastern question solved*, 1881

Budrys, Algis [Algirdas Jonas] *The furious future*, 1964
- *The iron thorn*, 1968
- *Some will not die*, 1964
- *The unexpected dimension*, 1962
- *Who?*, 1962

Bullock, Shan F. *The red leaguers*, 1904

Bulmer, Henry Kenneth *Behold the stars*, 1966
- *Challenge*, 1954
- *The changeling worlds*, 1961
- *City under the sea*, 1961
- *Defiance*, 1963
- *The demons*, 1965
- *The Doomsday men*, 1968
- *Earth's long shadow*, 1963
- *Empire in chaos*, 1953
- *Encounter in space*, 1952
- *The fatal fire*, 1963
- *Galactic intrigue*, 1953
- *No man's world*, 1962
- *Of Earth foretold*, 1961
- *The patient dark*, 1969
- *Quench the burning stars*, 1970
- *Secret of ZI*, 1961
- *Space salvage*, 1953
- *Space treason*, 1952
- *Stained glass world*, 1976
- *Star trove*, 1970
- *The stars are ours*, 1953
- *To out run Doomsday*, 1975
- *The ulcer culture*, 1969
- *The wind of liberty*, 1962
- *World aflame*, 1954
- (ed.) *New Writings in SF 22*, 1974
- (ed.) *New Writings in SF 23*, 1974
- (ed.) *New Writings in SF 24*, 1974
- (ed.) *New Writings in SF 25*, 1975
- (ed.) *New Writings in SF 26*, 1975
- (ed.) *New Writings in SF 27*, 1975
- (ed.) *New Writings in SF 28*, 1976
- (ed.) *New Writings in SF 29*, 1976

Burdekin, Katherine *The rebel passion*, 1929

Burdick, Eugene [Leonard] and Wheeler, [John] Harvey *Fail-safe*, 1963

Burgess, Anthony (John Burgess Wilson) *A clockwork orange*, 1962
- *The wanting seed*, 1962

Burgess, Eric and Friggens, Arthur *Anti-Zota*, 1973
- *Mortorio*, 1973
- *Mortorio Two*, 1975

Burgoyne, Alan Hughes *The war inevitable*, 1908

Burke, John [Frederick] See Burke, Jonathan
- *Moon Zero Two*, 1969
- *Expo 90*, 1972

Burke, Jonathan (John Frederick Burke) *Alien landscape*, 1955
- *Deep freeze*, 1955
- *The echoing worlds*, 1954
- *Hotel Cosmos*, 1954
- *Pattern of shadows*, 1954
- *Pursuit through time*, 1956
- *Revolt of the humans*, 1955
- *Twilight of reason*, 1954

Burke, Norah *The carlet vampire*, 1936

Burkett, William R. *Sleeping planet*, 1965

Burkitt, William T. *The coming day*, 1913

Burns, Alan *Europe after the rain*, 1965

Burroughs, Edgar Rice *The Moon Maid*, 1972

Burroughs, William Seward *Nova Express*, 1966
- *The wild boys*, 1972

Burton, Francis George *The naval engineer and the Command of the Sea*, 1896

Butler, Sir William Francis *The invasion of England*, 1882

Buzzati, Dino *Larger than life*, 1962

Byatt, Henry *The flight of Icarus*, 1907
- *Purple and white*, 1905

Bywater, Hector Charles *The great Pacific war*, 1925

Caidin, Martin *Cyborg*, 1973
- *The last fathom*, 1969
- *Marooned*, 1964
- *The Mendelov Conspiracy*, 1971
- *Operation Nuke*, 1974

Caine, [Sir Thomas Henry] Hall *The eternal city*, 1901
- *The White Prophet*, 1909

Caine, William and Fairbairn, John *The confectioners*, 1906

Cairnes, Capt. William Elliott *The coming Waterloo*, 1901

Calderon, George *Dwala*, 1904

Caldwell, Taylor *Your sins and mine*, 1973

Calisher, Hortense *Journal from Ellipsia*, 1966

Calvin, Henry (Clifford Leonard Clark Hanley) *Take two popes*, 1972

Davidson, Avram *(ed.); contd.*
- *Or all the seas with oysters*, 1976
- *Rork!*, 1968

Davies, Leslie Purnell *The alien*, 1968
- *The artificial man*, 1965
- *Dimension A*, 1969
- *The Groundstar conspiracy*, 1972
- *Twilight journey*, 1967
- *What did I do tomorrow?*, 1972

Davis, Brian *(ed.) The best of Murray Leinster*, 1976
- *The old masters*, 1970

Dawson, Alec John *The message*, 1907

Dawson, William James *A soldier of the future*, 1908

Dearmer, Geoffrey *Saint on holiday*, 1933

De Banzie, Eric See Baxter, Gregory *(pseud.)*

De Bury, Madame F. Blaze See Dickberry, F. *(pseud.)*

De Camp, Lyon Sprague *The Continent Makers*, 1974
- *The floating continent*, 1966
- *A gun for Dinosaur*, 1974
- (Campbell, H. J. *(ed.)) New anthology of science fiction*, 1953
- *A planet called Krishna*, 1966
- *Rogue Queen*, 1954

De Chair, Somerset *The Teetotalitarian State*, 1947

Deegan, Jon, J. *(pseud.) Amateurs in alchemy*, 1952
- *Antro*, 1953
- *Beyond the fourth door*, 1954
- *The corridors of time*, 1953
- *Exiles in time*, 1954
- *The great ones*, 1953
- *Underworld of Zello*, 1952

Dekhnewallah, A. *(pseud.) The great Russian invasion of India*, 1879

Delany, Samuel Ray *Babel-17*, 1967
- *City of a thousand suns*, 1969
- *Dhalgren*, 1975
- *The Einstein Intersection*, 1968
- *The fall of the Towers*, 1971
- *The jewels of Aptor*, 1968
- *Nova*, 1969
- *Out of the dead city*, 1968
- *The Towers of Toron*, 1968

Delius, Anthony *The day Natal took off*, 1963

Dellbridge, John *The Moles of Death*, 1927

Del Martia, Astron *(pseud.) One against time*, 1969
- (John Russell Fearn) *the trembling world*, 1949

Delmont, Joseph *Mistress of the skies*, 1932
- *The submarine city*, 1930

Del Rey, Lester *Badge of infamy*, 1976
- *(ed.) Best science fiction stories of the year, 1*, 1973
- *(ed.) Best science fiction stories of the year, 2*, 1974
- *(ed.) Best science fiction stories of the year, 3*, 1975
- *(ed.) Best science fiction stories of the year, 4*, 1976
- *The sky is falling*, 1974

Dempsey, Hank See Harrison, Harry *(pseud.)*

Demure One *(pseud.) The Battle of Boulogne*, 1882

Dent, Guy *The emperor of the If*, 1926

Derleth, August [William] *(ed.) Beachheads in space*, 1954
- *(ed.) Far boundaries*, 1965
- *(ed.) New worlds for old*, 1955
- *(ed.) The other side of the Moon*, 1956
- *(ed.) The outer reaches*, 1963
- *(ed.) Portals of tomorrow*, 1956
- *(ed.) The time of infinity*, 1961
- *(ed.) Worlds of tomorrow*, 1954
- *(ed.) The time of infinity*, 1961
- *(ed.) Worlds of tomorrow*, 1954

Dermott, Vern *Planet finders*, 1975

De Rouen, Reed Randolph *Split image*, 1955

Desmond, Hugh *Fear rides the air*, 1953
- *Suicide fleet*, 1959
- *Terrible awakening*, 1949

Desmond, Shaw *Black dawn*, 1944
- *Chaos*, 1938
- *Ragnarok*, 1926
- *World-birth*, 1938

Detre, Professor L. *War of two worlds*, 1936

Detzer, Diane See Lukens, Adam *(pseud.)*

Devinne, Paul *The day of prosperity*, 1902

Dexter, J.B. *The time kings*, 1958

Dexter, William (William Thomas Pritchard) *Children of the void*, 1955
- *World in eclipse*, 1954

Dick, Philip Kendred *Clans of the Alphane Moon*, 1975
- *Counter-clock world*, 1968
- *Do androids dream of electric sheep?*, 1969
- *Dr. Futurity*, 1976
- *Eye in the sky*, 1971
- *Flow my tears, the policeman said*, 1974
- *The galactic pot-healer*, 1971
- *The game-players of Titan*, 1969
- *A handful of darkness*, 1955

Duncan, Ronald [Frederick Henry] *The last Adam*, 1952

Dunkerley, William Arthur See Oxenham, John *(pseud.)*

Dunn, Saul *The coming of Steeleye*, 1976
- *Steeleye – Waterspace*, 1976
- *Steeleye – The Wideways*, 1976

Dunsany, Lord Edward John Moreton Drax Plunkett *The last revolution*, 1951

Dyas, R. H. *The Upas*, 1877

Dye, Charles *Prisoner in the skull*, 1957

Dyson, S. S. *The melting pot*, 1932

E., A. (George William Russell) *The Interpreters*, 1922

Eardley-Wilmot, Capt. Sir Sidney Marow See Searchlight *(pseud.)*
- *The next naval war*, 1894

Earnshaw, Brian *Planet in the eye of time*, 1968

Eastwick, James *The new Centurion*, 1895

Eaton, Benjamim Vandemark See Valentine, Victor *(pseud.)*

The Editors *The Saturday Evening Post Reader of fantasy and science fiction*, 1964

Edmonds, Harry [Moreton Southey] *The professor's last experiment*, 1935
- *The red invader*, 1933
- *The riddle of the Straits*, 1932
- *The rockets*, 1951

Edmonds, Helen See Kavan, Anna *(pseud.)*

Edmondson, Garry Cotton *Chapayeca*, 1973
- *The ship that sailed the time stream*, 1971

Edwards, Charman (Anthony Frederick Edwards) *Drama of Mr. Dilly*, 1939
- *Fear haunts the roses*, 1936

Edwards, Gawain (George Edward Pendray) *The earth tube*, 1929

Edwards, Peter *Terminus*, 1976

Effinger, G. A. *Escape to tomorrow*, 1974
- *Planet of the Apes*, 1975

Egbert, H. M. (Victor Rousseau Emmanuel) *Draught of eternity*, 1924
- *The sea demons*, 1924

Egleton, Clive *The Judas mandate*, 1972
- *Last post for a partisan*, 1971
- *A piece of resistance*, 1970
- *State visit*, 1976

Ehrlich, Max [Simon] *The big eye*, 1951

Eidlitz, Walther *Zodiak*, 1931

Elder, Michael *The alien Earth*, 1971
- *Centaurian quest*, 1975
- *Double time*, 1976
- *Down to Earth*, 1973
- *The Island of the Dead*, 1975
- *Nowhere on Earth*, 1972
- *Paradise is not enough*, 1970
- *The perfumed planet*, 1973
- *The seeds of frenzy*, 1974

Eldershaw, M. B. (Flora Sydney Patricia and Marjorie Faith Barnard Eldershaw) *Tomorrow and tomorrow*, 1949

Ellern, W. *New Lensman*, 1976

Elliot, Lee *Overlord New York*, 1953
- *The third mutant*, 1953

Ellis, A. W. *To tell the truth*, 1933

Ellis, Havelock *The Nineteenth Century*, 1900

Ellis, T. Mullett *Zalma*, 1895

Ellison, Harlan *Again, Dangerous visions*, 1976
- *All the sounds of fear*, 1973
- *Approaching oblivion*, 1976
- *The beast that shouted love*, 1976
- *Dangerous visions 1*, 1971
- *Dangerous visions 2*, 1971
- *The time of the eye*, 1974

Elmore, Ernest *The Steel Grubs*, 1928
- *This siren song*, 1930

Elton, John *The green plantations*, 1955

Elwood, Roger *(ed.) Continuum 1*, 1975
- *(ed.) Continuum 2*, 1976
- *(ed.) Dystopian visions*, 1976
- *(ed.) Flame Tree Planet*, 1973
- *(ed.) Frontiers 1: Tomorrow's alternatives*, 1974
- *(ed.) Frontiers 2: The new mind*, 1974
- *(ed.) Future city*, 1976
- See *Ghidalia, Vic*, joint author

Emanuel, Victor Rousseau. See Rousseau, Victor *(pseud.)*

Emanuel, Walter [Lewis] *100 years hence*, 1911

Erdmann, Paul *The billion dollar killing*, 1973

Ernsting, Walter and Mahr, Kurt *Perry Rhodan 4*, 1974

Ertz, Susan *Woman alive*, 1935

Eton, Robert (Laurence Walter Meynell) *Not in our stars*, 1937

Evans, Idrisyn Oliver *(ed.) Science fiction through the ages 1*, 1966
- *(ed.) Science fiction through the ages 2*, 1966

Everett, Frances *John Bull, socialist*, 1909

Follett, James *The Doomsday Ultimatum*, 1976

Foot, Michael Mackintosh See Cassius *(pseud.)*

Ford, Douglas Morey *The raid of Dover*, 1910

– *A Time of terror*, 1906

Ford, Ford Madox (Joseph Ford Madox Hueffer) *Vive le roy*, 1937

Ford, W. W. *Psyche, 1902*, 1901

Foreman, Russell *The Ringway Virus*, 1976

Forester, Cecil Scott *The peacemaker*, 1934

Forrest, David *After me the Deluge*, 1972

Forster, Edward Morgan *The machine stops*, 1928

Forth, C. *The surprise of the Channel Tunnel*, 1883

Forster, Alan Dean *Icerigger*, 1976

– *Star Trek Log 1, 2, 3, 4, 5* See *Note 12*

Forster, Richard (Kendell Foster Crossen) *The rest must die*, 1960

Fowler, Sydney (Sydney Fowler Wright) *The adventure of the Blue Room*, 1945

Fox, Samuel Middleton *Our own Pompeii*, 1887

Fox-Davies, Arthur Charles *The sex triumphant*, 1909

Frame, Janet *Intensive care*, 1971

France, Anatole (Jacques Anatole Thibault) *Penguin island*, 1909

– *The white stone*, 1909

Francois, Yves Regis *The CTZ Paradigm*, 1976

Frank, Pat (Harry Hart) *Alas, Babylon*, 1959

– *Mr. Adam*, 1947

– *Seven days to never*, 1953

Frankau, Gilbert *Unborn tomorrow*, 1957

Fraser, Sir Ronald [Arthur] *The flying draper*, 1924

Frayn, Michael J. *A very private life*, 1968

Frazee, Steve [Charles] *The sky block*, 1955

Frazer, S. *A corned hog*, 1933

– *A shroud as well as a shirt*, 1935

Freemantle, Brian *The November man*, 1976

Freese, Stanley *The ten year plan*, 1932

Friedberg, Gertrude *The revolving boy*, 1967

Friend, Oscar Jerome *The kid from Mars*, 1951

Fryers, Austin (William Austin Clery) *The Devil and the inventor*, 1900

Fullerton, John Charles [Mark] *The man who spoke dog*, 1959

Furnill, John *Culmination*, 1932

Fysh *(pseud.)* *Planetary war*, 1952

Gale, Frederick See Wykehamicus, Friedrich *(pseud.)*

Gale, J. E. Like an evening gone, 1972

Galouye, Daniel Francis *Counterfeit world*, 1964

– *Dark universe*, 1962

– *The last leap*, 1964

– *The lost perception*, 1966

– *Project barrier*, 1968

Gandon, Yves *The last white man*, 1948

Gantz, Kenneth Franklin *Not in solitude*, 1966

Garden, Donald J. *Dawn chorus*, 1975

Gardner, Alan [Harold] *Assignment Tahiti*, 1965

– *The escalator*, 1963

Garfield, Brian Wynne *Deep cover*, 1972

– *Line of succession*, 1974

Garner, Graham *Rifts of time*, 1976

– *Space probe*, 1974

– *Starfall Muta*, 1975

Garner, Rolf (Bryan Berry) *The immortals*, 1953

– *The indestructible*, 1954

– *Resurgent dust*, 1953

Garner, William *The Us or Them War*, 1969

Garnett, David S. *Cosmic carousel*, 1976

– *The forgotten dimension*, 1975

– *Mirror in the sky*, 1973

– *The star seekers*, 1975

– *Time in eclipse*, 1974

Garratt, Evelyn R. *The cry*, 1919

Garrett, Randall [Phillips] *Unwise child*, 1963

Garrod, John William. See Castle, John *(pseud.)*

Gary, Romain *The gasp*, 1973

Gaskell, Jane (Jane Lynch) *A sweet sweet summer*, 1969

Gastine, [Jules] Louis *War in space*, 1913

Gay, J. Drew *The mystery of the shroud*, 1887

Geen, Eric *Tolstoy lives at 12N B9*, 1971

Geissler, Ludwig A. *Looking beyond*, 1895

Griffith, George; contd.
- *Olga Romanoff*, 1894
- *The outlaws of the air*, 1895
- *The raid of 'Le Vengeur'*, 1974
- *The syren of the skies*, 1894
- *A woman against the world*, 1903
- *The world masters*, 1903
- *The world peril of 1910*, 1907
Griffiths, John *The survivors*, 1965
Grinnell, David (Donald A. Wollheim) *To Venus! To Venus!*, 1971
Grip *(pseud.) How John Bull lost London*, 1882
- *The monster municipality*, 1882
Grisewood, Harman [Joseph Gerard] *The recess*, 1963
Groom, [Arthur John] Pelham *The purple twilight*, 1948
Grousset, Paschal. See Laurie, André *(pseud.)*
Grove, W. *The wreck of a world*, 1889
Groves, John William *The heels of Achilles*, 1969
- *Shellbreak*, 1968
Gubbins, Herbert *The elixir of life*, 1914
Guerard, Albert Joseph *Night journey*, 1951
Guest, Ernest *At the end of the world*, 1929
Guggisberg, Capt. Sir Frederick Gordon. See Ubique *(pseud.)*
Guin, Wyman *Beyond Bedlam*, 1973
Gull, Cyril Arthur [Edward] Ranger. See Thorne, Guy *(pseud.)*
- *The air pirate*, 1919
- *The city in the clouds*, 1921
Gunn, James Edwin *The Immortals*, 1975
- *The joy makers*, 1963
- *(ed.) Nebula Award stories 10*, 1975
Gurney, David (Patrick Bair) *The "F" Certificate*, 1968
Guthrie, John (John Brodie) *Is this what I wanted*, 1950
Guttenberg, Violet *A modern exodus*, 1904
Gutteridge, Lindsay *Fratricide is a gas*, 1975
- *Killer pine*, 1973

Hadfield, Robert L. and Farncombe E. *Red radio*, 1927
- *Ruled by radio*, 1925
Haggard, William (Richard Henry Michael Clayton) *The conspirators*, 1967
- *The high wire*, 1963
- *Slow burner*, 1958

Haig, J. C. *In the grip of the trusts*, 1909
Haile, Terence *Galaxies ahead*, 1960
Hailey, Arthur *In high places*, 1962
Haines, Donal Hamilton *Clearing the seas*, 1915
Haining, Peter [Alexander] *(ed.) The future makers*, 1968
- *The hero*, 1974
Haldane, Charlotte *Man's world*, 1926
Haldeman, Joe *The forever war*, 1975
Hale, John *The paradise man*, 1969
Hale, Col. Sir Lonsdale Augustus *The horrors of war in Great Britain*, 1910
Hale, Martin *The Fourth Reich*, 1965
Hall, George Rome *Black fortnight*, 1904
Hall, Ronald *The open cage*, 1970
Halsbury, Earl of (Goulburn Giffard Hardinge) *1944*, 1926
Hambrook, Emerson C. *The red tomorrow*, 1920
Hamilton, Andrew *Host man*, 1975
Hamilton, Bruce *Traitor's way*, 1938
Hamilton, Cicely [Mary] *Lest ye die*, 1928
- *Theodore Savage*, 1922
Hamilton, Cosmo *The passing of Arthur*, 1904
Hamilton, Edmond *Battle for the stars*, 1963
- *City at world's end*, 1952
- *The haunted stars*, 1965
- *The horror on the asteroid*, 1936
- *The star kings*, 1951
Hamilton, Ernest Graham. See Graham, H. E. *(pseud.)*
Hamilton, Leigh Brackett. See Brackett, Leigh *(pseud.)*
Hamlyn, W. Ashton *Strange weather!*, 1941
Hanks, Keith *Falk*, 1972
Hanley, Clifford Leonard Clark. See Calvin, Henry *(pseud.)*
Hanley, James *What Farrar saw*, 1946
Hannan, Charles *The betrothal of James*, 1898
Hannay, James Frederick Wynne *Rebels' triumph*, 1933
Harding Ellison *The woman who vowed*, 1908
Harding, Lee *A world of shadows*, 1975
Harker, Kenneth *The flowers of February*, 1970
- *The Symmetrians*, 1966
Harness, Charles Leonard *The paradox men*, 1964
- *The Ring of Ritornel*, 1968
Harris, John *Right of reply*, 1968

Hutchison, Graham Seton. See Seton, Graham *(pseud.)*

Huxley, Aldous [Leonard] *Ape and essence*, 1949
- *Brave new world*, 1932

Hyams, Edward [Solomon] *The death lottery*, 1971
- *The final agenda*, 1973
- *Morrow's ants*, 1975

Hyder, Alan *Vampires overhead*, 1935

Hynam, John Charles. See Kippax, John *(pseud.)*

Iggulden, John Manners *Breakthrough*, 1960

Ingham, L. H. *The unknown dictator*, 1937

Ingram, [Archibald] Kenneth *The Premier tells the truth*, 1944

Ingrey, Derek *Pig on a lead*, 1963

Innominatus *(pseud.) In the light of the twentieth century*, 1886

Irving, Clifford *The 38th floor*, 1965

Irwin, H. C. See Mark Time *(pseud.)*

J.J.J. *The Blue Shirts*, 1926

J.A.C.K. *Golf in the year 2000*, 1892

Jackson, Basil *Epicenter*, 1976
- *Supersonic*, 1976

Jackson, Shirley *The sundial*, 1958

Jacomb, Charles Ernest *And a new earth*, 1926

Jaeger, Muriel *The question mark*, 1926
- *Retreat from Armageddon*, 1936

Jakober, Marie *The Mind Gods*, 1976

James, L. *The boy galloper*, 1903

James, Laurence W. *Simon Rack: Back flash*, 1975
- *Simon Rack: Earth lies sleeping*, 1974
- *Simon Rack: New life for old*, 1975
- *Simon Rack: Star cross*, 1974

James, Rowland *While England slept*, 1932

Jameson, [Mararet] Storm *In the second year*, 1936
- *The moment of truth*, 1949
- *Then we shall hear singing*, 1942

Jane, Frederick Thomas *Blake of the "Rattlesnake"*, 1895
- *To Venus in five seconds*, 1897
- *The violet flame*, 1899

Janifer, Laurence Mark *(ed.) Master's choice*, 1967
- *(ed.) Master's choice 1*, 1969
- *(ed.) Master's choice 2*, 1969

Janson, Gustaf *Pride of war*, 1912

Jefferies, [John] Richard *After London*, 1885

Jeffries, Graham Montague. See Armstrong, Anthony *(pseud.)*

Jenkins, Geoffrey *A grue of ice*, 1962
- *Hunter-killer*, 1966

Jenkins, William Fitzgerald. See Leinster, Murray *(pseud.)*

Jensen, Axel *Epp*, 1967

Jensen, Norman *The galactic colonizers*, 1971

Jeppsen, Janet O. *The second Experiment*, 1975

Jerome, Jerome Klapka *The new Utopia*, 1891

Johannesson, Olaf (Hannes Alfven) *The great computer*, 1968
- See Nolan, William Francis, joint author

Johnson, George Clayton See Nolan, William Francis, joint author

Johnhett (John Hettinger) *Our glorious future*, 1931

Johnson, Le Roy Peter Vernon (Peter Vernon Le Roy) *In the time of the Thetans*, 1961

Johnstone, Frank. See Wilson, Angus *(pseud.)*

Jones, Arthur Mervyn Keppel *When Smuts goes*, 1947

Jones, Dennis Feltham *Çolossus*, 1966
- *Don't pick the flowers*, 1971
- *Implosion*, 1967

Jones, Ewart [Charles] *Head in the sand*, 1958

Jones, Glyn *The blue bed*, 1937

Jones, Gonner *The dome*, 1968

Jones, Langdon *(ed.) The new SF*, 1969

Jones, Margaret *The day they put Humpty together again*, 1968

Jones, Mervyn *On the last day*, 1958

Jones, Raymond F. *This island earth*, 1955

Jorgensen, Ivar *Whom the gods say*, 1973

Joscelyne, Cyril *When the Gubbins rules*, 1923

Joseph, Michael Kennedy *The hole in the zero*, 1967

Judd, Cyril (Cyril M. Kornbluth and Judith Merril) *Gunner Cade*, 1964
- *Outpost Mars*, 1966

Junius J. *(pseud.) Pope Pacificus*, 1908

Juniper, Laurence, M. *A piece of Martin Cann*, 1973

Kapp, Colin *The patterns of Chaos*, 1972

Karp, David *One*, 1954

Kaul, Fedor *Contagion to this world*, 1933

Llewellyn, [David William] Alun *The strange invaders*, 1934

Lloyd, Roger [Bradshaigh], *The troubling of the city*, 1962

Locke, George *(ed.) Worlds apart*, 1972

Logan, Charles *Shipwreck*, 1975

London, Jack [John Griffith] *The iron heel*, 1908
- *The scarlet plague*, 1915

Long, Frank Belknap *It was the day of the robot*, 1964
- *John Carstairs*, 1951
- Monster from out of time, 1971
- *This strange tomorrow*, 1966

Long, George *Valhalla*, 1906

Long, Patrick *Heil Britannia*, 1973

Long, Paul and Wye, Alan *The remnants of 1927*, 1925

Loomis, Noel Miller See Water, Silas *(pseud.)*

Lopez, Anthony *Second Coming*, 1975

Lord, Graham *God and all his angels*, 1976

Lorraine, Paul [John Russell Fearn] *Dark boundaries*, 1953

Lorraine, Paul *(pseud.) Two worlds*, 1953
- *(pseud.) Zenith-D*, 1953

Lott, Stanley Makepeace *Escape to Venus*, 1956

Low, Archibald Montgomery *Adrift in the stratosphere*, 1937
- *Mars breaks through*, 1937
- *Satellite in space*, 1956

Lucian *(pseud.) Dips into the near future*, 1919

Ludwig, Edward W. *The mask of John Culon*, 1971

Lukens, Adam (Diane Detzer) *Sons of the wolf*, 1963

Lundberg, Knud *The Olympic hope, 1958*

Lundwall, Sam J. *Alice's World*, 1974
- *2018 A.D. or the King Kong Blues*, 1976

Lunn, Hugh Kingsmill See Kingsmill, Hugh *(pseud.)*

Lymington, John (John Newton Chance) *The coming of the strangers*, 1961
- *Froomb!*, 1964
- *The giant stumbles*, 1960
- *Give Daddy the knife, darling*, 1969
- *The green drift*, 1965
- *The grey ones*, 1960
- *The hole in the world*, 1974
- *Night of the big heat*, 1959
- *The night spiders*, 1964
- *The nowhere place*, 1969
- *The screaming face*, 1963
- *The sleep eaters*, 1963
- *A spider in the bath*, 1975

- *The Star Witches*, 1965
- *A sword above the night*, 1962
- *Ten million years to Friday*, 1967
- *The Year Dot*, 1972

Lynch, Col. Arthur Alfred *Seraph wings*, 1923

Lynch, [John Gilbert] Bohun *Menace from the Moon*, 1925

Lynch, Jane See Gaskell, Jane *(pseud.)*

Lynn, G. *The return of Karl Marx*, 1941

Lyon, Capt. Edmund David *Ireland's dream*, 1888

M', Mc, Mac, Mack are treated as Mac

M., J. W. *The coming Cromwell*, 1871
- *The siege of London*, 1871

McAllister, Alister See Wharton, Anthony *(pseud.)*

McCaffrey, Anne *Decision at Doona*, 1970
- *Dragonflight*, 1969
- *Dragonquest*, 1973
- *Dragonsong*, 1976
- *Restoree*, 1967
- *The ship who sang*, 1971
- *To ride Pegasus*, 1975

Macaulay, Clarendon (Walter Marsham Adams) *The carving of Turkey*, 1874

Macaulay, L. *The decadence*, 1929

Macualay, Rose *What not*, 1919

McCauley, Motley Ranke *(pseud.) Chapters from future history*, 1871

MacClure, Victor *Ultimatum*, 1924

McCutchan, Philip [Donald] *The all-purpose bodies*, 1969
- *Bluebolt One*, 1962
- *Bowering's breakwater*, 1964
- *Bright red business men*, 1969
- *The Day of the Coastwatch*, 1968
- *Hartinger's Mouse*, 1970
- *This Drakotny*, 1971
- *A time for survival*, 1966

MacDonald, John Dann *Planet of the dreamers*, 1954

McGivern, William *Caprifoil*, 1973

MacGregor, James Murdoch See McIntosh, J. T. *(pseud.)*
- *From a Christian ghetto*, 1954

MacIlraith, Frank and Connolly, Roy *Invasion from the air*, 1934

McIlwain, David See Maine, Charles Eric *(pseud.)*

McIntosh, J. T. (James Murdoch MacGregor) *Born leader*, 1955
- *The cosmic spies*, 1972
- *The fittest*, 1961

Mars, Alastair [Campbell Gillespie] *Arctic submarine*, 1955
- *Atomic submarine*, 1957
Marsh, Carl [David] *And wars shall cease*, 1939
Marshall, Bruce *Marx the First*, 1975
- *Peter the Second*, 1976
- *Urban the Ninth*, 1973
Martin, David S. *No lack of space*, 1967
Martin, Peter *Summer in three thousand* ,1946
Martin-Fehr, J. *The end of his tether*, 1972
Marvell, Andrew *Minimum man*, 1938
- *Three men make a world*, 1939
Masefield, Lewis [Crommelin] *Cross double cross*, 1936
Mason, Colin *Hostage*, 1973
Mason Douglas Rankine See Rankine, John *(pseud.)*
- *The end bringers*, 1975
- *From Carthage then I came*, 1968
- *The Janus syndrome*, 1969
- *Landfall is a state of mind*, 1968
- *Matrix*, 1971
- *The Omega Worm*, 1976
- *The Phaeton Condition*, 1974
- *Ring of violence*, 1968
- *Satellite 54 – Zero*, 1971
- *The Tower of Rizwan*, 1968
Mason, Sydney Charles See Carr, Charles *(pseud.)*
Masson, David Irvine *The caltraps of time*, 1968
Mastin, John *The stolen planet*, 1906
- *Through the sun in an airship*, 1909
Matheson, Richard *Born of man and woman*, 1956
- *I am legend*, 1956
- *The shores of space*, 1958
- *Third from the Sun*, 1961
Matthews, Ronald *Red sky at night*, 1951
Mattingley, Sidney *The terror by night*, 1913
Maude, Col. Frederic Natusch *The new Battle of Dorking*, 1900
Maugham, Robin (Robert Cecil Romer Maugham, 2nd Viscount Maugham) *The 1946 MS.*, 1943
Maurice, Michael (Conrad Arthur Skinner) *Not in our stars*, 1923
Maurois, André *The next chapter: the war against the Moon*, 1927
- *The thought-reading machine*, 1938
Maxwell, C. F. *Plan 79*, 1947
Maxwell, Edward *(pseud.) Quest for Pajaro*, 1957
Mayne, John Dawson *The triumph of socialism*, 1908
Mead, Harold *The bright phoenix*, 1955

- *Mary's country*, 1957
Mead, Shepherd *The big ball of wax*, 1955
- *The carefully considered rape of the*
- *world*, 1966
Mears, Amelia Garland *Mercia*, 1895
Melling, Leonard *First man on Mars*, 1971
- *The great beyond A.D. 2500*, 1955
Mendes, Henry Pereira *Looking ahead*, 1899
Merak, A. J. *Dark Andromeda*, 1954
- *Hydrosphere*, 1958
- *No dawn*, 1959
Mercier, Louis Sébastien *Astraea's return ; or the halcyon days of France in the year 2440*, 1797
- *Memoirs of the year two thousand five hundred*, 1772
Meredith, Edgar *Our stranger*, 1936
Merle, Robert *Day of the dolphin*, 1969
- *Malevil*, 1974
Merril, Judith *(ed.) (Josephine Judith Pohl) The best of Sci-Fi 1*, 1963
- *(ed.) The best of SciFi 2*, 1964
- *(ed.) The best of Sci-Fi 4*, 1965
- *(ed.) The best of Sci-Fi 5*, 1966
- *(ed.) The best of Sci-Fi 9*, 1967
- *(ed.) The best of Sci-Fi 10*, 1967
- *(ed.) The best of Sci-Fi 12*, 1970
- *(ed.) Beyond the barriers of space and time*, 1955
- *(ed.) Beyond human ken*, 1953
- *(ed.)Daughters of earth*, 1968
- *(ed.) SF: The best of the best*, 1968
- *(ed.) SF: The best of the best Part One*, 1970
- *(ed.) SF: The best of the best Part Two*, 1970
- *Shadow on the hearth*, 1953
- *(ed.) The space-time journal*, 1972
See Judd, Cyril M. *(pseud.)*
Merwin, Samuel Kimball *Killer to come*, 1960
Meyers, Roy *Destiny and the dolphins*, 1971
Meynell, Laurence Walter See Eton, Robert *(pseud.)*
Michaelis, Richard *A sequel to Looking Backward*, 1891
Michelson, Miriam *The awakening of Zojas*, 1910
Middleton, John B. *The god of this world* 1905
Miles (Stephen Southwold) See also Bell Neil *(pseud.)*
- *The gas war of 1940*, 1931
- *The seventh bowl*, 1930
Milkomane, George Alexis Milkomanovich See Borodin, George *(pseud.)*

Moorcock, Michael; contd.
- *The Oak and the Ram*, 1973
- *Phoenix in obsidian*, 1970
- *The Queen of the Swords*, 1971
- *The quest for Tanelorn*, 1975
- *The rituals of infinity*, 1971
- *The Runestaff*, 1969
- *Sailor on the seas of fate*, 1976
- *The shores of death*, 1970
- *The singing citadel*, 1970
- *The sleeping sorceress*, 1971
- *The stealer of souls*, 1963
- *Stormbringer*, 1965
- *The sundered worlds*, 1965
- *The Sword and the stallion*, 1974
- *The Sword of the dawn*, 1969
- *The time dweller*, 1969
- *The traps of time*, 1968
- *The twilight man*, 1966
- *The winds of Limbo*, 1970
- and James, Philip *The distant suns*, 1975
- and Jones L. *(eds.) The nature of the catastrophe*, 1971
- and Platt, Charles *(eds.) New Worlds 6*, 1973
Moore, Arthur See Oriel, Antrim *(pseud.)*
Moore, Brian *Catholics*, 1972
Moore, Catherine Lucille *Doomsday morning*, 1960
- *Shambleau*, 1961
Moore, Ward *Greener than you think*, 1949
Morel, Dighton *Moonlight red*, 1960
Moresby, Lord Charles *(pseud.?) A hundred years hence*, 1828
Morgan, Arthur and Brown, Charles R. *The disintegrator*, 1892
Morgan, Dan *The concrete horizon*, 1976
- *Country of the mind*, 1975
- *High destiny*, 1975
- *Inside*, 1971
- *The richest corpse in show business*, 1966
- and Kippax, John (John Hynam) *The neutral stars*, 1968
- *Seed of stars*, 1974
- *Thunder of stars*, 1968
Morgan, Dave *Genetic Two*, 1976
- *Reiver*, 1975
Morice, Charles *He is risen again*, 1911
Morison, Frank (Albert Henry Ross) *Sunset*, 1932
Morland, Dick *Albion! Albion!*, 1974
- *Heart Clock*, 1973
Morris, Alfred *Looking ahead*, 1891
Morris, Edita *A happy day*, 1974
Morris Gwendolen Sutherland See Sutherland, Morris *(pseud.)*

Morris, John *What will Japan do?*, 1898
Morris, William *News from nowhere*, 1891
Morton [Canova] Henry Vollam *I James Blunt*, 1942
Morton, John Bingham *Drink up, Gentlemen!*, 1930
Mosely, Maboth *War upon women*, 1934
Moskowitz, Samuel *(ed.) A sense of wonder*, 1967
Motta, Luigi *The Princess of the Roses*, 1919
Mottram, Ralph Hale *The visit of the Princess*, 1946
Moudy, Walter *No man on earth*, 1966
Moxley, Frank Wright *Red snow*, 1931
M. Pee *(pseud.) Hibernia's House*, 1881
Mr Dick *(pseud.) James Ingleton*, 1893
Muir, John Ramsay Bryce see Slack, Solomon *(pseud.)*
Mullally, Frederic *The Malta Conspiracy*, 1972
- *Venus afflicted*, 1973
Müller, Ernst See West, Julian *(pseud.)*
Muller, Paul *Brother Gib*, 1975
- *The man from Ger*, 1974
Muller, R. *After all, this is England*, 1967
- *The lost diaries of Albert Smith*, 1965
Münch, Paul Georg *Hindenburg's march into London*, 1916
Munn, Bertram *The skeleton man*, 1919
Munro, Hector Hugh See Saki *(pseud.)*
Munro, John *A trip to Venus*, 1897
Murray, Violet *(Mrs. Violet Torlesse) The rule of the beasts*, 1925
Murray, William *The Messiah*, 1927
Murry, Colin Middleton See Cowper, Richard *(pseud.)*

N., J. *Cuttings from 'The Times' of 1900*, 1873
Nathan, Robert *Road of ages*, 1935
- *They went on together*, 1941
Nation, Terry *Survivors*, 1976
Naval Officer, A *Great was the fall*, 1912
Navarchus (Patrick Vaux and Lionel Yexley) *The world's awakening*, 1908
Nedram *(pseud.) John Sagur*, 1921
Neeper, Cary *A place beyond man*, 1976
Netterville, Luke (James Standish O'Grady) *Queen of the world*, 1900
Neville, Derek *Bright morrow*, 1947
Newcomb, Simon *His wisdom, the defender*, 1900

Newman, Bernard *Armoured doves*, 1931
- *The blue ants*, 1962
- *The flying saucer*, 1948
- *Secret weapon*, 1941
- *Shoot!*, 1949
- *The wishful think*, 1954

Newte, Horace Wykeham Can *The master beast*, 1907
- *The red fury*, 1919

Newton, Wilfred Douglas *The North afire*, 1914
- *War*, 1914

Niall, Ían (John McNellie *The boy who saw tomorrow*, 1952

Nicholl, Maurice Sèe Swayne, Martin Luttrell *(pseud.)*

Nicols, Robert *Fantastica*, 1923

Nicholson, Harold [George] *Public faces*, 1932

Niemann, August *The coming conquest of England*, 1904

Nisbet, Hume *The great secret*, 1895

Nisot, Mavis Elizabeth See Penmare William *(pseud.)*

Niven, Larry *The flight of the horse*, 1975
- *A gift from Earth*, 1969
- *A hole in space*, 1975
- *Inconstant Moon*, 1973
- *Neutron star*, 1969
- *Protector*, 1974
- *Ringworld*, 1972
- *World of Ptavvs*, 1968
- and Pournelle, Jerry *The mote in God's Eye*, 1975

Noel, Leonard (Leonard Noel Barker) *The golden star*, 1935

Noel, Sterling *I killed Stalin*, 1952

Nolan, William Francis *(ed.) Almost human*, 1966
- *(ed.) The pseudo people*, 1967
- *(ed.) A sea of space*, 1970
- *(ed.) 3 to the highest power*, 1971
- *(ed.) A wilderness of stars*, 1970
- and Johnson, George Clayton *Logan's run*, 1968

Norman, Barry *End product*, 1975

North, Delaval *The last man in London*, 1887

Norton, André *The Sioux spaceman*, 1976
- *The X Factor*, 1967

Norway, Nevil Shute See Shute, Nevil *(pseud.)*

Nostradamus, Merlin (Francis Power Cobbe) *The age of science*, 1877

Nourse, Alan Edward *Beyond infinity*, 1964

- *The counterfeit man*, 1964
- *PSI High and others*, 1968
- *Tiger by the tail*, 1962

Nowlan, Philip Francis *Armageddon 2419 A.D.*, 1976

Noyes, Alfred *The last man*, 1940

Nunsowe, Green *(pseud.) A thousand years hence*, 1882

Nuetzel, Charles *Last call for the stars*, 1972

Oakhurst, William *The universal strike of 1899*, 1891

Observer, The *A.D.2500. The Observer Prize Stories*, 1955

O'Connor, Patrick See Wibberley, Leonard *(pseud.)*

October, John *The anarchy pedlars*, 1976

Octogenarian *(pseud.) The British*
- *Federal Empire*, 1872

Odle, E. V. *The clockwork man*, 1923

O'Duffy, Eimar [Ultan] *Asses in clover*, 1933
- *King Goshawk and the birds*, 1926

Offin, Thomas William *How the Germans took London*, 1900

O'Flannagan, Right Hon. Phineas *(pseud.) Ireland a nation!*, 1893

Ognall, Leopold Horace See Howard, Hartley *(pseud.)*

O'Grady, James Standish See Netterville, Luke *(pseud.)*

Oldmeadow, Ernest [James] *The North Sea bubble*, 1906

Oldrey, John *The devil's henchmen*, 1926

Oliver, Chadwick [Symmes] *Shadows in the sun*, 1955
- *The shores of another sea*, 1971

Oliver, George See Onions, Oliver *(pseud.)*

Ollivant, Alfred *Tomorrow*, 1927

Oman, Sir Charles William Chadwick *(ed.)The reign of George VI*, 1899

Omen, E. *Nutopia*, 1908

O'Neil, H. *Two thousand year hence*, 1868

O'Neill, Joseph *Day of Wrath*, 1936

Onions, Oliver (George Oliver) *New moon*, 1918

Oppenheim, Edward Phillips *The dumb gods speak*, 1937
- *Exit a dictator*, 1939
- *Gabriel Samara*, 1925
- *Matorni's vineyard*, 1929
- *Mr. Mirakel*, 1943

Robinson, Frank M. See Scortia, Thomas
Nicholas, joint author
Rochester, George Ernest *The black
octopus*, 1954
Roger, Noëlle (Hélène Pittard) *The new
Adam*, 1926
Rogers, Michael *Mind fogger*, 1973
Rohmer, Sax (Arthur Sarsfield Wade)
The day the world ended, 1930
– *The Emperor of America*, 1929
Rolfe, Fr. (Frederick William Serafino
Rolfe) *Hadrian the Seventh*, 1904
Rolls, Brian *Something in mind*, 1973
Romano, Deane *Flight from Time One*,
1973
Rose, Frederick Horace [Vincent] *The
maniac's dream*, 1946
Rose, George. See Sketchley, Arthur
(pseud.)
Roshwald, Mordecai [Marceli] *Level 7*,
1959
– *A small Armageddon*, 1962
Ross, Albert Henry. See Morison, Frank
(pseud.)
Ross, Major-General Charles *The Fly-by-
nights*, 1921
Ross, James *The god killers*, 1970
Ross, Jean *A view of the island*, 1965
Ross, Joseph (Joseph Wrocz) *(ed.) Best
of Amazing*, 1968
Rosse, Ian *(pseud.) The Droop*, 1972
Roth, Philip *Our gang*, 1971
Rotsler, William *Patron of the arts*, 1976
Rousseau, Victor (Victor Rousseau
Emanuel) See Egbert, H. M. *(pseud.)*
– *The apostle of the cylinder*, 1918
– *The messiah of the culinder*, 1917
Rowe, Hunter *(pseud.) The power box*,
1971
Rowland, Donald Sydney *Despot in
space*, 1974
– *Master of space*, 1974
– *Nightmare planet*, 1976
– *Space Venturer*, 1976
Russ, Joanna *Picnic on Paradise*, 1969
Russell, Arthur James *Christ comes to
town*, 1935
Russell, Eric Frank *Dark tides*, 1962
– *Deep space*, 1956
– *Dreadful sanctuary*, 1953
– *Far stars*, 1961
– *The great explosion*, 1962
– *Like nothing on Earth*, 1975
– *Men, Martians and machines*, 1956
– *Next of kin*, 1959
– *Sentinels from space*, 1954
– *Sinister barrier*, 1943
– *Somewhere a voice*, 1965
– *Three to conquer*, 1957

– *Wasp*, 1958
Russell, George William See E., A.
(pseud.)
Ryder, James *Kark*, 1969
– *Vicious sprial*, 1976
Ryman, Ras *The Quadrant War*, 1976
Ryves, Thomas Evan *Bandersnatch*,
1950

Saberhagen, Fred *Berserker*, 1970
– *Berserker's Planet*, 1973
– *The Black Mountains*, 1973
– *The Broken lands*, 1973
– *Brother Berserker*, 1969
– *Changeling Earth*, 1974
Sacks, Janet *(ed.) Best of "Science
Fiction Monthly"*, 1975
Sackville-West, Hon. Victoria [Mary]
Grand Canyon, 1942
Sadler, Adam *Red ending*, 1928
Saki (Hector Hugh Munro) *When William
came*, 1913
Sale, David *Come to Mother*, 1971
Slainger, Pierre *For the eyes of the
President only*, 1971
Sallis, James *(ed.) The war book*, 1969
Samuel, Horace Barnett *The Quisto-box*,
1925
Santesson, Hans Stefan *(ed.) Fantastic
Universe Omnibus*, 1962
– *Gods for tomorrow*, 1967
Sarban (John W. Wall) *The sound of his
horn*, 1952
Saunders, Hilary Aidan St. George See
Beeding, Francis *(pseud.)*
Savage, Richard *When the Moon died*,
1955
Savarin, Julian Jay *Beyond the Outer
Mirr*, 1976
– *Waiters on the dance*, 1972
Scheer, Karl-Herbert *Perry Rhodan 7*,
1975
– *Perry Rhodan 13*, 1976
– and Ernsting, Walter *Perry
Rhodan 1*, 1974
– *Perry Rhodan 2*, 1974
– and Mahr, Kurt *Perry Rhodan 5*,
1975
Schmitz, James H.*The demon breed*,
1969
– *The eternal frontiers*, 1974
– *The Lion Game*, 1976
– *The Telzey Toy*, 1976
Schutz, J. W. *The Moon Microbe*, 1976
– *People of the rings*, 1975
Scortia, Thomas Nicholas *Earthwreck*, 1975

Water, Silas (Noel Miller Loomis)
    The man with absolute motion, 1955
Watkins, William Jon The God machine,
    1974
Watlock, W.A. The next 'Ninety-three',
    1886
Watson, Henry Crocker Marriott Decline
    and fall of the British Empire, 1890
—   Erchomenon, 1879
Watson, Ian The embedding, 1973
—   The Jonah kit, 1975
Watson, Sydney In the twinkling of an
    eye, 1910
—   The mark of the Beast, 1911
Watten, Bowen Stratharran, 1887
Watts, Newman The man who did not
    sin, 1939
Waugh, Evelyn Love among the ruins,
    1953
Way, Peter The Kretzmer Syndrome,
    1968
Weatherhead, John Transplant, 1969
Webb, Jane (afterwards Loudon, Mrs.)
    The mummy, 1827
Wedlake, G.E.C. The wrecking ray, 1935
Weekley, Ian The moving snow, 1974
Wellard, James [Howard] Night in
    Babylon, 1953
Wells, Angus (ed.) The best of Isaac
    Asimov, 1973
—   (ed.) The best of Arthur C. Clarke,
    1973
—   (ed.) The best of Robert Heinlein,
    1973
—   (ed.) The best of Frank Herbert,
    1975
—   (ed.) The best of Frank Herbert
    1952–64; 1965–70, 1976
—   (ed.) The best of Fritz Leiber, 1974
—   (ed.) The best of Clifford D. Simak,
    1975
—   (ed.) Tjhe best of A.E. Van Vogt,
    1974
—   (ed.) The best of John Wyndham,
    1973
Wells, Herbert George All aboard for
    Ararat, 1940
—   The autocracy of Mr. Parham, 1930
—   The dream, 1924
—   The food of the gods, 1904
—   The holy terror, 1939
—   In the days of the comet, 1906
—   Scientific romances, 1933
—   The shape of things to come, 1933
—   The sleeper awakes, 1910
—   Tales of space and time, 1899
—   The time machine, 1895
—   Twelve stories and a dream, 1903

—   The war in the air, 1908
—   The war of the worlds, 1898
—   When the sleeper wakes, 1899
—   The world set free, 1914
Wells ,Robert Candle in the Sun, 1976
—   The Parasaurians, 1974
Wentworth-James, Gertie de S. The
    television girl, 1928
Wessex, Martyn The chain reaction,
    1976
—   The slowing down process, 1974
West, Anthony Another kind, 1951
West, Julian (Ernst Müller) My
    afterdream, 1900
West, Morris [Langlo] The shoes of the
    Fisherman, 1963
West, Paul Colonel Mint, 1973
Weston, George Comet "Z", 1934
Weston, Peter (ed.) Andromeda 1, 1976
Wharton, Anthony (Alister McAllister)
    The man on the hill, 1923
Wheatley, Dennis Black August, 1934
—   Sixty days to live, 1939
Wheeler, Paul The friendly persuaders,
    1968
White, Frederick Merrick The white
    battalions, 1900
White, James The aliens among us, 1970
—   All judgement fled, 1968
—   Dark inferno, 1972
—   Deadly litter, 1968
—   The dream millennium, 1974
—   Hospital station, 1967
—   Open prison, 1965
—   The secret visitors, 1961
—   Star surgeon, 1967
—   Tomorrow is too far, 1971
—   The watch below, 1966
White ,Jane Comet, 1975
White ,Ted (ed.) The best from Amazing,
    1976
—   (ed.) The best from Fantastic, 1976
White, Terence Hanbury Gone to
    ground, 1935
White ,William Anthony Parker. See
    Boucher, Anthony (pseud.)
Wibberley, Leonard (Patrick O'Connor)
    The mouse on the moon, 1963
—   The wrath of grapes, 1955
Wicks, Mark To Mars via the Moon, 1911
Wignall, Trevor C. and Knox, Gordon
    Daniel Atoms, 1923
Wilding, Philip See Haynes, John Robert
    (pseud.)
—   Shadow over the Earth, 1956
—   Spacefilght Venus, 1954
Wilhelm, Kate Andover and the android,
    1966

Wilhelm, Kate; contd.
- *The killing thing*, 1969
- *Let the fire fall*, 1969
- *Nebula Award stories 9*, 1974

Wilkinson, Burke *Night of the short knives*, 1964

Williams, Charles [Walter Stansby] *Shadows of ecstasy*, 1933

Williams, Eric Cyril *The call of Utopia*, 1971
- *Flash*, 1972
- *Monkman comes down*, 1969
- *Project: Renaissance*, 1973
- *The time injection*, 1968
- *To end all telescopes*, 1969

Williams, Islwyn *Dangerous waters*, 1952
- *Newbury in Orm*, 1952

Williams, Lloyd *The great raid*, 1909

Williams, Robert Folkestone *Eureka*, 1837

Williams, Robert Moore *Beachhead planet*, 1970
- *Now comes tomorrow*, 1971

Williams, T. Owen *A month for mankind*, 1970

Williamson, Jack. See Stewart, W. *(pseud.)*
- *After world's end*, 1961
- *Bright new universe*, 1969
- *Dragon's island*, 1954
- *The humanoids*, 1953
- *The Legion of Time*, 1961
- *The Moon children*, 1976
- *Seetee ship*, 1969
- *Seetee shock*, 1969

Willis, George Anthony. See Armstrong, Anthony *(pseud.)*

Willis, Ted *Death may surprise us*, 1974

Wilson, Angus (Frank Johnstone) *The old men at the Zoo*, 1961

Wilson, C. *The mind parasites*, 1967

Wilson, Herbert Wrigley and White, Arnold *When war breaks out*, 1898

Wilson, J. *When the women reign, 1930*, 1908

Wilson, John Burgess. See Burgess, Anthony *(pseud.)*

Wilson, Richard *Girls from Planet 5*, 1968
- *Time out for tomorrow*, 1967

Wilson, Robert Hendrie *Ring of rings*, 1976

Wilson, Steve *The lost traveller*, 1976

Winsor, George McLeod *Station X*, 1919

Wintle, Harold *The cleansing of the Lords*, 1905
- *Until the day*, 1912

Vinton, John *The fighting Téméraire*, 1971

Wise, Arthur *The day the Queen flew to Scotland for the grouse shooting*, 1969
- *Leatherjacket*, 1970
- *Who killed Enoch Powell?*, 1970

Wise, C. *Darkness and dawn*, 1884

Wodehouse, Pelham Grenville *The swoop!*, 1909

Wolf, Gary K. *Killerbowl*, 1976

Wolfe, Bernard *Limbo '90*, 1953

Wolfe, Gene *The fifth head of Cerberus*, 1973

Wollheim, Donald A. See Grinnell, David *(pseud.)*
- *(ed.) Flight into space*, 1951
- *(ed.) The 1973 Annual World's Best SF*, 1973
- *(ed.) Prize stories of space and time*, 1953
- *(ed.) Trilogy of the future*, 1972
- *(ed.) The World's best SF short stories No. 1*, 1975
- *(ed.) The World's best SF short stories No. 2*, 1976
- and Carr, Terry *(eds.) World's best science fiction 1968*, 1969
- *(eds.) World's best science fiction 1970*, 1970
- *(ed.) World's best science fiction 1971*, 1971
- and Saha, Arthur W. *(eds.) The 1972 annual world's best SF*, 1972

Wood, Samuel Andrew *I'll blackmail the world*, 1935

Wood, Walter *The enemy in our midst*, 1906

Wood, William *The news from Karachi*, 1962

Woodman, George [David] *The heretic*, 1963

Woolfolk, William *The overlords*, 1973

Wootton, Barbara [Frances] *London's burning*, 1936

Worts, George Frank. See Brent, Loring *(pseud.)*

Wright, Charles John Cutcliffe. See Cutcliffe-Hyne, Charles John *(pseud.)*

Wright, Henry *Depopulation*, 1899

Wright, Lan *Assignment Luther*, 1963
- *A man called Destiny*, 1961
- *A planet called Pavanne*, 1968
- *Space born*, 1964
- *Who speaks of conquest?*, 1961

Wright, Sydney Fowler. See Fowler, Sydney *(pseud.)*
- *The adventure of Wyndham Smith*, 1938
- *The amphibians*, 1925
- *Beyond the rim*, 1932
- *Dawn*, 1930

Wright, Sydney Fowler; contd.
- *Deluge*, 1927
- *Four day's war*, 1936
- *Megiddo's Ridge*, 1937
- *The new gods lead*, 1932
- *Power*, 1933
- *Prelude in Prague*, 1935
- *The throne of Saturn*, 1951
- *The world below*, 1929

Wrocz, Joseph. See Ross, Joseph *(pseud.)*

Wyatt, Patrick *Irish Rose*, 1975

Wykehamicus, Friedrich (Frederick Gale) *Anno Domini 3867*, 1867

Wylie, Philip [Gordon] *The disappearance*, 1951
- *The end of the dream*, 1975

Wynd, Oswald *Death the red flower*, 1965

Wyndham, John (John Beynon Harris) *The Chrysalids*, 1955
- *Consider her ways*, 1961
- *The day of the Triffids*, 1951
- *Jizzle*, 1954
- *The John Wyndham Omnibus*, 1964
- *The Kraken wakes*, 1953
- *The man from beyond*, 1975
- *The Midwich cuckoos*, 1957
- *The secret people*, 1972
- *The seeds of time*, 1956
- *Sleepers of Mars*, 1973
- *Stowaway to Mars*, 1972
- *Trouble with lichen*, 1960
- *Wanderers of time*, 1973
- and Parkes, Lucas *The outward urge*, 1959

Wynne-Tyson, Esmé. See Beresford, John Davys co-author

X (Fawkes, Frank Attfield) *Marmaduke, Emperor of Europe*, 1895
- *The setting sun*, 1904

Yexley, Lionel. See Navarchus *(pseud.)*

Yolen, Jane *(ed.) Zoo 2000*, 1975

Yorke, Henry Vincent. See Green, Henry *(pseud.)*

Yorke, Preston *Space-time task force*, 1953

Youd, Christopher Samuel. See Christopher, John *(pseud.)*

Young, A.M. *The Aster disaster*, 1958

Young, Bertram Albert *Cabinet Pudding*, 1967

Young, Florence Ethel Mills *The war of the sexes*, 1905

Young, Michael *The rise of the meritocracy*, 1958

Young, Robert (Pierre Stephen Robert Payne) *The war in the marshes*, 1938

Young, Robert Franklin *The world of Robert F. Young*, 1966

Z, X.Y. *The Vril staff*, 1891

Zamyatin, Yevgeny Ivanovich *We*, 1970

Zebrowski, George *The Omega Point*, 1974

Zeigfreid, K. (Robert Lionel Fanthorpe) *Android*, 1963
- *Atomic Nemesis*, 1962

Zelazny, Roger *Damnation alley*, 1971
- *The doors of his face*, 1973
- *The dream master*, 1968
- *Isle of the dead*, 1970
- *Lord of light*, 1968
- *Nebula Award Winners 3*, 1968
- *A rose for Ecclesiastes*, 1969
- *This immortal*, 1967
- *Today we choose faces*, 1975
- *To die in Italbar*, 1975

Zerwick, Chloe and Brown, Harrison [Scott] *The Cassiopeia affair*, 1968

Zetford, Tully *Hook: Boosted man*, 1974
- *Hook: Star City*, 1974
- *Hook: Virility gene*, 1975
- *Hook: Whirlpool of stars*, 1974

Zola, Émile [Édouard Charles] *Fruitfulness*, 1900
- *Truth*, 1903
- *Work*, 1901

PART 4 NOTES TO THE CHRONOLOGICAL LIST

1   Although Mercier stated in a later edition that *L'An 2440* was first published in 1770, the internal evidence suggests that the book was first published in 1771. The best discussion of this point is the article on Mercier in: Pierre Versins, *Encyclopédie et l'utopie, des voyages extraordinaires et de la science fiction*, 1972.

2   The first *Anticipation* started a series of pamphlets on the matter of the debate of November 1778, and these continued until 1794. For additional titles see the British Museum *Catalogue of printed books*.

3   A full account of the *Battle of Dorking* episode will be found in: I.F. Clarke, *Voices propheysing war*, 1966.

4   The preface by the historian Sir Charles Oman gives a valuable commentary on the themes and personages in *The reign of George VI*. It is of interest to note that until he came upon the book, when he was 'working through the wrecks of an eighteenth-century library in the old-world town of Burford', Oman had not been aware 'how far back the *catena* of this prophetical literature could be followed.' There has been a recent edition by Cornmarket Reprints, 1972.

5   The theme of *The Green Ray* is typical of some 58 adventure stories issued by the firm of John Hamilton in *The Ace Series* during the 1930s. With the exception of Helder's *The war in the air, 1936* (1932) the general style of stories favoured exciting adventures that turned on some secret danger to the nation or the world. This is known only to handful of dedicated heroes and villains. For want of satisfactory internal evidence, the publications in the series have to be left in the limbo of a possible future; they are not, therefore, entered in this bibliography. The principal authors were Captain W.E. Johns, Covington Clarke, David T. Lindsay, and G.E. Rochester.

6   The C.S. Lewis trilogy presents a problem that tests the principles of this bibliography. The first two stories, *Out of the silent planet* and *Perelandra*, are not entered because internal evidence shows that the action does not take place in the future. With *That hideous strength*, however, the scale of the events and the many indications of national actions and reactions in the story point to a time, presumably in the near future, for the context of the narrative.

7   John Russell Fearn was an exceedingly prolific writer of popular fiction who seems to have established the world record for the use of pseudonyms. Some thirty-four have so far been established. For a full examination of Fearn's many stories see: Philip Harbottle, *John Russell Fearn: The ultimate analysis*, 1965; and *The Multi-man*, 1968. This bibliography is indebted to Philip Harbottle for the work he has done and

for the light he has shone on Fearn's publications, and especially for his elucidation of the pseudonyms he shared with E.C. Tubb (Volsted Gridban) and for the more doubtful attributions of the Paul Lorraine, Astron del Martia, and Brian Shaw pseudonyms.

8   The publishing firm of Curtis Warren seems to have had a brief existence in 1953 and 1954, and was then recorded in *Whitaker's* as 'Gone from last known address'. Most of the publications are not available in the copyright libraries.

9   Paul Harbottle considers that *Dark boundaries* is the only story by Fearn under the Paul Lorraine pseudonym, and *Z formations* is the only story by Fearn to appear under the Bryan Shaw pseudonym, and *The trembling world* the only story by Fearn under the Del Martia pseudonym.

10   The many stories written by R.L. Fanthorpe were published by Badger Books. Most of these are not available in the copyright libraries. A list of these and a note on his various pseudonyms will be found in: Donald H. Tuck, *The Encyclopedia of Science Fiction and Fantasy*, 1974.

11   Kenneth Robeson was the pseudonym used by Norman A. Daniels, William C. Bogart, and Lester Dent for the Doc Savage stories in the *Doc Savage Magazine* from 1933 to 1949. The hero is a superman – intellectual and physical – and has been described as 'tougher than Tarzan and braver than Bond'. In all about 180 stories were written and many have been issued as paperbacks. By reason of their plots many of the stories are clearly set in the near future, since the national or international calamities that face Doc Savage and his friends have not yet begun to endanger the world. For a full account see: Pierre Versins, *Encyclopédie de l'utopie et de la science fiction*, 1972; and Philip José Farmer, *Doc Savage: his apocalytpic life*, Doubleday 1975, Panther 1975.

12   Like the very popular *Doc Savage* and *Perry Rhodan* series the heroic exploits of the crew of the *USS Enterprise* have promoted a cult that flourishes in many societies and in conventions of 'Trekkies'. The publishing history begins with *Star Trek 1*, Bantam Books, U.S. 1967. The following, all written by James Blish, have been published by Corgi Books as U.K. editions of the American originals:
1972 *Star Trek 1, 2, 3*
1973 *Star Trek 4, 5, 6, 7, 8*
1974 *Star Trek 9, 10*
1975 *Star Trek 11*
In addition to the above there have been hard-back publications: *Star Trek 1*, White Lion, 1974; *Star Trek 2, 3*, White Lion, 1975.
The following have also been published by Corgi Books:
1975 Foster, A.D. *Star Trek Log 1, 2, 3*
1976 Foster, A.D. *Star Trek Log 4, 5*

Further information can be found in: Lichtenberg, J. and others *Star Trek Lives!* Corgi, 1975; and Whitfield, S.E. and Roddenbury, G. *The making of Star Trek*, Corgi, 1976

3   The *Perry Rhodan* stories are the work of several German writers, in particular of K–H. Scheer, Walther Ernsting, Kurt Mahr, H.G. Ewers and others. The British editions have been translated by Wendayne Ackerman and were first published in the United States. The style of writing is in the superman mode, and they are a German version of Flash Gordon, Doc Savage, Captain Future and the rest. Since the beginning of the series in 1961 the adventures of the Peacelord of the Universe have proved exceptionally popular: they appear weekly in Germany in editions of 200,000, and they have a faithful following in the hundreds of *Perry Rhodan* clubs throughout the world.

PART 5 BIBLIOGRAPHY

British Museum. *Catalogue of printed books*, 1881–1900

British Museum. *Subject index of modern works acquired*, 1881 to date.

The British national bibliography, 1950 to date.

Classified index to the London Catalogue, 1816–1851

The Cumulative book index, 1928 to date.

The English catalogue of books, 1837 to date.

Extrapolation, *Newsletter of the Modern Language Association of America on Science Fiction*, 1959 to date. College of Wooster, Wooster, Ohio 44691.

Library of Congress. *List of references on utopias*, 1922

Library of Congress. *List of references on utopias (supplement)*, 1926

Library of Congress. *List of references on utopias (supplement)*, 1940

A London bibliography of the social sciences, 1931–1932. *(Supplements v.5–9).*

London Library, *Subject index of the London Library*, 1908 and supplements covering 1909–1953

Mudie's Library Catalogue, 1904, 1906, 1919.

Paperbacks in Print, 1962 to date.

Science Fiction Studies, v.1, 1973–to date

The Times Literary Supplement, 1902–to date

Whitaker's Cumulative Book List, 1958–to date

Aldiss, B.W. *Billion Year Spree,* 1973.

Amis, K. *New maps of hell,* 1960.

Armytage, W.H.G. *Yesterdays tomorrows,* 1968.

Bailey, J.O. *Pilgrims through space and time,* 1947.

Baker, E.A. and Packman, J. *A guide to the best fiction, English and American,* 1932.

Bleiler, E.F. *(ed.) Checklist of fantastic literature,* 1972

Block, A. *The English novel, 1740–1850,* 1939.

Bloomfield, P. *Imaginary worlds,* 1932

Clareson, T.D. *(ed.) SF: the other side of realism,* 1971.

Clareson, T.D. *Science fiction criticism: an annotated check list,* 1972

Clareson, T.D. *(ed.) A spectrum of worlds,* 1972.

Clarke, I.F. *Voices prophesying war,* 1966.

Cotgreave, A. *Analytical or subject index to English prose fiction,* 1890.

Cotton, G.B. and Glencross, A. *Cumulated fiction index, 1945–1960,* 1961.

Crawford, J.H. *"333": a bibliography of the science-fantasy novel,* 1953.

Dixson, Z.A. *The comprehensive subject index to universal prose fiction,* 1897.

Dupont, V. *L'utopie et le roman utopique dans la litterature anglaise*, Paris, 1944.

Elliott, R.G. *The shape of utopia*, 1970.

Gerber, R. *Utopian fantasy: a study of English utopian fiction since the end of the nineteenth century*, 1955

Gunn, J. *Alternate worlds*, 1975.

Hertzler, J.O. *The history of utopian thought*, 1922.

Hevesi, L. *Biblioteca Utopistica* (1914), 1977.

Hillegas, M.R. *The future as nightmare*, 1974.

Kaufmann, M. *Utopias; or, schemes of social improvement from Sir Thomas More to Karl Marx*, 1897.

Ketterer, D. *New worlds for old*, 1974.

Knight, D. *In search of wonder*, 1960.

Lem, S. *Fantastyka i futurologia*, 1973.

Locke, George, *Voyages in space: a bibliography of interplanetary fiction, 1801-1914*, 1975.

Masso, G. *Education in utopias*, 1927.

Nicolson, M.H. *Voyages to the moon*, 1948.

Parrington, V.L. *American dreams: a study of American utopias*, 1947.

Peddie, R.A. *Subject index to books published up to and including 1880.*
First series, 1933. *Second series,* 1935. *Third series ,* 1939.
New series, 1948.

Polak, F.L. *The image of the future*, 2v, 1961.

Ross, H. *Utopias old and new*, 1938.

Rottensteiner, R. *The science fiction book*, 1975.

Russell, F.T. *Touring utopia*, 1932.

Scholes, R. *Structural fabulation*, 1975.

Smith, R.F. *Cumulated fiction index, 1960–1969*, 1970.

Smith, R.F. and Gordon, A.J. *Cumulated fiction index 1970–1974*, 1975.

Sonnenschein, W.S. *The best books*, 3rd ed., 6v., 1910–1935.

Tuck, D. *The encyclopedia of science fiction and fantasy*, 1959 and 1974.

Tymn, M.B., Schlobin, R.C. & Currey, L.W. *A research guide to science fiction studies*, 1977.

Worcester Public Library *Guide to prose fiction*, 1899.

Versins, Pierre *Encyclopédie de l'utopie, des voyages extraordinaries et de la science fiction.* Lausanne, 1972.

Walsh, C. *From Utopia to nightmare*, 1962.